POLITICS
and
PHILOSOPHY

POLITICS
and
PHILOSOPHY

~

An Anthology
Edited by
WILLIAM F. PRAY

Creative Director: Susan Shankin
Cover Designer: Barbara Garibay
Interior Designer: Andrea Reider

ISBN: 978-0-9863321-9-7

Firebird Rising Publishing
Printed in the United States

CONTENTS

ACKNOWLEDGMENTS

Over the years that the website *PoliticsandPhilosophy.com* was up and running there were so many contributors, interested parties and encouraging fans, that singling out folks for special recognition is all but impossible. The readership for *PoliticsandPhilosophy.com* was worldwide, as were the contributors, and I thank them for their many compliments and suggestions. Obviously, the staff at Firebird Rising deserves enormous credit for standing behind the year-long development of this book, and that includes The Rhino (RW Klarin), the mastermind behind the "new" Firebird. Let's not forget my editor Amanda Freeman for her tireless effort at juggling her babies while simultaneously making this book a readable reality; Jon in Seattle for insightful suggestions; Dr. Gregory Fried of Boston College, for reading several of the articles with a wise critical eye; and Susan Shankin for bringing the book's design together. All you folks have my deepest gratitude. If this collection is a success, if it delivers greater understanding and wisdom, it is mightily due to you.

PREFACE

Philosophy always includes politics in much the same way that politics usually precludes philosophy. Unpacking this statement indicates that if the search for truth is the prime directive of philosophy, that directive would necessarily include the search for truth in political issues. However, truth, philosophic or otherwise, is very often the first causality in political struggles, often a struggle for survival. This apparent conflict between politics and philosophy is the gateway to this collection of articles.

Philosophy has always argued *veritas animvs* (truth is liberty). Dispensing with truth immediately hollows our political discourse. Relieved of truth, reason becomes moot and openly abandons liberty to the faction with the biggest guns. In this book, as in the original website of *PoliticsandPhilosophy.com*, from which this collection is derived, the search for truth is primary. Truth is the finest tool in our intellectual kit for the exploration of our environment, of which politics is a most omnipresent and dangerous element. Philosophy, with its overriding commitment to truth, is the best and surest way to dissect the politics of power and survival at their most fundamental level.

The political questions examined in this volume are not necessarily contemporary and therefore do not agitate feelings of "them-or-us." The issues examined here are universal and therefore lack the partisan urges typically animating political doctrine. A brief review of the table of contents will reveal such timeless topics as political violence, the moral value of personal honor in statecraft, the historical development of Christianity ideology in political discussion and decisions, the appropriateness of torture as a frank and forthright reply to terrorism, the political impact of a hyper development class consciousness, *et al.* Bottom-line: the articles found in this book will not be quickly dated nor are they supportive of current political dogma.

The website *PoliticsandPhilosophy.com* has now been taken down. The original purpose of the site was to offer young post graduate students a platform to experiment with publication minus any strenuous, nerve-wracking, and often destructive peer review. It was felt that offering this kind of stress-free platform would allow for free reign in developing their pet projects and controversial ideas. And second, the site was intended to offer a jump start to the publication train all academics must ride.

Two unexpected consequences arose from this approach. First, because of the controversial nature of the website, it almost guarantees that the essays published would be philosophically forward looking rather than a white-wash of rear facing ideas such as nationalism, mystical notions of racial superiority, predestination, etc. For the editors of *PoliticsandPhilosophy.com*, this was an exciting prospect. Second, due to the unorthodox and frequently contentious ideas the site was designed promote, many authors have chosen to write under pseudonyms; this was unexpected, but understandable. The articles are of a rigorous academic nature and therefore are professionally researched and documented. However, many of the pieces are controversial enough that subsequent and some potentially unknown effect on one's career had to be considered.

Regarding the continued use of pseudonyms, I have elected to continue their use. Partially, this decision was made because contacting some of the authors has proven difficult. Further, for professional or personal reasons the authors we successfully contacted expressed a wish to continue with the *nom de plumes*. Wherever the authors of these article have found themselves currently—in what profession, or stage of career—we should respect the original wishes and not link their names to politically and philosophically intriguing if speculative positions. We often assign audacity to youthful adventurism, yet we must remind ourselves that youth has produced much of lasting importance: Newton invents calculus at 24, Einstein published on special relativity at 26, and who can overlook Beethoven composing concertos at 15 and 16. And regarding names, Beethoven's 9th would be no less overwhelming were the composer unknown. Recall too, that one of the greatest of all documents in American history was written under pseudonyms: The Federalist Papers. We feel we are in good company as we continue that storied tradition.

INTRODUCTION

The editorial staff of *PoliticsandPhilosophy.com* have selected a baker's dozen of these provocative articles to be bound in this volume. For the reader's benefit, it should be noted that due to the type of material presented, many topics are examined multiple times from different angles and by different writers. For example, the very meaning of truth, intrinsically, is discussed in several of the articles. Following that, the meaning of truth is analyzed from a political point of view, from a social perspective, then finally from a philosophical standpoint. If there is contention here, it would be over the meaning of truth and not the meaning of the political and social issues; those issues might be considered more of a foil for a discussion of reality. At the most general level, understanding political reality depends on understanding truth. If the editors at *Politics andPhilosophy.com* had a battle cry, it was surly *veritas animvs* (truth is liberty). To that reality, we remain committed today.

Finally, following the primary twelve articles there is an epilogue, of sorts: A final, thirteenth piece which examines the role of personal honor in politics. Personal honor is not to be confused with integrity. The author of this piece argues that honor and integrity, while having points of intersection and overlap, are nonetheless, not at alike. At first glance, personal honor would appear, at best, to be a tangential and antiquated topic—and possibly a chauvinistic and melodramatic one—a glittery bit of pomp, minus substance. The author rejects this trivialization of honor as he dissects honor as a vital part of not only our personal lives, but our political lives as well. Plunging into personal honor will unpack an analysis of a forgotten and ignored subject. Personal honor is not only a topic with contemporary value and importance, but also a subject with far reaching implications for the emotional and mental health of an ethical world. As this analysis demonstrates, both men and women share in this world of honor and the responsibility that follows from the implications of a world without honor.

Make no mistake. This is a book of philosophy and not of politics, *per se.* This combination of politics understood through philosophy made for an exciting website that in the twenty years of its lifetime was accessed thousands of times from all over the world. The editors would offer enjoyment as a motive for delving into these articles, but the bold nature of the pieces allows more for pondering and rumination than amusement. So, the editors invite the reader to take the subjects and research within this small volume with all the seriousness inherent in each analysis. If any of the pieces bring insight, change or enlightenment, our goals have been met. The editors invite you to enjoy.

W.F. Pray, Reno, NV

AM I DUMB?
OR
WHY POLITICS IS BORING

EMMA BORDEN

Abstract: The article explains why keeping abreast of "political" development is a confusing and often tedious business. The author takes the approach that most often what we see is government and not politics, government being the mask behind which political struggle takes place. The organized face of government is in place to shield the citizenry from the deadly and vicious struggle that takes place behind its seemingly innocuous façade. Look behind the mask and much of the boredom disappears as survival and self-interest stake claim to your undivided attention.

I am a native-born American citizen and I hate politics. To most Americans that statement comes as no great surprise. Watching the political news drives the vast majority of us into a state of confusion, irritation, and ultimately, boredom, not to mention deflated and utterly helpless. These feelings are not unusual and as I have said, come as no great surprise. The question of what precisely provokes these feeling is the topic of this essay.

Personally, I find that the moods mentioned above never come on in the same order, but boredom is always high on the list. I suggest that this sense of boredom is kindled by political news that conjures only apathy as the spawn of helplessness. This is followed swiftly by boredom as some kind of private apology for apathy.

Does any of this mean that I am dumb? Perhaps it does, or perhaps it will end by *making* me dumb—but as I said, I'm not alone in this. Countless Americans feel the same alienation and helplessness as I, followed by apathy and boredom. For evidence, look at how few of us Americans vote. Statistically, only slightly more than half of the eligible voters in the United States bother to go to the polls. Perhaps hating politics is an American pastime, or maybe it's some kind of world-wide phenomenon? I am undecided on the world-wide aspect, but I do live in the United States and I know that helplessness, alienation and a strong dislike for the stench of politics is part of the atmosphere we all breathe.

I have friends, a few, who tell me that to avoid boredom I need to pay greater attention. Yes, they say I should pay close attention and I'll learn how politics affects me, how politics makes my life either livable or a living hell. The desire to survive and survive well will keep me from suffering boredom. But is this accurate? Sure, politics affects my life and the life of every American. Unfortunately, paying attention might have the opposite effect. Perhaps keeping my finger on the pulse of the American political system will have the reverse effect and throw me into an even deeper mood of despair. Being overwhelmed by helplessness can surely do that.

But why pay attention in the first place? Here is an answer, and a good one. No one denies that a central feature of politics is that it is the overall process that determines who gets what, how much, and when. That being the case, it follows that understanding it ought to make me

2

wiser and more fully engaged. However, again the opposite might be true: understanding might lead to the conclusion that all this parceling out of the nation's goods through the political process is, more often than not, unequal and unfair. Despite all the official denials, we certainly suspect that unequal distribution is the norm and not the exception. This realization can quickly lead to painful consequences and occasionally to violence. Sometimes this pain will be mine. Sometimes the pain will belong to others. But inevitably, and at some level, this process of "understanding" will draw me, my life, my surroundings, my wants and needs, into the great political maw to be emotionally chewed, digested, and excreted—very often without me being consciously aware of anything except the helplessness and apathy. My friends insist that there is no escaping this political process and the pain and struggle it produces. Like it or not, I am engaged, and should not ignore the engagement. Yet, isn't it also a serious possibility that a full-blown *consciousness* of this engagement, of this suspected unfair and unbalanced distribution of the social wealth, is the surest avenue for feelings of helplessness, alienation and its companion, boredom?

With full consciousness, however, there also comes a deeper peeling back of the scars of alienation to reveal the size, depth and nature found at the root of helplessness. While examining this root we must first consider that while I must take serious note of the suffering roiling across the world's stage, I should also carefully observe a revealed cause for this aversion to the politics at work behind these horrors. To be specific, a conscious analysis should start with the consideration that while I witness the events of the world I will rarely *see* anything I might accurately describe as *politics*, the struggle. What I *see* is the public face of the struggle: that is, government, or governments.

Conscious analysis should quickly reveal that it is a fundamental misunderstanding of the purpose and role of government, rather than politics, *per se*, (the underlying—and typically unspoken—social relations at work in deciding the allocation of material resources), which leads to the fuzz of helpless confusion that precipitates political withdrawal and alienation. Obviously, government is clearly connected to political relations, even so, it is not precisely the same creature. Government draws its design, meaning and energy from political relations, but government is

3

political relations only in the sense that lava is a volcano: lava is not the source of the volcano, the volcano is the source of the lava. Government is not the source of politics; politics is the source of government. Government is the creature of politics not the other way around. Obviously government and politics are intimately related, yet if we are to lift the veil on political alienation and its primary symptoms of withdrawal and boredom, I will need to draw a clear descriptive distinction between political relations, *per se*, and their formal, structural reification: government. In addition, I will need to specifically address how and why these political relations are often obfuscated by government, an obfuscation that is sometimes deliberate, but more typically simply an inherent part of the structural process.

To get at the feeling of helplessness, let us roll with the distinction between politics and government.

I. Politics or Government? So before anything else, how do we define political relations, or more simply, what is politics? Giving a definition to politics seems simple enough. At its most fundamental level, politics is the process by which the social product is distributed, which is to say, the pathway by which it is decided who gets *what part* of the social product, *how* much of that *what* they get, and *when* they get it; politics is the prioritizing of distribution. The *what* in this case is the sum total of the communal or collective product (which includes services) of a given society. A "given society" can mean the immediate locale, or it can mean the world-wide human community; that is, "society" can range from the very micro, as found in the family and neighborhood, to the very macro, as found in the nation-state and even beyond to that to entities found in the international arena. Whatever the locale, the distribution of the collective social product is always a negotiated feature of all organized societies. It is this distribution of goods and services that is the pivotal factor found at the heart of the human struggle, and it is this struggle that is called *political relations* or politics.

One simple way to get at the heart of all this politicking, this struggle, is to view it as a form of negotiated discrimination. Politics can be accurately viewed as a process that sorts and prioritizes, and thus in the end discriminates insofar as it decides to whom and how the social product is distributed. The formal controlling apparatus by which this negotiated discrimination is accomplished is government, which can take many unexpected forms: for example, a family unit where children might struggle for a greater portion of the collective income in the form of a larger weekly allowance. The governing apparatus that determines a child's portion of the distribution may be determined democratically (decided by family vote) or autocratically, where one of the parents comes to the fore as government (i.e., in this case a dictator). The politics involved is how the children go about influencing the outcome of the governing apparatus: the vote of the family members or the parental, governmental decision making.

The more important political relations do not involve everyone in a given society, only particular social and economic factions. Different factions of a society receive, according to bias, unequal amounts of the social product. I believe this inequality in distribution is obvious without belaboring its development. These distinct social factions are typically arranged in a hierarchal class structure that is protected by the controlling apparatus—government. This is a way of saying that government is built *around* discrimination in the distribution of unequal shares of the product. However, successful government presents itself, not as the protector of class interests, but as the benign face of justice and impartiality. As far as the successful government is concerned this protection of class bias is hidden from direct view behind a complex façade of *legitimacy*.

Without a doubt, all of this discrimination provokes a sense of tension for all members within the given society, no matter the class. This tension over the unequal outcome of distribution revolves around the issues of *fairness* and *justice*. Both of these concepts can best be understood as forces acting to legitimize the discrimination at work in the allocation of goods and services. If the discrimination is perceived in a way that allows for a commonly held sense of satisfaction, all is well and good, legitimacy would seem to prevail. However, if the perception of fairness seems lacking, and should the dissatisfaction be rank enough, the controlling apparatus must act. Simply put, governments can respond to the dissatisfaction in two possible ways. *First*, government can step forward to address the dissatisfaction and take steps to locate the causes of the unfairness then take corrective action, or, *second*, government can emerge as the leading agent for hiding or obscuring both the actuality as well as the causes for the misallocation in distribution. In this second sense,

5

government acts to conceal any lack of fairness, while at the same time offering the appearance of being a neutral and objective tender of justice and fair play. This effort might take some form of sheltering maldistribution beneath supernatural or magical causations such as the "invisible hand of the market," or "trickle down" economics, etc. Since this second way that government hides its true intent is a foremost cause for the feelings of unhappiness and helplessness, I will place my focus here.

Typically, obscuring some lack of fairness in distribution is accomplished by throwing up a cluster of legal rules and legislative principles designed to deflect criticism and dissent (citing the Constitution, for example) while at the same time using those same rules to obscure any bias that might exist, hidden within those rules. It is at this point that the very beginnings of estrangement and alienation, powerlessness and helplessness, begin to emerge. It is this obfuscation that we are interested in analyzing.

The controlling apparatus, that is, government, often acts as a deliberately confusing montage rather than a lens for clarity. This obscuring can be a byproduct of the evolution of a particular type of government, but more often the obscuring is a predetermined feature embedded into the apparatus from the onset of its construction; it is deliberately built into the design. The cause of this predetermination is found in the revealed reality that the political relations *have already determined* the pattern of distribution, and a controlling apparatus (i.e., government) is erected around that pattern in order to protect and if possible hide the unequal nature of that distribution.

If the controlling apparatus is successful, the benign mask of complexities and obscurities that are presented to the citizen has had the desired effect. The average citizen, though outraged by a sense of injustice, or feeling that the allocation of resources is grossly and unjustifiably unequal, is left mired in impotency and cursed with a directionless animus. Of course, behind the mask of obscurities the true benefactors of the unequal allocation have played the system through the predetermined rules to its logical conclusion: an unequal distribution of the social product upward to a specific segment of the social order. The peaceful success of this upward distribution depends upon utilizing government as a means of presenting the unequal distribution as fair and just and legitimate.

The lack of clarity, of course, serves the interests of its benefactors. Only hours of detailed study can unravel the tortured turns of parliamentary complexities, pierce the fog of legal jargon, and grasp the murky subtleties of unequal allocation. Human justice should be clean, direct and immediately understandable. Yet the human agency of government eviscerates the clarity and obscures the precise nature of the political struggle; this lack of clarity, as we will see, is most often a deliberate facet of governmental policy. Alienation and helplessness first arise as we confront this obscurity.

The question of "why" surfaces here: why must government, almost necessarily, be the presiding agent for alienation, helplessness and boredom? However, before we can discuss motive, let us turn to the mechanics of "how". How is it that the workings of our political world are so difficult and elusive? The answer is found in two of the many roles played by government.

II. Two Roles of Government. In its position as prioritizer of distribution, government exercises many functions. In the case of this essay we are concerned with two of the most overriding characteristic roles of government: *mediation* and *coercion*, both of which, in their own way, contribute to obscurity. And both can be further distinguished by their *overt* and *covert* aspects.

a. 1ˢᵗ Role. Mediation. The first of these roles played by government is political mediation. A first and most practical function of government is to establish the rules of the political contest, and then act as referee. This practicality is the *overt* purpose of the role of mediation; this is another way of saying that a foremost and obvious role of government is to establish and exercise a practical methodology for the safe, non-violent management of *discrimination* in the distribution of social wealth.

There is no society where the social wealth is distributed equally. Discrimination in distribution exists everywhere and the discrimination is in the hands of the deciding power at work in mediation. This is overt and should be obvious. Historically, there is almost no governmental legislation or decree that cannot ultimately be traced to some facet of wealth distribution, usually unequal distribution—to create it, reinforce it, manage it, or hide any visible signs of malfeasance.

To offer a few examples of the *overt* in mediation: certain aspects of a government's foreign policy can be traced to a controlled and peaceful management of the friction caused by international economic relations—a friction which is made ubiquitous by the never ending push toward an unequal trade advantage. A government losing control of peaceful mediation can result in trade wars, and in extreme cases, expensive and disruptive shooting wars.

Another example of overt purpose in mediation: a huge expectation of the effects of civil rights legislation is to head off the cost and widespread economic dislocation produced by mass civil disobedience—a civil disobedience that is itself a symptom of the maldistribution of wealth. The failure of quick mediation in the face of civil unrest can result in far greater dislocations (e.g., revolutions).[1]

And one more example: fiscal policy. A government's design in currency manipulation is easily traced to maintaining consistency in capital-intensive stock trading, stability in banking, and favorable balance of trade. These overt mediations in fiscal policy rarely promote equal distribution of social wealth. Such mediations in monetary policy ultimately fall favorably on the side of the ruling class.[2]

Governmental mediation may be corrective, prescriptive, retroactive or proactive, but at the end of the day all the actions can best be understood in terms of the preservation of a certain economic status quo advantageous to one social class over another. Of course, these actions are not presented in such blunt terms i.e., as an overwhelming advantage to the ruling class. In fact, this maintenance of class advantage is able to vanish beneath other more general and positive terms. For example, a good foreign policy can head off wars, civil rights legislation can and does appeal to a sense of fairness, and currency manipulation can halt runaway inflation. However, hidden behind the "positive effects" of these governmental actions is the ever-present fact that the promoted economic mediation generates a class advantage and is the foundation of economic inequality and the social tension that goes along with it.

A precise understanding of the reasons *why* particular types of methodologies arise is beside the immediate point of this discussion. The why will vary greatly from situation to situation. It is sufficient to note that the methods are adopted from what history puts forth as being both available and conforming to the existing political relations and the ideological atmosphere. What is immediately pertinent to us here is that the methodology used in the process of mediation also generates an important *"covert"* role for government. It is this covert role that moves us toward the heart of powerlessness, helplessness and boredom.

This *covert* role, as derived from the methodology and the structure of mediation, is designed to cloak both the unequal distribution, and perhaps more importantly to the favored class, the reasons behind it. The methodology, in a general way, typically blends a procedural mist with popular messages of patriotism and chauvinism. The intent, employed with great success, is to blanket and disguise the crude political struggle for the communal product that is at work behind the mediation. Rather than employ a methodology designed for a rational distribution of the communal product, the covert design is meant to hide the basic fact that the mediation is intended to preserve some basic status quo, a status quo that is fundamentally unequal.

Armed with enough facts and education, this veil can be pierced and drawn aside. For example, even a brief study will reveal that distributing income upward to the wealthy classes may be hidden behind a surge of "tax cuts for all." To illustrate: a 2% tax cut for income earners making $30,000 means a savings of $600.00, while the same tax cut for incomes of $3,000,000 means an increase in income of $60,000, or an income boost of twice the total yearly income of the earner of $30,000. This is upward distribution of wealth is cloaked beneath a popular "tax cut" for all. Such legislative maneuvering on behalf of the elite is not uncommon, but behind this parliamentary smoke and mirrors most voters never really witness the strong bias toward the upper classes. It is the covert role of mediation to make certain that this legislative bias never sees the light of day. Given the unequal distribution of power, every governmental effort at mediation from budget cuts to governmental agency appointees is tipped toward the elite. This literally means that government as a whole is covertly tipped toward socioeconomic inequality.

On what is, and what ought to be. Some of this hidden bias in mediation is obvious, even to the casual onlooker[3]. Other forms of class bias are less obvious[4]. The less obvious is because the covert role of government need not necessarily be of direct or deliberate intent. This covert role may be so completely integrated in the ideological playing field that it all but goes unnoticed by the majority of the players[5]. The referee (i.e., government) instead of searching out a pattern for more rational and equal redistribution of the communal product according to need and social contribution, finds the fact of social injustice and bias appropriate and even natural to mainstream political doctrine. This "natural" feel is a shield for the biased mediation and is provided by the prevailing cultural winds, those found in harmony with the dominate ideology. Unequal teams playing on a rigged field become far less obvious and more natural when seen through the lens of an ideological system that substitutes the idea of "what ought to be" for the actuality of "what is the reality." For example, we are all equal before the law, as the "what ought to be," which acts as a mask for the actuality of "what is the reality." In other words, the concrete reality of unequal social and economic wherewithal, which tips the scales of justice in favor of the moneyed classes and hides behind the fairy tale of "equality before the law."

The thing to notice about this rigged field is that the referee, that is *the government*, finds facilitation of class bias easier to negotiate behind the ideological shield of "what ought to be" (that justice is blind) as opposed to the actual of "what is" (economic and political position that lays a thumb on the scales of justice). The first (what ought to be) being the public face for the hidden effect of the class bias (the concrete reality).

It should be noted that there is a drawback to injecting the "what ought" into the material field of "what is." Such an injection tugs at the edges of the ideological cloak. The idealized "what ought" inevitably comes into conflict with the "what is" of governmental institutions, especially in "democratic" societies. Often this provokes confusion and a conceptual stalemate. And sometimes it generates governmental paralysis, as in the case of the presidency of James Buchanan, or worse, a governmental panic, as in the case of the Weimar Republic naming Hitler Chancellor of Germany. Between the two, stalemate or panic, stalemate is more common, though such a tension will not last very long without resolution.

Here is a paradigm illustrating the development of this stalemate and eventual resolution: what happens when the ideology that suggests how things "ought to be" comes into direct conflict with a governmental structure that is rigged to preserve a concrete "what is?" This becomes visible when an idealized reflex rises that tells us that we "ought" to live in an egalitarian society, a society where cooperation and common goals will benefit all. This idealized reflex is opposed by the very real, but cloaked, "what is" of a socioeconomic inequality that receives active support from the governing establishment. Such a situation was quite evident in the years following the American Civil War. The idealized equality of the new Freedmen came into direct conflict with the governing institutions dominated by Southern planters and Northern mercantile interests. For economic reasons necessary to the survival of these southern and northern financial interests, the governing apparatus came to support a system where the Freedman continued to labor under near slave-like conditions in order that the country's greatest product, King Cotton, continue to reign.[6] In this case, slave like conditions continued for the southern Black, fully sanctioned by government fiat and decree. The tension that was engendered by this conflict between "what ought" and "what is" had to wait until the middle and late 20th century for legislative redress and resolution.

   b. 2nd Role. The second *overt* role of government is the application of force. Except for the application of legitimacy, there is no attempt to hide this role. However, this role is not necessarily the direct application of violence, but an ongoing and systemic coercion that plays out through the monopoly on violence in the form of police agencies and a military at the beck-and-call of governmental institutions. So by "force," we mean force in its broadest sense, the *threat of violence* as well as its actual application. This role of government maintains the social order with the coercive agencies by which political decisions on the distribution of the communal product can be enforced, should voluntary compliance be lacking. Typically, the mere awareness of the threat of violence is enough to gain compliance from the populace. The policeman's gun can remain holstered, but its presence alone states the stark fact that playing outside of the rigged field can lead to loss of liberty and even life.

   The *covert* role of force and violence is to secure *legitimacy* for the uneven playing field. This path toward legitimacy begins with the presentation of coercion and enforcement as natural and just. This mask of legitimacy for state violence is presented by legal rituals and constitutional mantras that serve to cloak force and violence behind the mantle of *legitimacy*—a mantle which is then protected by the threat of the violence it legitimizes. The apparent symbiotic relationship between legitimacy and state sanctioned violence is real and covertly serves to stabilize the unequal scales of justice by laying on a heavy thumb.

   The covert application of legitimacy behind state-controlled coercion often serves government as a misdirection of focus from the very real and unequal distribution of social wealth. Legitimacy also acts to cloak the nature of the force involved in winning the power struggles. The near divinity of legal rituals provides the glue binding legitimacy with violence. By extension, the fulfillment of legitimacy allows for force, or the threat of force, to be applied against any resistance to legitimacy and do so with a minimum of debate or resistance. Legitimacy offers immediacy and moral sanctuary for its chief protector: state-controlled violence.

It is important to note here that the direct governmental application of force and coercion is only one form that political violence can take. The others forms of legitimate force and violence are less understood governmentally and more understood socially and economically; nonetheless, they are political in cause and effect. To offer a few examples of social and economic violence: depressing income through the dismantling of a unionized work force, discrimination in housing and education, and restricted or blocked access to medical facilities, all serve as examples of the "legitimate" use of social and economic violence against citizens, and all this is done in the service of unequal distribution of communal goods and services.

To be fair, it should also be noted that not all coercive acts by government are negative or abusive; there is nothing automatic here, or an abusiveness beyond human intervention. In the examples mentioned above, where housing opportunities and access to various educational facilities are largely controlled by economic class, governmental roles of mediation and occasionally force can step in for redress of the more egregious violations. We see this in the intervention of federal troops in the case of the desegregation of public schools in Little Rock during 1957, the coercive force of the Civil Rights Act of 1964, the introduction of the Dream Act to block forcible deportation of Americanized immigrants. One could argue, I suppose, that the entire civil rights movement was only an effort to clean up the ugly image the US presented to the world-at-large. On balance, however, Eisenhower's motives (and a decades later, Lyndon Johnson's and Obama's) no doubt stemmed as much from a sense of justice and fair play as it did from *Brown vs. The Board of Education*. However, all too often the citizen's experience with government feeds cynicism, making decent motives difficult to see.

III. An assessment of governmental roles: The roles of mediation and force work hand-in-hand because, to be completely realistic, the distribution of the communal product means that someone's gain is almost always due to someone else's loss. Politics is the intense struggle for the goods and services provided by the social order. This makes for dog-eat-dog political relations and plenty of ensuing frustration and anger. This is not a pretty picture, but due to the nature of scarcity, and the caprice of human desires, such an intense struggle is an accurate image of the politics of socioeconomic relations. As a consequence, it can be argued that what would be taking place in the absence of government processes is a fierce, often violent and unrelenting free-for-all over possession of the communal product. This was the point of view of political relations and an argument for the necessity of government advanced by Thomas Hobbes. And Hobbes' argument on behalf of government's major roles of mediation and force seems to have held together for quite a while now.

The level of ferocity in this carrot-and-stick, carefully managed free-for-all, depends on the proximity of two elements. One element is the *availability* of the communal product, and other element is the *control* over distribution of the communal product. Keep these two factors in mind, "availability" and "control," These operators, more than any other, serve to govern the level of coercion and violence necessary in any given social order. Government is both the mask behind which this struggle is carried out and the negotiator that attempts to keep the ferocity of the struggle from spilling over into open warfare. Throughout various societies these two factors (availability and control of the communal product) that manage political relations might be configured and arrayed differently, but they are always present to one degree or another and always in play—again, to one degree or another. The political relations that define the players in the struggle also vary greatly, and of course, this variety greatly affects the nature of the government that keeps all the players in check. In this real world the struggle that is political relations is always present behind the mask of government. Governments always attempt to present a benign front of legitimacy behind which real world discrimination and control are always at work.

The methods of government action—the overt and covert—are interwoven elements. They are also, to a considerable degree, symbiotic. The very visible machinery of mediation provides the legal infrastructure that covertly legitimizes and shields both the methods of control as well as the factions involved in the struggle over social wealth. The second role of government, that of providing the concentration of force that safeguards the unequal distribution of social wealth, also generates the covert misdirection by a legal "understanding" of force. This "legal understanding" goes a long way toward providing the fog of legitimacy that disguises and facilitates the suppression of agitation for some change in distribution patterns. This fog of legitimacy surrounding control and suppression is particularly keen and visible when democratic forces press for changes in distribution. For their part, the "rewarded factions," in exchange for their hiddenness and gain from peaceful distribution, steadily and positively bolster government's legitimacy in the control and suppression of agitation for change.

For the vast majority of us it is natural to sense something in the complex methodology of governing that, if not openly hostile, feels oppressive and beyond our control. Most individuals in any given society see this picture of alienation simply as an inevitable outcome of the size and machinations of government. The majority of citizens are remote from government and estranged from the intimacies of politics that afford command over the distribution of the communal product. These citizens need no elaborate descriptions to justify their sense of alienation (how do you fight city hall?). For them, government is witnessed as a hurtful and depriving entity. The fog of government does not allow for fast and ready analysis of the legitimacy of the underlying politics. Without the time and wherewithal to acquire or purchase expertise, the citizenry suffers frustration, depression and boredom. Is this frustration, depression and boredom warranted? It would seem so. It is this built-in, nearly impenetrable fog of government, in the service of mediation and coercion, that is the progenitor of voter apathy.

For those who benefit from the status quo the opposite is the case. The more one receives from the political mediation, the more government appears in a favorable light and the more involved you are likely to become in the processes. For those who acquire the lion's share of social distribution, government is not seen merely as good and temperate, not merely as a cornucopia of beneficence, but a legitimate protector of the status quo. For these few, the natural inclination is to support the source of this plenty with all the resources at hand, i.e., money and influence.

With this understanding of overt and covert, it is easy to grasp that the *seeing* of government, rather than politics, generally accounts for why most activities in the political arena are confusing, difficult to understand and disturbing to follow. It is always best to remember that it is politics, not government, which is the actual struggle to determine the distribution of the communal product as a whole. Government is the agency that legitimizes the distribution. This distinction is more than analytically useful. This distinction between politics and government will go a long way toward charging your interest in the political world.

IV. Gaining a Point of View. There is one thing that should not be a mystery. Alongside the mediating efforts of government, the actual fogging—i.e., constructing a lattice of constitutional frameworks and legalities—that conceals the real power relations is not readily available for viewing. This cloaking of the real relations by rituals of legitimacy is interwoven with the ideology of the times. Recognition of stark political reality depends largely on the position, the expertise and the sensitivity of the viewer. This is to say that exactly how the dynamic between the real struggle and the façade is perceived depends largely on whom the viewer is and where the viewer is positioned in relation to the operation of the distributive processes. A closeness to the decision-making process causes the viewer to see the relations as less enigmatic, less threatening, and more manageable than for those standing further away. When one stands close enough to the levers of power to actually influence their pulling, the process of distribution appears natural and appropriate to the events of the day. But regardless of position, the process must fit into current ideological interpretation, otherwise legitimacy could not occur. Under the most benign of circumstances, which is best exemplified by some form of a parliamentary government, the power structure must be ideologically viewed as "democratic" and a representative system seen as standing "for and by the people." In the absence of this perspective legitimacy might well collapse, often with grave consequences for the status quo.

Legitimacy seems to fare best in the flexible atmosphere of "representative democracies" as the representatives at least give the appearance of offering support to the ideals of justice and equality. The reality, as opposed to appearance, is that the distribution of the communal product acts according to the very real, material power relations, that is, the socio-economic, structural reality that animates and directs the government's distributive goals. Behind the fog and the legal and constitutional veneer that shield these relations from view, the "representatives" front for certain socio-economic groups, and typically these are not the groups suggested by the legal and constitutional façade. Because the ideology of legitimacy serves to mask the real political relationship, as well as the actual nature of the distributive process to the roles of government, even the players themselves can be fooled into denying the underlying power struggle. This is, however, not as common with the hands-on players as it is with the estranged bystanders. As pure democracy remains a theoretical entity—where the population at large would directly pull the levels of power and distribution—it is difficult to determine the practical consequences to social distribution under such a forthright democratic system.

V. Political Relations in Everyday Life. My every activity is a part of political relations, although because of the fog of ideology daily activities are not often regarded as such. To be more precise, acting out "political relations" can mean deciding which restaurant to eat at, or which book to buy, or simply getting up in the morning and going to work. All of these activities represent aspects of the communal product, together with the management and distribution of that product. Of course, describing these commonplace activities as "political relations" sounds strange, as one is inclined to think of some or all of these acts as being trivial, voluntary and far removed from issues of force and power. But consider: what if everyone stayed home today instead of going to work? This is typically called a general strike, and is an overt political tool used at times to bring down governments. Distribution of communal product can be disrupted by voluntarily boycotting particular commercially available items. Deliberately disregarding civil or even criminal laws—this is usually called civil disobedience—has an immediate impact on government and will quickly activate the two roles of government. These are mass movements and require the participation of large numbers of people. A single person's action is easily contained by the machinery of government, but it remains recognizable as micro civil disobedience. Likewise, continuing in a mode of obedience, rather out of fear or out of belief, is also political, and outwardly reinforces the legitimacy of the governing system.

A complete consideration of the above seems to provoke a secondary issue. This issue can be best stated by asking the question: are not these voluntary acts of obedience, and many other mundane actions, such as going to a movie, selecting a newspaper, and so on, completely free of overt coercion, that is, free of the active "intrusion" of government? For if it were true that my daily life is non-political, then the decisions I make in my daily life would be free of coercion, or so it would seem. But is this really the case, and do I honestly feel this way?

Consider first that government, while having a monopoly on "legitimate" violence, is only one face of political coercion, and that every one of my actions, no matter how pedestrian, is locked into the web of social experience and political relations in which I live. Ponder the above illustration of the general strike. Were I to alone refuse to work—act out my own mini general strike—I would suffer the force and power of the social order in short order. My action would not only be contained and go unnoticed, but likely cripple my life's chances. The matrix of these social relations that crushed my little protest is ultimately rooted in the relationships of power existent within my society. These actions are not always governmental, but are political. Let me make this point with a more positive example: the restaurant in which I decide to eat is within my "free" decision-making range principally because of the power of a politically managed economy that widely influences employment, income, advertising, food distribution, mortgage lending, and the business class to which the owner of the restaurant, and myself, belong, etc. Even this seemingly prosaic action is interwoven with many of the social and economic elements within which I live and make choices. Without being aware of it, a system of subtle economic and social force guides my actions through the decision-making surrounding events. Even within these social and economic actions that seem trivial and relatively unimportant, political coercion is at work.

The fact that we do not ordinarily consider such daily activities where we bank, shop or eat, as in any way coerced by the existing power relations is a testimonial to the pervasiveness of an ideology that obscures and misdirects much of our thinking. The media and government offer legitimacy to these modes of thought easily making them appear axiomatic and beyond question. These modes of thought, facilitated by mass decimation, are the primary way in which we are turned away from acknowledging the power relations at work that influence even apparently random decisions. We are turned away from realizing life itself as political and are instead channeled into viewing government as politics, or rather I should say the fog of government as politics. To escape helplessness and boredom I need to recognize that with very little exception, every act has some implication for this web of power relations. My every act is, to some degree, political in nature.

It is also true that seeing the extent of this system of thought may be beyond our prevailing consciousness. You and I, as distasteful as it is to contemplate, are creatures (though not marionettes!) of coercive (i.e., political) forces of which we are typically unaware. Material coercive forces (e.g., police) are not ghosts or spirits that live inside the social machinery. But what about the cohesive ideas in our heads? Vaporous, intangible, invisible—some allow us to seamlessly negotiate our way through actions that make up the circumstances of our everyday lives; others acts as a brake to action, or as a stern guide to behavior that is non-threatening to the social order. We are immersed in the ideology of our society to such a degree that we give this coercion not a thought, for the ideas we employ seem to us as natural as seeing the hands at the ends of our arms.

VI. Why I feel dumb. The role of government, while having considerable bearing on questions of distribution, is also a dominate player in why I feel stupid in the face of "politics." As government is a mask for the raw, underlying political struggle, it must misdirect my attention elsewhere into "safe" understandings of the political relations and their tireless jockeying for position. The real divvying up of the communal product, which might be of genuine interest to me, is spirited away behind a bland and boring apparat soup that is intended not to excite my interest lest I be tempted to enter the struggle actively. This last, my actively entering the struggle for communal product, is never a desirable factor for the power relations, relations that are the structural determinates of society. This reality seems most obvious in a "democratic" society, where the *appearance* of participation must overwhelm the reality of alienation, apathy and anomie. In actuality, however, my every move is wrapped up in this struggle for the communal product.

It is important to note that political factors blend into the social matrix in such a way as to misdirect an accurate view of the power arrangements guiding distribution of the communal produce. In addition, this blending and misdirection often causes the coercive factors to appear normal and fitting, that is, make coercion appear *a-political*. This misdirection represents another transforming power of the prevailing system of ideas (i.e., ideology). In the most general sense, all of my social relations (e.g., who I choose to marry, what university I plan to attend, etc.) are political in that the parameters of my living are expressions of historically determined power relations. Living within this idea system means that from the moment of my birth I have inhaled the idea-system of my time, making all that I witness seem as normal as water to a fish. Where I am born, into what time in history, into what class, into what race, has profound implications for me and the idea systems that influence my thinking. I am consciously aware of actions overtly related to the governing structure of our society—elections, party affiliation, taxes collection, police activity, and so on—but all of my other acts, no matter how trivial, and most of my thinking, have elements of power relations about them and are also political, only I am not completely conscious of them. It is actually more accurate to say that I am politically unconscious of the world around me, which makes me feel stupid and bored in the face of politics. Only I am not stupid or dumb; I am simply so immersed in the ideology of the times that I only seem unconscious of the power relations swirling around me. In a sense, I might say that I am conscious of the unconsciousness if only because I can trace my feelings of powerlessness to a sense of compulsion and coercion that direct my actions in ways that are often not so subtle, yet are visibly obscured. I must file taxes, sign up for the selective service, buy auto insurance, and so on. We do not know who the people were who first put these rules in place yet violating any of them can bring dire effects. There is greater subtlety in actions such as choosing the college I'll attend, where I'll live, the medical care I'll receive. I am guided by all of these choices, only the guiding machinery is more obscure and the principles more difficult to understand. All this seems very tedious and although I may understand it, I would prefer not to dwell on it. Many times the obscuring mist and the underlying ubiquitous threat of force actually provoke one to prefer unconsciousness to political consciousness.

VII. Fixing Dumb. It is not that government represents an outright lie; that government is an outright lie is not only a cynical view, but an incorrect view. Government, in terms of alienation and confusion, is like a river stone distorting the flow of political consciousness. Government is misdirection, an obstacle to clear thinking about where I am in relation to the struggle for the communal product. This is a challenge and one that I must accept in order to surmount the anger working against a clearer vision of my world and my power in it. Once I look deep, push past that veneer of government, my interest is piqued by tapping into the real social factors that jockey for possession and control of the forces of production and distribution. I can see that the real forces at work are human forces, acting on real human emotions, only hidden by working through the apparatus of government. The value of studying government is to see where it is going about its business, working through the rituals, the procedures, and how this offers clues as to the nature of the social forces involved in the struggle. Through the workings of government I can begin to grasp the alignment of these social forces with the governmental overlay, understand how the forces direct the levers of government to accomplish the self-serving tasks, and get it as to why the obscurity is necessary to the subterfuge. In short, the true value of studying government is found in using the acquired knowledge to push beyond the artificial contrivances of legality and legislative ritual to a naked vision of the social forces struggling for control of the communal product. The veil of government must be pushed aside, and that can only be accomplished through a deep study of the veiling process.

On another level, clear vision demands that I focus on the possibility for the introduction of high doses of *direct democracy*.[7] Besides bringing presentation in line with reality it would bring the actual power relations into much sharper relief. As stated above, it is not clear how the actual practice of direct democracy would work in reality, but as the introduction of direct democracy would cause governmental interference to be a minimal factor in obscuring a correct view of power relations, its consideration cannot help but produce clarity. Partly because of the practical changes a form of direct democracy would bring, and partly because of the change in perception it would produce, there is also a very good chance that the power relations would be strongly encouraged to reconfigure. Real, direct democracy can do such things. Whether such a change is for the better is a question of point of view, which is dependent of on the position of the individual in relationship to the communal product. But one thing seems certain. Being dumb is to a great extent a political act. It is an act driven by helplessness in the face of impersonal government, but not in the face of the actual power relations. Even the contemplation of direct democracy would give me the feeling of having my hands on the levers of power, give me a direct view and not a misdirected view of the distribution of the communal product, and thus empower my vision to blow away the fog of being dumb.

At the very heart of this awakening is the understanding that politics is not government, as government is merely an expression of politics. Government, as such, is a serious misdirection, a distraction working against a true understanding of political relations. Getting at an accurate picture of the true power relations is a liberating experience that correctly directs my energy at the actual nature of the struggle over the communal product. This is a struggle I cannot avoid, not ever, as I am part of my society's political relations from my birth to my death.

Notes

1. In no way does this suggest that none of the people involved in civil rights legislation were urged on by a desire to see justice done for rebellious repressed minorities, but only that a leading cause for such a civil rights movement was the preventing of future economic damage and dislocation. If I may: the squeaky wheel gets the grease.

2. I use the term "ruling class" advisedly, for there is nothing inherent in the expression that excludes the possibility, at least theoretically, that in a communist or democratic society the ruling class would be the working class, the underclass in a bourgeois social order.

3. As an additional example, look to pork-barrel legislation as a type of mediation understood as deliberately biased, though often in favor of a local elite rather a national elite.

4. The class bias is less obvious in such as anti-labor, right-to-work laws, hidden under the ideological guise of promoting individual freedom for the worker.

5. We might compare and contrast *Jim Crow Laws* as in overt conflict with western ideologies of equality, with that of *voter suppression*, which while accomplishing the same thing as Jim Crow, can be more easily integrated into cloaking ideologies promoting equality and fair play (i.e., fair elections).

6. For probably the best treatment of this shameful era of governmental oppression of the Southern Blacks see: Eric Foner, *Reconstruction, America's Unfinished Revolution*, Perennial Classics, (New York, 2002). Especially see chapter six.

7. Direct democracy (or pure democracy): where the people vote on initiatives directly; this as opposed to a representative democracy, where the people elect representative who are promised to act on behalf of the voters. While direct democracy is less open to corruption than representative democracy, it is also more difficult to establish as a working model.

ANARCHY
AND
THE CASE FOR GOVERNMENT

MARTIN BLISS, PH.D

Abstract: This article discusses the rise of government and the running thread of anarchist theory that has always existed in tandem and counter to government. The essay is written in two parts: The first part of the essay offers some of the more widely recognized philosophical premises to justify the existence of the political state, especially the modern liberal, political state. The second part is an analytical discussion of the historical reality and how anarchist theory would treat the discrepancy between liberal philosophy and historical reality. This historical treatment on the rise of government takes the reader into a theoretical journey through Plato and Aristotle, then Hobbes and Locke. The analysis then compares these several theories with the best research on the rise of "government" provided by up-to-date paleoanthropology. As it turns out, according to Dr. Bliss, the science *does* support some of the conjecture of the philosophers, but with certain caveats.

Government: *a political directorate exercising control over inhabitants of a community or society.*

Anarchy: *a state of society without government or law.*

Part One: The Case for Government

We will begin with a positive, affirmative argument for the existence of the state. Going back as far as any written record will allow there have always been the ruled and their rulers. Governments, as defined as entities exercising control over inhabitants of a community or society, are ubiquitous. This universality is so obvious that debates concerning "government," as such, generally revolve around types and not some overall argument for their existence. The existence of "government" has always been taken for granted; "government" is an assumed entity—end of discussion! But suppose we question this apparent axiom. Suppose we ask ourselves what exactly makes up the foundation for the assumption of government as necessary and omnipresent. Precisely how theoretically sturdy are the philosophical underpinnings for the ubiquity of government?

Thomas Hobbes is undoubtedly the first spokesperson that comes to mind when we casually consider the typical justification for government. In a dedication to one of the editions of *De Cive* (The Citizen), Hobbes states, as it is usually paraphrased, albeit somewhat clumsily, that "Man is wolf to man."[1] This is, however, only a thin slice of the famous statement by Hobbes. The complete statement found in the 1651 dedication of *De Cive* is as follows:

> "To speak impartially, both sayings are very true; That Man to Man
> is a kind of God; and that Man to Man is an errant Wolfe. The first
> is true, if we compare Citizens amongst themselves; and the second,
> if we compare Cities."

The complete quote raises innumerable questions as to what exactly Hobbes means when he speaks of human nature as opposed to the nature of political organization; we will look at this statement in greater detail a bit further down. However, before going further into Hobbes it will serve our purpose in questioning the assumption of government to look further back in history. First are the observations on the origins of civil government made by Plato and Aristotle.

At the time of Plato, the Greeks lacked extensive resources to study the history of humanity. As a consequence, much of their speculations were a bit fanciful and based largely on reason and acceptance of current reality as somehow the way things always were. As we will see further on, their speculation was actually not that far off the mark.

Plato (427-347 BCE). In book three of *The Laws*, Plato, taking the part of the Athenian Stranger, speculates somewhat briefly on need for government. This was not a "man in nature" theme as was later contrived by Hobbes and Locke, but a position based on the notion that a great deluge had destroyed all city-states, which is to say that civilization as the Greeks knew it was all but washed from existence, leaving our species in a primitive state.[2] Plato then suggests reasons why cities and government would start up anew.

In the dialogue, Plato claims that the few survivors of this catastrophe were well disposed toward one another, as their small number caused all in nature to be in great abundance. Natural abundance would cause strife and warfare to be minimal or non-existent. In this bygone era, Plato speculates, because all metal like gold and silver had disappeared, there was no class mired in poverty, and no class steeped in riches. Given the lack of enmity, or all things being equal, Plato asserts, "The fewness of the survivors would make them desirous of intercourse with one another."[3] Here Plato suggests that people are by nature social and even gregarious, enjoying each other's company.

Plato remarks:

"Hence in those days mankind were not very poor; nor was poverty a cause of difference among them; and rich they could not have been, having neither gold nor silver; such at that time was their condition. And the community which has neither poverty nor riches will always have the noblest principles; in it there is no insolence or injustice, nor, again, are there any contentions or envyings (sic). And therefore they were good."[4]

Yet even here, where there was no need to control a population because of disparity in wealth, Plato claims that there were lordships of sorts. Families were governed by the eldest who rendered laws and judgments to the wives and children. Such a governing structure was endemic to the nature of the family. To support his claim of early paternal lordships, Plato cites as evidence the works of the poet Homer.[5]

Plato suggests that after many generations, the natural sociability of humanity drew them into collections of greater numbers, at which time they turned to husbandry and farming, which required a restructuring for their new agrarian lifestyle. This was a lifestyle that involved the difficult organization of common defense and a more complex system of food production.[6] As the population grew, the people got together to select a council of arbitrators for the purpose of selecting from among the conflicting decrees those which would best serve the interests of the whole. These were presented to the king for him to choose those he thought best. This was the beginning of legislation and aristocracy, for the aristocracy surely developed out of this class of arbitrators.[7]

At this point Plato goes on to analyze the several forms that government can take, which is beyond the scope of this paper. In any case, three things clearly emerge from this look into Plato and the case he presents for government. The first is that according to Plato governments emerge naturally from the patriarchal family structure he was familiar with, and second, that government cannot be destroyed except by the rulers.[8] And finally, he says, a need to settle disputes becomes increasingly critical with the transition from the primitive family structure to the more complex extended agrarian community. All three of these notions found in Plato will be subjected to scrutiny and debate in the following portion of the paper devoted to an anarchist response.

What is crucial in Plato's position—in making the case for government—are two implicit assumptions: (1) Domination and authority are built into the structure of the human family, the underlying theme being that given the basic nature of human organization there are always the ruler and the ruled. (2) As societies transition from an archaic hunter-gatherer state to a complex agrarian state, the need to resolve disputes breeds a sovereignty that becomes more complex and more entrenched. Due to a complete lack of historical resources, the first claim was, in Plato's day, impossible to explore and verify. The running dialogue makes clear that the Greeks of Plato's time were simply unable to imagine a time when there was not some kind of authoritarian organization.

One cannot fault Plato for this lack of historical insight as such exploration only became possible in the last couple hundred years with the arrival of advanced paleo and anthropological tools and study. And it should be noted that in contemporary times, while there are such tools available, the common notion remains that there was always some kind of authoritarian structure no matter how rudimentary the society.

Aristotle (384-322 BCE): Aristotle, in keeping with his characteristic style, is more richly detailed than Plato, and lengthier in the systematic elucidation of his argument. Aristotle begins his famous work *Politics* with the statement:

> "Every state is a community of some kind and every community is established with a view to some good; for everyone always acts in order to obtain that which they think good. But, if all communities aim at some good, the state or political community, which is the highest of all, and which embraces all the rest, aims at good in a greater degree than any other, and at the highest good."[9]

There is a vague quality about this statement. The first basic question that should emerge is what does Aristotle mean by "the highest good." The good for Aristotle, which is the aim of the State, means far more than just the supplying of material products and services, though Aristotle clearly understands that these are necessary.[10] For Aristotle the highest good, as he also states in his work the *Ethics*, is the attainment of happiness, which for Aristotle is only found in a life of excellence and contemplation.[11] There are controversial aspects of Aristotle's vision for the State, such as the implied elitism and the reliance on a class of individuals at the bottom of the social ladder (in his day, slaves) so necessary for the comfortable support of the contemplative life. These objections are to be noted here, and then set aside, as a lengthy criticism of Aristotle's vision is beyond the scheme of this treatise. Instead, we will consider that the purpose of the State, in Aristotle's vision, is the fulfillment of humanness, which is to say, the achievement of virtue and excellence through rational contemplation.

As to the origin of the State, Aristotle first attests that before all else "there must be a union of those who cannot exist without each other; namely, of male and female, that the race may continue, and of natural ruler and subject."[12] Aristotle then claims that "out of these two relationships the first thing to arise is the family."[13] Aristotle next describes the family as "The association established by nature for the supply of men's everyday wants."[14] As wants grow beyond basic needs, collections of families, in the form of villages, arise. These villages are composed, as a most natural form, all of the same blood.[15] The villages are ruled by kings of the same blood as that of the collected families.[16] Like Plato before him, Aristotle's general outline appears to balance against whatever evidence was provided the Greeks by Homeric sources.[17] However, in going back further, to the prehistory of the "family," to a time which we today understand as the hunter-gatherer clan, Aristotle's position does not square up particularly well with the paleoanthropology. He is not wildly off, but enough so that his claim of natural ruler and ruled is a slippery one. But in making a *case* for the State, the actual facts of the matter are of less immediate importance than the argument itself. The historical facts will be considered in due course.

It is at this point that Aristotle makes his argument for the State. He writes:

"When several villages are united in a single community, large enough to be nearly or quite self-sufficing, the state comes into existence, originating in the bare needs of life, and continuing in existence for the sake of the good life. And therefore, if the earliest forms of society are natural, so is the state, for the end of them, and the nature of a thing is its end[18]. . . Hence it is evident that the state is a creation of nature, and that man is by nature a political animal."[19]

Further, Aristotle goes on to assert that:

"The state is by nature clearly prior to the family and to the individual, since the whole is of necessity prior to the part[20] . . . The proof that the state is a creation of nature and prior to the individual is that the individual, when isolated, is not self-sufficing; and therefore he is alike a part in relation to the whole. But he who is unable to live in society, or who has no need because he is sufficient for himself, must be either a beast or a god; he is not part of a state."[21]

We need to exercise a bit of caution when reading Aristotle. By the above passage he does not mean that the individual or the family would disappear or otherwise unravel in the absence of the State, but rather that the individual and the family become something less than fully human without the State. Therefore, as suggested before, for Aristotle the State bestows the quality of "humanness" to the individual and the family. The individual in the family or the village (i.e., collection of like families) can satisfy basic needs and wants; but when separated from law and justice (i.e., the State), individuals are reduced to "The most savage of animals, and the most full of lust and gluttony."[22] In these remarks by Aristotle there is certainly more than a glimmer of the commonplace assumptions concerning Thomas Hobbes.

Like Plato before him, Aristotle hints at a pre-state condition, a collection of like families, as in villages, where law and justice achieve prominence and dominance. The "good" that was spoken of so ambiguously earlier has come to mean that the State allows for the fulfillment of human design. The State cannot exist without the human, nor the human exist without the State.

Aristotle is very much aware that the State is made up of various parts, some intended to rule and others ruled. In a section ostensibly intended as a discourse on slavery, Aristotle momentarily digresses to claim: "That some should rule and others be ruled is a thing not only of necessity, but expedient; from the hour of their birth, some are marked out for subjection, other for rule."[23] Aside from remarks on slavery as a natural condition, there is little room to doubt that Aristotle considers women subservient to men.[24] But other than these specifics, equality among free citizens is left a somewhat a blurry picture, although he does consider there to be superior citizens and inferior.[25] A detailed analysis here of the *source* of unequal authority is beyond the primary question of this paper. However, the issue of inequality will arise again and again as we consider the case and justification *for* authoritarian rule.

29

Even so, Aristotle, very much like Plato, considers that authoritarian rule begins with the family and is refined in the political State. Therefore, that there are always the rulers and the ruled is indisputable. So, in making a positive case for government, Aristotle, in a similar manner to Plato, suggests (1) that authoritarian rule is according to nature and cannot be avoided, (2) that the first authoritarian structures (families and collections of families) were proper and expedient for meeting basic needs, and (3) that the State, as a refinement, codifies authoritarian rule in order that the greater good be achieved.

∽

For Aristotle and Plato, the case for government rests on elements in nature that support the meeting of human needs through a hierarchal power structure. This is to say that for our two Greek philosophers, the basic needs for sustenance, shelter and defense are best executed through a system of ruler and subject. Government, for both these ancients, supplies the necessary requirements for a just distribution of these basic necessities. The types of government thought best by Plato and Aristotle are beside the immediate point. Suffice it to say that neither of the philosophers favored democracy, that is, rule by the people. Yet government, it was thought, was for the attainment and fulfillment of humanness, and was in the best interest of all, ruler and governed alike. In addressing justification for government, we will see that the arguments presented by Plato and Aristotle are largely pressed forward by Hobbes and Locke, though the question of origin shows some considerable difference.

Thomas Hobbes (1588 - 1679) and **John Locke** (1632-1704). Neither Hobbes nor Locke presupposed the existence of the State. Both these philosophers start with human beings and build the State around their understanding of our species. They will argue that the State is a necessity given the nature of our species in natural and uncontrolled circumstances. For them the State becomes necessary because of the way that human beings are in a raw "state of nature," an imaginative thought experiment designed to argue the necessity of the State given the unattractive core nature of human beings.[26] This presentation of the "true nature" of human beings explains, in part, why these two philosophers have had a much greater impact on modern political thinking than either Plato or Aristotle.

Hobbes is more forthright, detailed and organized than Locke. He is also more bold in his assertions—so bold in his thinking that he had at least one conservative scholar, Leo Strauss, maintaining that Locke saw it as his personal duty to mitigate the teachings of Hobbes. Strauss thought that Locke caused Hobbes to be more palatable for his time by turning the need for government as an institution for outright self-preservation into an institution for the protection private property.[27] As the right to private property is only one aim of one form of government, we will set a direct study of Locke aside for this project. Thomas Hobbes, as a proponent of strong government—and ostensibly advocating no particular class interests (though clearly certain classes have expropriated his position)—advocated a strong hand for all citizens in his call for the Leviathan. No doubt Hobbes would argue that class interests were a byproduct of his position, or more likely a presumption of the byproduct.

Thomas Hobbes and the Social Contract. Hobbes argued that human beings, being the radical individuals that they are, primarily possess only the need to survive; there is no lust after power for its own sake, but only the lust for survival and security which power can provide.[28] Human beings are not evil. In fact, according to Hobbes, there is no such thing as good and evil, apart from the persons using the terms.[29] Human beings, Hobbes declares, are equal in nature, equal in their wants and desires, and therein lies part of the problem. There is nothing wicked in this—it is just the way nature has arranged matters. As people try to gain their ends, which are, by the reality of things, often the same ends, they come into conflict and act as enemies to one another. There comes a time when the many collect to deprive the one of the fruits of labor, and sometimes of life and liberty.[30] Thus Hobbes asserts that when everyone is potentially everyone else's enemy in a state of nature, a perpetual state of war exists in which there can be no security, no industry, no fruits of labor, no society, nothing "but continual fear, and danger of violent death; and the life of man, solitary, nasty, brutish, and short."[31] In this war there is no sin or injustice, for in this state of war where there is no law there is no justice and even the notions of right and wrong have no place amongst people.[32] But for Hobbes there are natural principles, which he calls the Laws of Nature, and in their desire to quit the state of war and gain peace, people following the rule of reason will understand and desire these Laws of Nature and should follow them.[33] Hobbes sees the Laws of Nature, those precepts which lead people to desire peace by their faculties of reason, as emerging from the basic principle found in the primacy of self-preservation.

A Law Of Nature is not a legislated law, but one that exists in advance of society, one that is a "general rule, found out by reason, by which a man is forbidden to do, that, which is destructive of his life, or taketh away the means of preserving the same."[34] This general rule leads to what Hobbes identifies as the Fundamental Law Of Nature: "That every man, ought to endeavor peace, as far as he has hope of obtaining it; and when he cannot obtain it, that he may seek, and use, all helps, and advantages of war." In other words, given the state of war that exists between everyone, it is a precept of reason that everyone has a right to everything, even to another's body, that might help preserve the individual's life and liberty.[i] That first branch of this rule, Hobbes states, is "to seek peace and follow it. The second, the sum of the right of nature; which is by all means we can, to defend ourselves."[35]

The Social Contract. Following the development of the Fundamental Law of Nature, Hobbes posits his second Law of Nature, which is derived from the Fundamental Law. This Second Law of Nature argues that the individual can set aside all rights to any and all practices necessary for self-preservation, when others are willing to also do the same, and bind themselves to mutual forbearance of destruction and war. Hobbes argues that this setting aside of rights can be done by contract—a *Social Contract.* By taking up this contract people will sign away the rights to all

---

i. Here it ought to be pointed out that it is this whole section that Locke was determined to amend and "mitigate" Hobbes teachings. In defending the rights of property, rights that Hobbes claimed were secondary to the right to life and liberty, Locke was determined to reverse these priorities. Locke was bent on making the defense of private property primary, or at least equal to the Hobbesian position on survival. Locke's emphasis on private property has great impact on the development of the "liberal" state, but not the rise of the State, as such. The crucial argument for the State, *per se*, was the bailiwick of Thomas Hobbes rather than Locke.

things necessary for self-preservation in exchange for safety.[36] Of course, the affixing of one's name (or mark) to a piece of paper is not actually done. Both Hobbes (and Locke) knew that this contract did not actually exist in this world. Instead, the "signing" of the contract can be inferred by either action or inaction. The mere living within a given domain connotes acquiescence to the supervision by a third party, a ruling body, *a Leviathan.*

The Leviathan is a necessary, nearly mandatory ingredient of the position taken by Hobbes. It seems quite clear that to Hobbes the Social Contract, once having been made, is no guarantee that all individuals will trust each other, or that all will abide by this Social Contract; therefore a common power must be set up to enforce the contract. This common power is necessary because the bonds of words are too weak to control ambition.[37] In short, Hobbes argues that the State is a necessity to forcibly provide for the social stability required for the safety and wellbeing of the population. The Social Contract is a device Hobbes conjures to offer plausibility for the force necessary to control and dominate the impulses of a subject population. It is important to note that although the notion of a Social Contract is pure conjuring, there is nothing overtly sinister in its construct. To Hobbes (and Locke) a strong government appears of omnipresent necessity. The imaginary Social Contract is merely a way of rationalizing the necessity of removing freedom of choice and controlling what appears to this philosopher as humanity's single-minded need to survive, no matter the cost to others. The Leviathan is there to save humanity from itself.

However, in *not* presupposing the existence of an organized society, Hobbes develops an argument for the State that is both compromised by the lack of this presupposition and weaker for the lack of a formal arrangement attesting to voluntary agreement. Rather than solving these two issues, (i.e., the assumption of human anti-sociability and the absence of any actual mechanism underlying contract theory) the devise of a Social Contract actually highlights these problems. This is an underlying problem with all Social Contract theories, as will become more apparent in the following part of the essay on anarchistic theory.

For the present, it is only important to recognize that for both Hobbes and Locke, and the liberal philosophers that followed, the case for the existence of government (i.e., the State) rests on the argument that in one

way or another the population being governed is better off for the governing. They argue that contentious situations will arise that find their best
and most peaceful solution by employing a third, more objective party
(e.g., a code of law and a legal system) rather than leaving the resolution
to a violent struggle. The existence of a governing body, in the form of
a single ruler, or a code of laws, or "representatives of the people" is
ultimately in the interests of both the individual and the population as a
whole; in other words, for the sake of survival, the State is inevitable. In
one way or another, the inevitability of the State is the position of all the
above philosophers, Plato, Aristotle, Hobbes, and Locke. It is an argument that is highly compelling.

Part Two: The Anarchist Replies

The anarchist—in the quest for a stateless society—is not left dumb-
founded and speechless in the face of the political philosophy espoused
by such theorists as Plato and Hobbes. The anarchist would reason that
the bulk of the arguments for the inevitability of the State rest on certain
assumptions about human nature that are opportunistically "revealed"
in thought constructs born of a fanciful "state of nature." These fictional
constructs are the flaw in their justification for the State. These flaws will
be revealed by the anarchist's reply. Of course, overall anarchist positions
for a stateless society are highly diverse,[38] but given the restrictive length
of this essay, undermining the dominant justification for the State seems
the most economical path to take.

A Fanciful State of Nature. The first thing to be noted is that the
base assumptions supporting the arguments presented by Plato, Aristotle, Hobbes, and Locke are, in one of two ways, pure fantasy. The first
fiction is that the starting points for human society as described by Plato,
then picked up on by Aristotle, are simply that: a myth. Through no
real fault of their own both philosophers lacked the empirical historical resources we, in modern times, have come to take for granted. The
second fiction is that the "state of nature" as described by Hobbes and
Locke, is not simply bad history (or in this case bad *pre*-history), but
is a deliberately imaginative construct—an illusory bit of intellectual
nonsense, but nonsense with a purpose. No such "state of nature" ever
existed, at least not as Hobbes and Locke conceive of it. This is probably

no surprise to the contemporary reader. Both these English philosophers, perhaps unconsciously concocted these imaginary circumstances in order to establish a premise for a desired conclusion, which is to say the existence of the political state—or rather, we should say, for a *certain kind of political state*.[39]

The Real State of Nature. At this point it will serve the purposes of this essay to draw on actual history. This will best be accomplished by looking at a picture of exactly how human beings lived and behaved in a real "state of nature" rather than an imaginary one. Here we must remind ourselves to avoid the temptation to assume that the actual, prehistorical "state of nature" was in any way an anarchist society. Prehistorical conditions denied human beings the technological and other sophisticated preconditions (principally language and literacy) for a functioning anarchist community.

Paleoanthropologists generally agree that unlike the image portrayed by the theories of Hobbes and Locke, humans were never solitary creatures, battling the world alone. As a species we humans were always social. Further, the first social bands of hunter-gatherers were small nomadic populations, highly transient and equalitarian in nature.[40] The equalitarianism was based largely on equal access to resources such as food and shelter, even when these resources were lacking in abundance.[41] It seems that the casual speculations of Plato and Aristotle are closer to the mark than those offered by Hobbes and Locke; the ancient Greek philosophers hewed to the claim that people were social, gregarious, and well-disposed to one another, or if not congenial, at least cooperative. If the anthropological research is correct, then what lay behind the sudden appearance of a competitive rancor and the sharp rise of hostility and violence that was to become so undeniably present in the world?

This discussion is not about personal or individual behavior. The personal is an area for the psychologist rather than the sociologist. The enmity spoken of here somehow springs from the group. In a "state of nature," at least that as described by anthropologists, decision making was largely spontaneous, *ad hoc*, and not hierarchical or repressive. Anyone could spontaneously act as a leader.[42] If hierarchy existed in the small band, it was the hierarchy of status, not of control.[43] This seems understandable and well fitted to the size of hunter-gatherer bands and the small and relatively uncomplicated scope of their activities. Therefore, the question that is here raised is a political one rather than a psychological one. The issue before us is what developments arose that brought about apparently unavoidable intragroup antagonism and aggression. This development is followed by the rise of the State which seems so necessary to control this emerging violence?

Anthropological research strongly supports the contention that it is not human beings living in the state of nature that produces antagonisms, but a new way of being in the world that developed out of a transition to a new set of social relations.[44] This social transition was to a more controlled, hierarchical and repressive political structure. That change seems to emerge alongside a later development during the Neolithic period, that is, the introduction of deliberate cultivation and a new sedentary lifestyle.[45] However, let it be quickly noted that cultivation is not to be interpreted as an introduction of contemporary notions of "private property," *per se*. Our modern concept of "private property" arose during Locke's time, not Neolithic time. Be that as it may, a look into the transition to agriculture will enlarge our understanding of the origins of the repressive political State and its seemingly apparent need.

Motivating factors for cultivation. What motivating factors pressed the hunter-gatherer bands to deliberate cultivation is a most interesting question, but not directly relevant to the focus of this small paper.[46] Even so, it is important to acknowledge that conditions for such a huge conversion to agriculture had to be ripe. The opportunity for deliberate cultivation must have been present in the form of post glacial environmental conditions making for a warm, temperate climate.[47] Of course, other environmental considerations must have also arose, e.g., geographic placement of the band, its proximity to reliable water sources, rich soil composition, and the absence of large predators, etc.

Beyond the above, and more pertinent to our study of political development, there must have been some sense of social incentive that moved a band toward the conscious planting and harvesting of food grains. This social incentive was no doubt energized by a desire to provide greater food stuff for the band or encouraged by a band-wide sense of competition with other nearby bands. Planting and harvesting would offer a sense of security *vis-à-vis* these competing bands.[48] Motivation and incentive could have been jump-started by competitive intra-band social demands, such as providing security for the increasing individual size of autonomous families.[49] And of course, one cannot overlook the obvious possibility that a turn to cultivation was motivated by the needs of a generally fast growing population.[50] Whatever the cause, at some point the emergence of deliberate cultivation, which provoked a necessary emergence of division of labor, seems to have led to the abandonment of equalitarian relations. The path from this abandonment of equal relations to a more disciplined and authoritarian social structure seems difficult to derail.

This emerging sedentary lifestyle turned the band—a collection of unrelated and transient individuals drifting in and out of various social groupings—into the clan—a more permanent and tightly bound grouping of individuals claiming common source of familial relationship, or at least homogeneity; this allowed for a greater understanding and permanence of position, duties and responsibilities. Eventually, this evolved into a political structure more easily and generally identifiable as a "tribe," which allowed for fixed, heredity leadership. Thus, with cultivation the familial clan, morphed into the larger, extended tribe, which became the first political entity that might be identified as a budding political state.

All of these are important and germane considerations. All the major anthropological theories indicate a motive for cultivation that was cooperative rather than competitive in nature. However, what is directly relevant to this study is that the impact of organized and deliberate cultivation 10,000 years ago brought profound changes in the social lives of small human collectives. This can't come as a surprise, but what were these changes?

Consequences of Deliberate Cultivation. It seems quite apparent that a sedentary lifestyle would be the first big change brought about by deliberate cultivation. This would have revolutionized the way in which the workloads were organized and distributed among members of small, previously equalitarian groups. Also, this turn to farming ultimately meant an increase in the need for a larger labor pool. This need would have opened the door for an increase in the number of males who might desire to begin distinct families within the clan. Increased number of families would have increased the labor pool. But coming along with this necessary labor pool came a considerable size increase in the population to be fed. In this way an increased population density would have been established, and, it should be pointed out, a growing density whose very increase fed on itself.

It must be emphasized that a first consequence of planting and harvesting was that the highly mobile lifestyle of the hunter clan had to be given up. This change brings about four not entirely obvious consequences. The first consequence is found when considering the way people understood their environment—that is, how the families of the clan came to perceive their relationship with the land on which agriculture and farming emerged. There is little doubt that the Neolithic human population came to view their relationship with the land in greatly changed terms and with it a new vision of their rudimentary society and the individual's place in it.

A second consequence was that the transition to domestication and a sedentary lifestyle inevitably brought cultural, ideological and psychological changes. Much of the way in which these Neolithic people came to perceive their relationship with each other as individuals underwent a radical change. There was a growing tendency to view each other through a practical and utilitarian glass. Such a tendency laid groundwork for estrangement, alienation and objectification. Such a disaffected view greatly facilitates a psychology of dependency and control that is still with us today.

Third, farming required a much different set of labor skills than hunting. This would have left a shrinking and increasingly specialized group of individuals in charge of hunting. In turn, this would lead to the development of a small group with a monopoly on weapons and expertise. This hunter sub-group, certainly in the beginning, would have been fully integrated into the farming occupations, yet distinct in that their knowledge and skill with weapons and hunting set them apart. This sub-group would have been distinguished not only by their skill in the handling of weapons, but also by the production of secondary resources and equipment necessary for weapons manufacture. By secondary resources we mean the making of such things as arrowheads, developing tools for the making of throwing sticks, spears poles, axe heads and handles, etc. In addition there would have been the development of secondary products associated with the hunt and animal domestication, e.g., pottery for transporting water and salt, wheels for carts, as well as the carts themselves, hide tanning for sturdy footwear, garments for harsh weather, pouches for traveling supplies, etc.

The fourth consequence of a sedentary life would have been the inevitable rise of barter and trade between families, bands and tribes. This would have been made possible by an increasing surplus of secondary products. Planting, harvesting, and tending to cultivation only take up so much time, leaving some left over for handicraft. As grain increased in abundance, and the storage for this grain became available, the temporary off shoot of craft-makers would become a semi-permanent and then finally a permanent occupational shift. The manufacture, nature and control of secondary products was to have far reaching effects.

At a certain point in the prehistory and early history of the late Natufian period (c. 10,000 BCE) there begins to be evidence of a surplus of hard goods. These goods ranged from obsidian and stone carvings, to pottery, shells, woven baskets, and stored seed grain, all of which suggests the development of trade between clans, which by this time may be more properly called tribal villages.[51] The growing size of villages also seemed to develop along with evidence of trade, as the discovery of sites such as Jericho attests.[52] All unearthed sites begin to show an accumulation of products not local in origin, but products which must have been transported from distant locales. The product accumulation also appears to have been unequal in its distribution among family sites.

Social Differentiation and Emerging Inequities. It is at this point that societal inequities begin to reveal themselves through such evidence as burial ornamentation; examples would be collections of household tools and agriculture implements, the accumulation of shells, pottery, sculptures, jewelry, etc.[53] What's to be noted here is that many of these secondary products are not directly related to survival and are apparently becoming amassed and heading into circulation for the express purpose of trade. Consequently, with the arrival of the circulation and exchange of goods, we can claim that there is an active economy in embryo. As the storing and circulation of these goods become increasingly obvious, so does their association with emerging social differentiation and a growing inequity in the accumulation of social wealth. With circulation these secondary products come to take on an inflated significance which adds an artificial value to the actual utility worth of the hard goods. It is not entirely accurate to title this additional value "profit;" nonetheless, accumulated value does bring new meaning to the relationship between vertical occupation and horizontal differentiation. The eventual disengagement of these two differentiations is the genesis of a social "faction."[ii] For the first time, circulation becomes structurally distinct from the actual production of material wealth. Consequently, what starts as exchange of secondary products ends with an accumulated added value that paves the way to a certain and obvious kind of social distinction that goes well beyond social differentiation and into the realm of horizontal *stratification.*

It seems clear that in an agrarian society the original source of wealth can be nothing other than the product of the land. From this wealth comes a surplus product to feed individuals beyond an immediate group or family. That is, from the original growing comes accumulated produce that exceeds the needs of the individual growers and harvesters. This overproduction can go to support the producers of handicrafts, weapons, ornamentation, etc. For the purposes of this study, the individual motivation for deliberately producing surplus matters less than the added value that comes to be invested in these secondary, more durable goods.[54] The concept of added value is derived from the original value of the agricultural product that is augmented via the labor it supports, and that added value goes into the manufacture of secondary products. It is with the arrival of these secondary durable goods, with their added value, that circulation, exchange and trade begin.

The added value supports not only the existence of a permanent group of secondary producers, but also a merchant faction whose self-serving function is to direct and control the exchange and trade of these goods.[55] This merchant faction is an economic factor that by virtue of its function must become distinct from both the producers of agricultural wealth and the producers of secondary products. Additionally, this merchant faction must insert itself firmly into any control of the exchange of goods. This merchant faction is a non-producing social group whose role greatly impacts the accumulation and guidance of the stream of wealth created by others. This faction, as it is non-producing itself, needs to quickly establish a firm control over not only trade, but also the structural roots of trade: the producers of material wealth themselves. The survival of this merchant faction, the authority of which is always tenuous and without solid guarantees of control, ultimately depends on domination over the

---

ii. It's not entirely accurate to call these factions a social or economic "class" in the contemporary sense.

social product and its producers. It is this domination over the social product that lifts this group vertically to a status identifiable not so much by accumulation as by control over production and distribution. It is fair to say, at this point, that a social and political "elite" has emerged horizontally, along with vertical differentiation.

Further, not only does this non-producing elite desire immediate control, but also it needs to pass this control over wealth on to generation after generation to foster control over a stable base necessary for permanent, hereditary elite status. The hereditary, hierarchal State, in its earliest forms of permanence, are typically of the type called chiefdoms, and eventually kingships. This is a probable model for how the earliest form of government as it was defined at the very head of this paper (i.e., *a political directorate exercising control over inhabitants of a community or society*) emerged from the survival needs of a non-producing class. In determining how this control and transmission of wealth is accomplished, we see how hierarchal structure develops into the permanent political State.

Paleoanthropologists have long suggested that societies must acknowledge some form of inequality based on something other than age or sex or intra-family position. The evolution of a hierarchical society demands a power structure that can guarantee the transmission of unequal wealth across generational lines. We see this when collections of households first combine to maintain their cross generational wealth. At some point, for reasons that vary, the households combine to recognize a particular elite house as a central power. Following that, the elite households themselves agree to become subservient to that one house and arrange themselves in some sort of hierarchy.

There are three key factors that act to stabilize a permanent hierarchical development of subservience, as well as a more general and practical governance of the inhabitants of a community of producers. These three factors of stabilization that can be seen in early Neolithic development are (1) the economic, (2) the military, and (3) the ideological.[56] It is the changing relationship between these three factors that gives rise to the possibility of *permanent* social differentiation, vertical (based on occupation) at first, evolving later into a fluid horizontal separation (based on control) separation. Because these three factors (economic, military, and ideological) seem to be of considerable importance for the case for government, this study will now move into an extended examination of their Neolithic development.

The Economy of Surplus Products. It is important to draw a distinction between surplus *product* and surplus *value*. Surplus value (certainly in the Marxist sense of the concept) derives much of its meaning from the existence of money and the exchange and circulation of commodities possessed of labor value converted to specie. In certain forms this would represent the primitive accumulation of capital. No such "primitive accumulation" happened in Neolithic times. In the context of this paper it is not surplus value which is described, but a kind of surplus product (or perhaps even surplus labor) in the form of crops utilized for the support of a non-agrarian population. In the absence of any written records during the Neolithic era the exact mechanism by which surplus labor was appropriated by—or exchanged with—a non-agrarian class is not clear, but what is certain is that the appropriations were made and then used in ongoing barter exchanges. There seems to be no other way some households would have been able to collect and store more hard goods than other households.

It is not accurate to call the appropriating a form of "tithing," in some medieval sense, as the land on which the produce was grown was, in all probability, *family owned*. The feudal manorial system, and any other similar system of hereditary indenturing, was a much later development. Here, in the Neolithic age, a surplus agricultural product developed that made possible the existence of secondary occupations (flint and stone workers, potters, tanners, jewelry makers etc.). However, it is highly doubtful that at this early stage there existed any lord of the land through which the primary products were filtered for distribution to secondary producers. It is far more probable that the primary distribution was spontaneous and direct. Even so, the important claim here is that surplus product made possible secondary producers and secondary products. As a consequence, and beyond the raw agriculture product, certain non-agricultural items became invested with value, a value which could be used for barter and trade. In this way it can be said that commodity circulation entered the world for the first time.[57] The arrival of exchangeable commodities marks the beginning of social stratification but does not directly cause it in some one-to-one relationship. The accumulation and control of commodities by a non-producing faction came to determine rank within the Neolithic community some four thousand years ago. Due to the lack of written documentation, a precise accounting of the origin and impact of commodity exchange is impossible, but it is reasonable to assume that certain individuals saw commodity exchange and the accumulation of certain products as highly advantageous,[58] and this marks the advent of horizontal differentiation and the foundation for social stratification and its subsequent effect on political power.

The Rise of Military Force. Here, the term "military" is used in the loosest of ways. The rise of the warrior does not automatically denote the existence of an organized military. A warrior faction does, however, demonstrate the concentration of potential violence within a distinct structural grouping, a societal grouping that possesses a monopoly of weapons and the skill necessary to use them. It must be added that although weapons during the Neolithic period were crude, even by the standards of the Bronze Age, their use required skills far different from a farmer or a potter. The warrior grew out of the hunter, whom we can see in a vertical social position, one complimentary to the potter and farmer. Sooner or later, concentration of different skills in certain segments allows for social position to be fixed and hereditary. The fixing of social position clearly allows for the emergence of a defined warrior faction that operates as an organized force both for defense of the community and also control *within* the community. Skill in weaponry now allows for a heavy-handed perpetuation in vertical status and hierarchy. There is little doubt that this secondary social structuring takes place by the opening of the 3rd millennium.[59] It is also around this time that separate, individual tombs are constructed for these warriors, as opposed to the mass burial sites for the population at large.[60] It is quite apparent that these warriors become increasingly revered and socially distinguishable from the rest of the community.

It should be obvious that given their monopoly on weapons and the skill necessary to use them, such a sub-group of warriors can dominate and direct a community. This direction can be done either on its own behalf or on the behalf of a more primary group, one with the wherewithal to support and maintain this warrior faction. Without making any judgments, or drawing any conclusions, this much appears objectively true.

Ideological Influences. The third factor, ideology, is most important because of a theme it supports that is closely associated with government.

That theme is *legitimacy*, that amorphous, nearly mystical, ideological concept that acts like glue to keep governing systems above question and in total command of the political environment. Loosely, and for our purposes here, ideology can be thought of as a worldview, a way of distinguishing and sorting things such as right or wrong which may have no ultimate meaning other than in terms of obedience to political norms. Legitimacy is one branch on the tree of ideology

Before about 5000 BCE, ideological influence is exceedingly difficult to track. There are no written testaments to give us a clue as to the worldview of the populace. Depending on the locale under study this problem continued for a considerable time. In Europe, for example, written documentation was completely unreliable until the coming of the Greeks and the Romans[61]—detailed written records were simply unavailable. Of course, this makes it impossible to directly peer into the mind of a Neolithic population. However, inferences can be made. These inferences are based on the study of artwork and burial sites.

Throughout the 4th and 3rd millenniums, Neolithic art is dominated by scenes of the hunt and of hunted animals. Such art was frequently interpreted as possessing some form of magical intervention that enhanced the hunter's success in bringing down large prey. This connects the importance of the hunt and the importance of the hunter to the notion of supernatural intervention.[62] We also know that primitive, religious superstition, in the form of magical cult activity, began around this period. Such cult orientated rituals were used in a manner that supported certain groups and activities while ignoring other factions and activities.[63]

It is possible to observe the effects of cult activity in the individual tombs of those of rank, complete with religious icons, fine jewelry, and stone idols. At the other end of the spectrum, the general population was treated to mass burials without markers or evidence of ceremony. Neolithic tombs are replete with suggestions of a sense of status and high regard for the bearer of weapons, weapons adapted to both hunting and warfare.[64] Cult objects are also found in the tombs of warriors, suggesting that the rising class of weapons bearers began to occupy an increasingly important role in the maintenance of social control together with the direction of community decisions. Cult activity was used to affect social control through the budding ideology supporting legitimacy through cult activity. Anthropologists have concluded that this warrior class developed into something very near to a cult of a noble aristocracy, and this by the end of the third millennium.[65]

How the State Comes About. As the above paleoanthropology strongly suggests, anything resembling organized politics and government was not the result of long term, structural planning, much less philosophical study and analysis. The opposite appears to be the case. The road to *legitimate* authoritarian rule was an unguided process—a coping process which evolved slowly over two millennium—developing somewhat differently in various parts of the populated world, but always closely intertwined with the three conditions cited above: (1) the circulation of commodities; (2) increasingly sophisticated weaponry; and most importantly, (3) ideology: a worldview regarding wealth, position, and legitimacy; a pattern of thinking hugely influenced by the control and distribution of commodities.

The first result of these three conditions is an embryonic horizontal pluralism of *status-as-influence* that admits of relations to power. This was not an overnight process, nor does it appear planned or calculated; but even so, social ranking associated with status-as-influence has been convincingly uncovered by paleoanthropologists.[66] If this status-as-influence were true in the hunter-gatherer bands, it no doubt continued in the emerging agricultural communities.[67] Unfortunately for those personages possessing this "influence" they were without direct access to any structural levers of power (e.g., organized military and police, laws courts, prisons, etc.), as these levers for widespread social control did not yet exist. It would seem that the eventual need to develop levers of social control came out of the quite understandable desire to stabilize the growing recognition of status-as-influence. This stabilizing process can be called the politicization of influence, which is to say seeking and organizing structural attempts at resolving the competitive struggle among influencing groups. It is within this stabilizing, this politicization of influence, that the evolving form of the State as a horizontal hierarchy is first found. The first result of this prehistorical politicization is that the social dynamic begins to lose its equalitarian resiliency and starts the long process of coalescing into the hierarchical, repressive and inflexible apparatus we see first in the prehistoric form of the tribe, then the kingdom, and eventually, the codifying of hierarchical control in the emerging State. All this was facilitated and made possible by the three evolving factors of stabilization cited above: circulation of commodities, weapons and ideology.

The long-term success of this politicization of status-as-influence depends on two key developments: (1) the *idea* of legitimacy, which, as detailed above, is a quasi-mystical derivative of an evolving ideological outlook, and (2) a monopoly of force. It is important to note here that class, as it is thought of in historical times, is not yet a function of differentiation and position within the social structure (although horizontally they are synergistically related). In early agrarian Neolithic society, social position as located in a hardened hierarchical structure was never a reality. What was experienced by Neolithic society was a social *relationship* to both advancing technology and growing exchange practices.[68] This relationship to exchange and technology eventually leads to a formalized horizontal positioning that can eventually be called "class" in something vaguely resembling the historical and modern sense of the term. The social *position* of class rests on factors commonly understood as politicization, (e.g., a consistent network structure; a supportive system of laws; clear ideological triggers; a functioning coercive apparatus; related political rituals, etc.), and not only on mere possession of production and distribution, which are *relational* factors—factors related to horizontal stratification, but not causing it. This apparent splitting of hairs is important to describe the point at which the fluidity of relationship becomes statically politicized, together with the entire top down coercive apparatus that politicization implies. This is a journey neither automatic nor forced. Before actual politicization can be fully achieved, the factors of relationship-to-production must first develop the structural levers of control over production and exchange. In the beginning, this politicization is relatively unsophisticated as it begins largely as a function of power and a monopoly over the exercise of force in its rawest form (i.e., violence). However, no State can safely remain in existence for very long if based entirely on force. The energy and resources necessary to maintain a State by raw force is a cost too high to sustain for very long. Eventually, successful politicization of hierarchy is only possible through the ideological function of *legitimacy*. The successful legitimizing of this hierarchical relationship to production and distribution largely emerges from an ideological view that blends awareness of social position with the concrete facts of power, which is to say, violence. In this way a budding politics of legitimacy, well stirred by fear and awe, comes about to ideologically cement a horizontal hierarchy in place. The question becomes: how exactly does this politicization of legitimacy, and not raw force, emerge as a long-term, deciding factor?

Monopoly of Force. Of the two developments cited above, (i.e., monopoly of force and legitimacy), force is the easier to consider and analyze. In the early transition from the band to the clan, to the tribe, the monopoly on force is the first development to emerge as a recognizable feature. Legitimacy, if it existed at all, was a feature far more difficult to ascertain and investigate. Legitimacy's ideological and mystical characteristics shroud the concept in an emotional fog that nearly defies penetration.

Regarding force, the physical material necessary is often ready at hand. Tools can quickly become weapons. Stone and flint axes can chop wood, and also kill human beings; arrows can kill deer, and humans, and so on.[69] There seems to always have been a certain status and reverence awarded to masters of weaponry—those that can take lives—even prior to the formal existence of the State.[70] From the clan to the State, social status and greater access to resources was awarded the hunter-warrior as provider, guardian and hero. It is the hunter-warrior, with a monopoly on weapons, who emerges center stage with the State as the direct controller, or as the agent of control. Deadly violence and the use of weaponry are the common dominators that link all States, regardless of historical time or philosophical design. In other words, the State possesses a non-criminal monopoly on violence.

The warrior as a distinct sub-group is a crucial and unique development—a development that was largely made possible by the existence of a surplus of agricultural product. As discussed above, such a surplus in agricultural production leads to the possibility of full-time secondary occupations and the development of commodities for exchange. Where agriculture offered only perishable food stuffs and domestic animals for trade, there now arose more non-perishable goods, everything from pottery to woven cloth to weapons that could be moved and traded among communities. Such mediums for exchange developed a new set of values for a new kind of permanent, commodity wealth. This new wealth led to the establishment of numerous individuals totally divorced from direct toil in production. As mentioned, one such group was the warrior, newly separated from the toil of both agricultural and commodity production. The ability to support the warrior sub-group gives to the State its axiomatic link to force, violence and coercion. This support is facilitated through the reverence and awe surrounding the warrior-hero. There are, of course, less than noble realities behind coercion—realities of coercion that are well camouflaged by the various contrivances of legitimacy. If the warrior is the physical cornerstone of the State, legitimacy anoints that cornerstone with a reverence for authority by cloaking the question of coercion beneath the ideological justification for a newly emerging political hierarchy.

At this point it seems appropriate to mention that the direct use of force by the State is often rationalized by the supposed evil in human nature. Promoters of state violence consistently put forth the argument that humans are possessed by some sort of selfish gene that demands people be controlled for their own betterment. If force is not threatened or applied, it is claimed, people will rape and murder one another in an uncontrollable plunge into hedonism and the expansion of power, wealth and rank. This argument holds that the only thing beating back the waves of chaos, bloodshed and pillage, is the strong arm of State authority with its threat of "legitimate" force and violence. As we will see, this notion of evil does not exactly square up with the Hobbesian notion of the Social Contract.

It is not the point of this study to present differing views on human nature, but rather to look into how such views provide a justification for government. The nature of the human species is a topic for psychology and not in-and-of-itself political science. Under the rubric of political science, using the "evil" lurking in our species as a justification for forcibly restraining human nature falls short of the political mark demanded by the Social Contract; recall that even Hobbes rejected "evil" as having any objective validity. Evil is not a stand-alone feature of reality independent of human action. In fact, Hobbes outright claimed that evil was merely a projection of the individual and had no real life of its own.[71] Further, Hobbes considers the quest for power to be only part of human survival strategy and not indicative of any innate "badness" in the human spirit.[72] One must look elsewhere for any rationale involved in the controlling of a population and the preserving of a status quo. Hobbes is quite clear in that the Social Contract rests on the abandonment of the kind of violence that springs from the scuffle for competitive survival needs and not on the supposed evil in human nature.[73]

The Idea of Legitimacy. It is the *sensation* of legitimacy—those seemingly preconscious, emotional excitabilities that sanctify obsequiousness, even glorify subservience to hierarchy—that is more difficult to grasp. No doubt the mystical and ideological roots of legitimacy are part of what makes an analysis of the "feelings" so elusive. These mystical roots are often sunk deep in the *sacred*: a calling on the spirit of god, the *zeitgeist* and the master race, tapping into the esoteric mythology of destiny, tribalism, the heroic ancestors, revisionist history and tradition, things all grander and more glorious than material reality (although we cannot overlook those base sensations that arise because of a simple fear of Moloch: legitimacy as a byproduct of fear). While these mystical qualities might be considered intangible, murky, not to mention vaguely pretentious and instigating of hubris, we must bear in mind that without the ideology of legitimacy, control by the State could never be fully realized. Paradoxically, these facts alone reveal and spotlight the central weakness of legitimacy: legitimacy is causally linked to nothing solid or concrete. It is an *idea*—a thing that exists inside the head and nowhere else. Threatened by veracity or intellectual integrity, analysis of legitimacy can quickly turn the idea into a wisp of smoke; either that or confirm legitimacy as springing from honest and forthright actions and desires of a given population. But in either case, deserved or not, loosen the grip of ideological legitimacy and any human grouping larger than a clan would forever be structurally dependent on naked violence to maintain control. Covert suppression of opposition forces by *an idea* is clearly the surest, most economical and self-regulating gatekeeper for social control.

Legitimacy can either support the needs of the group or repress those needs. Legitimacy is a fine agent for covert suppression. It allows for self-policing behavior—control, typically guided by laws, without a need for overt violence. This is so even where legitimacy honestly reflects a society's aspirations and where all the needs of the society are thoughtfully met. Legitimacy can have both a positive function in supporting a free and egalitarian society and it can have a detrimental one operating in support of a repressive regime.

Law cannot create legitimacy, but legitimacy can create respect and even devotion to law. The making of law is a (if not "the") principle *legitimatizing* function of government; penal codes and constitutions legitimize the state. Then, through this legitimacy, the State (i.e., government) manipulates the use of laws to suppress certain activities and certain societal groups and urge these groups toward activities deemed by the State to be benign. The *idea* of legitimacy generates the energy to maintain the suppression lying deep within the "dominated" population itself. This monopoly on violence gives the State the ready capacity to become an oppressive apparatus; however, by dint of the State's revered hold on legitimacy the usual overt expressions of violence are uncalled for. Concealed within legitimacy, covert suppression is the real source of power, a covert power underwritten by a powerful system of ideas (i.e., ideology and its transformational stepchild, political doctrine). When considered carefully, it can be seen that the dominated population participates in its own suppression by adhering to powerful ideological worldviews that sanctify the legitimacy of current political doctrine—and all of this without an ounce of self-awareness.

Ideologies are, to put a point on it, merely the *systems of ideas* that we humans use to organize and make sense of our experience. This organizing of experience is done in order to understand the world around us and to understand ourselves and our place in this world; ideologies are everywhere and everywhere ideologies tell us who we are and what are we doing here.[74] Just as important, the organizing of experience often serves in one way or another to *control* the world around us—or at least make some sort of peace with a world that can often seem angry, hostile and unforgiving. In these senses, both science and religion have always been leading (if antagonistic) ideological forces. Both these idea systems can be used as markers to grasp the mind set of many societies, even the very earliest. But our concern with legitimacy as a basis for social control leads us to focus attention on the more spectral ideological factors and not the empirical or concrete, which form the basis for scientific understanding. After all, social control happens most successfully when it starts in the mind, even the pre-historic mind. One paleoanthropologist explains earliest social control thus: "This control may have been accomplished by ritual and ideological means rather than by more overt expressions of power. The elaboration of cult objects at this period [Neolithic] indicates the existence of ritual codes shared by all communities."[75]

When examining the tombs of the Neolithic period, paleoanthropologists find that the most affluent members of society possess a great many cult-like statues and relics.[76] This would seem to indicate an investment in religion by an emerging "upper-class" faction. This may not be a cynical and calculated move on the part of this faction, as they might have been true religious believers. Even so, it is difficult to entertain the possibility that they did not recognize the status enhancement offered by being central figures in cult worship. And while we do not know the precise configurations and spiritual details of Neolithic religion, it can certainly be surmised that there were magical and otherworldly elements that would have cast the central figures in a shroud of superiority—the superiority of being seen as close to god or god-like, or even an actual minor deity. We can find support for this contention by examining the religious rites and influence in the earliest societies with literate ability (e.g., Samaria and Egypt). The written evidence of these early socio-political groupings demonstrates that a celebrated, ideological link was fashioned between the ruling class and the "Gods." Archeological study concerning Samaria, for example, shows that as early as 3000 BCE a great time of warfare produced king-generals who quickly took up the mantle of the gods, and along with their priests became a ruling elite entrusted with interpreting divine will.[77] There is little reason to think that people of preliterate societies, such as those found in the Neolithic era, possessed a different ideological outlook. It is very likely, therefore, that from the very beginning the "citizens" of the State looked at the world in much the same way as the Sumerians. That is, the State was legitimized through an ideological system fundamentally derived from mystical principles and not the harsh reality of violence.

The entire edifice of State legitimacy rests on one of two premises, one enigmatic and the other intellectually flimsy. (1) Either some supernatural phenomena cause authoritarian governments to spring into being, as in the case of the assumed divine right of kings, or (2) the case for government is grounded in some sort of societal agreement as that seen in the Hobbesian "Social Contract." Either of these two (sometimes comingled) bestow legitimacy on governing bodies, thus granting them authoritarian prerogatives. Since both these ideological constructs (i.e., divine right and the social contract) are at best mystical entities, or at worst utterly fanciful fictions, it is clear that legitimacy is not automatically made real and concrete. In fact, legitimacy—even the "good" kind—rests on a foundation only as strong as the spiritual argument behind it. It is also clear that once simple faith in legitimacy is broken and brushed aside, the violent face of the State is all that remains as the sole controller of the social order.

Conclusion. The facts of history fly in the face of Hobbes' Second Fundamental Law and the Social Contract. The rise of the political state, as a *real* historical episode, did not develop out of some rational thought process grounded in Hobbes and Locke, but out of real and tangible material relations. The social contract can be presented as a "voluntary" process only in the most absurd sense, *viz.*, you can either stay on board or jump into the sea. Simply put, the State arose not out of a voluntary association, but out of a natural material and historical development, i.e., the transition from the nomadic hunter-gatherers to the sedentary farmer, and from the clan to the tribe. This transition was quickly followed by secondary commodity production (which itself rested on an increasing division of labor), and by a commodity circulation that provoked exchange and trade. This increased economic activity evoked a political structure divided along the lines of producers on one side and appropriators on the other. Again, it is fair to assume that none of these developments were the result of some process of collective rational decision making. The actual evolution from the hunter-gatherer clan to the first political entity, the tribe—that entity where leadership first became hereditary and supported by a monopoly of force—can be said to have developed out of free choice only given the unlikely probability that the vast bulk of producing individuals collectively came to desire their social and political subservience to a ruling class. For obvious reasons, such a fully conscious self-divestiture is not a likely scenario.

Putting Plato and Aristotle aside for the moment, the Hobbes–Locke philosophy underwriting the modern liberal-democratic State collides with the historical actualities surrounding the origin of the political state. Everything in Hobbes rests solely on an assumed "state of nature" with its centerpiece of the "war of all against all." When factoring in the historical reality, the only recourse the classic Hobbesian liberal has is to claim that Hobbes (or Locke) never intended his "state of nature" to be anything other than a purposeful, if imaginative, piece of fiction.

But of course, an important consequence of admitting that this "state of nature" is a made-up thing, along with the "war of all against all," is that it undermines the Second Fundamental Law which supports legitimacy *via* the Social Contract. This leaves the political state wide open to the anarchist charge that the state is not deserving of legitimacy at all, as the Social Contract portents, but is based purely on coercion, and ultimately violence, albeit thinly disguised. From the very beginning, the anarchist would say, the State was a socio-political machine whose primary purpose was the exploitation of the many for the benefit of the few—the actual and deliberate consciousness of such a primary purpose notwithstanding.

Strictly in the sense of evolving political dynamics, rather than conscious decision making, Aristotle and Plato were closer than Hobbes to the actuality of events. They did not credit the rise of the State with voluntary actions, but with a circumstantial processing of events the power of which makes human beings the flotsam rather than helmsmen. Few among us fully grasp the outcome of immediate events, much less long-term complexities. We often drift with the tide to arrive at shores not of our conscious election, and frequently not even to our recognition. Locked into the prison of our own idea-systems, we are often kept from fully grasping and successfully organizing the concrete reality around us. Inaccurate or inadequate ideologies tangle the pathway to our own self-interest. False ideologies make us alone, frustrated, depressed and at odds with events.

The anarchist would encourage us to wonder that if the "divine right" of kings is a recognizable piece of fiction, why is it so difficult to recognize the same thing about the Social Contract? Why is it that so few recognize that the Social Contract is a fuzzy intellectual concoction, completely divorced from reality—a fanciful brew rationalizing the newly emerging 16th Century political order? This concoction subsequently works its way into dominating modern ideology—to mask the lopsided economic and political realities of the liberal state. The modern liberal state is not, and was not, founded on some voluntary association; rather, it is the result of changing material conditions that resulted in an historically sharp division of labor leading to vast disparities in wealth and power. Following this "conspiracy of history," the new division of labor and wealth, unguided, leads directly to a hierarchal society with those at the top enforcing their "good fortune" through a monopoly of force and a shimmering idea-system that ultimately seeks to control the destiny and labor product of the bulk of the population. This is what the material realties of history teach—realities that are typically at odds with liberal ideology, thus making the Lockean-liberal case for government an overwhelming piece of fiction and not a realistic argument. Remove the fiction, asserts the anarchist, what is left is that the factual case for government rests, as it always did, on coercion and violence aimed at delivering the good life for the few and a life of toil for the many.

A question lurks in the weeds. from the anarchist point of view, what is the remedy for this dismal state of affairs?

First, are facts and truth. We immediately need to recognize that nearly all rational arguments for government on the scale to which we are accustomed are specious. The *necessity* for the great masses of people to be controlled by a few for the benefit of those same few is worse than a fiction, or even a travesty. It is an infinitely long trail of crimes of violence against a suffering humanity. The velvet glove of reason is stretched mightily thin when used to cloak the naked violence that lies behind the "rational" arguments for government.

Second, as remedy, the anarchist would suggest closing the circle. Politically—and I say this at the risk of sounding preposterous—return to the *political* spirit of the hunter-gatherer bands roaming the Savannah in Neolithic times. This was a time when equality and crude democratic impulses were taken for granted. I said it sounds preposterous, and that is . true, but what is not preposterous is learning that the single most defining feature of the Neolithic hunter-gatherer bands is what allows for equality and democracy. That which separates the band from the other social bodies, the clans and the tribe, and the State: *Size!*

At this point we might reflect on the words of Abraham Lincoln when he suggest that the legitimate object of government is "to do for the people what needs to be done, but which they cannot, by individual effort, do at all, or do so well, for themselves." This speaks directly to size. Obviously, we can all tie our own shoes without government help, but what about the lead poisoned water in Flint, Michigan. It is quite apparent that the very size of the US government has worked against any serious action regarding a permanent fix for the Flint water system. This goes well beyond individual political interests; the sheer size of the state and federal bureaucracies has adversely impacted any speedy action and recovery of a safe water supply. However, give local people the authority and power necessary, and the problem with Flint's water would be taken well in-hand long before the government agencies had even begun a study of the problem. Massive government agencies and a meridian of bureaucrats far removed from the scene might be well meaning, but nonetheless, they still clog the system and bring it to crawl.

The anarchist project may be only a dream, but size does offer a simple explanation as to why the Israeli kibbutz can operate anarchistically while the *state* of Israel cannot. The bottom-line question seems to be that while the anarchist can argue the evil of the State and call for its dissolution, can the anarchist develop a realistic rubric for a stateless society? There are those who say yes.[78] The existence of the kibbutz certainly demonstrates that anarchy is largely a matter of size linked with organization.[79]

However, going any further with discussing the practical application of anarchy would result in writing another paper—and one probably much longer than this one. It is enough to say that further reading and discussion is definitely warranted before any offhand dismissal of the practical application of anarchist theory. The anarchist would also advise further reading and critical discussion into the ideological justification for the hierarchical state.

Notes

1. It is well to note that this quote often attributed to Thomas Hobbes goes back much further, to at least the Greek playwright Plautus (254-184 BCE).

2. In passing, it should be noted that the Greeks of Plato's time lacked the same vision of history possessed by modern thinkers. It was difficult for the ancient Greeks to imagine a time without some form of civilization and organized societies.

3. Plato, *The Laws*, chapter III

4. Ibid.

5. Ibid.

6. Ibid, and it should be noted that Plato seems to be suggesting a change from what we today would call a hunter-gather society to an agrarian social system. One has to be careful not to stick too many words in Plato's mouth, but this clearly seems to be one plausible reading of the text.

7. Ibid.

8. Ibid.

9. Aristotle, *Politics*, 1252a1, Jowett translation.

10. 1323a25, 1323b15

11. 1281a1, 1295b1, 1323b1, 1323b20

12. 1252a25

13. Ibid, 1252b10

14. Ibid, 1252b10

15. Ibid, 1252b15, 1252b20

16. Ibid, 1252b20

17. For example, see: M.I. Finley, *The World of Odysseus*, (New York Review Books, New York, 2002) especially chapter 4.

18. *Politics, op. cit.* 1252b28

19. Ibid, 1253a3

20. Ibid, 1253a20

21. Ibid, 1253a25

22. Ibid, 1253a35

23. Ibid. 1254a21. It is possible to argue here that Aristotle is merely carrying through with his thoughts on slavery. But in this passage and for some lines after, Aristotle continues to discuss rulers and subjects without ever mentioning slaves. Most scholars would maintain that Aristotle was consistent in his belief that rulers and ruled were according to nature.

24. *Politics, op. cit.* 1254b13-14

25. See *Politics*, Book VII, part 3

26   The intellectual construct of a "state of nature" did not originate with Hobbes. It can be traced to the writing of Thomas Aquinas. The notion is important for Catholic theology and the theologies "natural law" theories.

27. Strauss, Leo, *What is Philosophy?*, from *What is Philosophy and Other Essays*, (University of Chicago Press, Chicago, 1988) p. 48

28. Hobbes, Thomas, The Leviathan, Prt. 1, Ch. XI, §2

29. Hobbes, *op. cit*, Prt. 1, Ch. VI, §7

30. Ibid, Prt. 1, Ch. XIII §1, §3

31. Ibid, Prt. 1, Ch. XIII, §9

32. Ibid, Prt. 1, Ch. XIII, §10, §13

33. Ibid, Prt. 1, Ch. XIII, §14

34. Ibid, Prt. 1, Ch. XIV, §3

35. Ibid, Prt. 1, Ch. XIV, §4

36. Much of chapter fourteen of the Leviathan concerns itself with the "contract," but sections five through fourteen mark the strongest and clearest expression of this Social Contract.

37. Ibid, Prt. 1, Ch. VIX

38. For example, see: Emma Goldman, *Anarchism and Other Essays*, (Dover Publications, New York, 1969)

39. It should be noted that J.J. Rousseau also began with a state of nature theme, but was driven by far different goals, and ended up in a far different place than either Hobbes or Locke.

40. Peter Bogucki, *The Origins of Human Society*, (Blackwell Publishers, Oxford, 1999), pp. 74-76

41. Ibid.

42. Keith Grint, *Leadership, A Very Short Introduction*, (Oxford University Press, NY, 2010) p. 113

43. Robert Wright, *The Moral Animal*, (Vantage Books, NY, 1994) p. 237

44. Price and Gebarer (eds), *Last Hunters—First Farmers*, (School of American Research, Sante Fe, NM, 1995) pp, 4, 8

45. Peter Bogucki, *op. cit*, p. 205

46. Peter Bogucki, *op. cit*, especially chapter 5

47. Peter Bellwood, *First Farmers, The Origins of Agricultural Societies*, (Blackwell Publishing, Maldin, MA., 2005)
pp. 19-22

48. Cowgill, G.L ., 1975 *American Anthropologist* 77: 505-25

49. Farrington, I and Urry, J., 1985, *Journal of Ethnobiology* 5:143-57

50. This is a general theme expressed by such works as that by Mark Cohen, *The Food Crisis in Prehistory*, (New Haven: Yale University Press, 1977).

51. Steven Mithen, *After the Ice*, (First Harvard University Press paperback edition, London, 2006) p. 50

52. Ibid. p. 68

53. Guilaine and Zammit, *The Origins of War, Violence in Prehistory*, (Blackwell Publishing, Oxford, UK, 2005) pp. 158, 159

54. Deliberate overproduction might be attributed to altruistic cooperative motivations, but it is more probable that particular individuals saw the advantage of accumulating value-added hard goods.

55. Brian Hayden, "Pathways to Power. Principals for Creating Socioeconomic Inequalities," From *Foundations in Social Inequality*, ed by Price and Feinman, (Plenum Press, NY, 1995) pp. 15-86

56. See Antonio Gilman, "Unequal Development in Cooper Age Iberia," *Specialization, Exchange, and Complex Societies*, E.M. Brumfield and T.K. Earle (eds), (Cambridge University Press, Cambridge, 1987) pp. 22-29

57. Guilaine and Zammit, *op. cite*. pp.170-171

58. John Clark & Michael Blake, "The Power of Prestige: Competitive Generosity and the Emergence of Ranked Societies in Lowland Mesoamerica," found in *Factional Competition and Political Develoment in the New World*, E.M. Brumfield & J.W. Fox (eds) pp. 17-30, (Cambridge University Press, Cambridge, 1994)

59. Guilaine and Zammit, *op. cite. P. 200*

60. Ibid. p. 200

61. Robinson, Andrew, "The Origins of Writing" in Crowley and Heyer (eds) *Communication in History: Technology, Culture, Society* (Ally and Bacon, Boston, 2003) pp. 35-36

62. Whitley, David, *Cave Paintings and the Human Spirit: The Origin of Creativity and Belief*, (Prometheus Books, Amherst, NY, 2009) p̄. 34 - 36

63. Andrew Sherratt, *Economy and Society in Prehistoric Europe*, (Princeton University Press, Princeton, NJ, 1997) p. 263-264

64. See Guilaine and Zammit, *op. cit.*, pp. 158-159

65. Ibid. p. 207

66. Ibid. p. 159

67. Robert Wright, *The Moral Animal*, (Vantage Books, New York, 1994) p. 237

68. E.M. Brumfiel & J.W. Fox (ed) *Factional Competition and Political Development in the New World*, (Cambridge University Press, Cambridge, 1994) pp. 17-30

69. Guilaine and Zammit, *op. cit.* p. 159

70. Robert Wright, *op. cit.* p. 237

71. The Leviathan, *op. cit.* ch. VI, §7

72. Libid. Pt. 1, Ch. XI, §2

73. Libid. Ch XIV, §5, 7, 18

74. For an elucidation of this topic see Louis Althusser, *For Marx*, (New Left Books, NY 1977), especially pp. 231-233

75. Sherratt, *op. cit.*, p. 264

76. Guilaine and Zammit, op. cit. p. 200

77. For a quick read of the early political history of Sumeria see: http://history-world. Org/sumeria.htm

78. See Noam Chomsky, *On Anarchism*, The New Press; 1st edition (November 5, 2013)

79. See, Ran Abramitzky, *The Mystery of the Kibbutz: Egalitarian Principles in a Capitalist World*, Princeton University Press (February 13, 2018)

CLASS AND
CLASS WARFARE

Daniel Shattuck, Ph.D

Abstract: Class warfare is a subject on quite a few lips these days. The discussion of this warfare begins by examining the various ways to define class, showing many of them to be faulty. The analysis then steadily works toward a definition of class-based material reality, building on an economic model which in turn is drawn on a production model. This definition is less Structuralist than it is neo-Marxist, but the definition offered is all but definitive and is far more satisfactory than conventional models that are wed to social status or income orientated definitions. At this point the article strikes out in an unusual direction: an analysis of the nature of war, but in a social and political context. Finally, the article provides a detailed look into different models for the resolution of class war—those that have be successful, and those that have not.

Class

The problem with class—and war. We scholarly types—especially in the US—tend to think of class as a socioeconomic category, the usefulness of which seems to be narrowly academic. For the majority of us non-academic citizens "class" tends to be a fuzzy concept at best and confusing at worst. Consider this definition of class from a well-known academic journal:

> "Nowadays people can define your class by what your interests are, what newspaper you read, what music you listen to or television shows you watch. You can also be defined by what status you have in society, and the status of the people you know, such as friends, family and business employees."

Then the authors admit:

> "However, introducing such a wide definition of class can make it quite hard to define where you actually belong."[1]

So, what is class? Is it how we define where we "actually belong" on the social ladder or is it an actual thing that confines and restricts us in our life's choices? And what exactly is the concept's useful purpose?

First, we ought to consider such vague definitions of class as that cited above as powerful propaganda weapons. By this we mean that "class" is a notion very often used by political forces to persuade, pressure, cajole, dissuade, mystify and sometimes outright bamboozle and confound both our friends and our enemies. Because class is all the nebulous things cited above, it is a slippery notion and often a deliberately unstable category. By the latter we mean that the instability itself may be a feature of political design.

While we will offer below a careful definition of class, it is worthwhile to keep in mind that class as a political and social division is also a category often denied—it is sometimes claimed that "class" doesn't exist at all. That's right, the existence of the concept itself is denied outright, and always with self-interest at the heart of the denial. What's the reason for the denial? Because the very concept of class seems to automatically give rise to the notion of inequality—a thorn in the side of contemporary democratic societies—and a particularly painful thorn to people who do not wish to have the issue of inequality raised in a way that seems to legitimize outrage and a demand for redress. Many images of class seem to do just that. The remedy for some is the outright dismissal of the concept itself.

Couple this slippery notion of "class" with the concept of "war" and the resulting mindset of "class warfare" becomes a dreaded anathema to those groupings of people most vulnerable to accusations of exploitation and greed. In contemporary parlance "those people" are identified most readily as the top 1%. To those atop this lofty perch the self-interested reaction to class war is understandable, as some form of class turbulence is an ever-present threat. Inequality very often provokes social movements at the bottom that agitate for redistribution of the wealth, or pressures to unionize for a greater a share of the product, or struggles for universal health care and universal education—all these speak to the various forms of class struggle. All are grounds for the upper classes to attempt to suppress strivings for redistribution by muddying the terms "class" and "class warfare." Suppression by "muddying" may take the form of various maxims: "Contrary to popular myth, we're *not* all in this together"—or "In the race for a fair share of the social product there are only clever and resourceful individuals"—or more directly, "There is no working class at all, everyone who is successful is of a middle class, a class composed of winning individuals." This suppression of a clear concept of a working class is partly responsible for the confusion in the lower 99% as to the means and purpose of class awareness.

At the end of the day, this bewilderment is completely understandable. Given that the confusion is not only definitional (what exactly is class) but also conceptually blurry (how exactly does class fit into the social structure), it is little wonder that class is typically omitted from most political studies. Not only that, but we also find that "class" gives every impression of existing in conflict with democratic ideals and accompanying doctrines touting equality. This conflict in doctrine emerges from the political filters that underwrite all our ideas of social and political reality. These filters that obfuscate class are politically expedient; they give every impression of being adopted and used intentionally by those at the top who control the narrative. By this we mean that for those at the bottom, strong feelings of social equality ("I'm as good as anybody else") hamper the class consciousness that presupposes understanding real material inequality as a function of economic position. If the chief ingredient of this understanding, that is, of *class*, remains a fuzzy concept, frustration within the ranks of the 99% stays manageable. Ignorance, while curable, requires social resources that are often willfully restricted. A widespread lack of class consciousness allows for the channeling of frustration and outrage into the relatively harmless avenues of representative democracy. As long as the focus is on the individual and not on the class of which the individual is a part, such outrage can be muted by confusion and lost in the labyrinth of bureaucratic and parliamentary dead ends.

All of this should prepare us for the realization that for the subject of "class warfare" to be properly discussed, both war and class must first be analyzed separately. In this way their precise meanings can be uncovered. Only after satisfying this descriptive prerequisite can the two concepts be synchronized for a harmonious fitting. I say "synchronized" rather than "aligned," for class and war in the form of class warfare are part of same *historical* process, a mostly objective process that is one of the main drivers of social change. To be clear, there is nothing about the concept of social class that makes it *definitionally* hostile to itself; nor is there some overlooked, inbred contradiction. To fully grasp the cause of class antagonism, class friction, and potential class warfare, a precise description of social class is the first condition, followed by a treatment on war.

First, as has been pointed out above, "social class" is prone to a wide range of interpretations, many of them far-fetched and self-serving. Much of this self-serving role in interpretation can be circumvented. This is most readily accomplished through careful phenomenal description. Such a careful description will set us up for a better understanding of the type of class relations that potentially result in serious class friction and class warfare.

A Definition of Class. Definition is a critical point for the emergence of a true class consciousness and understanding. Academic economics and sociology are the primary sources for general descriptions of social class. However, quite often these descriptions are, as we have pointed out, vague and confusing. There are quite a few reasons for the vagueness, but one such is simple self-interest. In a very real analytical sense, the obscuring of class has the power to twist any notion of class warfare into a non-sequitur, a genuine non-starter. It is easy to see that a dismissal of class, along with class conflict, is highly useful to individuals and groups interested in deflecting the reality of inequality in a society stabilized by a vision of social equality. This desire to dodge the implications of "class" through confusion will be especially appealing in pseudo-democratic societies.

To offer a few recent examples of the indistinct quality found in describing class: It is sometimes claimed that there is no such thing as class at all, but only *social groupings*—that is, "collections of people who interact on the basis of shared expectation regarding one another's behavior."[2] These grouping are typically seen as vertical social arrangements rather than horizontal, which discourages visualizing them as hierarchical or providing fodder for social friction. In a similar vein, it is sometimes concluded that there are no sharply definable "class" distinctions at all, but only a gradual shift in differing life styles and life defining experiences (education, professions, etc.).[3] It is easy to see that when alternate, social (i.e., non-economic) standards are applied, exacting and meaningful class differences can be fuzzed over and obscured.[4] These inchoate typologies all sidestep economic models—models which tend to sharpen class distinction and often lead in the direction of confrontation among certain political and social groups. At the very least, clearly defining class will render those at the top vulnerable to criticism and isolation.

Much closer to an economic model is that featured by Michael Zweig, who defines class in a political sense. Class, Zweig states, is:

"In large part based on the power and authority people have at work. The workplace engages people in more than their immediate work, by which they create goods and services. It also engages them in relationships with each other, relationships that are controlled by power. A relative handful of people have great power to organize and direct production, while a much larger number have almost no authority. In a capitalist society such as ours, the first group is the capitalist class, the second group the working class."[5]

With this definition, Zweig makes a foray into an economic profile that can most usefully characterize class as it appears in its more pugnacious form. However, this definition does not take into account the pivotal agent of economic authority. What Zweig says of work-a-day

65

power is true enough, but by sticking with the "political" relations he avoids a direct examination of the economic relations lurking beneath a politicized surface—those economic relations that give politics its form and character. This becomes most clear when Zweig gets into defining the "middle class" as the small business owners and professionals—a "class" that stands between the capitalist and the worker.[6] The introduction of this "middle class" permits him to say that there is no real structural line separating classes, or that the separations are at best arbitrary and lack practical importance. It is quite correct, as Zweig says, that class is characterized by power relations, and unequal power relations at that, which can lead to political struggle; but it is only a logical next step to ask: from where does that unequal power derive? Political struggle is clearly an expression of unequal power and by its very nature represents a battle over economic resources, but the term "politics" is also a slippery polemical device. Politics and political rhetoric can be used to disguise the precise dynamic of the underlying economic struggle—in this case, class struggle—rather than bring that struggle to light for effective analysis. Pure political wrangling must be brushed aside to get at the underlying economic causes for the struggle between classes, those not struggling for their place in the sun, but for their place at the dinner table.

All the above definitions serve to confirm the confusion over the meaning of class. Without clear and sharp distinctions, the use of class becomes a weak variable to insert into any analysis of class driven social friction. Additionally, these definitions depend widely on interpretation, subjective assignment, and above all, value judgments. Who is to assess the value and meaning of a "life-style," and does not "the power and authority people have at work" beg the question of the assigning of authority? Such value laden assessments are the opposite of a phenomenological approach. In order to promote true understanding, clarity must be brought to the subject of class warfare.

In a very interesting book,[7] Alejandro Portes lists four insights that make analysis of social class genuinely possible:

1. Social phenomena are not explainable by their surface manifestation. There is 'deep structure,' defined by durable inequalities, among large social aggregates.

2. Classes are defined by their relationship to one another and not simply by a set of 'gradational' positions along some hierarchy. In this sense, status rakings are a manifestation, not a defining feature of class.

3. Classes are defined by differential access to power within a given social system.

4. Class position is transmissible across generations.[8]

Portes identifies two general classes, the dominate class and the subordinate class. Both are identified by the class-member's need to sell their labor or skill. The dominate class, as one might suspect, lives free of any need to sell their labor time. Portes next subdivides this dominate group into the *rentires*, those who live off passive investments, the *capitalists*, who actively engage in the management of their investments, and the *Grand Capitalists*, those whose vast wealth allows them to impose their will on wide sectors of the political economy.[9]

The second class, the subordinate class, are all those who depend on their labor and skill to survive. Portes further sub-divides this subordinate group into *Elite Workers*, which are skilled professional workers such as doctors and college professors—and who are quite often poised to cross the class divide—and *Common Workers*, whose manual skill is sufficient to make a living but insufficient to acquire and amass wealth.[10] This is a class description similar to what Marx describes in *Grundrisse*, where the worker is separated from the means of production[i] by the need to sell labor to acquire the basics of subsistence.[11]

These descriptions, as Portes outlines them, are drawn *by inference* from the relationship these groups bear to the means of production as reflected in marketplace dynamics. The worker is an individual that has turned the "self" into a labor commodity presentable at the marketplace. This working class produces use-value—that is, through the direct

---

i. The "means of production" of a society include all of the physical elements, aside from human beings, that go into producing goods and services, including the natural resources, machines, tools, offices, computers, and means of distribution, such as stores and the internet; in our modern world the "*mode of production*" related to the means are either capitalism (private ownership) or socialism (public ownership).

production of material consumer goods (automobiles and dinner rolls) or indirect service goods (waiting tables and mowing lawns). The capitalist is the consumer of the labor commodity found at market for the purpose of commanding and transforming that labor commodity into a stored use-value (typically in some form of money or other commercial securities). These two groups, the capitalist and the worker, exist in contingency with each other. The marketplace relationship that creates use-value through the means of production is in command of this contingency. It is not enough to say that one group *owns* and the other group *works*. The actual definition of these two classes depends more on the structural relationship each bears to the marketplace, i.e., the marketing and consumption of use-value rather than the actual work performed.

We might say that the "dominate" group owns, but this consideration is separate from the actual process of production except insofar as it comes to command and consume the use-value produced by the subordinate group. The "subordinate group" is far more fully integrated into the productive process and largely exists as an integral component of the means of production. What sets this description apart from the above descriptions is that these two groups have an indirect relationship with each other; these two groups relate to each other only through the marketplace and its command over use-value. For these two groups, their portfolios are clearly economic rather than political or social. Such a marketplace description satisfies the definitional prerequisite for a concrete analysis of class.

What Portes describes in this way is nothing other than the deep structural and durable political and social inequalities that are market driven definitions of any contemporary socio-economic order. Such a phenomenological portrayal offers up a clear and useful delineation between those that produce use-value and are subordinate, and those that command use-value and are dominant. It defines contemporary class structure in such a way as to give a real sense of legitimacy to the pervasive mood of class antagonism.

Even from the point of view of the academic and the successful artist, i.e., societies' intellectuals, if you will, such a use-value description might be considered a downgrade in status—from a respected member of the elite worker to that of lowly, common worker. Obviously this is a psychological reaction and not an objective one, a reaction springing from the values of a commercial social order rather than an objective universal system highlighting contributions to the social harvest brought by use-value. The concept of "worker" has certain grimy connotations that can get under the nails of even the most sympathetic of intellectuals. Being lumped in with a mechanic or carpenter is awkward for the would-be elitist—never-mind the necessary social usefulness of these trades, the profound contribution to the social aggregate; the fashion statement of wearing Armani is preferable to that made by Dickies, at least in commercial society.

And what about those who seem to have a foot in both camps, for example, the restaurant owner that is also the cook, or the plumbing contractor who labors daily alongside employees? Under purely Marxist description, these groups are referred to as *petit bourgeoisie*, which introduces an important subgroup. In the Portes analysis, however, it is most appropriate to see this group as capitalist, for although they are directly involved in the productive process, they also command the use-value brought about by their labor—and that of their employees.

The "common worker" also has a status issue to bear. The feeling of being tossed to the bottom of the social heap may provoke a denial reaction. Proletarian status in American society is not a desirable position, regardless of the actual social usefulness of the skill or trade and the worthiness of the individual wielding such a trade. The worker as hero is not an image the average American has of those who labor to produce the necessary goods and services we all consume.

Such descriptions as Portes suggests, while clear and properly functional, uncover two problematic issues. The first problem is that social status, as it is commonly thought of in commercialized societies, becomes a two-edged sword. That is, in societies where amassed wealth is the leading indicator of status and authority, those with the greatest wealth and power are often those who contribute the least to the social aggregate.[12] The second issue is that "class awareness," as it affects the producing class (i.e., the worker), often becomes negatively charged in such a way that class consciousness turns into an alien and hostile entity, causing the worker to be self-loathing. This self-deprecation operates in a way that turns class antagonism inward, generating apathy and depression. Of course, this underlying self-loathing by the common worker is not universal, but even slight elements of such negativity are the kind that the dominant class cultivates in order to express its superiority.

Even given the "drawbacks" of Portes' quasi-Marxist description of class, it would seem that identifying class on the basis of a use-value relation to the means of production—the working class, those who produce use-value, and the owning class, those who expropriate that use-value—is the most phenomenological way of arriving at an empirical understanding class. Of course, such a description eliminates the middle class. Phenomenologically, there is no way to introduce this subclass (i.e., a middle class) without the introjection of a subjective, descriptive interpretation: getting back to a mix of income, lifestyles, education level, etc. Eliminating such subjective assignments and value judgments is desirable for the purposes of research, making the elimination of "middle class" a beneficial elimination. It seems that while the class description put forward in this article—relationship to the means of production—is the most analytically appropriate, it is not without its psychological impact. This impact creates a real barrier to acceptance. It is simply a reality that status is far more important than we would like to admit. For the capitalist, and certainly the Grand Capitalist[13], such description (relationship to the means of production) defines the self as a kind of useless social canker, and for the worker, such a description is pregnant with the possibility of self-loathing. Additionally, drawing strict lines such as these is not desirable to a pseudo-democratic political process that seeks to dodge the optics of inequality. Even so, for objective analysis, the relationship to the production and command of use-value found through those relationships to the means of production, remains the best tool to describe the deep structural social differences that manifest themselves politically. The political manifestation of these structural differences is what opens the door to class friction and on to class warfare.

Class Warfare

Background to Modern Class Warfare. Class, as defined above, did not begin to take concrete form until somewhere around the turn of the 16th century. There was no clear cut point of departure from a time of "pre-class" (that is, adopting "class" as it is defined in the above section), a time where individuals might be more realistically assigned to a "caste system" (serfdom) rather than a class system. The end of feudal relations and the development of new urban centers, together with the rise of mercantilism (as an obvious innovation in socio-economic relations between competing groups) were not legislated into existence. These structural economic changes came about developmentally through a very uneven historical transformation process.

Consequently, prior to the 16th century class warfare was an event more akin to slave revolts than class struggle. For example, the issues that the Spartans had with the Helots, who outnumbered them at various times ten to one, lay at the root of many Spartan problems. The Athenian statesman Thucydides maintained that most Spartan institutions were designed with a view to suppressing the Helots, an underclass of forced labor whose status fell somewhere between slave and the medieval serf; Aristotle compared the Helots to an internal enemy that lay perpetually in wait. Next, consider the three Roman Servile Wars, ranging from 135—71 BCE, with the famous Spartacus-led gladiator uprising being the Third Servile War (73- 71 BCE).[14] Closer to our own time, there was the much touted Virginia slave revolt in 1831, led by Nat Turner. The Turner revolt was crushed somewhat quickly, but it serves to underwrite that even in modern times, slaves, as a socio-economic group, were always consciously antagonistic to both their status and position in the economic framework. This self-conscious antagonism also strongly suggests that slaves, as an oppressed group, fit into the social milieu quite a bit differently than the wage-earner who does not seem to automatically possess this self-aware class antagonism.

In more modern times, Machiavelli identified class conflict as "those natural enmities which occur between the popular classes and the nobility, arising from the desire of the latter to command and the disinclination of the former to obey, and are the causes of most of the troubles which take place in cities [bearing in mind that the cities of which Machiavelli speaks were the *political-states* of 15th century Italy and not modern urban centers]."[15] The attitude of the "popular classes" was different from that of the slave. In these "modern times" the popular classes were no longer "fixed" in place in the manner that social position was fixed for the slave or the serf. Urbanization meant that the population was no longer bound to the land, and this generated a kind of rootlessness that, while promoting social anxiety, also brought a larger sense of freedom. There was a much grander sense of entitlement, down to a budding sense of equality.[16] For the popular classes a wider vision of the world developed, bringing with it rebellious sentiments of "liberty, equality and fraternity," and along with those modern ideas came a feeling that a greater "fairness" was due them.

The point of all this is that while the potentiality for social strife has always gone cheek to jowl with political states, the development of urbanization, along with the new forms of production, and the changes in relationship they brought, produced changes in the nature of social antagonism. The pertinent question for us seeking a resolution to class antagonism, and especially class warfare, is to study its new sources and directions. Is it possible to resolve class antagonism in a non-violent way? Let us be clear, resolution through non-violence has not been the historical way. However, if a new sense of resolution can be uncovered, a resolution that stands a greater chance of non-violent success, we must begin with study, analysis of the violent struggle for equality. There are no guarantees of non-violence, for either class. The non-violence approach has a dismal record of success. Ironically, any positive search for a non-violent path must begin with a greater understanding of the violent path. For class warfare, this starts with on the meaning of war—class war through non-violent means. This will lead us to see how the non-violent approach favors the ruling class.

The Meanings of War. What exactly is war, that thing from which we derive the notion of class warfare? This is a question basic to our point. As nearly all this examination rests on the subject of warfare, an acceptable descriptive summary of the meaning of war seems necessary and appropriate. Von Clausewitz, a reigning master of the art of war, explains its meaning through an analogy for war as a contest of wrestlers. Clausewitz states that as "each [wrestler] tries through physical force to compel the other to do his will; his *immediate* aim is to *throw* his opponent in order to make him incapable of further resistance....*War is thus an act of force to compel our enemy to do our will*."[17] Of course, Clausewitz recognizes that there is a problem with this definition, *viz.*, what is the meaning of force? So further, Clausewitz says: "Force...is thus the *means* of war, to impose our will on the enemy the *object*. To secure that object, we must render the enemy powerless, and that, in theory, is the true aim of warfare."[18] So war, which is an act of force, is the means of imposing our will on an enemy by rendering the enemy incapable of further resistance. And, as any elementary physics text will reveal, force is any influence that causes an object to undergo a change. In the realm of physics, force typically means a change in either direction or speed. In the realm of politics, force means a change in immediate or long-term behavior. The question then arises: Does force always mean violence and bloodshed? No, not necessarily. In fact, one of the better-known statements by another master of the craft of war, Sun Tzu, explains: "Those skilled in war subdue the enemy's army without battle...They conquer by strategy." This famous pronouncement by Sun Tzu has far reaching implications that will become clear a bit further on.

For now, let us put the above considerations with another universally recognized observation by Von Clausewitz: "War is the continuation of politics by other means." Such an observation raises possibilities. A first possibility would be that if, as Clausewitz claims, war is a force applied to compel an enemy to do our will, and if subduing the enemy can be done without battle, then force can be applied through any number of non-violent, coercive means. It follows that such non-violent methods not only come in a variety of forms but are very frequently preferable. Non-violence is part of the art of winning through a system of *non-battle*, as Sun Tzu carefully states, the preferred strategy that the skilled warrior would adopt.

More or less overt acts of violence by non-violent force are common throughout history. Laying siege to a fortified position comes immediately to mind. Starvation is clearly an act of force—and violence. In modern times, the coercive impact of the embargo is the preferred version of the siege and is widely recognized as an act of war. Intimidation is also a suitable act of war. Often it is enough to gain compliance by menacing an opponent with embargo, or tariffs, or merely threatening the use of violence. Imperialism is a violent foreign policy, and military occupation of conquered land is clearly a picture of a people living under the continual threat of violence. The quartering of troops, for example, is a most visible sign of force being used to gain compliance and "to render the enemy powerless." According to of Von Clausewitz, any deep feeling of helplessness is a transparent indicator that some form of force is being applied and the "enemy" (whichever class is involved in initiating the struggle) is engaging in the psychological process of urging compliance through the non-violent application of force—which is to say, non-violent violence.

Non-violent war through methods such as the coercive power of tariffs and embargo, and even military occupations, are routinely dressed up in the garb of legal niceties. Obviously, any new rules set in play by the conqueror must be rationalized and communicated; laws and edicts promulgated by an occupying force often represent, or at least imply, such rationalizations of force. The poor laws of old, and more recent laws governing apartheid, and the current laws concerning same sex marriage, all may serve as obvious, even bald-faced examples of legally rationalized compliance by the threat of violence and force. Military occupation of any kind would be extremely difficult if the subjugated population did not know the new rules in play. We don't often think of the law itself as a fact of force, but certainly what stands behind the law (i.e., the potential for police violence) is clearly force. These rules by themselves represent coercion, a form of force, and like the wrestler cited by Clausewitz, these rules and laws are intended to render the opponent helpless.

A second consideration would be that if war is an extension of politics, is not politics a form of war? Such a question brings this descriptive analysis to an interesting point. Might not law, even as an abstract entity, be considered a means of war? While at first glance, such a notion appears awkward, or even silly, is not crime frequently presented as a war, as in the case of the "war on drugs"? Clearly, laws meant to prevent murder have widespread practical and beneficial intent and are not entirely delineated by class considerations; but other laws, such as apartheid laws, are meant to openly oppress and hold powerless huge segments of an occupied population. We might call this a form of domestic imperialism, where segments of the population are held in a quasi-colonial status through legalized, political force. This understanding of apartheid makes obvious the use of the law as blunt force trauma.

The Law as a Means of War. An unusual claim, I know, but let's examine it. In an occupied territory, laws favoring the occupier are clearly an extension of a war of conquest. Stripping the population of rights, forced quartering of troops, taxation to support the occupation, curfews, usurping the judicial system, ethnic or internal passports, etc., are all covert (and sometimes overt) signs of a continued war against a conquered and now occupied population. Attack and suppression of a conquered population are not always the final results of warfare. Occupation and colonization are very often the continuation of warfare in its non-violent form. The control and management of a conquered people will require many different laws and methods of enforcement. These are the extensions of war by legal means, which is to say by political means.

In a most general way, laws are a way of regulating and guiding behavior in a manner that is beneficial to certain socio-political groupings. In the case of a conquered people, these laws typically support the conqueror over and against the conquered. But what about under "ordinary" circumstances? Sometimes the "socio-political group" *is* the society at large, which is reflected in wide ranging criminal statutes. But sometimes that group is smaller, and the laws more specifically honed to meet the structural circumstance surrounding the exploitation of a subordinate class. This is obvious, in such as we would find in a colonial setting. In a domestic setting, however, it is not so clear; legal advantage that protects and enhances a privileged class is usually tucked away and out of sight. Through analysis, however, the murky outlines of hidden advantage in the law become more distinct and can reveal structural privilege in positioning. By way of contrast, laws against burglary, for example, generally benefit a wide swath of society, while on the other hand, laws preventing the hoarding of gold, or laws against patent infringement, are aimed at a much narrower social target. Laws against trespassing and copyright violation say something about how force is applied on behalf of both physical and intellectual property; laws regarding prostitution and gambling speak to force governing cultural and moral attitudes and standards. If there are laws against homicide, except in the name of the state, the neutral political "position" of the state is exposed (along with our tolerance for moral contradictions). However, since the state is rarely neutral, few laws emerge from the state that can be identified as neutral. Laws are a symptom leading to precise diagnosis concerning the nature and direction of non-violent control of the state. Laws especially answer the question of "*whose* state are we talking about"? The nature of a state's legalisms, and on whose behalf those legalisms are enacted, reveal the direction of force, and who benefits by the force that is being "non-violently" applied.

Regarding class war, the above observations lead to questions of perspective. How are we to view domestic laws in general? Do laws pertaining to an original, domestic population, a population against whom no violent war was ever declared, show any tell-tale signs of intent to subjugate? Can laws reveal such a thing as a form of domestic imperialism or internal colonization? To what degree can those laws not directly pertaining to common criminal behavior represent a means of war, or at the very least, leave a footprint of the conqueror in a conquered land? As it would seem that certain laws favor certain groups (e.g., laws protecting the accumulation of wealth), we can conditionally say yes and recognize the legal outlines that of protect a lopsided distribution of wealth. By way of illustration, and without condemning wealth, *per se*, it would seem that short-selling, public bailouts of private financial institutions, favorable tax laws, or even laws protecting simple usury (e.g., credit cards), all represent a few of the many routine forms of protection for accumulated riches possessed by certain groups. It is also easy to see that such legal fortification for the accumulation of wealth sets up the conditions for conflict between the two major socio-economic classes (i.e., the producing class—vs—the expropriating class).

Furthermore, political laws that suppress those who possess neither wealth nor power clearly exist. For both ideological and doctrinaire reasons, these laws are notoriously difficult to describe in terms of class war. However, the use of police power can be a tip off to class war, and more particularly, the nature of class war. In the U.S. we might look to historical events such as the commutation fee that allowed the rich to avoid fighting in the Civil War, a law which sparked the Draft Riots of 1863; fast forward to the assault by federal troops on the Bonus Marchers of 1932, or the evicting of residents from the many Depression Era Hoovervilles that sprung up across the US in the nineteen-thirties, and the more recent dismantling, along with numerous arrests, of the citizens acting within the "Occupy Movements."[19] It's painfully obvious that none of the "suppressed" in these illustrations were of the capitalist class, those owners and controllers of the means of production. It is noteworthy that the above examples lack any racist component of legalisms such as voter suppression, or criminal possession of small amounts of marijuana. In fact, all these groups cited above were highly representative of a distressed white working class being pressed by difficult economic and/or political circumstances which led to a round of revolt and suppression. It is no stretch at all to interpret these, and many other episodes like them, as representing the laws of a suppressing occupying force. All these assaults on the lower classes were enacted under the guise of law and authority.

Class war from above. As Von Clausewitz's exposition of warfare illustrates, the examples cited represent controlled non-violent violence

76

being applied to force "the enemy" to submit to the will of superior might; in war, the conquered submits to the conqueror. As specifically outlined in these terms, class warfare clearly, by descriptive analysis, exists in Western democracies seemingly in perpetuity.[20] It is where force is being applied, against whom, and by whom, that should cause us to rethink the typical, mainstream analysis of class warfare.

When we consider class warfare and how it is generally handled by politicians and the media, we tend to think of those struggling at the bottom (i.e., the working class) attacking those at the top (i.e., in most contemporary societies, the capitalist class) through strikes, rioting and mayhem, and the occasional rebellion. But as pointed out above, given the wide range of the laws regarding both labor and privilege, it seems to be that the ongoing and unrelenting class warfare presses in the other direction, a ruling elite suppressing the class beneath it. Through an examination of such laws as the anti-labor laws, voter suppression laws, various tax laws offering advantage to one class as opposed to another, and many others, it can be convincingly argued that those at the top are waging a continuous war of occupation on those at the bottom. Even aside from these examples (and there are many more), it is always the case that the nature of the established laws is to protect and offer permanency to the status quo. Given the primacy of the status quo, it is difficult to disagree with the fact that laws are discriminatory, and that they offer advantage to one social group as opposed to another. The status quo in western democracies is a hierarchy that places the moneyed class at the top both as the rulers of the economy and as the dominate political elite. Does society look any other way, even to the casual observer? If we agree with Von Clausewitz that politics is an extension of war by other means then it follows that class warfare is largely perpetuated by the ruling political elite against the working class. We might say, adopting more contemporary usage, that class war is largely initiated and institutionalized by the 1% against the 99%, with occasional revolts from below (e.g., occupy wall street), revolts all too quickly suppressed by legal action.

Naturally, such a description as we have offered is anathema to the perpetrators of class force and violence. Any image revealing the nature of legalized class warfare will be resisted by representatives of the status quo and resisted by any and all means possible. Publicly, this resistance by the powers-that-be typically takes the form of psychological manipulation of political doctrine. Before any suppression in the form of police violence comes non-violent suppression by canard, perhaps appeals to patriotism or Christian values, or even outright stoking baser prejudices such as racism, misogyny or homophobia. Only after these have failed is police violence threatened and applied.

To be specific, the first go-to for public manipulation is a touting of political canards that insist that the playing field is level for all (in other words, that what you are seeing is not what you are seeing); that all citizens of western-style democracy are created equal and all citizens have equal access to great wealth and elite status. Despite the absurdity of this claim (that we are all born equal), it is heavily relied upon by members of the ruling class in order to deflect the images of oppression. This manipulation depends on spreading the belief that the laws of the land are sacred, fair and unbiased. Manipulation publicly offers a nearly religious, sacred interpretation of the law as a gift, almost as though the laws came down from on high and human beings played no role in their construction. Most distortion of class war by the perpetrators of class violence takes a variation of one of these two paths. Masking and deflecting analysis and criticism is a chief survival tool for the ruling elite.

A second go-to is to cause the image of class war to be flipped, reversed in an attempt to show that the 1% are the victims rather than the bottom 99%. This is somewhat difficult to carry out as how it runs defies even causal optics and evidence and the commonly held understanding of what society looks like. So it is here that well developed prejudice is pressed into service: the "American Way of Life" is under attack by everything from foreign engineered, communist conspiracies to home grown cheats, e.g., the welfare queens. And of course, the reliance on dog-whistle expressions also would include simplistic, jingoistic appeals to patriotism and Christian values (e.g., "my country, right or wrong," or "one nation under God").

Finally, there is, as a last resort, the threat of imprisonment and police violence. Those who resist the inequality, and do so forcefully enough, find themselves tied up in a maze of legal constraints backed by the threat of police violence. These legal constraints include a long list of legislation that limits rights to collectively organize for negotiating contracts (Right-to-Work Laws are an obvious example, but also the very recent legislation by Wisconsin, Tennessee, *et al.*, to cause public employee unions to be illegal), and the use of violence authorized in the use of federal troops to squash rebellious workers (e.g., Grover Cleveland and the use of Federal Troops to crush the Pullman Strike is a well-documented case), not to mention the imprisonment of their leaders (e.g., Eugene Debs, imprisoned during the same Pullman Strike).

The reason these deflections are not more widely recognized and can hide in plain sight, is that class warfare is a *lawful system of repression* rather than a sudden and arbitrary frenzy of violence. This lawful system is the result of a successful warfare that has moved from open and periodic violence into the occupation phase of war, a lawful occupation that can last scores of years, and even centuries. It is not farfetched to say that class warfare has never ceased; it is tireless, changing its legal form as dictated by historical transformation and the English Enclosure Movement and the wholesale dislocation of Native Americans are centuries apart and appear to be quite unalike, but they actually bear many similarities in both law and social violence. The greatest similarity of all can be found in the legal trappings which surrounded and cloaked the oppression and subjugation of the populations involved. Consider the actual ante-bellum law which stated that: "Slaves cannot redeem themselves, nor obtain a change of masters, though cruel treatment may have rendered such change necessary for their personal safety."[21] Of course this came to an end, but only after the most violent war in American history.

In a very real sense, violent revolution is the most obvious reaction to this class warfare from above. Revolution is the antithesis of repression, its rejection, its dialectic dance partner, if you will. Revolution is the sharp unmasking and rejection of class warfare from above. That this happens so rarely is testimonial to the stupefying, cloaking power of ideology and political doctrine.

However, this antithetical expression of class warfare is far more dramatic and abrupt than institutionalized oppression, as it seems to come from nowhere. This expression of class violence is also rarer, though not, by any means, completely spontaneous. Both rebellion and revolution (two different political events) clearly arise in response to the above described system of class occupation and oppression. As revolution is the face of class war that attempts to overthrow the existing intuitions, it does not, and indeed cannot, hide in plain sight. The oppressive origins inspiring revolution may hide like a coiled spring in a legalistic jack-in-the-box, but not the eventual release. Revolution, and to a lesser extent, rebellion, are the most obvious and dramatic expressions of class warfare from above.

The Resolution of Class Warfare. It would seem that class warfare, as described in one of the two ways above: (1) suppression and occupation, or (2) revolution, is all but omnipresent, with suppression and occupation being the most prevailing outcome of the warfare. Given this understanding, we should look with special care into the desired resolution of class warfare from above as it is the likely provoker of revolution.

Recall first that in western democratic societies, class war from above often goes completely unspoken and largely unrecognized, cloaked as it is by legal and constitutional niceties. Thus, the commonplace and lawful occupation of an entire social system or sub-system (such as race, class, or religious systems) often goes largely unrecognized for what it is. Typically, any person pointing out or resisting this type of class warfare is, as the situation warrants, identified a common criminal, or insane, or a foreign agent, rather than a political enemy. In this way, the political side of the oppression can continue to hide behind the legal framework provided by constitutions and the courts. A self-evident and ongoing example of this type of legalized suppression is easily found by drawing attention to the plight of labor unions. Having all but been destroyed in the 1970s and '80s, labor unions are in an uphill struggle for recognition and better, more equitable treatment for the working class. By the way, this struggle by the working class for union recognition is international.

In this sense, a particular country's domestic population is treated in a similar manner to that of an occupied nation. Once conquered, the first social elements suppressed are labor unions and intellectuals, which include publications and the media; labor leaders are arrested, universities and media outlets are closed. The Nazi conquest and occupation of France (and virtually any other German occupied nation) and Pinochet's violence against the Chilean people stand as examples of these techniques used to crush working class aspirations toward equality. In countries where domestic occupation and suppression are long standing, anti-union legislation and legal action against workers are so commonplace that it all but goes unnoticed. At the same time, general education is underfunded and left to languish, and teachers constrained and controlled, often told what to teach and how to teach it. Mass media (sometimes called the Fourth Estate), which is typically in the hands of intellectuals, is brought under control only to be resurrected as communication organs for the conquerors. Providing the 99% with the tools to analyze social circumstance and spread the analysis (such as this paper is doing) is the last thing desired by the ruling elite. It is not for nothing that this Fourth Estate always draws ire and hostility from the ruling elite. Remember that education—of which the media is a powerful factor—is often dependent on a free and persistent uncovering process, and elites can only rule in comfort when ruling in secret. This suppression of the supporting elements of the 99% (unions, the media, and education) is a deliberate policy of the 1% and never a product of happenstance, though where possible it is made to appear so.

The ubiquity of these policies raises a question: can there ever be any resolution to class warfare? Even though any answer must be abstract, ideal and theoretical, we must remind ourselves that we are restricting this ideal answer to satisfy the concept of class as described in its economic relations, as laid out by the Portes model above. Any answer here, in this paper, cannot hope to cover "differences in life-styles," or who has "managerial" authority in the workplace, or who is thought of as "intellectual" or "professional." We will concern ourselves with "class" as it relates to the means of production and distribution (a more or less strictly structured understanding of "working class"). This seems less confusing and more directly related to the most visible elements of class and class warfare.

As the means of production and distribution tend to evolve slowly, they therefore appear fixed in place, and can not be done away with in any practical sense. Resolution of class friction (i.e., class warfare) can thus take only one of two paths: accommodation or elimination. As elimination of class appears to be an impractical solution, accommodation of the friction becomes the only alternative. Describing the details of accommodation is less difficult than one might suppose, but the practical implications for politics are another matter.

To *accommodate* class friction and antagonism, it would be necessary to either alter the *consciousness* of the antagonism or change the *perception* of the friction. In either an emotional or a structural sense, this is not an easy process. Such an accommodation or acceptance of class friction usually implies the acceptance of some doctrine fostered by a corporatist image of the social order. A typical example of this approach would be that advocated by fascist theory. Much fascist theory is woven into discussions of social peace far more often that one might suppose. In fact, most forms of resolution-by-accommodation bear some of the earmarks of fascist doctrine.

The Fascist Resolution. The very idea of fascism, at least under the aegis of western democratic thought, is always dished out with a strong dose of disapproval. The name itself, "fascism," is often presented as an ugly vilification.[ii] Looked at objectively, however, fascism should not be dismissed out of hand. It must be noted that, to an extent much greater than we typically realize, most western democracies contain numerous fascist elements, though they are not usually picked up and analyzed as such (e.g., top down political authority, state control over societal elements such as police and education, an impenetrable elite, etc.). Having made that clear, we will return to our focus on class relations as directly impacted by fascist political theory. We need only stress that doctrinaire prejudices often prevent us from clearly seeing important perspectives offered by other points of view.

The fascist point of view seems almost automatically distasteful, particularly as fascism is very often equated with Nazi Germany. It ought to be noted that this comparison is a much debated issue among scholars, and typically considered a mistaken view.[22] Nazism, as a totalitarian doctrine, took little direction from either the owners of the means of production, and none at all from the working class. Nazi totalitarianism was thorough and absolute, whose leaders saw themselves as having risen above messy class distinctions. Although the last is a tenant of fascist doctrine, the actual reason that there was no noticeable class conflict under Nazism was because both the actors of the conflict, the capitalist and the worker, were under strict state control; such tendencies toward social control exist within all fascist doctrine, but not in the single minded manner as that seen in Nazi totalitarianism. Fascism is not, by any structural necessity, a totalitarian theory. Fascism requires control of the leadership of the state, but there is nothing automatic about the theory that requires

---

ii. For instance, fascism is often conflated with Nazism. They are not necessarily the same. To offer one example, anti-Semitism and racism are not automatically a part of fascism.

a totalitarian rule such as Nazism. Rather than absolute obedience, which is a cornerstone of Nazi totalitarianism, fascist doctrine requires absolute *cooperation* from all classes with state-political leadership. This statement is a bit more than a substitution of words.

Seen from the perspective of fascist theory, the individual, *as individual,* together with the individual's class, is not only accepted, but is a positive and functional necessity of a prosperous socio-economic system. Under Mussolini's fascist doctrine, "cooperation"—albeit a guided cooperation—was critical to the successful working of the state. Thus individualism, with an emphasis on cooperation and coordination was, in Mussolini's words, gathered into a system he called *corporativism.*

> "The Corporation is established to develop the wealth, political power and welfare of the Italian. Corporativism means a disciplined and therefore a controlled economy, since there can be no discipline which is not controlled. Corporativism overcomes Socialism as well as it does Liberalism: it creates a new synthesis."[23]

Objectively, this type of social cooperation (i.e., fascism) is arranged through a horizontal structure, somewhat like a train pulling forward toward a distant, prosperous horizon. However, *theoretically* the system is not presented as horizontal, but as a vertical system, thus making it more palatable. The structure is based on an organic model of the social order where each part (individual and class) contributes to the overall betterment of society as a whole. The individual, along with the individual's class, draws significant benefits from this new reality of a fulfilled society. However, all this is accomplished under the controlling guidance of a political elite acting as the helm for the state. This elite are members of a political class and not an economic class; thus they are able to act in the unbiased interests of all segments of the social order. Each part of the social order will prosper to the degree that the whole will prosper, and safety and security will surely follow from this cooperation as structured through fascist corporativism.[24]

> "The nation is seen as a biological organism that lives, breaths, grows and, presumably dies, while individuals are seen as cells that perform their function and achieve fulfillment only insofar as the entire organism is healthy. The individual simply does not exist

without the nation, for humans are by nature social animals and can realize themselves only as members of a collectivity."[25]

We see in fascist theoretical doctrine that class and class warfare are no longer problems, as each class is fully integrated into a common collective process lead by the wise men of the state, the engineers of the locomotive, guiding the organism for the betterment of all. According to fascist theory, in place of class warfare comes class cooperation, cooperation for the common good. There is no need to represent class in terms of the exploited and the exploiter, as this is like saying that the transmission of a car is being exploited by the fuel pump, or the stomach is exploited by the liver. All the parts of the organism are necessary for the survival of the whole, and both the individual and the individual's class prosper because the collective effort is for the betterment of all. This is quite literally the burial of class conflict beneath the mantle of organic harmony, an idealistic version of class cooperation rather than class warfare.[26] If in the above one detects a subtle contradiction, it is not a misreading. In theory, fascism paints a picture of a cooperative, vertical pluralism; in reality, the controlling parts are hierarchical in arrangement. Let's examine this by a closer look at the *theoretical* model of fascism.

By no means did this organic model promoted by fascism originate with Mussolini. The organic model can be traced back to Plato—a philosopher much admired by Mussolini—and Plato's *Republic*, which sketched individuals as working for the betterment of the whole by carrying out their assigned (predetermined) functions. This is a very attractive model, especially for those in possession of the self-described "higher functions." It goes without saying, however, that those whose functions reflected a lowlier social station may not have been so pleased with the "organic" arrangement. Organic theory assumes a vertical, cooperative model in which a selfless human nature would come into it own and cause all to be pleased with the unequal rewards due their various stations in life—a problematic assumption at best.[iii]

---

iii. To be fair to Plato, the philosopher was opposed to great wealth and degrading poverty, and though not entirely consistent or deliberate, supports the idea of a more equal distribution of wealth, a narrowing of class distinctions as a necessity for the survival of the state. See Plato's *The Republic*, esp., chapter four.

This leads to a striking difference between the fascist model and fascism in practice, as witnessed in fascist Italy or Pinochet's Chile. In real-time, the vertical promise is a hierarchical structure in practice, and "fascist cooperation" leads to something other than the betterment of all; the "betterment of all" turns out, in reality, to be the betterment of those at the top of the hierarchical structure. Under the fascist model, private property, that is, the means of production, remains private and inviolable, with the owners of the means of production consuming the profits of production. Again, in the words of Mussolini, the father of modern fascism:

"The corporative economy respects the principle of private property. Private property completes the human personality. It is a right. But it is also a duty. We think that property ought to be regarded as a social function; we wish therefore to encourage, not passive property, but active property, which does not confine itself to enjoying wealth, but develops it and increases it. The corporative economy respects private initiative."[27]

As the means of production remains in private hands, class cooperation comes to mean something other than political equality and betterment for all. Mussolini makes it clear that the state, under the guise of equal reward, merely acts as the ombudsman for the owners of the means of production. Class is still present, an elite is still in control, the owners of the means of production still the principal beneficiaries of all this social cooperation. Under fascism, the social organism is still organized for the purpose of class warfare and suppression—a repressive system drafted under a different guise.

The Anarcho-Communist Resolution: Just do away with class. End social inequality based on its relationship to a privately held means of production. Of course, to upend the economic system is easier said than done. Nonetheless, this abolition of privately held means of production and distribution is the prescriptive resolution advanced by that part of the left represented by orthodox Communist (the socializing of production and distribution) and Anarchist theory (the ending of authoritarian rule from above).[28] Karl Marx, in the Manuscript of 1844, said rather bluntly that:

"Communism is the positive abolition of private property and thus of human self-alienation and therefore the real re-appropriation of the human essence by and for man."[29]

Whereas the fascist finds the need to do away with (or explain away) class warfare through the medium of social and economic cooperation, the communist would go directly after the cause of social friction. If the warring factions find themselves on opposite sides of a barrier built by capitalism, then the solution would seem to be to tear down the barrier. Rip down the privately held means of production and build up a socially responsible system of production and distribution. Construct a political system responsive to the needs of an entire society rather than the needs of the few, or in the current vernacular, the 1%.

The communist is not so naive as to think that this will do away with individual distinction, or group differentiation, or even some measure of social pedigree (nor is there any compelling reason to eliminate such differences); however, the anarcho-communist does theorize that such a change will eliminate the more ugly rancor stemming from a vastly unequal distribution of wealth and political power that plagues contemporary western democracies. Again, all concerned realize that attempting to fix these problems through the abolition of private ownership of the means of production is more easily theorized than achieved. The overthrow of class hierarchy and authoritarian control is often preceded by a violent confrontation with the old order, with results that are far from predictable or conclusive. History has clearly revealed the truth of this claim. Having made note of that, the mechanism of revolution, for this brief paper, is of less analytical importance than the end result of a possible communist victory, i.e., an anarcho-communist resolution to class warfare. The issue before us at this point is to uncover what such a resolution of class warfare through anarcho-communist theory would look like in practice.

First, a glance at the theory. To paraphrase a modern patriarch of anarchy, Peter Kropotkin, anarchy is the no-government system of socialism. In somewhat more detail, Kropotkin writes that anarchy is:

"A principle or theory of life and conduct under which society is conceived without government—harmony in such a society being obtained, not by submission to law, or by obedience to any authority, but by free agreements concluded between the various groups, territorial and professional, freely constituted for the sake of production and consumption, as also for the satisfaction of the infinite variety of needs and aspirations of a civilized being. In a society developed along these lines, the voluntary associations which already now begin to cover all the fields of human activity would take a still greater extension so as to substitute themselves for the state in all its functions."[30]

In this no-government system, the individual is expected to contribute according to talent and ability and take from the common aggregate according to need. To fully grasp this, we will need illustrations, as without examples words become little more than canards and platitudes. For fascism, we have the illustration provided by Mussolini's Italy, but what about the actual practice of anarcho-communism?

The Israeli system of the kibbutz can stand as a real-life example both of anarchism and communism:

"The kibbutz is a voluntary, self-governing community, administered democratically by its members with neither legal sanctions nor any framework of coercive authority to ensure conformity to its collectively-agreed upon behavioral norms. The source of political authority in the community is the general assembly of all members in which every member has an equal vote on every matter relating to kibbutz life, with decisions made by majority vote."[31]

The political and economic structure of the kibbutz is based on the idea of communal ownership and direct democracy; that is, a living system based on a communist economic structure and anarchist political principles. With the ownership of the means of production held in common, privilege based on the economic division of society is no longer a threat to democratic principles. With a common ownership of production, the political influence of great wealth is done away with, and a direct democratic power structure is not only made possible but seems to follow nearly axiomatically. Democratic, political equality is no longer sidelined by the economic power of the owners of the means of production. The problem of a corrupted and privileged pseudo-democratic political structure is in great measure solved by a system of communist ownership.

The actual day-to-day routines involving production and distribution within the kibbutz are run by elected committees that function in a series of rotation. This is a horizontal rather than hierarchical system of management.

"A horizontal management structure composed of a network of managerial committees, democratically elected by the general assembly of members and operating via a system of regular rotation. To each branch was assigned a branch manager, with each branch consisting of several autonomous units operating independently[32]....Decision making within these groups was carried out on a directly democratic basis with each team free to choose a supervisor responsible for the day-to-day operations of the team. The supervisor divided tasks among team members who then decided for themselves how to perform the work, and kept an overview of the work process."[33]

After more than half a century of operation, the Israeli kibbutz system has shown remarkable resiliency and structural integrity. This anarcho-communist system continues successfully to the present day. At the time of the present writing (c. late 2019), while much of the original system has been privatized, there remain over 250 kibbutzim in operation.[34]

None of this description is intended to imply that ordinary, day-to-day human squabbling has ceased under this economic system; rivalry, jealousy, envy, and just plain human rascality, are not done away with. But the description and the actuality of the kibbutz seems to indicate that the squabbling is personal rather than some ongoing result of social friction based on unequal power and authority.

However, there are downsides. Due to the lack of authority and coercive power, anarchy cannot guarantee any democratic outcome; enforcing *ad hoc* democratic rulings has proven extremely difficult. Size is another problem. In place of laws, *ad hoc* democracy seems ineffective beyond small scale enterprises. One might consider this to be the greatest and most general problem with anarchy. Laws give consistency and predictability. Functioning without these pillars of social stability leaves democratic decision making open to societal angst, exacerbating a general atmosphere of insecurity. It seems fair to say that widespread, direct democracy is inherently unstable and unenforceable, and this would be a great source of anxiety for a good many people. Living with freedom is hardly casual and never free.

> "Anarchist ethical action lacks the coercive muscle that accompanies state law. This approach to politics, therefore, prioritizes action and life over effectiveness, result, or outcome. Anarchy thus seems to promise few guarantees in terms of specific outcomes, which means that it will probably be unlikely to be persuasive to those who insist on the kind of social engineering that is justified by its outcome."[35]

All of the above provoke a sticky question: whether to possess a security and predictability that can be had through the muscle supplied by a strong, top-down, authoritarian state, or to suffer the unease and apprehension that can arises from a purely democratic setting. This is not an easily answered question. It represents an extreme form of existential tradeoff, a tradeoff tinged with strong, even compelling emotional overtones: Does one want security or does one want freedom?

> "If it is the result that matters at all costs, it will usually seem most guaranteed by resorting or appealing to institutions of power and coercion—that is those that can promise a result. But if what matters more is the self-discovery of humanity, and if that self-discovery is dependent on humanity's own action in the world, then what we have at hand is a process that cannot be foretold."[36]

Again, freedom is hardly free. The anarcho-communist path might look appealing at first blush, but the choice for taking this leftist position demands that one also pick up enormous personal responsibility, a personal responsibility necessary for the freedom to carry out self-determined decisions with no else to blame. The removal of economic (i.e., class) distinctions based on a market relationship to the means of production also weakens the power to guide, to control, to decide, to direct, to establish those factors of safety and security without which many individuals will feel adrift and frightened. The choice presented by anarcho-communism, that is, the choice between freedom and security, is both personal and difficult.

Summation: We began this project by demonstrating that the many descriptions of class based on social factors such as lifestyle, status and professional position, are uncertain, ambiguous and altogether inadequate for a rigorous analysis of social conflict. Further, by description, we revealed that the best empirical explanation of class friction seems to be based on the conflicting economic relationship social groups have to the means of production and distribution. Adopting the Portes model, this relationship separates society into two distinct groups. These are the two groups we typically see exhibiting antagonism toward each other: the capitalist class of elites who consume labor and the working class who produce labor, *a la* Portes. Class conflict can best be seen as an outgrowth of the divergent way in which these two classes draw their unequal share of the common yield from their relative position to the means of production and distribution.

Next, we found that class war, based on the general descriptions of war by Clausewitz and Sun Tzu, covers both violent and non-violent struggles, with the exploitation of occupied zones coming under the definition of war. Through phenomenal analysis, class warfare can be seen as coming from both directions, from the bottom to be sure, but far more often from the top, that is, a class war carried out by the 1% against the 99%. We were able to tie the class warfare of the top against the bottom to a legal system acting in support of such warfare. This supporting legal system often takes on the feel of a hostile occupation. This examination of a lawful means of occupation excluded common criminal codes but revealed how such occupation laws frequently hide beneath the cloak of criminal codes. The unequal share of the common yield is held firmly in place by these laws.

Finally, we looked into two theories, with empirical support, for resolution of class warfare. The first to be examined was fascism; the second was anarcho-communism.

The first, fascism, attempted to resolve class warfare through a model of *cooperation*, a model that Mussolini called *corporativism*. Through the fascist system, all aspects of the social order draw life and substance from the collective effort, with each part of society doing its fair share and drawing its fair share. The capitalist does their part and the producing classes do their part, with a political class (the fascist party) riding at the top of the pyramid, a vantage point from where they can best guide the state. According to the fascist, antagonism between classes is an absurd contradiction to the well-being of the social order, much like suggesting that the stomach wages war against the liver. In practice, however, fascism supports private property and private holdings of the means of production, and class conflict is not so much turned into a system of cooperation as it is suppressed. The needs of the state are always paramount. The Italian state, under fascist rule, was supported and supportive of the elite capitalist class, and class cooperation. This last, class cooperation was largely a myth. In reality, working class institutions such as trade unions and worker collectives were ruthless suppressed.

The second theory—anarcho-communism—resolves class conflict by simply doing away with a capitalist ownership of the means of production and distribution. Instead, the anarchist institutes a collective ownership and control of production. The doing away with private control over the means of production and a radically direct democratic structure, meld anarchy with communism. By illustration we have demonstrated that this admittedly idyllic approach works successfully on a small scale within the modern kibbutz system. This collective, democratic system has been in operation for several generations and while personal conflict between individuals remains, structural, economic conflict between groups of individuals seems to have been eliminated. There are, as yet, no large-scale examples of an anarcho-communist system, which represents a downside to the system; how to enlarge this system to encompass a society larger than a few hundred individuals remains for future analysis. Other drawbacks to the system are found in such as the lack of enforceability for democratic rulings, or the often tedious and time-consuming meetings of the collective required for even the smallest decisions, and the tendency to drop out of the ongoing democratic process, etc. While structural conflict seems to be minimized, the lack of a legal framework makes large scale institutionalization a paradoxical hurdle anarcho-communism struggles to get over. Although attempts have been made to solve this problem, the successful anarcho-communist system thus far remains a small-scale enterprise. Anarcho-communism seems out of reach to the great majority of the world's citizens. It remains, almost exclusively, an idealized goal for the left.

~

Future Considerations: In the absence of direct democratic institutions and the continued private ownership of the means of production, friction and class warfare seem inevitable, at least for the foreseeable future; that is, unless fascist theory is eagerly embraced by all classes of society. However, the acceptance of fascist doctrine by the working class seems highly unlikely; this, of course, depends on propagandist packaging. Therefore, it appears an inevitable conclusion that until such time that direct democracy can be instituted and the means of production and distribution can be re-assigned for large scale social well-being rather than private consumption, class warfare (with the emphasis on class warfare directed from above) is here to stay.

Size seems to be a central issue. A monopoly on violence and coercion has offered the fascist model viability on a widespread political plain. All actual large-scale political entities possess some form of top-down, class dominated authoritarian rule. In a sense then, the fascist model already exits as the most common form of political expression and organization.

Anarcho-communism is another matter. Its seeming resistance to large scale institutionalization has minimized its attractiveness as a political alternative. Future analysis may open a pathway to the general institutionalization of more widespread democracy and more equal distribution of the social yield. For now, anarcho-communism remains mostly a thought experiment by which to measure practical, political realities.

If anything is taken away from this brief study, it is that class warfare is inherent to current western democratic structures, and that it involves predominately top-down class warfare. Further, the abolition of class warfare is dependent on the institutionalization of authentic and direct democracy and collective ownership of the means of production and distribution, no matter how impractical that might appear to us at the current time. Practical resolution of this dilemma awaits future analysis.

Notes

1. https://www.ecnmy.org/learn/your-society/status-in-society/socio-economic-class/

2. William Kornblum, *Sociology: The Central Questions*. (Belmont CA: International Thomson Publishing, 1998) p. 72

3. See: Paul Kingston, *The Classless Society*, (Stanford: Stanford University Press, 2000)

4. For example, see Andrew Cherlin, 'Between Poor and Prosperous', in *Social Class and Changing Families in an Unequal America*, ed. Carlson and England, (Stanford: Stanford University Press, 2011) pp. 68-84

5. Michael Zweig, *The Working Class Majority: America's Best Kept Secret*, (Ithaca NY: Cornell University Press, 2001) p. 3

6. Ibid. pp 27-37

7. Alejandro Portes, *Economic Sociology, A Systemic Inquiry*, (Princeton: Princeton University Press, 2010)

8. Ibid. p. 79

9. Ibid. pp 80-82

10. Ibid. pp 83-84

11. See: Marx, Karl *Grundrsse*, (New York: Vantage Books, 1973) p. 284

12. In a rather odd admission of this non-producing status of the wealthy, Jamie Dimon, CEO of JP Morgan Chase, stated during the financial crisis of 2008: "They [the public at large] want Wall Street to pay…They think we're overpaid assholes. There's no politician, no president, who is going to sign off on a bailout." Then in a moment of supreme clarity, he added: "And why would you try to bail out people whose sole job it is to make money." As reported by Andrew Sorlin, *Too Big To Fail*, (New York: Viking Penguin, 2009) pp. 335, 336

13. Again refers to Portes' descriptive categories, ibid. pp 80-82

14. It's of interest to note that only about half of the Roman gladiators were slaves, with the other half being contract gladiators, men who signed up for the fabulous pay and the fame. It should also be noted that only about 10% of the gladiators were put to the sword. The death of a gladiator meant that the organizer of the games had to pay the cost of replacement, a highly expensive luxury.

15. Niccolo Machiavelli, *History of Florence*, (New York: Harper and Row, 1966) p. 108

16. See Machiavelli on: *Discourses*, translated by C.E. Detmold, (New York: Modern Library, 1950) p. 149

17. Carl Von Clausewitz, *On War*, (New York: Everyman's Library, Alfred A. Knoph, 1993) p. 83

18. Ibid. p. 83

19. For example, see the "Occupy Wallstreet" protests of Fall 2011

20. I am ignoring *intra*-class warfare, that is war between members of the same class, which is represented by nearly all international wars, as it is beyond the scope of this paper. It is enough to say that this model of class warfare is the better known, and the most costly in terms of lives and material.

21. https://www.bowdoin.edu/~prael/projects/gsonnen/page3.html

22. Ingersol, Matthews & Davidson, *The Philosophic Roots of Modern Ideology*, (New Jersey: Prentice Hall, 2001) p. 214

23. Benito Mussolini, as quoted in Herman Finer, *Mussolini's Italy* (New York: Grosset & Dunlop, 1965) p. 502

24. Zeev Sternbell, "Fascist Ideology," from *Fascism, a Readers Guide*, ed by Walter Laqueur, (Berkeley: University of California Press, 1976)

25. Ingersoll, Matthews, & Davidson, *op. cit.* P. 219

26. For example, see: http://www.openyear.org/super-earners/class-cooperation-not-class-warfare/

27. Benito Mussolini, as quoted by Gaetanho Savemini, in *Under the Axe of Fascism* (Oxford: Hesperides Press, 2008) p. 134

28. Obviously, right wing anarchy (e.g., Libertarianism) is not considered in this article as unequal distribution and economic class are not done away with through Libertarianism, but only arrived at by other means.

29. Karl Marx, *Early Texts*, ed by David McLellan, (Oxford: Oxford Press, 1971) p. 148.

30. Peter Kropotkin, "Anarchism," from the 11th edition of the *Encyclopedia Britannica*

31. James Horrox, *Living Revolution. Anarchism in the Kibbutz Movement* (Edinburgh: AK Press, 2009) p. 7

32. Ibid. p. 68

33. Ibid. p. 69

34. http://www.kibbutz.org.il/eng/

35. Mohammed A. Bamyeh, *Anarchy as Order* (New York: Rowman & little, 2009) p. 34

36. Ibid. p. 34

DEFINING THE LEFT
AND THE RIGHT

WILLIAM F. PRAY

Abstract: The article opens with the historical origins of the highly charged words "Left" and "Right," and from where they derive their political meaning. The piece then goes into the most common misconceptions surrounding the political concepts of Left and Right. Following that, a more appropriate and consistent definition of class is introduced, one based on differing views concerning the foundation of all political doctrines, "human nature." Then, given the Right's and the Left's opposing positions on human nature, various political doctrines are measured up against these different understandings of "us." At this point, it is then shown where and how these differing positions on the inner nature of our species influence behavior and thinking in the real political world of power and position.

Welcome to Political Science 101. This article will track and explain what should be a basic part of such a course: an understanding of our political spectrum and where we as citizens fit on that scale. Then further, how that understanding (or more likely, mis-understanding) affects our political conversations and decisions. In other words, are you a Right-Winger, or a Lefty? This is not so obvious as we have been led to believe by newscasters and pundits.

What is the political Left and what is the political Right? We use these political terms often enough—Left and Right. We see these terms in print. We hear them in media outlets. Yet, how many of us really understand their meaning? Do we fully comprehend the philosophical arguments and positions that lie behind the words, Left and Right? What exactly distinguishes the political Left from the political Right? If we were to fully grasp the ideas and elements that distinguish one position from the other, would it change our minds on any political debate? The answer is unequivocally, yes, quite likely it would. Education (i.e., knowledge and how to use it) in any respect readjusts our alignment to whatever subject is under study. Knowledge of the real difference between the Left and the Right will blow away much of the absurd and pernicious propaganda that swirls around political wars.

History of the words and background to the debate

The words themselves: Aside from simple curiosity, knowing the origin of the words will provide a convenient foot-hold on their political importance. That foot-hold starts with the history of the words. Getting at the origin of Left and Right is not really essential to defining the words. However, following this path will help us to understand the political impact brought about by the words and the concepts that underwrite them.

During the **French Revolution** (1789-1799) those members of the National Assembly that favored strong constraints on the monarchy and the adoption of a republican form of governance—that would be the radicals of their day—sat to the *left* of the podium, a podium nominally occupied by the King. Those members of the National Assembly who stood in opposition to radical change and favored a continuation of the monarchy and the aristocratic order—those easily identified as the conservatives of those heady days—sat to the *right* of the podium, and the King. The physical positioning of the Assembly members by political disposition caused the word "Left" to become synonymous with progressive and sometimes revolutionary movements, while the word "Right" was to become synonymous with resistance to change and a plethora of conservative positions.

While the proffered background for these words is historically accurate, our political language has evolved considerably. The basic picture remains, crudely, but evolution has made the original meanings important primarily for a grasp of depth. Today these definitions are an oversimplification. There exists in our world a wide variety of left-wingers who show a good deal of unevenness in their desire for change, and the types of change. And of course, there are right-wingers for "progressive" (sometimes inaccurately referred to as "populist") change. At times the Left seems to reflect much of what we would tend to call conservative analysis and judgment, and at times the Right seems equally prone to uttering what would appear to be leftist sentiments.

Consider one illustration: "rational self-interest." Both the Left and the Right claim it, but with far different outcomes. Understanding human self-interest, upon which personal survival hinges, seems to demand an unvarnished view of the basic and pure workings of the political mind. Such a pure reflection of rational self-interest would seem to go a long way toward making visible the boundaries between the Left and the Right. Yet even when this line is successfully drawn, it is not typically pointed, or even politically helpful. For example, how are we to understand why it is that some people with apparently no self-interest in furthering the existing social order continue to support it; or why many individuals who have self-interest in the old way of doing things, want to do away with it? We cannot take the meaning of "rational self-interest" for granted. Self-interest—whether the Left variety or the Right—is often so ginned up with passion and emotion that reason and intelligible argument are all but lost. Self-interest may be present in the political position, but often as a symptom and not as a cause. If anything, trying to reduce concepts of Left and Right to self-interest creates more confusion than it resolves. If there is not a universal, self-evident understanding of the meaning of "self-interest," then self-interest must rest on something even more fundamental. This is just one example of why we need to get at the basic ideological *substructure* which supports the *superstructural* positions held by the Left and the Right. This is a way of saying that we must get at the philosophy behind the politics.

First, we must uncover the unspoken, rudimentary distinctions that cohere with those super structural concepts such as self-interest—distinctions with which we are more familiar. To do this we must bring the assumed features of the Left and the Right to the surface. One way to approach this is to deal with one type of misconception that not only hampers a clear understanding of Left and Right, but oddly, a misconception that can also steer us in the direction of a correct view of Left and Right.

A confusing misconception about the Left and the Right.

Let's look at an early and faithful misconception: "The political spectrum is circular!" Yes, and how any times have we heard that major allegation? This claim is made by some and believed by many: the political spectrum is circular rather than a straight line. In this way the extreme Left and the extreme Right can be made to appear symmetrical, a mirror image, instead of polar opposites. This incorrect analysis is based on a representation which, when pushed to their extremes, shows that the Left and the Right, will meet in a dictatorial system where freedom and civil rights are suspended in favor of absolute totalitarian control. The examples of Stalin's USSR (representing the Left) and Hitler's Germany (representing the Right) are frequently offered in support of this circular conceptualization.[1] In closing the circle, the Left and the Right meet, blur together, merge. This circular model is not simply incorrect, but often intentionally incorrect. It is a weaponized view that is most often aimed at the Left rather than the Right.

To the casual observer these two examples of political societies offered above (those societies fomented by Hitler and Stalin) do appear to share many of the same features. Looked at superficially—like a visitor from another planet might observe the superficial similarities of our race and those of chimpanzees and conclude that we are of the same species—the optics of these two social orders are similar enough to generate a misinterpretation. For our visitor from another planet, it would take a good while to unravel and analyze enough of these "similar features" to understand that humans are not chimpanzees, nor of the same species. Likewise, it would also take a considerable amount of time to establish a background sufficient for the casual political observer to discern the actual differences between Nazism and Stalinism,[2] or for that matter to recognize the differences between the British Parliamentary form of government and the US Congressional form of government. The casual observer may even find it difficult to have the differences explained coherently in a brief minute or two.

It is possible to bypass such a lengthy process and still get at a root of the misconception by identifying *the* crucial understanding that distinguishes the Left from the Right; not just distinguish, but zero in on that understanding so that we can quickly demonstrate that the Left and the Right are opposites. We need to examine the basic "given" that supports the philosophies of the two ways of looking at what is practical in the world. That basic "given" is that there are two very different understandings of the *nature* of the human species (detailed below). Having brought this "given" to light, we can then connect it with the consciously articulated arguments. That "given" falls under the general heading of *human nature*. There are two principle (and opposing) views of human nature. Exploring these two views on is the fastest and most certain way to segue into a complete understanding of the difference between the Left and the Right.

Human Nature

At the most basic level, we must look at the way in which the two perspectives, the Left and the Right, view the complete operating mechanisms of the biological system, *genus Homo*—or what we might choose to simply call human nature. As trivial as it might seem at first, it is on the basis of this orientation toward human nature that all else rests concerning the political ideas of the Left and the Right. We will demonstrate how this different understanding of human nature develops into the politics of the Left and the Right.

The Right's view of humanity

The Right's view of humanity's basic nature is one of the most commonly held views. It is arguably the less complicated of the two positions,

Left and Right, though its development into political theory is far from smooth and uncomplicated.

There are two views held by the Right. While they are similar, they should not be overlapped. One view we might call **Hobbesian** (after the 17th century British philosopher **Thomas Hobbes**), and the other view **theological** (in the western world, **Christian-Judeo-Islamic**) in orientation. This second, the theological view, is often coupled with an incorrect understanding of Hobbes.

Hobbes: At the very beginning of his much misunderstood work, *The Leviathan*, Hobbes states: *"Homo homini lupus,"* or "Man is wolf to man."[3] It is here that the misreading of Hobbes typically begins. Hobbes did not intend for this statement to imply that Homo sapien was wolf by nature, or that human nature contains within itself some corrupting seed of violence or evil. Rather, what Hobbes meant was that the malice of all against all was the inherent result of the emergence of humanity in a world he described as a "state of nature."[4] By "state of nature" he implied a situation lacking any governing authority that would keep individuals, in their fundamental quest for survival, from tearing at each other's throats.

Hobbes rejected a state of original sin, or some notion that innate evil lurked within the human breast—unless we are willing to declare that basic survival is an evil. As a consequence, Hobbes considered that such a state of the "war of every man against every man" was merely the logical outcome of each rational individual's egoistic, subjective relativism, coupled with the solitary struggle for personal survival. To correct this situation where "life is solitary, poor, nasty, brutish, and short," a strong, authoritarian government (i.e., *The Leviathan*) must rise too artibrate the struggle for personal survival. That governing state, *The Leviathan*, would move toward ending this intolerable condition where a "state of nature is a state of war."

Different readings of Hobbes have facilitated right-wing conclusions concerning the nature of an appropriate government. One such reading and interpretation of Hobbes' *Leviathan*, sees him as promoting government as an arbitrator between conflicting individuals and is favored by those of a libertarian (i.e., Right-Libertarianism[5]) persuasion. A reading of *The Leviathan* as promoting an authoritarian government that would hold human passions in check by coercion, blends well with various totalitarian ideologies.[6] A typical representation of this latter interpretation of Hobbes can found in most theories of fascism.

The Christian-Judeo-Islamic view: It is not much of a secret that worldviews dominated by a spiritual or mystical perspective tend to lead the believer in the direction of strong conservative bias.[i] In order to hold such views as fluoride gives you cancer, or measles vaccines lead to autism, or one race is intellectually superior to all others—in other words, views for which there is absolutely no scientific basis—*all* material evidence must be regarded with extreme suspicion or rejected outright. Among other things, this lack of regard for material evidence tends to color all aspect of reality, including any need for social or political change, especially when that change appears to violate the tenets of a spiritual world. For example, a great deal of the hostility toward political changes that would legalize abortion is driven by a supernatural belief in the soul.[7] But this suspicion of material reality dives even deeper, striking at the very root of change: curiosity. According to Saint Augustine:

> "There is another form of temptation, even more fraught with danger. This is the disease of curiosity...It is this which drives us to try and discover the secrets of nature, those secrets which are beyond our understanding, which can avail us nothing and which man should not wish to learn."[8]

Why is curiosity dangerous and to be avoided? Because it leads to the death of God. Nietzsche was not the first philosopher to claim that God is dead, but he was at least one philosopher who identified the weapon: human curiosity—our very love affair with the truth.[9] But regardless of where you find yourself in this debate, it is clear that without curiosity the road to social change will be blocked. Even though it appears obvious, we should note that theological suspicion and rejection of curiosity, and its hindrance of social change, serves the interests of the governing elite; in many respects, spiritualism marches in lock-step with the interests of those benefiting from the status quo.

---

i. By "mystical perspectives" I refer to political views that would include such elements as racial purity or national destiny, and other such notions for which there is no material evidence.

By way of contrast, the common spiritual or theological view of human nature differs in one key way from that held by Hobbes. Mainstream western religious philosophy places at the center of our species a seed of sin that is more condemning than the egoistic, subjective relativism of Hobbes. For the spiritualists of this persuasion, we humans cannot escape the wickedness of our original, sinful nature. This view finds its way into the notion that the evil existing at the heart of humanity is baked into the cake and must be contained and dominated by strong authority, both ecclesiastical and temporal. This view of human nature as crippled by original sin cannot be called freedom in any sense, nor can it be outrun or negotiated away. Only by accepting original sin and embracing it can our nature be transcended, or at least, ameliorated. This idea of an uncompromisingly flawed humanity opens the gates for justification of the most harsh and authoritarian of governments.

Of the two positions—the Hobbesian or the religious view of a deeply flawed humanity—the Left has the most difficult time coming to grips with that view of humanity as put forth by Hobbes. Material reality and scientific exploration have been chipping away and weakening the grip of mysticism for centuries. A more serious difficulty for the Left is that Hobbes, as a materialist, seems less definite in his concept of human nature as ultimately evil. For Hobbes human nature is not evil in some mystical or innate sense. According to Hobbes human nature is merely self-serving. This is a position that is difficult to argue with. The theological position lacks the realistic straightforwardness as represented by the Hobbesian position. The religious perspective is ethereal and other-worldly, and therefore more vulnerable to reason and logic—at least from the point of view of the Left. Hobbesian materialism represents a far more serious obstacle for the Left.

The Left's view of humanity.

In going behind appearances, we see that the leftist position on humanity is far more complex that that held by the Right. There is little doubt that diving into the substructural scaffolding supporting external presentation generates a mosaic of causal relations that makes the Left's position arguably more difficult to sustain than the Right's. The leftist position truly does seem to fly in the face of simple "common sense" and the "evidence" of everyday experience.

Like the Right, the Left would advance two views on the human condition. The first perspective would find that **human nature is positive**. Secondly, and as convoluted as it might appear, this view finds that **human nature is a myth**—that there is no such thing as human nature.

Human nature as positive: This view of human nature states simply that we Homo sapiens possess a nature that is complex and multi-dimensional. Among those dimensions is one that is characterized by a well meaning altruism and beneficent impulses. According to the Left, we humans, by our nature, tend to be cooperative and protective of other humans in our social circle, or tribe, if you will. A vigilant sense of empathy and a sense of responsibility are wired into our genetic makeup by evolutionary design.[10] Those who display a watchful protectiveness over others around them have the greatest chance of seeing their genetic material passed on to the next generation. It's evolution one-oh-one, the leftist would say.

Obviously, such a view judges humanity in positive terms, rather than negative terms. Political theories such as those espoused by the Enlightenment philosopher **J.J. Rousseau** and those of the 18th century Russian anarchist **Peter Kropotkin** emerged from variations on this positive view of human nature. It should be noted that neither Rousseau nor Kropotkin are as naive as a superficial reading of this position on the human condition would make them appear. Their two views, while different, are rationally grounded and coherent enough to have withstood the considerable test of time.

Rousseau. This philosopher would not have taken the position that our species was good in some absolute spiritual or moral sense. It was Rousseau's position that in "the state of nature" human action was animal action, where notions of good and evil simply do not apply. Like all the animals on our planet, Homo sapiens living in a "state of nature" were merely attempting to survive with as little conflict as possible. In a "state of nature" our species, the same as any animal, shows a disinclination toward violence for its own sake, and takes to violence only for the purpose of basic survival; this would include violence associated with mating. Other than that, Rousseau would claim that Homo sapiens, like all animals, avoid violence that would be issued solely for some perversely wicked "inner need," or for the sake of some artificial ideal. Wanton violence, according to Rousseau, is a product of a civil society that was built on a corruption of the basic animal need for survival. Rousseau often stated that the first person that ever fenced in a piece of land and declared: "This is mine!" was the inventor of civil society, and was also the necessary inventor of the violence needed to keep that plot of land the personal property of the claimant. According to Rousseau, this is the origin of violence beyond the human need to survive, and violence for the sake of an abstract ideal, i.e., private property. It is civil society itself that is the creator of good and evil, and is the corrupter of human nature. We human beings, by our very nature, are without sin or any impulse to do evil, *per se*.[11]

Peter Kropotkin, the 19th century Russian anarchist, would have taken a different view. Kropotkin, much more than Rousseau, adopted a firm belief in the defining characteristic of humanity as possessing a thing called "human nature." Kropotkin based his view on the assumption that in nature, the animal species that survived best possessed an innate instinct which triggered mutual aid and mutual protection for the species. Evolution, according to this leftist vision, had generated an "instinct" to cooperate.[12] In this way, Kropotkin adopted the Darwinian argument to suggest that the animal species which demonstrated the greatest propensity for mutual aid would survive the best and thus pass these genes for cooperation along to their descendants.[13] He argued that not only lesser animals, but also human beings showed this inclination to aid and protect for cooperation and sheltering, which accounted for their success as a species. For Kropotkin—as for Rousseau—it was civil society that distorted "human nature," though in Kropotkin's case it was a human nature that was innately cooperative rather than merely empathetic.

There is no such thing as human nature. This, the Left's second perspective on the human species, formally emerged in the early 19th century as one of the numerous forms of existentialism and continues into the 21st century. Within many of the constructs of existentialism is the view that human nature is a myth, a fanciful and imaginary social construct. The concept of human nature, according to the existentialist, is well intended, but wrong, generating more problems than it solves. By the lights of this philosophy, there is no human nature, not as held by Rousseau, or Hobbes, and certainly not Kropotkin. We might take **Karl Marx** and **J.P. Sartre**, both highly recognizable as icons of the Left (though the former not as an existentialist), as proponents of this philosophical point of view. Though both Karl Marx and J.P. Sartre would deny the existence of an innate human nature, the two differ somewhat in their positions.

Karl Marx is complicated when it comes to the question of an innate human nature. His writings are voluminous, and he was not shy about using the term "human nature," but he is not entirely clear in the use of the word and concept. It would seem that on balance Marx considered that we humans have basic drives we all recognize. We humans possess drives to reproduce and sustain ourselves, which of course can also be said about dogs and caterpillars. This is largely a matter of interpretation, and the interpretation of human behavior offered by Marx is that these basic animal drives are shaped by the cultural rituals governing sexual reproduction and the manner in which we physically produce the substance we need for survival.[14] In other words, Marx would claim that human nature is malleable, and as far as the basics of survival and sex are concerned, these drives are sculpted by the forces of society and history, both large and small. Aside from our hardwired sexual drive (seen as a social drive) and the need to feed ourselves (seen as an economic drive), those elements we could call our "animal nature," there is nothing fixed in our human system. Bounded by history our "human nature" is created and established by the social and economic forces around us, constrained only by circumstantial reality.

J.P. Sartre. This 20th century philosopher will press the envelope on this issue of the denial of human nature. According to Sartre, our individual "nature" is formed by our choices. For Sartre even these sexual and survival "needs" are not beyond choice. The only unalterable element to our existence is freedom, not nature. We are utterly and completely free. We can choose or not choose to engage in sexuality. For that matter, we can choose life, which is to survive or not survive. Certainly, for Sartre, the forces of history are not the determining factor in some construction of a human nature. For Sartre there is no determining factor beyond what we choose. For Sartre we are the creators of our own human nature. This leads to a sort of irony which Sartre recognizes. Our nature must be the freedom to choose our nature.

Of these two positions, *viz.*, that there is a human nature which is positive and cooperative (exampled by Rousseau and Kropotkin), or there is no fixed human nature (see Marx or Sartre), the Right has the more difficult time with the latter. To say that there is no human nature, other than that which is constructed by the forces of society and history, or drafted by the individual facing the "moment," makes for an elusive political target—one that sifts like sand through the fingers of a changing history.

Where our view on human nature will lead us.

At this point it should not be a big leap to reach the conclusion that the political philosophies of the Left and the Right derive a huge portion of their ideological superstructure from these substructureal and assumed givens on the state of human nature—or lack of it. Both the Left and the Right espouse political theories that are (or should be) founded on these underlying axioms of the human condition; at all events, the theories should be demonstrably compatible with the assumptions.

The Right.

From the point of view long held by the Right, it is useless to attempt to change that which cannot be changed. Therefore, given the generally negative and fixed view of human nature adhered to by the Right, it follows that changes in the structure of the social order will do nothing to change that nature. Put another way, it is easy to see that the selfish and violent nature of the human animal would be unaffected by the design of the cage. The Right will argue that the wickedness inherent in our species is utterly immune to any alteration of the political, economic or social structure. They claim that the evidence is readily available. One need only look around, the Right will assert, to experience, to grasp the history of change and its minimal impact on human behavior. Societal change in an attempt to alter the egoistic selfishness lodged at the very heart of human nature is more than a waste of time. It is much worse. It is unabideably cruel to hold out rays of hope where none exist.

To fully understand the reach of this right-wing perspective on human nature we need to look at the possible ends of the thinking. The view of humanity as being acquisitive, grasping and selfish, will support two radical extremes—the fascist and the libertarian. These two systems of thought are far from mainstream conservative thinking, and also quite dissimilar from each other. Surveying these two extremes will offer a quick look into the overall philosophical position of the Right.

Fascism and libertarianism, as political philosophies, share very little in common. While their views of human nature bear underlying similarities, those similarities make for two political theories that lead in two vastly different—we might even say "opposite"—directions. Fascist theory rallies for total government control and domination, while Libertarianism presses for the complete (or nearly complete) absence of government coercion. Quite different indeed, it would seem.

For the fascist, freedom is a myth. The fascist will argue that freedom in a state of nature is only the freedom to rape and pillage. One can find genuine freedom only in a strong political state where human passions can be corralled and controlled.[15] For those on the extreme Right, the sad fact is that freedom is not freedom to do, but freedom from—from the fear of all that is human. Egoism must be channeled, and cooperation coerced. In this forceful way, we can find the only true freedom, the freedom from the wickedness of our own inner human nature. People must be compelled to act in their own best interests. Though it seems a logical conclusion, this is Thomas Hobbes pushed to an extreme he would not have sanctioned.

For libertarianism, by way of contrast, freedom is only possible in the absence (or near absence) of coercive interference from the political state. Fascism insists that the overall good of society can best be brought about by a political system which will dominate and control the corrupting elements within human nature. Libertarianism presses for a non-coercive, indeed, non-governing civil society that takes these "evils" in human nature for granted as inescapable. However, it is through the intelligent release and protection of these egoistic forces inherent to human nature that the overall good of society is achieved.[16]

These two ideological derivatives from a similar starting point on human nature could not be more different. How can the fact of different conclusions derived from similar beginnings be most instructive? First of all, a common premise with inconsistent conclusions might imply that there is something fundamentally wrong with their assumed premise. That is, if their shared understanding of human nature arrives at divergent conclusions, then it is possible that there is a problem with their basic reading of human nature. A thorough going analysis of this premise and divergent conclusions lies well beyond the scope of this paper. What is emphasized here, in a paper defining the Left and the Right, is that fascism and libertarianism derive almost nothing in common from a shared premise. One should not need a Ph.D. in logic for this awkwardness to give us pause when considering the validity of the premise.

The more orthodox rightist philosophy will center itself in mainstream conservative views: Namely, that social change is not merely irrelevant to the nature of humanity but is in fact dangerous for two reasons. *First*, it is dangerous in that upturning an established social order is dangerous, as the results are of such an upending are unpredictable; rather than harmony and order, chaos is likely to ensue. The most probable outcome of wholesale change, given the unchangeable nature of humanity, is the swapping of one ruling elite for a different elite, and perhaps a more vicious elite. Here the Right offers as an example the Russian Revolution, whereby the aristocracy was dumped for Stalin—not a good deal by any reckoning. *Secondly*, even to suggest that solutions can be discovered in fomenting fundamental change to the social order will only fuel false hope that social change will somehow transform the immutable nature of humanity. Mainstream right-wing conservatives ultimately justify resistance to change because of the assumption that human nature is irredeemably egoistic and self-serving. The conservative might ask: Why change a known for an unknown? Attempts at social change would either be irrelevant or actually serve only to promote greater friction and tumult within civil society.

The Left

Although more hopeful, the position of the Left is far more argumentative. And indeed, paradoxically, even if more contentious, the Left's position tends to show greater consistency. The leftist position is contentious because their perspective on human nature seems to fly in the face of the evidence, which creates the greatest, fundamental problem for the Left. The leftist position offers greater consistency because even extreme leftist positions tend not so much to differ in kind, as for example do fascism and libertarianism, but to differ only in degree. Socialism and anarchy appear to be extremely different, but at bottom both these positions are founded on a faith in egalitarian and democratic principles.[17] Socialism and anarchy tend to differ by the degree of democratic reform, not the kind.[18]

Throughout the Left there is the feeling that if human behavior is conditioned by the social and historical forces in which the individual finds themselves, then a change in the surrounding social forces will open for us many different choices in individual behavior. On the left, both the Marxist and the Sartreian will agree that we are free to choose, but we must choose among exiting alternatives. To paraphrase Marx: we humans are free to make history, but not exactly as we please. Some form of this reasoning is consistent throughout the Left. The individual will learn only what the situational environment has available to teach. The individual is free to grasp the deepest precepts of the cultural mores and choose a style of life and a way of being from among the recognizable, existing alternatives. Place the individual in different circumstances with different cultural mores, and the individual will learn differently, choose differently and behave differently.

The American liberal is clearly not a democratic socialist, just as the democratic socialist is not an anarchist. Yet all these positions would adopt the same opinion that a changed social system will bring a change in human activity and behavior. Both the liberal and the democratic socialist would agree that people will steal food because they are hungry and not out of avarice. The remedy seems simple enough: offer people a safety net that includes food and the hungry will stop stealing food. By way of contrast, the conservative might resist this opinion, as they consider stealing endemic to human nature: in other words, give people bread and they'll steal cake. While this illustration might sound cynical and a bit harsh, it is not too far off the mark and aptly illustrates the nexus of origin: the conservative starts with innate, inner forces, while the left starts with controlling, external forces.

While internally consistent within their viewpoint, the leftist viewpoint rests on a contentious premise. That uneasy premise is the ultimate malleability of human behavior. This in turn is based on the leftist notion that human behavior either rests on a structure of emotional neutrality—an absence of structure (i.e., human nature)—or a strong sense of goodness and fair play at the heart of human behavior. This view of the human condition as the ultimate *tabula rasa*, a blank slate, sees a human being as an empty vessel into which social norms are poured. The other leftist point of view sees humans not exactly as benign, as would be the case of a *tabula rasa*, but preprogramed in elements of cooperation and goodness.

To demonstrate the extent of the contentiousness of the position, the Right would counter the Left by stating that there clearly is a human nature, and that nature is neither blessed nor good. Even with full bellies, unrestrained people will rape and pillage. Just examine the evidence of everyday life or look back through history. *No matter how much you give a human, they still want more.* Human beings, no matter the social system or the social relations, are relentless in their aggrandizement. Greed is in their nature; a greed that is insatiable. You can spit it in any direction and see evidence for this, the conservative would say.

The resulting and often acrimonious debate surrounding "human behavior" versus "human nature" poses the greatest difficulty for the Left. Do we witness behavior or do we witness innate characteristics? To see a person stealing food is one thing. To say that the act is the result of hunger requires a brief logical extension that requires at least a modicum of training and education, not to mention evidence. On the surface this seems to be a small difficulty easily surmounted: When people are hungry they will steal food. The left's position seems secure, but what about the Right? The Right's counter to the Left also seems secure: look at the egregious opulence desired by humanity. A simple grave is not enough for the dead. To satiate human greed, a pyramid is required, and never mind that ten thousand human beings died in the building of it.

But forget ancient pyramids. Consider modern ones—that is, the pyramid structure of your typical Ponzi scheme, or insider stock trading.[ii] The inside trader might already have billions in the bank, so why does the trader "need" more? The trader is not "hungry" so why the criminal behavior? It is easy to see greed as the link, the culprit and human nature as the ultimate villain.

The Left is not caught flat-footed and without a reply to this "evidence." If there is a problem with a reply, it is proportional to its

---

ii. Ponzi scheme: a form of fraud in which belief in the success of a nonexistent enterprise is fostered by the payment of quick returns to the first investors from money invested by later investors.

complexity. As the actions become increasingly complicated, the reply becomes increasingly complicated. Here the explanation becomes a creature of greater education and training. The explanation for inside-trader, "white collar crime," for example, brings in culture, ideology, sociological and psychological paradigms, etc., all learned designs, according to the Left. To be consistent, the leftist would insist that the more complex explanation is the correct one and not the simplistic "human nature is evil" explanation offered by the Right. This complexity increases the difficulty for the Left to insist that human behavior and human nature are learned structures and not innate. A lack of background in this regard makes both insight and discussion difficult, but not completely impossible.

The bottom line here is that the Left can and will take the stand that if human nature exists in any form, it is driven by positive internal forces and the witnessed bad behavior is a corruption of those forces. It does not really matter if the Left takes the view that there is an innate nature to humanity, or there is no innate nature; the Left will consistently argue that social environment is *the* strong determinate in human behavior. Freedom and choice are matters of learned response to available alternatives. If changes are made to the alternatives within the social environment, human behavior will change accordingly. The Left has remained consistently loyal to the heart of these more or less feisty claims.

A Summation

First. Let us be clear. There is an oppositional, ideological understanding that distinguishes the Left from the Right. Contrary to a common misconception, the political spectrum does not represent a closed circle. The political spectrum can best be visualized as a line. On this line, the Left and the Right start at opposing ends. The Left and the Right begin from entirely different places and show a marked difference in their views on what drives human behavior—views on what we have come to think of as "human nature." These opposing views on what constitutes human nature have a huge impact on topics like social engineering.

Second, either human behavior is derived from an inherent predisposition to act in certain ways, or human behavior *is not* the result of any predisposition.

The Right's claim is clearly expressed: there is a fixed human nature such that the individual is disposed to act primarily in predictable ways. Humanity, by its very nature, will almost exclusively behave in ways that satisfy and promote their own individual, selfish interest. Look back through history, the Right will say. The evidence for this dismal point of view is as obvious as the nose on your face. In addition to this material point of view, a theological perspective is sometimes offered up, one that characterizes human behavior as a reflection of an innate, inherent evil, a species wide flaw, such as the concept of original sin.

The Left is less clear on the existence of a human nature. In general, the Left would hold that either human behavior is the result of a learned pattern of behavior or can be seen as the result of rational choices made from understood alternatives. In any case, for the Left, bad behavior is either a perversion of the natural inclination toward benevolence and cooperation, or the result of choices made from misunderstanding, or fearfulness, or some other rational, existential factor. Human nature, if it exists at all, is an empty vessel filled by absorbing a whole range of current mores and cultural markers.

Third, all the political theories and arguments between the Left and the Right are, from the very onset, a reflection of this background position on human nature.

Fourth, as these assumed positions on human nature are irreconcilable, any Left-Right debate that ignores these differences is superfluous and extraneous and nearly hopeless at finding a resolution. A successful conclusion to the Left-Right debate presupposes a philosophical reconciliation over the nature of the basic human condition.

In the end, this presupposition and reconciliation does not depend on professional philosophers, but on the determination of the average Joe on the street. How the above sits with Joe-average will determine successful social changes, or firmly establish a resistance to change.

Notes

1. To show how confused and sometimes bizarre this circular position can become, study a by no means unusual offering at http://www.oicu2.com/afc/leftright.html

2. This in no way denies the similarity of many elements that appear in all authoritarian societies. In fact, concerning Stalinist regimes, and fascist regimes, many elements are similar, even if their espoused goals are different. This has led many to claim that Stalinist regimes are actually more fascist than socialist, or to use the vernacular of this study, more Right that Left, and the vocalized justifications for the similarities are more rationalization and propagandistic apologies for the authoritarianism. Whether this represents an accurate picture depends on individual analysis and sometimes the underlying motives for such an assessment.

3. Hobbes is not the first to use this expression, "man is wolf to man." It can be traced back through many writers at least to the Roman playwright Titus Macchius Plactus.

4. The phrase, *state of nature*, is a commonly employed construct used by political philosophers to indicate a situation where there is no governing authority with the power to use coercion to gain obedience. Political philosophers are quite aware that such a condition has probably never existed in historical times and may well have never existed. The "state of nature" is part of a "thought experiment," constructed solely for the purpose of theoretical discussion.

5. There is a Left-Libertarianism, but due to the constraints on this brief examination, this minority view, will not be considered. The term Libertarianism in this paper will be used in all cases to mean Right-Libertarianism.

6. By no means is this the only conclusion for the Right to draw. Libertarian theory (occasionally, though not completely correctly, referred to as Right-Wing Anarchy) will typically also draw from Hobbes a picture of a rational humanity lost in struggle. Their conclusion (see Ayn Rand) is that the state of nature is not a state of war, but a state of freedom. The struggle represents freedom and the best appropriate action is to let the struggle ensue. This is an oversimplification of Rand's philosophy, but it is fair to say that from the libertarian point of view the best, wisest, and most deserving individuals will use this freedom to gain the greatest advantage, and this is deservedly so since it is the outcome of a free and open contest. Consequently, a role for government should be minimal, if existent at all. This libertarian perspective is a minority viewpoint. The major players on the Right (e.g., Plato, Thomas More, and a few of the more sophisticated, modern

fascists) have drawn conclusions more in keeping with the Hobbesian tradition of the necessity of an authoritarian and absolutist ruling body to control the human condition.

7. For a lengthy treatment as to how abortion, and the destruction of the soul, can interfere with God's plan, see https://www.catholic.com/encyclopedia/abortion

8. As quoted by Charles Freeman, *The Closing Of The Western Mind*, Vintage Books, (New York, 2002), p. 143.

9. https://academyofideas.com/2012/11/nietzsche-and-the-death-of-god/

10. "Traits of human nature were adaptive during the time that the human species evolved, and those genes consequently spread through the population that predisposed their carriers to develop those traits. Adaptiveness means simply that if an individual displayed the traits, he stood a greater chance of having his genes represented in the next generation than if he did not display the traits." Edward Wilson, *On Human Nature*, (Harvard University Press, Cambridge, 1978) p. 32

11. This leaves open the question of whether Rousseau thought there was such an element to humanity as an innate human nature. There is some debate on this point, but it seems clear that if Rousseau did have such a belief in a universal human nature, it was a weak belief.

12. It is not difficult to understand that the group made up of individuals who protected each other would see their genetic material passed on to the following generations. Thus, it is argued, that this "passing-on" gives empathy and safe-guarding others in the group a genetic base.

13. There is a good deal of modern research that encourages this evolutionary point of view; for example, see: Nigel Barber, *Kindness in a Cruel World*, (Prometheus Books, Amherst, NY, 2004)

14. Marx's interest in sexual activity was generally restricted to the cultural and political implications of sexual ritual. The psychological dimension of sexuality, *per se*, was left to later individuals with an interest in Marxism such as the psychoanalyst Wilhelm Reich (1897-1957)

15. For detailed analysis of fascism, and telling quotes concerning the nature of fascism by one of its founders, Benito Mussolini, see Ingersoll and Davidson, *The Philosophical Roots of Modern Ideology*, (Prentice Hall, New Jersey, 2001) especially p. 219

16. For an elucidation of libertarian theory see David Boaz, *Libertarianism, A Primer*, (The Free Press, New York, 1997)

17. The question of whether or not liberalism truly represents a leftist position is a legitimate one, but one beyond the scope of this paper. Sufficient to say that Liberals often present a confused picture of a philosophy that at once wants to argue for the underdog as a victim of circumstances, yet without showing any serious interest in changing the fundamentals of those circumstances.

18. Identifying socialism as anti-democratic, or dictatorial, is the result of a misreading of mainstream socialist theory. In any case, socialism is predominantly an economic theory, not a political one.

ON RAISING POLITICAL CONSCIOUSNESS

The Political Landscape Beneath our Conscious Thinking

RICHARD WU

Abstract: A philosophical question for the ages: What is human consciousness, and how is it different from raw animal awareness? Analysis of this important distinction is followed by an in-depth treatment of human consciousness. This paper then considers the impact of consciousness on political thinking, and how the elevation of consciousness impacts political thinking. This leads to a discussion of what a raised consciousness looks like and how the raising of consciousness can be achieved by a contemporary electorate. Raising consciousness involves the utilization of all four of these factors—(1) the ability to reason, (2) accumulating knowledge, (3) use of imagination, and (4) empirical grounding in the real world. The first three are a natural part of our humanness and need only refinement through use. However, the last—empirical grounding for the use of reason—depends on the *development* of the first three. The growth and advancement of political consciousness depends on all four.

Human consciousness is not merely awareness. At its most basic level, to be aware means to feel sensation, in one of its many internal or external forms. To be conscious means to reflect on that sensation, to contemplate, to mull over that "feeling" of sensation. Consciousness is strictly a human condition. There is no scientific evidence that a cat, for example, can either contemplate an awareness of itself or grasp the nature of itself as it is entangled with its environment. The cat may be aware that it is hungry, and that delicious edibles are to be found in the cupboard below the sink, but this is rote learning through awareness and not discovered through a process of reflection and reasoning. Consciousness, as revealed through reflection and reasoning, is solely the purview of our human species.[1] A question then comes about: can we alter our state of consciousness? What is the impact of reflection and reasoning on our state of consciousness? Can we lift our consciousness to a higher plane, deepen our understanding, elevate our grasp of the world around us for both our internal satisfaction and our external well-being?

The phrase "raising consciousness" has typically been used to refer to the lifting of *political* consciousness to a higher level of political understanding—which is to say a greater understanding of our external state of well-being. As we'll discuss later, this political understanding, this understanding of our well-being, refers to a higher level of insight and discernment concerning the social and economic environment in which we live. Beyond that, this "raising of consciousness" is generally thought of as not only the expanding of one's own political consciousness, but the expanding of political consciousness in those around you. In this paper I give to "raising consciousness" both these meanings. It is, however, the nature of *personal* political consciousness that will be the focus of the study. If you are asking yourself why this topic would be of importance to you, I hope the next section, the introduction, will provide an answer.

Introduction

First, let's address the term, *political*. When I say "political" I do not mean the political party you belong to, or the protest demonstration in which you participated, or even the act of voting. While these things are political, and of importance, "political" has a wider, more socio-economic meaning. "Political" can include actions like deciding which restaurant to eat at, or which book to buy, or simply getting up in the morning and going to work. This notion sounds strange, as you think of some or all of these acts as being trivial, voluntary and far removed from issues of power. The question arises: are not these, and many other mundane actions, completely free of coercion, which is, after all, a central feature of political relations?

Recognize first that every act, no matter how pedestrian, is locked into the web of social experience and relations in which you live. This matrix of social relations is ultimately rooted in the relationships of power located within your society. Let me make this point with an example: the restaurant in which you decide to eat is within your decision-making range principally because of the power of a politically managed economy that widely influences employment, income, advertising, food distribution, mortgage lending, and the business class to which the owner of the restaurant, and you, belong, etc. Even this seemingly prosaic action is interwoven with many social and economic elements. Without your being aware of it, a system of subtle force guides you through the decision making of even seemingly trivial actions.

The fact that we do not ordinarily consider these activities as pressed by power relations is a testament to the pervasiveness of inherited idea systems (ideology) that obscure and direct much of our thinking. Ideology is the premier primary force obscuring the power relations at work to influence even apparently random decisions. With very little exception, every act has some implication for this web of power relations. It is also true that seeing the extent of this system may be beyond our prevailing consciousness. You and I, as distasteful as it is to contemplate, are creatures (not marionettes) of political forces of which we are typically unaware. Part of the raising of political consciousness is the drawing back of this curtain, allowing us to see the reality of these power relations that guide our thinking and decision making.

Political considerations that decide winners and losers blend into the social matrix in such a way as to veil the power arrangements and make these considerations appear normal and fitting; that is, as far as it is possible, make them appear a-political. This veiling represents the transformative power of the prevailing system of ideas (ideology). In the most general sense, all of my social relations (e.g., even who I choose to marry, or who I choose to befriend, etc.) are political in that the parameters of my living are expressions of historically determined power relations. Where I am born, into what time in history, into what class, what race, have profound implications for me and the idea systems that influence my thinking. I am consciously aware of power relations in actions overtly related to the governing structure of our society—elections, party affiliation, tax collection, and so on—but all of my other acts, no matter how trivial, and most of my thinking, have elements of power relations about them and are also political, only I am not completely conscious of this fact. All this seems very tedious and although I may understand it, I would prefer not to dwell on it. Many times I actually prefer unconsciousness to political consciousness. This represents a serious problem in the raising of consciousness. To get at this and other issues concerning political consciousness, a general background grasp of the topic of consciousness will provide clarity for later in this paper.

The Nature of Consciousness

What follows will seem a lengthy epistemological detour from our main subject, but it is necessary for a full and complete understanding of consciousness. To begin with, consciousness is a very different creature from awareness. They are both present in my humanity as brute fact but are distinct. It is important to grasp this distinction. Both "awareness" and "consciousness" have an identical starting physicality: the neural gestalt of the central nervous system, (i.e., the brain). After this jumping off point, the two (awareness and consciousness) develop separately and uniquely. It is easy for me to understand that my "sentient reaction" is a product of certain bio-chemical reactions built into my central nervous system. For certain, I understand that a "survival instinct" (i.e., as an awareness reaction) is part of my mental makeup which I share with most animals. Consciousness, on the other hand, while very frequently provoked by awareness, is something apart from sentient awareness. We have a sense that consciousness is something higher than awareness. This is not to say that consciousness is something spiritual, but rather something telescoped, broader and deeper, networked, an encompassing thing that is uniquely human. For example, I have no trouble saying that my dog is aware of my presence in the room. I am certainly part of her sentient sense of well-being and survival. However, there is a natural hesitation in saying that my dog is conscious of my presence in the room. To say "conscious" would imply that the dog has a separate, abstract "idea" of me apart from my immediate presence in the room. To be conscious implies something more than what we suspect animals of being capable. On the other hand, I can be both aware of my dog in the room, and at the same time be conscious of "dog" in an abstract sense.

Regarding awareness, then, I am going to make the claim that awareness is rooted directly in that self-serving part of my instinct for well-being and survival; awareness acts as a homeostatic governor on our sense of well-being that is triggered by our biological drives for survival and procreation. In this way we share awareness with the rest of the animal world. Consciousness and awareness, as in a Venn diagram, overlap, and therefore bear a strong, and occasionally awkward, affinity for each other, but it is awareness rather than consciousness that is instinctual. Consciousness can enhance awareness but cannot produce it. Awareness can enhance consciousness but should not be confused with it. Again, they come from the same human facticity, but serve that facticity in distinct ways.

Here is another angle on their difference: to be aware is a *passive* process. I can be aware of things outside of me. Awareness knocks against me. Awareness is that sentient part of me. In a very real and immediate sense, awareness puts my feelings of well-being on alert. To be conscious is an *active* process. When I am conscious I am reaching out to engage with things in the world of my experience. I am extended into a host of things and events both inside and outside of myself in a pro-active way. There is something about me that has reached out and is happening to things, both internal and external. Those "things" can be outside, can be concrete, as when I consciously consider a tree, another person, or clouds. These "things" can also be internal products of my mind, as when I consider the abstractions of love, or happiness—or human rights versus political power. This does *not* mean that my happiness cannot have a concrete dialectical *expression* outside of me—for example, the person I love as both the provocation and object of my love. Awareness alone can clearly stimulate conscious interest, as in the arousal of sexual interest, but awareness does not cause me to love; clearly love and sexual interest can be related but are not identical. Happiness has no *meaning* outside of my conscious (or perhaps subconscious) grasp of a thing or event.

Happiness is an engaging process, a conscious product of my mind. I am conscious of happiness rather than being aware of it.

Consciousness, while related to awareness, discloses its distinct energy along the line of focused, intentional curiosity. Intentional curiosity is part of a syndrome unique to humans. Of course, many animals do show an interest in things in their immediate environment. They do exhibit behaviors that are sometimes referred to as "curiosity." But this is not *intentional* on the part of animals. They are engaged, are seized, if you will, from without by things and events having direct relationships to aspects of their survival and well-being (e.g., predators or food). However, to suggest that animals other than humans have a special curiosity about such things as the nature of clouds, the history of their species, or magic, is absurd. These are the products of intentional curiosity. They are part of a curiosity syndrome that energizes only humans. Animals other than humans are aware, not conscious; they are engaged rather than engaging.[2]

Of course, all animals—including humans—are aware; this is part of the instinctual, survival makeup common to all animals. All animals have senses that are receptive to stimulation from the world around them, a receptivity that is the neurological pathway to a sentient reaction. As stated above, I hold that this awareness is quite distinguishable from "consciousness," in the same way instincts for survival and well-being are distinct from the development of abstract curiosity about the nature of well-being. However, I will argue that the instinct for well-being is the trigger for this curiosity, abstract and otherwise. To be sure, the ultimate manifestations of curiosity (e.g., what is dark matter, is there a soul, etc.) appear so remote from a raw, animal instinct for survival and well-being that any connection between the two can seem tenuous at best. Nonetheless, I am confident that a rearward looking analysis will trace "curiosity" to material factors originating in our historical need to survive and thrive in the most general sense. As strange as it might sound at first, it might even be said that the awareness of death is the universal human instigator for our sense of curiosity; ironically, both religion and science, incomparable as they are, spring from this same instigator.

Further, I do not consider that this use of the words "aware" and "conscious" is in any way part of a private language, or private understanding. We all have a reasonably strong grasp on the words, and we

understand that the words "conscious" and "aware" are similar by implication, yet we also understand that they do mean something different in
their application.

None of what I have said above is to be construed to mean that awareness is a secondary factor to consciousness, or a thing of less importance.
While they are distinct, awareness can be a powerful force on its own,
a force of great moment for humans. It is fair to say that awareness and
consciousness very often act in concert, like two individual people on a
dance floor, with awareness frequently the leader of the dance team. This
leads to an important consideration in our study: awareness can provoke
sudden shifts in consciousness. Certain key events of awareness can trip
a powerful response in consciousness. Awareness can impact people in
such a way as to force sudden and compelling changes in consciousness.
In a manner of speaking, awareness can flip the switch on the proverbial
"light bulb," unexpectedly, and often with virulence. However, the "light
bulb" itself is internal.

Unlike awareness, to say that I am "conscious" is to suggest that
something about my being is active rather than passive.[3] Consciousness
is that part of my being that actively "reaches out to engage" with things
beyond me, beyond my individual state. This "reaching out to engage" is
driven by that basic human ability to be curious, itself a manifestation of
deeper needs for well-being. This reaching out is aided by another human
ability: focus. I motivate this focus, this willful "reaching out," by intentional curiosity, which directs focus outward, toward something. To say
"directing outward" or "reaching out" does not necessarily mean reaching toward something outside of my individual being, but only something
distinct from my consciousness, *per se*. For example, I can direct my consciousness at internal things as well as external things. I can also direct
consciousness at itself in what we typically call self-consciousness. This
thing, this *focus*, is an intentional or willful act: I *intend* to do this thing.
To say that I *intend* is to acknowledge that I have a conscious understanding of future time. This recognition of time is yet another uniquely human
"understanding."[4]

Focus goes beyond reaching out to a thing. Focus, as part of the
curiosity syndrome, is also an *envelopment* of the thing. Focus, as an
intentional act, is a tool of consciousness that envelops the thing aimed
at by consciousness, and then separates this thing from the surrounding

environment for an internal viewing. The separation I will call *uncovering* and the internal viewing *reflection*. This last is rooted in another uniquely human capability: the ability to arrange and rearrange complex and unique patterns of the thing uncovered. These newly emerging patterns constitute a form of *revealing*. Thus reason, or reflection, is nothing magical, but is part of our natural hardwiring, an ability built into the neurological gestalt. This gestalt must possess things previously revealed—that is, grasp things previous uncovered on which to build a reflecting surface. Reflection is the bouncing of the enveloped thing off arranged and rearranged patterns, *qua* abstractions, previously revealed—these abstractions are integrated and secured in a place that for the sake of simplicity I will call *knowledge*. In this context I might say that reflection acts as an internal pinball machine, reflecting things off solid knowledge, shaping them until the perfect slot is found. The development and nature of these slots increases the overall stability of a growing intellectual gestalt.

This ability to reason, this reflection, also possesses a *willful* or intentional element, and is both a tool and a result of consciousness. The precise origin of will is, for now, uncertain,[5] but it seems clear that will (and intent) exist tangentially to our ability to reflect, and reflection is a development of "understanding" which is rooted in knowing. Will and reflection are powerful tools in a human arsenal that augments instinctual survival and well-being to a level much higher than that experienced by other animals. More pointedly, these tools are what make us uniquely human, for only humans have the capacity to *know* in the abstract sense (i.e., to hold reflection in suspension).

So, consciousness is not merely the reaching out to things, but also, by the medium of focus, consciousness is the drawing in of things for an extensive search and grasp of the uncovered, which leads to the revelation of meaning through intentional reflection. Focus is the active envelopment and removal of things from background clutter. Focus allows for intentional reflection and manipulation by knowledge of the enveloped things. Meaning is revealed, and advanced, through willful envelopment and manipulation of those things that we already know. I advance the uncovered by "reflecting" the uncovered off the mirror of my previous knowledge, guiding it toward the appropriate slot in my intellectual framework. This framework grows and develops according to the level of dedication applied to the process described.

Thus, consciousness exists within a dialectical reality: consciousness is both a product and a provider of revealed meaning. This advancement in reflective ability is a dialectical aggrandizement unique to our species. This reaching out, or aiming, and manipulation, is part of the process of "thinking," but it is not identical with thinking. Do we not seem to understand that consciousness and thinking are not exactly the same things? Rather, I might say that thinking is the intermediary, the faculty that binds consciousness to knowledge. That thinking and consciousness are not the same thing can be illustrated by the reality that I can be conscious—that active reaching out—without thinking, but I cannot be thinking without being conscious. Consciousness precedes thinking. Without consciousness there can be no abstract knowledge, and without knowledge there can be no thinking.

If the difference between consciousness and awareness still seems obscure let me offer an example. A deer may become *aware* of wolves in the vicinity. Awareness is the alertness, the ringing of the survival bell. The deer's well-being is clearly at stake. At this point evolutionary programmed instincts take over the deer's behavior as the deer reacts to those things acting on it. The deer is not curious about the wolves; the deer does not direct a reflection on the meaning of the wolves, or reflect on what it knows about the behavior of the wolves (indeed, if it truly knows anything about wolves in some abstract sense), nor does it consider alternative actions regarding the wolves. The deer is aware rather than conscious of the wolves and merely reacts within the limited scope that evolutionary instinct has provided. A human, once made aware, can exhibit curiosity, can reach out with focus. That is to say, a human being *can* direct consciousness in a probing way at the meaning of the wolves, and then can "reflect," amble across the web of knowledge he or she possesses about the wolves, and then select a course of action based on a variety of alternative actions abstractly known about the wolves and the nature of a particular situation.[6] It is clear that these pro-active elements of focus and reflection, which are adjunctive tools of consciousness, are factors uniquely human. Yet, even given the originality offered by *humanness* there exists only the *possibility* that a willful focus followed by reflection can happen. As with the deer, instincts are present in the human. These instincts *can* be overridden by the curiosity syndrome, by focus and reflection. However, reactions can be programmed in such a way by prevailing idea-systems so as to short-circuit reflection and cause actions to be reflexive. Therefore, intentional, focused reflection is only a *possibility* for our species. Ideological programming will have great impact on the possibility of raising consciousness in general and raising political consciousness in particular.

Although it seems unnecessary to add, I feel the need to point out that I can exist in a state of both awareness and consciousness at the same time; this might be filed under the heading of being consciously aware. These two things, awareness and consciousness, can also come in either order, i.e., sentient awareness can precede conscious, or visa-versa, focused consciousness can precede sentient awareness. Although this arrangement, where consciousness precedes awareness, is a rare event, which is no doubt facilitated by *imagination*—i.e., the creative reflection and rearrangement of known things that leads to some unexpected or serendipitous revealing (i.e., meaning) of an unknown thing. Imagination might, in some sense, be dubbed the basis for genius. However, even deep genius must be in possession of many known things. In the absence of a store of knowledge there would be nothing on which for the genius to exercise his or her imagination.

With this epistemological detour under our belt, we can now proceed with the main topic—raising consciousness in general, then raising political consciousness in particular.

Raising Consciousness in General.

If the development of consciousness turns on the development of a knowledge necessary for reflection, as it clearly seems to do, then raising consciousness must be part of a process concerned with the *augmentation* of knowledge. This augmentation is not the same thing as learning more, although "learning more" is, without a doubt, a necessary ingredient of the changing patterns of augmentation. Knowledge, in the way in which I use it here, is the revealing of "meaning" rather than a manner or mode of thought or analysis which is more in the arena of intentional reflection. "Revealing meaning" might make it appear as though the raising of consciousness is as simple as merely reading another book. This is too superficial an understanding of the process. The raising of consciousness presents a far more delicate arrangement of the intellectual factors involved in the process of envelopment and reflection. The intellectual factors must be arranged in such a way as to make two things possible: (1) to make the envelopment conform to true and actual reality and (2) to allow for the knowledge matrix demanded by precise reflection. This arrangement is not so easily accomplished. Reading another book is a helpful factor but is not a complete answer. A discussion of these factors in total, and why the arrangement of these factors is so difficult, is the first step leading to understanding the raising of political consciousness.

A simple example will provide an illustration as to the arrangement and development of these intellectual factors. Consider the solar eclipse. Today, in the modern world, I think little about the mechanics of an eclipse. A solar eclipse, while an awesome spectacle, is not a mysterious or supernatural event. I also know that this was not always thought to be so. While astronomers have, for a very long time, had a realistic grasp on principles surrounding a solar eclipse, for the human population at-large an eclipse had definite overtones of supernatural intervention. An incident involving the pre-Socratic philosopher, Thales of Miletus (ca. 624-546, BCE), serves to illustrate the arrangement and development of these intellectual factors required for envelopment and reflection.

It is reported by Herodotus that Thales successfully predicted a solar eclipse in 585 BCE (modern astronomers place the date at May 28, 585 BCE).[7] On that date there was a battle raging between the Medians and the Lydians. On seeing the eclipse both armies threw down their weapons and refused to fight, the soldiers believing that the eclipse was of supernatural origin and showed divine disapproval with the bloodletting. This event ended a bitter five-year war between the two states. What does this situation tell us? It tells us that the masses of the army and their rulers were superstitious enough to think that the solar eclipse was a sign from their gods. Thales, of course, understood the event in other terms. This demonstrates that there existed two very different grasps on reality at work that day. We also now know that Thales' understanding of this event was not merely different but was an accurate and true picture of a universal reality; Thales' consciousness was functioning on a "higher" level than that of the army and its generals. To understand Thales' grasp of the situation I must come to grips with the intellectual factors leading to his correct interpretation of reality as opposed to the masses of Medians and Lydians whose idea system lead them to a dramatically incorrect interpretation.

We know from historical writings that Thales tended to explain natural phenomena using rational principles as opposed to supernatural principles. This ran counter to the superstitious, ideological order of the day, an order that consistently advanced supernatural explanations for natural events. Thales was able to step outside of and reject the prevailing idea system (ideology). We know also that Thales had a good working knowledge of geometry. We do not know of the exact methods he used, but he was certainly aware of solar eclipses as they occur worldwide at different places for different observers at least twice a year. He also knew of their relation to the cycle of the new moon. This was enough information to give him a jumping off point. Without these empirical observations made by Thales and others, the average person of his day would have had no tools other than superstition to reveal the meaning of an eclipse. Thales possessed a store of knowledge not widely available at the time.

What can I learn from Thales about revealing the meaning of things? What was it about Thales' intellectual processes that made his grasp of reality accurate and true? How is the example of Thales relevant to the consciousness achievable by all human beings? To begin with, there are four identifiable and relevant factors. The first three are endemic to human physicality: (1) Reason; (2) accumulation of knowledge; and (3) imagination; and the fourth, (4) empirically grounded observations, leads to separating the real from the fanciful, a big step in the quest for truth.

The actuality of the first three factors cited above certainly seems inherent in the human neural system and is in no way mysterious or spiritual. The fourth factor is a derivative of practical, material experience. It is the conviction that things occur in the real and physical world and not in some spirit world. This anti-superstitious conviction emerges as a result of the first three factors tampering with experience and is no way an innate or instinctive reaction. We might say that this fourth factor represents the ability to pierce through the suffocation of inherited idea systems (ideology) such as, in this case, superstition. I should add that the first three are outgrowths of the universal human characteristic of curiosity, which is itself rooted in the instinct for survival and well-being shared by all animals. This was detailed above.

Let me now apply these factors to the Thales situation.

First, Thales utilized the power of reason as the basis for understanding the world. Reason is clearly a human faculty made possible by neural hardwiring. This faculty assembles the raw material we have gathered through our senses and social relations facilitated by what appears to be a natural human predisposition to orderly (i.e., logical) structuring. Reason is the manner in which we form combinations of observed reality, the way in which we track down links between events. Reason can be, and ought to be, a creative, fluid process that avoids the rigid idea-systems that provide prefab answers to real world issues and events.[8]

How and why Thales achieved this critical understanding and reliance on reason is not known, but there can be no doubt that not only was Thales possessed by curiosity—that ultimate enemy of superstition[9]—he was also a keen observer. It follows that he must have also possessed the tools to accurately observe. We know that Thales had a superb educational background that gave him the intellectual tools he needed.[10] Thales was not merely aware; he was conscious of possible alternative explanations for events such as a solar eclipse. The possibility of alternative explanations, alternatives made available by the human gift of imagination, was chief among his tools. Both reason and the recognition of possible alternatives rest on the second factor, a rich storehouse of knowledge.

Second, knowledge is hard to avoid. We are constantly taking in information and warehousing it. It is in the nature of the warehousing that the difficulty begins. Our knowledge can and often does involve raw information developed in pattern formation via the process we call reason. However, and unfortunately, we all too often store knowledge in a prefab structure. The design and structure of the "storehouse" is one of many possible ideologies we are presented with upon our arrival in his reality. Depending on a prefab ideological structure usually means the jettisoning of any experiences that conflict with the ideology. In making the preservation of the ideological structure predominate, much knowledge is lost. The dominant idea system may not be the best to advance the third and most vital factor: imagination. Most ideologies are impediments we must overcome with the aid of reason and imagination. Generally speaking, suspicion of dominant ideas systems is always justified and warranted.

Third, besides reason and the storing up of information there is a factor truly unique to our humanity: Imagination. Imagination is the projection

129

of all of what I know about certain types of events into a current perception of reality. I then work to combine, recombine, tweak, fiddle and adjust the things and events in creative ways until a combination matches up with current perception. It is entirely possible that pattern formation is hard-wired into our neural gestalt. Some of us possess the imaginative ability to an extreme. We call these people geniuses. However, imagination is ultimately (and perhaps ironically) grounded in accumulated knowledge. Even a genius must possess knowledge to realize the potential of his or her gifts. If that knowledge is faulty, our current perceptions (or those of a genius) will not properly align with reality and thus a crippled imagination—one lacking sufficient components of knowledge—can lead us in a fruitless direction.

Fourth, Thales' rising consciousness convinced him that physical explanations, rather than supernatural explanations, led to a true under-standing of the world around him. An empirical grasp of the world is a vital step in gaining material truth. Superstition is an old and oppressive enemy of humanity. Therefore, overcoming an ideology of superstition proves to be a crucial factor in the revealing of true and accurate meaning behind events and things.[11]

Raising consciousness involves the utilization of all four of these factors—(1) the ability to reason, (2) accumulating knowledge, (3) use of imagination, and (4) empirical grounding in the real world. The first three are a natural part of our humanness and need only refinement through use. The last depends on the development of the first three. All are necessary tools for the advancement of consciousness.

I speak of these four factors as vital to the revealing of *realities*. These realities are often a web of circumstances or situations which are clearly related to "knowing," but are not empirically obvious. Remember that although I am speaking of consciousness in general, I will next address *political* knowledge of material relations, and how these relations are typically concealed from us. The concealing is sometimes deliberate manipulation by the power relations themselves. After all, secrecy is a primary source of political power. Sometimes the concealing is historically "deliberate" in the sense that it is a product of inherited idea systems. These things make the uncovering and revealing of political relations a far more difficult task all the more dependent on the above four factors.

Political Consciousness.

Now that I have introduced general consciousness, the question becomes: what is political consciousness? Political consciousness begins its actualization along similar lines as general consciousness: that is, a reaching out to engage. The difference is specificity. Political consciousness is a reaching out to willfully engage the power relations found in a specific social order.

Political consciousness, like consciousness in general, is engendered by the "curiosity syndrome," that derivative of my instinct for survival and well-being. It utilizes the tool of focus to envelop specific things and draws them back in for intentional (which is to say willful) reflection. There are, however, levels and degrees, and the objective of political consciousness is stated as specific. In other words, political consciousness has a distinguishing intention that sets it apart from general consciousness. It is curious about power relations.

To illustrate this specific intention let me look into a most basic level of political consciousness, which is not a true political consciousness at all but a reaction I will call political *awareness*. I am using "awareness" in the same sense as outlined in the above discussion of general consciousness, that is, awareness as a manifestation of more fundamental instincts of survival and well-being. This political awareness is an awareness of power that lacks the fully conscious grasp of power relations. This awareness is aroused by the force of power acting on it. This merits some elaboration.

By definition, all things political are a reflection of power relations. In some form or another all societies cohere in the way that they do because of the specific arrangements of power within that society. For me, the solitary individual, the social pressures that guide my daily decisions and movements are located within the power relations found in the social structure in which I find myself. This is a basic description that cannot be avoided in any study of the social process; in the last analysis we are free to choose, but this is not always obvious. Choice is hemmed in and guided by political arrangements.

These power relations are usually veiled, but the veil can be drawn back. The uncovering of power relations is the first step in raising political consciousness. Through the processes described above, the uncovering then leads to the revealing of specific meaning in the observed power relations. As this happens the ideological façade will fall away, and the revealed relations will lose their mystery. Often the revealing process itself will lead to the power relations being stripped of much of their revered legitimacy, thus undermining political authority.

In so stating I am claiming that much of political "authority" is granted by a sense of *reverence* that leads to an atmosphere of legitimacy. Much of political legitimacy and authority are actualized through reverence for mystical principles (e.g., nationalism, sanctity of law, racial purity, etc.). A grasp of this sense of "reverence" serves to illustrate the difference between political awareness and political consciousness. Reverence veils the power relations behind arcane and esoteric principles, leaving one with a vague sense of the coercive forces at work without any clear grasp of their true origin and purpose. I am "aware" of the coercive forces at work around and on me, but I fail to fully understand them. Consequently awareness, as opposed to consciousness, tends to "feel" political pressure rather than grasp and understand it. Awareness will usually view political authority through an esoteric lens of legitimacy, *per se*, leaving the actual working of the power relations behind the legitimacy as wholly misunderstood or veiled and out of sight.

To elaborate: in the case of "political awareness" the individual is only passively aware of power relations. I can get a parking ticket, receive a tax bill, or denied medical coverage, and all this can happen to me without my possessing any precise knowledge of the power arrangements at work behind these events. I am aware only that something disagreeable is happening to me. I am compelled to move here and there without understanding the exact reasons compelling the move. Drawing on the example offered previously, the deer is aware of the wolves in the same way that I am aware of being acted upon by forces outside of myself. Like the deer, I move, almost instinctually, responding to an unseen threat, but understand very little of those forces making up the threat. I am *passively aware* of the power in the vicinity and have only a vague notion of the nature of the power behind the threat. This pawn like response is the lowest level of political sensitivity. This level of political sensitivity (i.e., political awareness) will tend to leave the individual feeling confused, powerless, dazed, and eventually angry in the face of the forces surrounding him. This state of confusion and helplessness is to the advantage of the powers that control the social structure and is often deliberately fostered.

In keeping with the defining characteristics of general consciousness, political consciousness is an active, engaged process. At the risk of pointing out the obvious, to engage requires faculties of engagement. The discussion now revolves around the questions: what is the nature of these faculties that facilitate political consciousness and from where do these faculties come?

Faculties of engagement. Passivity requires only inactive reception. This is not to say that passivity represents a pervasive dullness, but rather an alertness that lacks intentional curiosity. As opposed to this, every form of reaching out must abandon inactivity and proceed actively; this is facilitated by the free reign of curiosity. While it is true that reaching out to engage springs from the curiosity syndrome, engagement must possess the power of dynamic action; that is, for me to actively reach out I must possess the dynamic tools to do so. Besides the obvious—that is, my central nervous system—what is the nature these tools? To reveal the nature of these dynamic tools for an active reaching out, let me try the type of simple illustration typical of philosophers.

I sit at my desk and I look over at the corner of the desktop. I see a coin. From where I sit I am only *aware* that the coin appears elliptical. I *know* it is not elliptical. In spite of how the coin appears to me from where I sit, I *know* the coin is round. Let me examine what has occurred in our illustration. I glance at a coin and what I *see* and what I *know* clash. I am aware that something is not quite right with what I see. My curiosity about what has happened to my "looking" is aroused. I now reach out to the coin with curiosity about what I see. I focus, that is, I *envelop* the coin. Next, with willful intent, I draw the vision of the coin back for an engagement with reflection against my previous knowledge of coins and looking. Through reflecting, the meaning of what I was seeing is revealed. I am now conscious that something that I *know*, which is a thing called "perspective," has caused the coin to appear elliptical. The chief dynamic tool that I used to actively engage and realign appearance with true reality was my knowledge about coins. The dynamic nature of the enveloping tool is focused curiosity. The reflection of the engaged against previous knowledge is the source of revealed meaning. This is

133

a very simple example. Yet even for more complicated or exotic issues, the dynamic nature of the engaging tools remains the same: they are primarily curiosity and knowledge. Without those dynamic tools awareness never reaches the level of consciousness.

Along with distinguishing political consciousness from political awareness, these factors of focused curiosity and knowledge not only allow me to actively and effectively engage with my environment—in the case of this study, my political environment—they also tend to replace the confusion and the feelings of helplessness—that drifting sense of powerlessness. It is also true that with knowledge comes frustration and anger, but without the helplessness that denies anger direction. Through knowledge, my frustration and anger can be directed. Through knowledge, I find myself feeling a sense of control rather than being controlled. With knowledge, I can anchor myself in the conscious world, not the aware world.

Raising *political* consciousness.

The first thing to note about political consciousness, and in particular the *raising* of political consciousness, is that this action will take place in a hostile atmosphere. It is a rare individual (or group of individuals) who would find himself sitting in the highest seat of power and at the same time show any interest in a growth of political consciousness within that social order. Political consciousness is one of the few authentic threats to the power structure. A poor education or better yet, no education at all, is a mainstay for any governing elite. Ignorance is a form of secrecy, and secrecy is a major source of control and therefore power. Make no mistake, where there is a political structure there is a political hierarchy with its own set of vested interests that are not intended to come to light. Transparency is a canard, a platitude, and never the desired outcome of any political arrangement. Lack of developed knowledge exacerbates a mood of helplessness and alienation. It is in the interests of the power structure to frustrate the free flow of information and knowledge, together with the acquiring of the tools to organize this information. The rigidity, ruthlessness and absoluteness of a political structure's governing elite vary only by degree. This is not a hopeless situation for the raising of consciousness. Knowledge by its very nature is universally available, and therefore "knowing" is always possible, even in the harshest of political environments. However, an inhospitable environment makes the achievement of political consciousness through knowledge a true uphill battle. The question is how to take that first step.

Let me return to the example of Thales offered above. Thales lived in a time when the real nature of material events was often shrouded in mystery. The chief ideological forms of explanation were variations of superstition. This bears a resemblance to the fog surrounding politics. Political institutions are typically shrouded in the psychotropic of patriotism, destiny, and duty, camouflaged in xenophobia and nationalism, wrapped in the gilded mysteries of the national or constitutional law. As a result, the real workings of power relations are largely unknown to the population at-large. Like Thales, I must come to the realization that something solid and real is going on here. The chauvinism of the state has a purpose, a design I am not meant to uncover. It is here that political *awareness* serves its best purpose as a jumping-off point.

The wolf and the deer. Like the illustration of the deer above, we humans also possess survival instincts, instincts that support an alert system I have been referring to as awareness. Awareness is opportunity. Awareness is a trigger for curiosity and therefore consciousness. How often have I heard my neighbor grumble about taxes, or those fools that keep plunging the country into wasteful wars and painful depressions, or the rich bastards that have everything while everyone else just scraps-by? This grumbling is an alert system. It is my political awareness. I am not imagining things. I am like the deer that knows wolves are in the area, and I am alerted. I need only trust myself, my own instincts: *what I think is happening is probably happening*. Like the deer I can ignore this alert, this awareness, but I do so at my own peril. At this point, possessing awareness alone, I am lost, not knowing which way to turn to escape the wolves; I can easily become their willing prey, even their accomplice in my own destruction.

Ideological claims: Taxes are my patriotic duty, I must sacrifice for the greater good of the nation, our leaders are wiser than me, the rich have worked hard and are deserving of their wealth, etc. These are common political claims in our modern world, yet often these claims feel wrong. This *gut feeling* that something is not quite right with some or all of these claims is my alert system at work. Like the deer, my first step is to trust my gut feelings, my survival instincts. The deer is an intimate of the terrain and knows the manner in which a twig snaps, or a stalk of grass bows, and senses when these events are not congruent with the landscape. Like the deer, I am an integrated component of the political terrain, and can sense or feel when events around me do not properly line up. Bottom line: when things feel out of place, I feel out of place. These feelings will prepare me to reach out to the situation or event with the best tools I find available.

First, I must judge the best direction to reach out. Here, I separate myself from the deer. My instincts will prove inadequate to proceed beyond feeling and awareness. Unlike the deer, the wolves in my life are not operating solely on instinct. These human wolves are highly skilled and have developed habits based on a cunning manipulation not only of their environment, but of knowledge concerning the terrain in which they hunt. There is always the danger that the wolf is more conscious than the deer. The terrain which both the wolf and the deer inhabit is the social and political landscape in which history has placed them. To elevate my consciousness, I must learn the social and political skills of the wolf. This learning is encouraged and fashioned by the nature of the political landscape. If I fail to learn the hunting skills of the wolves, along with their integration into the political turf, I will be their accomplice, their willing quarry. If I do not come to understand the participants and the terrain I will not survive. I will be eaten.

Raising my political consciousness means a more careful study of the power relations in which I live. It is vital to understand that I, myself, will be initially resistant to this kind of reflection. This is a natural reaction. I am not lazy or stupid, but alienated in much the same way as the victim who would say: "Who cares, and anyway there is nothing anyone can do about it!" Rather than being stupid, lazy or uninterested, I am overcome by an apathy that has its roots sunk deep in those feelings of powerlessness and alienation.

One of the goals of power is to promote these feeling of alienation and apathy. The cleverest power relations actively program this alienation into the political landscape. Often, this is accomplished through a legal framework that causes change to be so time-consuming, arduous, expensive, or even dangerous, that frustration leads to a desire for unconsciousness. To be unconscious shields me from my own powerlessness; it turns aside my anxiety, blunts my anger. To desire relief through a lack of consciousness is a natural reaction. It is also a mark of an extraordinarily successful ideology that it not only inculcates a feeling of powerlessness in the general population, but also blinds the population to the source of these feelings. To blind the population to the nature of the power structure is a heady accomplishment for any ideology. To cause the population to *want to be blind* is the ultimate achievement for any power structure. It is easy to judge the power of the political hierarchy by how much the populace wants to avoid political involvement. For example, low voter turnout is one apt indicator of a successful campaign against the engagement of a conscious electorate.

The terrain of my political world is the entirety of the social matrix in which I live. More specific to my point: the political terrain in which I find myself is a system of power relations, networks or alliances. These networks do not merely surround me, these alliances are a fully realized system into which I am fully integrated. It is this landscape of power relations that I must uncover and reveal in order to acquire the tools to reach out and fully grasp the things and events that attempt to manipulate and control my life. I must first realize that the totality of the circumstance in which I find myself is *real*, not fantasy, not metaphysical, not surreal. This means that I must first suspect that the tools I was given by my inherited idea-system are part of the trap. I must begin with an examination of myself, uncover the ideology that compels me, the ideology that organizes my vision of the world. This uncovering of "myself"—that is, the discovering of the consciousness that defines me, is the first step in the process we call the raising of political consciousness.

We must also realize that the real, concrete terrain into which we are integrated is different for everyone. No two individuals stand in the same place at the same time, or are in the grip of the exactly the same idea system, or share the same view of the landscape; so as I am different from you, my consciousness will be different from yours. This fact alone goes a long way toward accounting for the vociferous disagreements between individuals regarding the issues our society faces. The problem may not alone be some hand-me-down ideology, but simply how our position in the terrain produces or promotes one idea-system as opposed to another. This is a way of saying that my position in the socio-historical landscape encourages an idea-system that defines my individual consciousness—that is, defines me. Although we may share many aspects of consciousness, no one will need to uncover and reveal the exact same features of the terrain to raise individual political conscious-ness. To a certain extent this streamlines the process. To be effective, every uncovering experience need only be appropriate to an individual's position in the social matrix, shared with others or not shared. Ultimately, it is an individual self-discovery, a self-revelation. This specific uncover-ing and revelation will change who I am and therefore greatly affect my position in the landscape. In this sense, political consciousness raising, even mass consciousness raising, is an individual process.

Understanding political consciousness through understanding who you are.

Who am I? This is probably the most penetrating and universal ques-tion I can ask to launch the search for individual consciousness. It is also the question I will ask to expand my political consciousness. The question—*Who am I?*—connects the personal world with the objective world. It greatly increases the possibility of a deeper consciousness of both worlds. The weaker my engagement with the facticity of my exis-tence, as that existence is integrated within a specific landscape, the more likely I will display a political schizophrenia in interacting with the power relations that work hard to define me. Under this weak engagement, my political responses will not just be inappropriate—perhaps even for my personal survival—but more vitally a failure of political consciousness that will cause me to lose a true sense of who I am.

In the earlier section on consciousness in general I suggested that consciousness was a bit like describing who you are, or somewhat oddly, how you are. Locating, uncovering, and revealing an answer to the ques-tion "who are you?" is a giant step. This giant step will locate your exis-tential position in your world. Knowledge of this position will put you in a place to actively reach out, engage and envelop the things in your world. To raise your consciousness, that is, make the most of this engagement, you will need to develop the relevant tools to reach out into the world, to connect with the facticity around you. I have already stated them above. You must come to see yourself as rooted in this real world. You already have the ability to reason, and imagination can be developed. The power of these elements (i.e., reason and imagination) is grounded in accumu-lated experience shaped by reflection off a general web of knowledge.

Knowledge is the central element to the process of raising general consciousness. Knowledge of power relations is the key to the process of raising political consciousness.

Knowledge is the basic tool, but not the process. Make no mistake, the raising of consciousness is *not* an easy process. The process of raising consciousness consumes both time and energy, and both in great amounts. Your existential position is a complex issue. You can start by understanding that as a human being you are social, historical and ontological; that is the nature of your being. This last—the "ontological you"—has far reaching implications in terms of your extended sense of reality, but for the sake of space, and immediate relevance, I must set it aside.

I will bypass the ontological issues when asking the question, "who are you?" and will bind the question in two ways. First, I will restrict the "you" with a defining reference to the immediate issues confronting you. Second, the consequence of the first restriction requires that who you are right now (i.e., confronting immediate situations) is all the outcomes of situations you have faced historically. In other words, who you are existentially (your immediate position in time and space) is the development of who you are historically (your presence in accordance with past actions, both individual and historical.) Together, this dialectical configuration reveals who you are socially and politically, which is another way of saying how you are integrated into the terrain which both defines and responds to your engagement. One implication of this relationship is that the raising of your political consciousness is a consequence of immediate activity that will develop a new historical you. Demonstrating how this development of a "new you" can happen is my next task.

Understanding Raising Political Consciousness by Illustration:

You are a sophomore student attending the University of California at Los Angeles. Your family is well off. You sit in a comfortable classroom and listen to a lecture on Beowulf. The study of medieval English literature may be interesting, and ultimately it bears some connection to the landscape in which you find yourself, but it is not of immediate, dialectical relevance to what you are beginning to confront in your contemporary world. You are chagrined to discover that much of your studies show this lack of immediate urgency and are consequently vaguely boring. They always seem to lack any sense of relevance (a common complaint with university students everywhere and at all times.) As a student you are in a uniquely opportune situation to tackle these issues.

You are looking into a world mired in pain and suffering. For reasons not fully understood by you, this worldview deeply affects you and who you are. The calluses of cynicism that block the light from your distressed spirit have yet to form. You are young and full of hope. Of great importance is the fact that you are still able to ask a deeply troubling, personal question: what can I do about all this? You have not yet been made indifferent by incessant exposure and you ache for an answer to this question so affecting your life. The "I" in this question is a critical turning point. Revealing an answer to "What can I do?" will change who you are.

As you view the world you wonder, is it sympathy you feel, or empathy, or perhaps you sense in the pain and suffering a direct but ill formed threat? These are "alerts" and any one of them can turn on the "curiosity syndrome." This is a positive turning-on. It draws you into the equation. In many ways your task is less demanding than those hounding your work-a-day contemporaries, your contemporaries that find themselves locked in a world of economic survival and have neither the time nor the energy to contemplate what they *feel* about the world. As I said, as a student you are in the perfect spot. You search only for relevance.

The *relevant* answer to your search is as easily defined as it is demanding. For example, the range of the troubles you see is too large to swallow at one sitting. Instead, you must pick an issue, but not an issue at random. Select an issue that is, for you, particularly irksome, plays on your mind, seems *personal*. Pick a situation that truly gets under your skin because it strikes you as "wicked," so incredibly stupid, and somehow menacing ("How could this have ever happened?" "Who's in charge here, anyway?" "Can't anybody see what's going on?" "Why can't we stop this?") Very quickly you will find that this irksome issue is in some way related to all the other "troubles." But this remains for you to uncover. The first task is to gather the tools you will need to reach out and grasp this personal, irksome issue.

A quick example of raising consciousness. Allow me to make a small digression as an illustration of how to proceed. For a variety of reasons I

140

have chosen an example removed from the political sphere, but also one reasonably well known. I refer to the discovery of psychoanalysis made by Sigmund Freud. As this example will demonstrate, the word "discovery" is often incorrectly used. "Discovery" implies a sudden sighting (Land Ho!) or a *satori*, (sudden enlightenment, if I might borrow a concept from Zen). Neither of these things was the case with the discovery of psycho-analysis, and certainly "discovery" is the wrong concept to apply. What Freud's work does illustrate is the uncovering and revealing process that I am calling raising consciousness.

Briefly, the facts of the Freud's revealing go as follows: At the age of seventeen, in 1873, Freud entered a university as a medical student. He immediately encountered the anti-Semitism so prevalent in the Europe of his day. Freud later wrote of this experience as being more puzzling than shocking, of his having developed an attitude more curious than hurt. There is no telling just how disturbing this encounter with anti-Semi-tism was for the young Freud, but it is clear that it troubled him.[12] His response—that of being puzzled and curious—is telling. In these early days as a medical student, Freud began to show more interest in psy-chology than medicine. Connecting the two—the encounter with racism and a curiosity about the workings of the mind—is in no way automatic, yet it seems plausible that the anti-Semitism directed at Freud offered him an element of a personal motive to be curious about those hostile attitudes operating beyond his reach. This curiosity clearly would have involved questioning who he was in relation to the real and threatening world around him. This awareness triggered a reaching out to the subject of mental disorders as a way for Freud to uncover something about him-self and his relationship with the world in which he was integrated.

From the opening of his studies to his co-authoring a first paper on psychoanalysis, his "discovery" took ten years of diligent work, hardly a *satori*.[13] During this time Freud studied with several individuals, each of whom possessed some of the keys to psychoanalysis.[14] It was through his association with each of these individuals that the dynamics of psy-choanalysis were slowly revealed to Freud. This was a slow process of uncovering the many pieces of the psychoanalytic dynamic. Although several other individuals who uncovered the pieces, it was Freud who finally came up with the revealed common denominator.[15] Freud took the newly uncovered pieces and imaginatively rearranged them to reveal the astonishing facts of the unconscious mind: the short version of Freud's arrangement is that symptoms of hysteria (e.g., neurosis) were impulses or past events that were suppressed and then re-appear as substitutes for the suppressed impulses.

What can we learn from Freud's experience? First, it seems clear that personal motives must be present to activate and energize the curiosity syndrome. It is not farfetched to suggest that Freud's encounter with anti-Semitism at the university triggered a primitive awareness for survival and well-being. This would not have been an unusual reaction, given the hostile atmosphere experienced by European Jews in the 19th century. It must have also been this reaction and awareness in Freud that led to the curiosity syndrome described above. Freud was not alone in this. This instinctual awareness operates within us all and leads to the same sense of curiosity. Next, Freud demonstrated all the other qualities human beings possess: he followed the reaching out by his curiosity with apparent dispassionate reason, accumulated knowledge, used his imagination to rearrange what he had uncovered, and above all, he avoided fanciful or spiritual answers in the process of his reflecting.

The practical application: How can I be instructed by this example? First, and especially in dealing with power relations, I must let my instinctual awareness lead the way. I must trust my instincts for survival and well-being. If I feel a sense of menace it stands a very good chance of being based in something real:

What I think is happening is probably happening.

Next, allow my curiosity, as intentional focus, to reach out and envelope and pull the thing that threatens me loose from the landscape. Envelope and separate the contentious thing from the background clutter. Pull it in for reflection, bouncing and shaping it off what I already know; if I do not yet know enough the reflecting itself will increase my knowledge, and hence the power of my reflection will increase in a dialectical manner.

So, pick an issue. No issue that troubles you is mundane or trivial. As we shall see, all that troubles you is in some degree personally triggered by your instinct for survival and well-being. So, pick an issue that is personally irksome. Be it the spread of HIV, the burden of taxation, capital punishment, abortion, famine in the Horn of Africa, the decriminalization of narcotics, or perhaps climate change. These are not trite issues. It is entirely realistic for you to feel a sense of personal menace stemming from any of these issues. They are not irrelevant. They occupy your thoughts and define you in dialectical relationship with the world. Each of them is threatening in its own way, though not in the same degree for everyone.

Consider climate change. It may well be that you live in a wealthy, developed country, and are a member of an elite class. This seems to put you beyond the threat of any immediate impact of climate change—or does it? When reflecting on what you know about climate change you feel a vague sense of uncertainty, and perhaps a little feeling of unease. No matter the cause of climate change you come to know that the change will produce worldwide shifts in population, mass migration, desertification, and a global short fall in both food and fresh water. Your unease is caused by a correct sense of this changing situation as a threat. You come to be conscious that wholesale climate change is a threat to the political security of your nation and almost certainly a threat to your economic station in the social system. This further piques your interest, your curiosity. So, where to look?

You must first define the thing on which you would focus. Like Freud, you must reach out to search through and grasp what others have uncovered. If the situation you perceive is a genuine threat, then someone has already done some work on the subject. This reaching out requires study and contemplation. This is not especially difficult, but it is time consuming. Absorbing what others have uncovered increases your knowledge base and therefore increases your powers of reflection. With increased reflection the knowledge base will develop a greater reflective ability, and so on. This is changing who you are.

But suppose no one has done any previous work on your subject? If your subject is real this is highly unlikely. It is more probable that you may not know where to look. Everything *real* makes an appearance somewhere in your environment—rather that environment is social or intellectual—although the appearing itself may not be in the form you expect. As in the case of Freud's "discovery" of psychoanalysis, the thing may only be waiting to be uncovered by imaginatively rearranging the position of the pieces uncovered by others. A new uncovering or revealing or rearranging might be accomplished by you.

Knowledge and its impact on your ability to reflect will personally change your position in the landscape. Again, I say "in the landscape" rather than "on the landscape" to remind you that we are all integrated *into* the landscape and not apart from it. We are both its context and its reflection. As you change your integration with the terrain it will change not only who you are but will also change your context. Most often these shifts are subtle. It is like moving down a highway with road signs leading off in a multitude of directions. As you pass, you will see things—the signs—from different angles, see different opportunities, be allowed different directions to travel to more distant landscapes. No matter the direction you choose to travel it will most likely lead to further study, but eventually as your context changes you will experience an expansion of consciousness. You will completely adjust to the nature of the threat and this will lead directly to an answer to your question: "What can I do?" An answer to this is facilitated by the change in who you are in relation to your context.

This is a time-consuming process. Raising consciousness is not a quick, one stop treatment. As a student you have both the time and resources at your fingertips. It is far more difficult to achieve the same consciousness once separated from these resources. Even so, this consciousness raising will progress whether you are a stock broker, or career military, or a timber worker. It will be a more demanding process if you are not a student, as you are not normally continually engaged in the process of uncovering. But it can be done.

Conclusion

Raising consciousness is not a one-shot deal. Because the landscape is nearly infinite, and so is your changing position in it, raising consciousness is an ongoing process with no end in sight; consciousness has no boundary because knowledge has no boundary, and neither do you. Everyone will find themselves starting in a different place in this process, but ultimately raising consciousness will impact all aspects of our human capabilities from physical survival of our species to the loftiest ethical considerations governing our daily lives.

I am also convinced not only that raising consciousness is a process available to everyone, but also that raising consciousness is a human duty that *obliges* everyone. It obliges because the ongoing process of expanding consciousness is the single greatest defining characteristic of our humanness. This assertion rests on the assumption that curiosity is a derivative of our survival and well-being instincts, which is to say that raising consciousness is the most fundamental ingredient necessary for the survival of our species. This does not imply that everyone will participate, or be able to, but only that my humanness, and yours, will suffer concomitantly from a lack of participation.

It is fair to conclude that raising consciousness develops in a dialectical relationship with human survival. Curiosity, the immediate derivative of well-being awareness, makes the accumulation of experience inevitable. However, experience is not knowledge. The greatest antagonist to the conversion of experience into knowledge, and therefore the expansion of consciousness, is a decadent or calcified system of ideas (ideology) that stands as a central obstacle to genuine knowledge. In the main, ideologies that hinge on vague mystical interpretations of reality such as astrology or witchcraft, or ideologies that serve as a flunky for superstition constructs such as the "national destiny" or "racial purity," are immediately suspect as detrimental to human survival. Expanded consciousness can overcome these handicaps.

A new, expanded political consciousness is linked to what for you would be a new theoretical framework by which to observe political events worldwide. This new consciousness is a giant step forward, a truly powerful tool for you and the world around you. More than anything else, the development of consciousness represents your individual history. In the raising of your individual consciousness you will be answering many of the questions surrounding who you are. This raising will also serve in answering the question of how you got to where you are, why you think what you do, and how you can contribute to a changing world.

Finally, this paper does not delve directly into the issue of what to do with political consciousness. Nor does it approach the subject of raising the political consciousness of those around you—a vital project for anyone politically conscious. Both of these topics must wait for another paper. For my current project it is enough to realize that the steps necessary to achieve political consciousness rest on what is innately human: (1) Pay attention to your base survival awareness. *What you think is happening is probably happening.* (2) This awareness will lead to what I refer to as a curiosity syndrome. (3) Following the lead of curiosity, you must ground of all your thinking in the real world; spiritual or mystical explanation will ultimately lead in the direction of wasted time, dead ends, and zero personal growth. (4) Glean the knowledge of power relations uncovered by others. Reach out and pull these uncovered relations into your consciousness for reflection. (5) Allow the reflection to be imaginative. Imagine how these power relations might be reshuffled and arranged for a different agenda. (6) Finally, you must possess the recognition that there is no final consciousness, only the ongoing process that is the unlimited raising of your own personal consciousness, both political and general.

Notes

1. For philosophers, distinguishing awareness from consciousness can be a much trickier and complex business than I have presented here. For example, see: Nelkin, Norton *Consciousness and the Origins of Thought*, Cambridge University Press, 1996; especially pp. 140 thru 146. For the purposes of this paper I have streamlined to reach the core differences between awareness and consciousness.

2. By "curiosity syndrome" I mean a group of related or coincidental things or actions that can be characterized as a "probing" to satisfy a uniquely human need.

3. When speaking of "Being" I mean "me" as a fact, that is, a facticity separate from the deterministic factors of time and place, separate from those elements in which I find myself and define me as who I am. Being is the "I" as a raw fact.

4. Space and time prevent me from going into the subject of time in any detail. However, our understanding of time may well be related to our abstract grasp of our own death, but it is beyond the scope of this paper to explore this dimension. Other philosophers, such as Martin Heidegger, have rather interesting and lengthy discussions of the subject.

5. Again, time and space prevent a detailed discussion, but "Will" may be a manifestation of desire, if I may follow Arthur Schopenhauer's suggestion, and thereby give will a possible origin in human biological drives. However, for the purposes of this paper it is only important to note that will and intention are a basic part of the human makeup.

6. We can see this at work in the delicate balance between environmentalists and livestock owners in the American northwest.

7. We do not know if Thales predicted a total or partial eclipse. Predicting a total eclipse would have been far more technically impressive.

8. For a more detailed philosophical analysis on reasoning and thinking see the study by Daniel Dennet, *Content and Consciousness*, Routledge and Kegan, London 1993.

9. As Nietzsche so keenly observed, curiosity led to the death of God.

10. As a pre-Socratic, little is known of the education of Thales. It is known, however, that he was from a patrician, Phoenician family. These families paid great attention to the education of their children, and Thales no doubt had the best tutors available. We know that he did receive his mathematical education from Egyptian priests whose interest in astronomy is well known. It is from them that he might have learned of solar eclipses, and some sense of how to predict them.

11. While many philosophers will disagree with me, I tend to house spiritual systems under the same roof as superstition. The reader is cautioned not to confuse abstract explanations with metaphysics.

12. For a highly readable elucidation of Freud's life and work the biography by Ernst Jones is highly recommended.

13. Freud first published a joint paper on the subject with Josef Breuer in 1893.

14. For example, Freud studied with the Frenchman Charcot and witnessed the effects of hypnoticis as a relief for maladies then called "hysteria." Later, through an association with Josef Breuer, Freud learned that through verbal expression, the revealing of some connection between symptoms and past events was possible. Through the verbalizing of the connection the subject could be relieved of the symptoms. It was at this point that Freud made the common connection that some forgotten event or impulse was suppressed by certain outside factors; this suppression caused the symptoms to appear as a substitute for the act or a twisted version of the original event.

15. To his credit Freud always gave acknowledgement to others (especially to Josef Breuer) for their significant contributions to his findings.

RIGHT-WING SOCIETY

What does the Ideal
Look Like in Real Time?

IGOR VLASOVA

Abstract: The article starts off with the question, what exactly are prototypical, right-wing societies supposed to look like? What's the vision? The vision held by the Right (or the Left) cannot be objectively labeled right or wrong, good or evil, true or false. Objectively, a general vision of either the Right or the Left is only that: a vision—a vision that will satisfy some and discomfort others.

This paper makes the central claim that the fundamental and elemental differences between the Left and the Right are lodged in the following:

(1) The attitude toward human nature.
(2) The attitude toward human equality.
(3) The attitude toward the existing social and economic order.
(4) The attitude toward reason vs custom.
(5) The attitude toward class and class relations.
(6) The attitude toward liberty and freedom.
(7) The attitude toward the social model.

The ideal society of the Right is described, compared and contrasted against these differences.

W hat exactly are prototypical, right-wing societies supposed to look like—in real time? While this would be of great interest, there are few detailed descriptions—however, there are plenty of hints that we will examine. Following this, we will ask: from where do these utopian perspectives come? These lofty visions don't jump up in the mind in full flower. They have a well-spring. We must find out what that bubbly spring consists of. Now, let me quickly point out that in this paper I will reverse the questions. Before sketching a picture of the right-wing quintessential social structure I'll first ask, what are the right-wing ideological ideals that project the vision? Then we'll move on to explore what exactly what are these primary, ideological ideals that shape a vision of an optimal, right wing social order.

~

To be right-wing (or left-wing) is to be a creature of ideology. To be wholly Right or Left is to be possessed of an encompassing world view, an idea system. Ideology is a semi-automatic, reflexive way of organizing our experience into a mediated settlement we can use to manage and negotiate our social environment. It does not robotically follow that ideology is either necessarily coherent or accurate. Nonetheless, ideology, though rarely articulated, allows the possessor to unconsciously, and nearly seamlessly, find their way through the social world with at least the appearance of understanding and propriety. For example, it was once thought that to read the entrails of a goat was a legitimate way to guide political and social policy. Of course, these efforts were neither coherent nor accurate, but because they were bathed in a certain ideological soup, such interpretations were thought routine, customary and appropriate. So, in order to get at the ideal of the Right (or any socio-political model) we must start with what supports right-wing ideology and the subsequent worldview. Ultimately, we will break down that worldview into its basic elements, then compare and contrast these right-wing elements with their counterparts on the Left. This will offer us the clearest view of the right-wing ideology that will underwrite the Right's own ideal social order.

I feel obliged to offer assurance that this critique is not politically driven. The paper is a study of right-wing thinking, and left-wing thinking will be brought in only to compare and contrast. I should also add that insofar as it is possible, I have struggled to keep this examination of the right-wing ideal objective and accurate and not a tedious and noxious diatribe against either the Left or the Right. Rational analysis is the goal. With that in mind I have sequestered my own perspective in an effort to offer an exacting insight into the vision of the political extremes. At times then, objectivity will make it appear that I am a supporter of the Right, then at other times, a supporter of the Left. Such is the curious nature of hermeneutic analysis.

The vision held by the Right (or the Left) cannot be objectively labeled right or wrong, or good or evil, or true or false. Objectively, a general vision of either the Right or the Left is only that: a vision—a vision that will satisfy some and discomfort others. A study that delves into what underlies and supports this vision will probably reshuffle who is satisfied and who is discomforted. Learning tends to do that: produce changes in thinking. But the changes must be voluntary, based on the material evidence and the logic of the position. With this is mind, I will struggle to keep the paper objective, but hopefully not too terribly dry.

The Right

What does it mean to be on the Right, politically and ideologically, as opposed to being on the Left? There are seven basic differences between the Left and the Right. I will list them (see below) in an order that will make each successive element an understandable derivation of the previous one. I will list them here quickly, then return for a closer inspection of each element, followed by a brief discussion of their differences with the Left.

The fundamental and elemental differences between the Left and the Right are lodged in the following:

(1) The attitude toward human nature.
(2) The attitude toward human equality.
(3) The attitude toward the existing social and economic order.
(4) The attitude toward reason and custom.
(5) The attitude toward class and class relations.
(6) The attitude toward liberty and freedom.
(7) The attitude toward the social model.

As said above, these are not presented in some sort of random order. Rather like building blocks, one might think of the above list as a sort of pyramid, rising in the order presented to form a structural relief that taken together makes up the right-wing ideal. After a brief analysis of each of these topics, I will return to show how each of them fits into an integrated whole that will flush out the ideal right-wing social order. We will start with self-perception.

Nothing distinguishes the Right from the Left more than the view of human nature. These divergent views are infrequently considered. Discussion between the Left and the Right most often involves the top elements of the pyramid: the social order and issues concerning liberty and freedom. Scant attention is given to the foundation of these quite different views; it is clear that many ideologues do not understand the well-spring of the thinking that ultimately organizes their life's experience. Such an analysis of those origins might well lead to a rethinking. So, let us begin with the foundation: *Human nature.*[1]

(1) Attitude toward human nature:

In general, the Right has a perspective on human nature that they believe to be realistic and genuine rather than merely dark and cynical. Taking the most expansive view of this conservative position we can identify a baseline of humanity as being one that is first and foremost survival orientated, ego-centered and independent. Consequently, as the Right would see it, human nature is energized primarily by the needs of the first law of life: self-preservation. That is, individual survival is primal and primary, which is to say that the bottom line of individual self-interest, in the form of survival, can only be overridden with the direst of consequences. The conservative view would claim that self-interest is only a form of the survival instinct, and that all our actions ultimately emanate from that instinct. There is nothing good or bad about this claim, or right or wrong, and it is a huge mistake to attach any moral sentiments to survival and self-interest. Reality is what it is and people are just people. They will obey this first and primal law.

However, it should be noted that in state-of-the-art, affluent societies, the concept of self-interest can be viewed as "well-being" or living well. For example, to live well in contemporary, industrial societies would mean, among other things, having the best, most reliable car, refrigerator and a house properly wired for internet and cable necessary for expansive entertainment centers. These examples of "survival" in developed societies are not outlandish in the least. One can quickly see the potential for conflict between individuals, all of whom are similarly motivated by individual needs for "well-being." Life becomes traceable to the survival instinct, a silent struggle to achieve "living well."

These identifiers of well-being and survival are all well beyond the reach of good and evil, right and wrong. They serve only as an objective descriptive consideration. As pointed out above, exactly what constitutes survival might change with time and circumstance. It should also be clear (at least from the conservative's point of view) that the fact that people are driven by these fundamental elements is not in dispute. It's all about survival and self-interest! Whether you are scratching for roots under a blazing sun on a desolate savanna or elbowing your way through surging Black Friday crowds at Best Buy, the impulse driving humanity is all but the same. People are people, driven by considerations fixed into the nature of our species.

According to that great conservative, Sigmund Freud:

"Psychological investigations show that the deepest essence of human nature consists of instinctual impulses which are of an elementary nature, which are similar in all men and which aim at the satisfaction of certain primal needs. These impulses in themselves are neither good nor bad. We classify them and their expressions in that way according to their relation to the need and demand of the human community."[2]

In other words, we humans are locked into an instinctual pattern not of our own choosing, a pattern loaded with evolutionary and biological triggers. This means that much of our social drivers are baked into the cake. We can push back, attempt to resist the triggers, but we cannot escape our mortal coil. Moral qualifiers, such as right and wrong, good and evil, exist within our thinking, but nowhere inside our "human nature." Good and bad, and for that matter, even the glowing light of justice itself is merely a contingency applied to the structural and cultural makeup of the community. Human values, morals, ethics, all our tossed salad of legal niceties, reside within our world view, our ideology, but they do not exist someplace out there in the objective, material world.

As the conservative, Thomas Hobbes argued:

> For those words of good and evil, and contemptible, are ever used with relation to the person that useth them: there being nothing simply and absolutely so; not any common rule of good and evil, to be taken from the nature of the objects themselves; but from the person of the man (where there is no commonwealth;) or, (in a commonwealth,) from the person that representeth it."[3] Thomas Hobbes

In the absence of a firm, structured social order (i.e., for Hobbes, the commonwealth) there is no common, objective rule for evil, or any moral values to be taken solely from the social objects themselves. The objective world is neutral. For good and evil we must look to the way people are, or rather to what underlies the way people are by a designing evolution: humans must obey the first law, *to survive*. To uncover the moral and ethical considerations draped around survival, we must look to the evolved social nature of our species.

Let's be clear then, from the right-wing point of view all the heinous, murderous and conniving impulses possessed by our species: greed, aggrandizement, jealousy, selfishness, etc. are, simply speaking, part of the way we are. We can't dodge us—who and what we are; we can't hide from us, so to speak, or out run us. We can only hope to contain, to bottle-up those dark, human urges. Control is ultimately achieved by threats of force, that is, control is backed up by threats of violence or incarceration. This is to say that eventually a legal framework must arise to constrain this fundamental law of survival. Thus, the connection and tension between constraint and civilization becomes ever more obvious.

This is not a paper examining the attitudes of the Left. Consequently, I will only say that the Left, as you might suspect, takes an opposite position from that of the Right. Most frequently, the leftist attitude toward human nature, in general, is one that suggests that there is no such thing as human nature:

"With the exception of the instinctoid reactions in infants to sudden withdrawals of support and the sudden loud noises, the human being is entirely instinctless....Man is man because he has no instincts, because everything he is and has become he has learned, acquired, from his culture, from the man-made part of the environment, from other human beings." Ashley Montagu [4]

It is either the above neutralist position, or the more controversial, leftist view that human nature is a thing hard wired into our species to make us helpful, cooperative, and empathetic, or at the very least benign. But according to either leftist position, those features of human "evil": the greed, covetousness, aggressiveness, etc. we all witness, emerge as a result of twists and turns in the objective, environmental world. We are greedy, according to the Left, when we see famine on the horizon, covetous when we see scarcity superimposed by rules and laws favoring the few, aggressive when threatened by scarcity or famine or other hostile humans.

This brings us to the second of the elements separating the Left from the Right: attitudes toward human equality, or human sameness.

(2) Attitude toward human equality

"Strip us all naked and we shall all be found alike. Dress us in their [the upper classes] clothing and they in ours and we shall appear noble, they ignoble—for poverty and riches make all the differ-ence." N. Machiavelli [5]

Strangely, despite to Machiavelli's much maligned reputation, he appears here (and elsewhere[6]) to be a humanist and a materialist:[7] beneath our clothing, Machiavelli declares for all to hear, we are all alike.

However, and bluntly speaking, from the viewpoint of the Right the above claim of equality is ridiculous, no matter who said it or for what rea-son. People are simply not the same. People are different and not equal to one another—except in "standing before the law" (and that claim is also not without its own level of controversy and detractors). There are varying

degrees of harshness to this point of view on natural differences leading to natural inequality, with some points of view being not particularly
forgiving. Largely then, the perspective on natural inequality amongst
human beings remains a high point of reference for the Right. Obviously,
in one of its more extreme forms this point of reference concerning natural inequality will break along racial, religious, ethnic or national lines.
Currently, this more aggressive version seems to be in recession in favor
of more subtle and more pointed points of illustration.

For example, human inequality manifests itself in all kinds of ways:
physical differences are obvious. I've always wanted to slam-dunk a bas-
ketball, but unaided and at five-foot-nine it's simply not going to happen. However, unlike physical distinctions, the emotional and mental
differences found in the multitude of personalities are not at all obvious.
That people strive for different goals, that they possess varying degrees
of wherewithal to achieve those goals, and that many are emotionally and
intellectually outfitted in very uneven ways, is not generally disputed.
But unlike the Left, the Right feels that these differences that lead to
inequality are a fact of life according to human nature, according to birth
and DNA. There is no worming out of this inbred diversity, the Right will
claim. Character traits are intrinsic, baked in at conception, traits that
have tipped the survival scale in favor of the uber-successful. Even looking at social distinction found in the earliest examples of human history
will show that changing status and power were largely an outgrowth of
human differences.[8] Of course, it is possible to push back against these
inbred boundaries—governments can do this, through legal devises and
coding infrastructure for equal access—but ultimately nothing can alter
the nature of our species and its effect on separating the winners from
the losers. Intelligence, courage, strength, etc., are all naturally given
differences that lead to inequality in the possession of power and wealth.
From the view point of the Right, we must make our peace with nature
and learn to adjust to the reality of human inequality. That there is no
objective, scientific proof alone makes this claim of inbred inequality
ideological rather than rational. But despite the lack of rigorous proof,
this perspective can certainly claim to be mainstream; so what are the
effects of this point of view?

According to the Right, humanity is driven largely by individual survival instinct and individual well-being. This brings egoistic individualism

center stage in the governance of social interaction. Individualism, when driving by survival, translates in a social behavior that quickly pivots to some version of "every man for himself." Of course, this will lead to each individual acting independently as he sees fit, and for goals of his own choosing. Here, "difference" rears its ugly head. Keep in mind that one man's basic survival is another man's basic opulence; difference does not automatically mean unequal, but difference in character and personality can certainly lead, and usually does, to unequal power and social standing, at least as they are defined by current standards.

This is so because *difference* makes acceptable the fact that divergent people frame survival and well-being in terms very unalike. In a sense the various attitudes toward survival frequently revolve around the old saw of seeing the glass half empty—vs—the glass half full. To illustrate: above I mentioned that in the contemporary world the possession of a reliable car (i.e., transplantation) is highly desirable. Only what does it mean to be "reliable," and for that matter what does "transportation" mean? For one person a dependable bicycle is satisfactory transportation, yet for another person only a Bentley will do. Obviously, the energy and the resources, not to mention the applied direction of these means, required by these two individuals are also completely different: One person seeks to be an artist while another looks to day-trading in stocks. The demands are different, and the rewards are equally different. These *differences* point directly to questions concerning the allocation of the energy and resources required to obtain reliable transportation.

But wait, you might object, isn't all this a matter of choice? As the powerful will say to the powerless: different people will make different choices, no? So, what's the problem? You made your choice to live a lifestyle compatible with bike riding, while I made choices more fitting to drive about in a Bentley. The raw truth is that I got rich and you got to paint pictures—pictures that I might buy some day. I don't mean to sound harsh, but our different personalities did steer us in different directions, resulting in different gains and losses, different social positions and consolidations of power.

In short, the Right believes that difference in personality and character can and do lead to inequality in resource distribution. According to right-wing philosophy inequality is mainly true because different people adopt different survival techniques. However, whatever path we adopt is constrained by what intellectual tools and gifts are offered to each individual at birth. The first law of survival has no play book, no set of do's and don'ts. It only admonishes us to survive and pass along our genetic material. For some, those few with superior tools, the chosen path leads to success in whatever capacity is determined by current conditions. Of course, for those others less well equipped for survival at a modern level, their choice lead to much less success, at least as a contemporary, capitalist society defines success.

The Left is not not blind-sided here. Briefly, and for comparison, the Left would identify the social environment and history as spoilers for the Right's point-of-view. Power and wealth accumulate over generations, the Left would point out. This accumulation is passed down from generation to generation, leaving the starting line for different people at different points relative to a successful life. The social constraints and barriers devised by circumstance and history govern who will succeed and who will fail to a far greater degree than individual character traits. It is important to note that the Left does not deny individual character traits, but instead reduces their importance when up against the reality of material life.

Obviously, the impact of DNA and genetic research remains a contentious point of friction between the Left and the Right. Given the entrenching of the two position, it is unlikely that the controversy will be resolved anytime soon.

(3) The attitude toward the existing social and economic order.

The Right will claim that formalized customs relating to wealth and power were developed by human social organization right from the very beginning of political governance. Translated: to the Right, "from the very beginning" means that social hierarchy based on wealth and position are the foundational and defining points of all civilizations—right from the very beginning of even the simplest, most primitive political organizations. As one leading anthropologist bluntly expressed it:

"Chiefdoms represent the formalization of inherited differences in access to status, power, and wealth." Bogucki, Peter [9]

According to the Right, in order for even the earliest forms of government to emerge certain structural conditions must have been present. For example, societies must recognize some form of inequality based on something other than age or sex—perhaps the important acknowledgment of the transmission of wealth across generational lines. When collections of households combine to uphold their cross generational wealth, social differentiation emerges and reaches the community level. This is the beginning of class differentiation and institutionalized protection of differences in class wealth. At some point, for reasons that may vary, the entirety of the households combine in recognition of an emerging elite as a central power. Further, for reasons having to mostly do with efficiency and security, these elites agree amongst themselves to become subservient to one of the key houses.

There are three primary factors behind the structured hierarchy and subservience: economic, ideological, and military. Consider: first, unequal economic differentiation acts as the instigator, second, ideology arises to offer legitimacy to the inequality, and third, the military, *qua* police, is poised to move on objectors if the ideological mask slips and force is required to maintain the hierarchy—along with the unequal economic and social structures that have arisen in support of the new pyramid. Thus, we crack the door on the bare beginnings of the political state.

That the impact of the above two previously discussed attitudes (*viz*, human nature and human equality) have a strong effect on the development of the social and economic order should come as no surprise. Political government is, after all, little more than a systematic codification and infrastructure of existing social and economic arrangement. A proper role of government is to legitimize and minimize friction between emerging classes. It follows, of course, that government is also the primary protector and guardian of these historically produced economic and social arrangements, unequal though they may be.

As John Locke points out the proper role of government in managing the types of conflict that can arise:

> "That it is unreasonable for Men to be Judges in their own Cases, that Self-love will make Men partial to themselves and their Friends... hence nothing but Confusion and Disorder will follow, and that therefore God hath certainly appointed Government to restrain the partiality and violence of Men." John Locke[10]

In short, even though "evil" has a certain cryptic and esoteric feel to it, both the Left and the Right agree that "evil" exists (e.g., war, theft, murder, etc.), but they disagree on the causes. For evil to exist, the Right will blame deficiencies in human nature. The Left, on the other hand, will blame historically determined conditions that preserve and foster inequality in resource distribution and the friction that inequality will produce.

Of course, where and when one finds oneself in space and time can determine if this mal-distribution is an issue born of scarce resources or is a result of political decisions. Even so, while both the Left and the Right would agree on the facts of mal-distribution, the Right would insist that equal distribution of these scarce resources is a fanciful, Pollyanna vision of how people determine their goals and strivings. The Right would maintain equal distribution based on altruistic sentiment is a Left-wing myth, which at bottom is only envy and jealousy of those who have struggled successfully to be able to afford an opulent lifestyle. According to right-wing thinking, life is a struggle for scarce resources, and the governing upper crust is in place to control that envy, jealously, covetousness, and rapacity found at the dark heart of human nature. One should be grateful that these efforts on the part of strong, ruling elites can bring about a temporary peace between the winners and losers in this race for survival. Given these realities, the social and economic orders are exactly as they should be. Governments by elites are established to prevent the type of chaos that would ensue from a radical and undeserved re-distribution of resources.

Given that the Right assigns blame for human woes on flaws in human nature, changing the political and social arrangements would make no difference as to how people behave—or misbehave. According to the Right, human beings are grasping and predatory by nature and social engineering can't change human nature. Human nature is fixed and immutable:

"I put for a general inclination of all mankind, a perpetual and restless desire of power after power, that ceaseth only in death. And the cause of this, is not always that a man hopes for a more intensive delight, than he has already attained to; or that he cannot be content with a moderate power: but because he cannot assure the power and means to live well, which he hath present, without the acquisition of more." T. Hobbes [11]

As a consequence, any social and economic order must be arranged and structured with this piteous, acquisitive side of human nature in mind. "Evil," in the form of greed and the rapacious violence often needed to keep the gluttony satiated, must be controlled. A firm hand must be in place. Without the strength of a powerful state to hold back these forces of evil, unrestrained violence and aggrandizement would make any kind of social order impossible. As Hobbes expressed it, only an all-powerful central government could hold back a war of all-against-all. The world is as it should be when a strong state is in the driver's seat to assure a peaceful existence for the social and economic order.

(4) The attitude toward reason and tradition

Obviously, force cannot be the only deterrent to prevent a war of all-against-all. If force and violence were the only alternative to dissatisfaction with the existing social order, then there would truly be an unending war. To synthesize Hobbesian thinking: the absence of a strong, central state would truly mean the war of all-against-all. Henceforth, a different type of control intercedes. We can effectively call it "thought control." And by thought control we mean a type of cognition that is not consciously or deliberately directed, but one possessed of an undercurrent "guiding" conscious thought seemingly without presence. Custom and tradition easily fall into this category, this undercurrent to thought. These represent ways of being in the world that are guided automatically; for example, wishing a stranger "good day," queuing up for an event, tipping a waitress, throwing rice at a wedding, all represent customary behaviors that are beyond conscious, directed thinking. These examples are harmless, but other types of tradition and custom are not so harmless. For example, events as diverse as college hazing to female circumcision, represent ritualized traditions that can lead to pain, sickness and death. Under the heading of negative "traditions," we might also include ugly axiomatic reactions toward the world such as xenophobia, ethno-nationalism, racism, *et al*. Furthermore, given the far-flung nature of so many unconscious patterns of behavior, it seems appropriate to identify thought control by a single, more inclusive handle: ideology.

By "ideology" I refer to an insensate idea system acting on human behavior prior to conscious thinking. The specific type of ideology we are interested in is one typically encompassing an idea system guiding coherent thought in ways unthreatening to the existing social order. Boiled down, ideology is an unconscious system of understanding, a pre-cognition underwriting conscious thought. This is a system that is produced by humans, but not directly. So what is ideology to the individual?

> "The real motive forces impelling [the individual] remain unknown to him; otherwise it simply would not be an ideological process. Hence he imagines false or apparent motive forces. Because it is a process of thought he derives its form as well as its content from pure thought, either its form as well as its content from pure thought, either his own or that of his predecessors. He works with mere thought material, which he accepts without examination as the product of thought, and does not investigate further for a more remote source independent of thought; indeed this is a matter of course to him, because, as all action is mediated by thought, it appears to him to be ultimately based upon thought." Fredrick Engels[12]

Obviously, in describing ideology in this way, Engels is describing an unconscious system of pre-cognition that has far more in common with tradition and custom than reason. For example, to say that "America is the greatest country in the world," is a canard hung on a traditionalist view of American patriotism. In no way does the canard depend on reason, or even reality. For what is the meaning of "great?" In many ways reasoning is the opposite of ideology and ideological canards.

> "The normal product of reasoning is an argument, a finite series of statement (premises) offered in support of another statement (conclusion)."[13]

Ideology is not a lattice of organized thinking; ideology is not an argument based on rules of logic; ideology is not so coordinated. There is no series of true statements to form the coherent structure of a logical argument or even an intelligible political position. With ideology there are only vague feelings that settle on us, propelling us to act. Ideology is a system of ideas that are the result of a timeless interplay between historically produced social arrangements and the emergence of new challenges and struggles. The manner in which this conflict between the past and the present is resolved generates fresh ideas that press toward modifying the system to accommodate this emerging present. This modification, of course, generates even newer ideas, and so on. The adoption of new ideas thus generated is often seamless, automatic, and therefore typically axiomatic.

That ideas spring from this simple dialectic seems reasonable: the emergence of new ideas and notions caused by the friction between historical circumstances when colliding with the challenges of the present. This would seem a reasonable explanation for both changing perceptions and the new interpretations of those perceptions. Although we might not be aware of it, gaining intelligibility and consistency from these new ideas requires deliberately directed analysis, reason and conscious thinking. Yet here's the rub.

Without saying as much, I presented the above sketch without revealing that it is the vision adopted by the Left; this for contrast. The Right has a far different point of view on the origin and development of ideas. The Right has never completely adopted a dialectical perspective.[14] The historical dialectic depends on conflict with the past for the emergence of new ideas. This represents an ongoing problem for the conservative, who venerates the past and has no interest in rejecting its many gifts. So, since the past is the "ideal," how can this perfect, quintessential past, provoke a dialectical conflict with the present? No—according the conservative, dialectics is not, indeed, cannot be the source of new ideas.

For that matter, the loss of "new ideas" is not even the "rub." Consider that for the Right there is no need for new ideas. The wisdom of the past is guide enough. Tradition and culture spell it all out. There are no good new ideas. As the great conservative Edmund Burke[i] put it, tradition and custom represent "the wisdom of the species."[15] What is best for society

---

i. I am calling on Edmund Burke as a highly recognizable icon of classic conservatism. At the same time, using Burke is unlikely to be offensive as he is seen as a both a prognosticator and a champion for modern conservative political parties.

is a worldview based on the accumulation of wisdom—this wisdom of the species for ages to come. After all, institutions that have survived the test of time are best for our species. Burke further discourages innovation and reform by asserting that those who would bring change have no empirical evidence that what they propose by way of reform would, in fact, be better. Would-be reformers have only "reason" to articulate their arguments, that is, a "reason" fallible and unreliable and often totally without material evidence; these are merely mind games. However, tradition, having stood the test of time, always trumps the mind game of reason. Tradition, having been tested time and time again, has shown its worth and mettle. It is by following the tenets of traditionalism that we have arrived at the best of all possible worlds and the best possible idea system.[ii]

For the Right, this "wisdom of the species" leads nearly immediately to "what is, is what ought to be," a familiar right-wing refrain. The Right will claim that all in this world is exactly as it should be. The historic gathering of collective wisdom has produced a tradition that has brought the social order to a point of perfection. That perfection should be left as it is. Again, "what is, is what ought to be." The existing social order, and the ideas that support it, are the best of all possible worlds. Let the wisdom of tradition and custom be the guide for society, not reason.

For contrast, it should come as no surprise that the Left sees matters in a much different light. For the Left there is an inherent conflict between reason and tradition. According to the Left, reason as a thought process is dynamic while tradition exists in a non-thinking, reflexive and static state. The two are only related through analysis. This boils down to what is reasonable (what ought to be) versus custom or tradition (what is current) in a contest that engenders an unending cycle of struggle between the old and the new. Here we see the Left adopting reason and pressing for the new and untried while the Right stands pat by tradition and custom, and holds fast to being the old guard preserving the safety and continuance of the rich ideals mined from the past.

Unfortunately for the Right, any analysis that connects past ideals with present circumstance always reveals that the main source of social

---

ii. It should be pointed out that the left would not define this as an "idea" system, but a "belief" system. This "defining" represents much more than a semantic difference. The implication should be clear.

change is the *conflict* between the past and the present. This conflict translates into an intractable ideological chasm between reason and custom. The Left, which champions reason, is always pressing for change and reform. The Right, on the other hand, whose interests are typically tied to the existing social order finds that the existing social institutions are what ought to be. This also stands true for current economic relationships. All is as it should be. No surprise here. Only it must be asked of the conservative, where do new ideas come from?

For the Right the emergence of new, reformist ideas is not so much the result of changing conditions, but rather is the result of new, emerging elites. For example, early in the 20th century the sociologist Vilfredo Pareto[iii] conflated changing historical conditions with what he identified as "a circulation of elites." Change arrived with arising, new elites; change didn't produce the elites, elites produced the change. Pareto clearly grasped the importance of ideology as a form of thought control. Ideology (or *residues* as Pareto referred to ideology in those early days) served only to support or undermine existing elites.[16] Elites are inevitable, according to Pareto (and most conservatives). The idea system(s) that surrounds and shields elites goes beyond reason. Ideology comes upon us as a representative of wisdom that has been built up over the eons, built up through tried and tested methods and accomplishments. Reason represents only feeble attempts to restrain the muscularity of tradition and custom—and ideology. Reason is the tool of the unsuccessful and the talentless in their relentless attempt to tear down a vibrant social order living out the promise of the ages. Such is the traditional way the Right views the world of success and failure.

(5) The attitude toward class and class relations.

Considering the Right's attitude toward the existing social and economic order, it should come as no surprise that the *class structure*, as found within a particular social order, is deemed appropriate and necessary for the well-being of the society as a whole. Yet at the same time the

---

iii. I am using Pareto in the same spirit as I used Burke above. Pareto is a past figure, well respected and not particularly controversial, and is uninvolved in current ideological disputes.

Right is not oblivious to the "optics" of oppression brought about by the very existence of a class structure. The top down design of the hierarchy offers the clear appearance of both order and control *and* domination. This "appearance" is one of the unavoidable optics behind most class relations. This is simple reality. Given the hierarchal design of nearly all political and social structures, someone has to be on the bottom, and notice that the bottom is the broadest, thickest of the steps. Optics or not, it is the masses of people that support the upward development of the pyramid. This is an unfortunate presentation of the social order, and one the Right would like to avoid. We will discuss their most successful ways in dismantling and revising these less than attractive images.

There are several divergent ways for the right to identify class—or deny that it exists. This idea that class as a socio-economic identifier does not exist I will ignore; the attempts at rubbing out class as a conceptual entity usually run from incomprehensible to downright stupid, and not worth going into.[17] Although identified by a variety of different markers, class certainly does exist, and it is important to view this reality through understanding the chief ingredients of class and the structure that makes class possible. Alejandro Portes identifies four core insights that make class visible to the social eye and make class analysis possible:

1. Social phenomena are not explainable by their surface mani-festation. There is 'deep structure,' defined by durable inequal-ities, among large social aggregates.

2. Classes are defined by their relationship to one another and not simply by a set of 'gradational' positions along some hierarchy. In this sense, status rakings are a manifestation, not a defining feature of class.

3. Classes are defined by differential access to power within a given social system.

4. Class position is transmissible across generations.[18]

You'll notice in #2 above, that Portes suggests (correctly, I believe) that class is defined by interaction as related to positioning. By positioning I mean the active role one class plays with respect to the other. In ortho-dox Marxist theory these relations are primarily found within the means of production; that is, the relationship of the individual to the means of production. In times past, this tended to point out two primary groups: (1) those individuals who work and produce societies' wealth and (2) those who expropriate that wealth. When considering this we used to imagine a manicured, cigar smoking, three-piece suit in contrast to the sparks and glow of molten metal and the steel workers who puddled and rolled the shiny metal bars. It was clear who we were talking about: the boss wore a suit, the worker wore overalls. In contemporary life this image no longer holds. Today we must trade the factory floor for the sparkle of the computer laboratory. The grunting, heaving laborer has now to be exchanged with the crisp white smock of the smiling lab worker—different workers, different production, different optics, yet one thing holds. It is the same expropriation of wealth by the owners of the "means of production."

For the Right, the attitude toward the varying roles within the different classes are seen as mutually supportive and compatible with regards to their function. This is to say that each individual function, each subset or grouping or by function, is seen as necessary to the harmony and well-being of the entire social organism. This view is usually called the organic social model. One advantage of this model is that it avoids the top down pyramid model and therefore discourages the appearance of domination.

The Left, as one might suspect, has a different view of all this necessary harmony. The Left takes the pyramidal image to heart, indicating that the top of the hierarchy is wholly supported by the bottom of the structure; that the pinnacle of the pyramid exists at all is due to the exploitation of the bottom. This means that not only are the classes not functioning in concert, but they are also virulently antagonistic: the top exploits the base, while the base resists the exploitation as best as it can. Typically, this worker resistance takes the form of work stoppages, strikes, and slow-downs. The top of the pyramid pushes back against the workers in the form of laws, ideology and, when deemed necessary, police action. Who wins? Power decides.[19]

Since in the world of the Right all appears as it should be, class structure is seen as appropriate, both in design and effect. Typically, the Right, in agreement with their view on human nature and their recognition that there are differences in talent and skill, see class as an inevitable and natural consequence of these differences. The degree to which race enters into the formula depends on the ideocracies of the movement. For example, while Nazi Germany made race one of its doctrinaire

167

foundations, Italy struggled with the impossibility of identifying the *Italian race*.[20] Keep in mind that race is much more of a social and political category than a biological one. As a consequence, race, *per se*, was never universally applied by the Right, even in fascist movements. The stress was always on function within the organism, with the weight falling on talents and differences. These, it was often believed, were a product of a fixed, genetic inheritance.

The recognition of class and class harmony as realities that exist for the betterment of the social order as a whole is a priority for the Right. To rid the world of harmful class antagonism, the Right struggles to convince those reluctant to get the idea that in order for society to survive for the betterment of *all* classes, social and economic functions need to be seen as working in harmony as guided by the upper classes. This is a sort of "we'll hang separately, or we'll all hang together" image that often drifts into the uber-patriotism and neo-tribalism that so often defines the Right.

As mentioned above, this view of the Right seeking class harmony is most accurately identified as the *organic view* of the social order. A prototype of this view would identify the nation and society as things very near to living biological entities—entities that live, breathe and function as any living entity. Individuals are seen as cells within the organism, with collections of cells gathered into functioning parts. The role of each of the parts is to ensure the survival and well-being of the total organism. The individual is neither safe nor secure without the entire organism, and the function of each of the parts guarantees the individual's security through the security of the entire organism (i.e., the state). The extreme right, say as exemplified by fascism, tends to use the term corporatism rather than organic, though the meaning is exactly the same. In the words of fascism's founder, Benito Mussolini:

"The Corporation is established to develop the wealth, political power and welfare of the Italian people. Corporatism means a disciplined and therefore a controlled economy, since there is no discipline which is not controlled. Corporatism overcomes Socialism as well as it does Liberalism."[21]

Bringing in ultra-right movements, such as fascism, allows us to see how racism and more commonly, xenophobia and ethno-nationalism come to play a role in this organic view. Except for such extreme factions as Nazism, neither of these categories is openly cited by the fascist political movement, *per se*; they are hidden behind such notions as supremacism, and patriotism. More accurately, it might be said that race and xenophobia were regionally located in places where tradition and custom (see above) bake such elements into the cake.[22] Regarding tradition and custom, consider the different accents racism plays out in such divergent regions as Russia and the US southern states. Russian tradition earmarks Jews, while US southern tradition singles out African-Americans. This is not to say that every Russian hates Jews, or that every southern conservative is a bigot toward Black Americans, but only that regional traditions make for an on-site, structural proclivity toward bigotry. Ultra-right groups, whether sincerely or not, play both into and play on those inclinations.

Rarely, however, does racism fit comfortably into the organic model. Race and xenophobia tend to produce antagonisms and friction with no positive upside for a model based on the political organism. Consequently, while supremacism would comfortably fit below the surface of ultra-right doctrine, it is not often brought into the light of public inquiry. Given the Right's view of human nature, the organic model is clearly simpatico with racially charged views, but is less concerned with those views than the view that individuals of any race hold radically different degrees of intellect, talent and skill. To simplify, there are, to draw from Plato's Republic, men of gold, men of silver, and men of bronze, each with a different role to play in the survival of the total organism—the state. Plato's views would no doubt receive a sympathetic hearing by the elite of the fascist state, at least by the ruling elite of that state. No doubt those individuals at the bottom of the pyramid would have a far different perspective—yet another reason for the elite to shun the hierarchical view in favor of the organic model.

(6) The attitude toward liberty and freedom

For the Right a problem quickly develops when discussing freedom and liberty and their impact on the social order. The problem of liberty arises because for the Right there are two main, divergent political extremes to handle freedom both in theory and reality: one would be libertarianism[23] and the other, fascism. Obviously, these two doctrines represent the outlying poles, extreme views not held by the majority of conservatives. However, these extremes project images stark enough that they can handily be used to afford a quick examination of the notion of right-wing freedom.

~

The first (i.e., libertarianism) gives the impression of absolute freedom. The other (fascism) seems to offer an authoritarianism hugely restrictive of individual freedom. Within fascist theory freedom is not only forgotten or dismissed, but is a thing defined as solely possible within the corporate social model. Right-wing thinking tends to bounce between these two poles—libertarianism and fascism—with the middle ground as the usual residence of mainstream right-wing doctrine. In this piece I will confine any extensive remarks to libertarianism, pointing out where appropriate that when the fascist uses the notion of freedom it is in a far different manner than the libertarian. For the fascist the state offers freedom *from*, not freedom *to*. According to the fascist the state is as a living thing that uplifts the individual through tradition and custom, offering freedom from violence, hunger and want. The state offers freedom from the "other." Simply put, fascism describes the state not in terms of pluralism, but of tribalism, a form of collectivism that proposes that the individual does not, and cannot, exist apart from the state. This is how Mussolini put it:

> "The state is the guarantor of security both internal and external, but it is also the custodian and transmitter of the spirit of the people, as has grown up through the centuries in language, in custom, and in faith. And the state is not only a living reality of the present, it is also linked and above all the future, and thus transcending the brief limits of individual life, it represents the immanent spirit of the nation."[24]

This means that what the fascist offers is a negative type of freedom. Again, fascism is a freedom *from*, a freedom largely derived from fear—fear of deprivation and arbitrary violence. Broadly put, fascism offers the individual a freedom from fear of the *other*. The paramount example of this national movement based on fear is Nazi Germany, but other, examples, Salazr's Portugal, Pinochet's Chile, Franco's Spain, all are based to one degree or another on fear of the *"other,"* e.g., fear of the communists, the Catholics, the unions, the Jews, the foreigners, etc. And of course, we know how those fascist experiments ended in failure.

On the other hand, the libertarian offers a positive type of freedom, a freedom to—to build, to develop, to advance according to individual talents and energy. Loosely speaking, it might be said that fascism caters to the paranoid while libertarianism caters to the egoistic. Whether any of libertarian theory can be trusted to mirror reality is another matter. To understand this we must return for a review of human nature as it relates to social development.

Recall that the view claimed by the Right is that human nature is primarily driven by self-interested survival and well-being. This need not be an opening for a discussion of some kind of supernatural force of an "evil spirit" driving humanity. One must keep in mind that survival is a natural drive, a reflexive impulse based on concrete, biological needs, not spiritual ones. The Right's view of humanity is harsh enough without the addition of evil monsters struggling for control inside our skins. Yet even given as harsh a view of human nature as the Right might claim, it is still within their advocacy to find a basis for absolute freedom, a freedom based on materialism and not spiritualty.

To reiterate, this view of nearly absolute and positive freedom most often appears under the heading of "libertarianism." This positive freedom is not often succinctly spelled out, but according to one prominent libertarian theoretician:

"Libertarianism is the view that each person has the right to live his life in any way he chooses so long as he respects the equal rights of others...Libertarians defend each person's right to life, liberty, and property—rights that people possess naturally, before governments are created. In the libertarian view, all human relationships should be voluntary; the only actions that should be forbidden by law are those that involve the initiation of force against those who have not themselves used force—actions like murder, rape, robbery, kidnapping, and fraud." Boaz, David[25]

This, of course is an ideal, and one bristling with loose ends. Reducing the power of the state does not necessarily reduce the power relations between people and between classes. Clearly, there are certain realities that can compromise these lofty ideals; thus, the reality of libertarianism is not without its detractors. In the words of one critic:

> "In reality, the 'strong do what they must and the weak suffer what they must.' Simply making the state not the "strong" in this case does not alter the validity of this condition between men, it just advocates making someone or something else "the strong" who force the weak to "suffer what they must" instead." Steven Maloney [26]

What we see here is that the very default setting of "human nature" being offered by libertarianism is its own blowback. It seems that the survival instinct that drives human beings, along with their innate differences, has undermined the libertarian argument. Freedom goes to the strong. The weak suffer not only the loss of freedom, but protection from the strong. That the Right makes a great deal of human "difference" seems to be the pivotal piece.

The above quote by Maloney makes the point that "difference" need not be one of talent. It might be, and often is, a difference of strength. Especially for libertarian theory, differences in power raise the question of how exactly one finds oneself in advantageous societal positions that translate into status and authority. At this juncture it is probably better to adopt the concept of "predilection" in place of talent; this implies bias without offering a source of the bias. In other words, while "talent" suggests something innate, predilection indicates only a leaning without a hard-and-fast claim as to the source, be it DNA or social conditioning. This is an important distinction. When survival and well-being are inherited positions rather than earned, such structural advantages rule out talent as the origin of success and social position. However, the social position gained through inheritance can lead to predilections in behavior and thinking. These predilections are acquired and adopted through the passive learning attained through social modification and practice. In this way, predilections can seem to appear to the casual observer as talent, inbred and ingrained.

Yet, under the sponsorship of libertarianism, such a view creates a serious speed bump for the delivery of freedom and liberty. If social positions are inherited (as is allowed under libertarian theory) then it is the political and social structures that are the source of power and inequality and not the predilections (or talent, if you will) of the individual. It should be obvious that the where and when of birth are pure happenstance and not the result of diligence and hard work. Therefore, it would appear that while freedom and liberty do exist to various degrees in a libertarian society, they are highly dependent on a fixed transmission of wealth as governed by the rules of the existing social structure. Quite literally, then, given that by design all individuals do not start from the same station in life, freedom takes a back seat to the structural tools presented to certain individuals by historical circumstance. A freedom that flows from historically determined material relations, and not individual effort, seems to be a direct repudiation to the libertarian ideal.

It is unlikely that libertarians would be willing to give up the transmission of wealth and position that locks them into the existing social order. Consequently, the libertarian must ignore, modify, or delete one of the central platforms of their doctrine, *viz*, that the individual, and the class which he represents, are, and should be, solely responsible for their success or failure in life. Given that the transmission of wealth depends on existing social structures, claims for individual freedom and reliance stand on shaky ground. For their survival and well-being, the libertarians (at least the elites) become just as dependent as the fascists on the existing material relations. This reduces the claim of the libertarian to a state of dependence. That is, a dependence for their "freedom" on the existing institutions and not on individual talents and energy. This point of view strongly contrasts with the Left, who would first abolish most of the existing institution as a precursor to liberty and marks a clean and strategic difference between the Left and the Right.

For the sake of space in my analysis of the Right I have turned this study more toward a treatment of libertarianism than fascism. Although fascism is a legitimate political position and a reasonably coherent doctrine, it has a far less appealing nature than libertarianism. The cause seems apparent: libertarianism attempts to hold the individual apart and above the state rather than a mere "unit" submerged, and subservient to the needs of the state. In most western-style democracies the libertarian message is more widespread and attractive than fascism. Be advised, however, that fascism is not a "dead" political doctrine. Fascism is alive and well, and according to the ideological tenets of the Right, still a viable alternative, given certain conditions.

To sum up, then, for the Right as whole, individual freedom depends on the forces of history at work in the design of existing institutions. Of course, we must understand that these "institutions" might certainly be castles in the sky—that is, ideological and cultural platforms that act to legitimize both station in life and the rules for survival and well-being. This indicates that for the Right, individual freedom is bound to be an adversary to change, as change violates both tradition and custom.

(7) The attitude toward the social model

We began with the question: What exactly would the proto-typical right-wing society look like? Following the above discussions, the answer to this question is nearly anti-climactic. Given the Right's attitude toward human nature and the inevitability of a hierarchy and expanding elites, it follows that the rest of the social body must be structured to accommodate the ensuing social and economic imbalances. This sounds rather harsh and not at all how a spokesman for the Right would put it. To counter this distressing tone, any coarse accusations can be addressed by the Right through ideological archetypes. Such extreme canards as racial superiority, tribalism, gender chauvinism, jingoistic nationalism, etc., need not be resorted to. Instead, and in terms of a less radical ideology format, the Right might stress freedom of choice, democratic equality and pluralism. Both are designed to obscure class structure and the image of dominance represented by the pyramidal structure; the latter is preferred as it is less abrasive and more difficult to refute.

Bearing this in mind, the Right has a solution. Pressing forward with their ideological position the Right attempts to portray the social organism as a harmonious whole without any antagonistic parts. Translated, this means viewing all parts of the socio-economic system as doing what they do best to preserve the survival and well-being of the whole. Given this vision, all of the parts of the social organism survive and prosper working independently, yet together for a common goal of survival and well-being. We have referred to this above as the "organic model," a central tenant of fascist doctrine. As Zeev Sternhell describes it:

"This view of man as an integral part of an organic whole is the basis of fascism's political philosophy. Fascism developed a conception of society which accorded moral privilege to the collectivity, its traditions, and particularly its juridical embodiment in the state as against the empirical and transient individuals which constitute its membership at any given time."[27]

To demonstrate shades of the above with a somewhat controversial claim: when John F. Kennedy famously posed a challenge to the American people, "Ask not what your country can do for you—ask what you can do for your country," it is assumed that he is calling on Americans to contribute to the greater, common good. However, underlying and supporting this supposed call to the common good is the implication of the *primacy of the state*. Both the "common good" and the "primacy of the state" have huge appeal to the gods and myths of the nation-state and the nationalism it provokes—sounds reasonable, until one considers the question of *whose nation-state are we talking about*? To be sure, the organic model works out a lot better than the pyramid model for the purposes of engendering loyalty and compliance. However, for those sections of society less privileged than the upper classes—the elites from which JFK emerged—the organic view tends to spread apathy, resignation, and a muted rage at the feeling of powerlessness.

Going back to 18th century Edmund Burke, we can see that even non-fascist conservatives tend to identify society as a living organism. As Burke and other conservatives maintain, any social community is larger than the sum of its parts, and much, much more than a set of atomized units:

"In a state of rude nature there is no such thing as a people. A number of men in themselves have no collective capacity. The idea of a people is the idea of a corporation." Edmund Burke[28]

Burke speaks in a foreshadowing of Mussolini and the Italian fascist doctrine. It is clear that the corporate image of the social order is raised much earlier than 20th century fascists, an image that stresses cooperation between the "parts" instead of antagonism and conflict. As Zeev Sternhell describes it:

"Fascism being highly nationalistic and socially concerned, thus achieved a harmonious synthesis between the forces of the past and the demands of the future, between the weight of tradition on the one hand and revolutionary enthusiasm on the other. It borrowed from both the right and the left. In practice, of course, fascism's insistence on the cooperation of all social classes and their reconciliation with the corporative regime through it irrevocably to the right."[29]

Again, the organic model appears. Furthermore, to claim the ascendency and primacy of the social order, Burke argues that society *precedes* the individual, and that the individual has no "natural right" to push back against the demands of the preeminent social order.[30] As society comes before the individual, the individual can be expected to be shaped and guided by society and not visa-versa.

"Society requires not only that the passions of individuals should be subjected, but that even in the mass and body as in the individuals, the inclination of men should be thwarted, their will controlled, and their passions be brought into subjection. This can be done by a power out of themselves; and not, in the exercise of its function, subject to that will and to those passions which it is its office to bridle and subdue." Edmund Burke[31]

All of this, of course, is designed to promote the "needs of life," needs that are best satisfied through social cooperation. Historically there has been an antagonism that exists side-by-side with the need for social cooperation—a contradiction that seems to arise. Here the Right would argue both human differences and Prateo's cycle of elites: What we see as friction and conflict from the bottom of the social order are merely the rise of new elites.

But what would the ideal right-wing society (or utopia) look like? We might go back to Plato and Thomas More to find lengthy descriptions,[32] but what about modern and contemporary thinkers? Again, let us look toward libertarianism. As I mentioned above, there is rarely any detailed description offered, or even attempted.[iv] However, one huge exception is

---

iv. In fairness, it should be noted that the Left also lacks any clearly presented image of their future utopia.

the often cited work by Robert Nozick, *Anarchy, State, and Utopia*.[33] The work itself advances libertarian philosophy in a carefully reasoned study. To remind the reader: I elected to discuss libertarianism as a generally acceptable view of the right-wing ideal, yet one not so negatively charged as fascism, the other extreme right-wing ideal.

In this monumental piece Nozick devotes much of the second half of his work to a presentation of the utopian libertarian layout. However, his description of the libertarian society conjures images he might not have fully intended. The description Nozick rolls out more closely resembles 10th century European feudal structure than what you might have anticipated from a political philosophy that purports to advance a radical individual freedom. Nozick's utopian layout depends almost entirely on voluntary compliance with a hierarchical model of society. While we can suspect that this is not what Nozick intends, it's difficult to avoid the conclusion that the organic model favored by conservatives fails almost at once. What we are left with here in Nozick's sketch is a struggle for supremacy with no arbitrator of last resort.[v] Nozick apparently thinks that the avoidance of war-of-all-against-all is apparently possible by a system of ethics that would need to be voluntarily accepted by all. The difficulty of this "voluntaryism"[34] and "need" is that in real-time, the actual history of libertarian society did not seem to work out very well. Let us travel back to the late 19th century to the days of the wild, wild west.

We all have some idea as to who the outlaw "Billy the Kid" was (i.e., William H. Bonney, or Henry McCarty, born 1859, died 1881). I mention the famous outlaw's name only to jog memories. Without the popular image of William Bonney, much of the Lincoln County War in the New Mexico Territory (1878-1881)[35] and its relevance to libertarianism, would be lost to us. As a backup to our discussion, we might also look to the Powder River War (*aka*, Johnson County War—1889-1893),[36] that took place in the Wyoming Territories just before the turn of the 20th century.

---

v. A single law appears to be all Nozick seems to suggest, a law that serves to enforce contracts. The question of how the "enforcers" are paid, organized and directed is left rather vague. It should be obvious that both the nature of the enforcers and their "handlers" are critical issues that create huge stumbling blocks on the way to utopia.

What is memorable to us in both of these contentious situations is the lack of any immediate, official authority. In both cases, in the absence of governmental authority a fierce and bloody struggle erupted between two competing elements, a competition over scarce resources and assets. In both cases, given the lack of any governmental arbitrators in these territories, all parties to the disputes were free to manufacture their own laws and hire their own lawmen (police). This led to the "wars" where during the ensuing years a long and violent struggle finally forced US military intervention: In Lincoln County the violence was interrupted by an army detachment commanded by Col. Nathan Dudley and in Wyoming by an army unit directly ordered by President Benjamin Harrison. These military interventions quickly halted the bloodshed, though the issues that prompted the conflict simmered for quite some time.

Given the actual history of the events, it is exceedingly difficult to see these two examples of libertarian conditions in a positive light. In the absence of any means of arbitration and compliance the situation quickly deteriorated into classic class warfare.[37] There are multiple histories of each of these events,[38] and even a perusal of the factual evidence shows that there were clearly two sides to the warfare, sides easily described by both their relation to wealth and their relation to the production of wealth. In both the Johnson and Lincoln County cases the two sides are shown to represent (1) the producers of wealth from open range cattle herding and (2) those wishing to control the direction and flow of wealth. Given theories outlined by Nozick, together with actual events that play out in real-time, it is hard to see how such an arrangement as libertarianism does not sharply deviate from the organic model and end (usually by violence) by supporting the hierarchical pyramid model. Further is it not clear how right wing anarchy (libertarianism) does not ultimately degenerate into chaos and a violent scuffle over the control of resources and production.

The fact that libertarian theory has been twice shown to be a failure in real-time needn't debunk the theory completely. "Real-time" has a habit of molding and shaping theoretical sentiments to suit actual, material conditions. As I suggested above, the right-wing model ultimately finds itself dancing between the two extremes. We, in western style democracies, tend to hear more libertarian ideals than fascist ones, yet as the quote from JFK demonstrates, the fascist idea of the primacy of the state is not altogether zeroed-out in public sentiment. This makes perfect sense in a top down social order hiding behind a mystical curtain of ideals.

Conclusion

We began with the question, "Thinking in terms of ideals, what exactly would the proto-typical right-wing society look like?" First, it must be pointed out that the ideals and the ideal image are very much alive and kicking, as we have demonstrated. We cannot dismiss these ideals entirely as a pie-in-the-sky ruse or ancient mythology. Today, these right-wing ideals very seriously motivate millions of people. Second, we need to take these ideals at face value, even if at the same time we realize that material and historical evidence suggests that any actual realization of these ideals has a very big hill to climb to become a practical reality.

We also ought to sum-up by restating our observation that while there is no exact standard, two right-wing archetypes do occupy opposite outlying positions. As related above, those two archetypes would be the fascist and libertarian ideals, both best presented in terms of the organic model. The fascist prefers the term "corporate" rather than organic, but the difference is largely semantic. Even so, both of the terms are intended to offer a gloss, a dress-up to enhance the desirability of the two political systems. It is said with great accuracy that in politics appearance is everything, an elemental reality that both the Right and the Left knows full well.

So, regarding appearance it would seem that only the organic model avoids the look and feel of Jack London's "iron heel" suggested by the top-down hierarchal model. Given the visual impression offered by the pyramid image, it's difficult to hide the overwhelming optics of inequality, oppression and control by the powerfully placed—optics the Right dearly wishes to sidestep. Unfortunately, the model that accomplishes this side-step best—the organic model—when superimposed on either the real-time libertarian or the fascist experiences, has been shown by historical experience to have failed to realize its promise. What does this mean for the ideal model(s)? First, it is apparent that there is a lack of coherence between the two models. Both the optics, for example, of Franco's Spain and the real-time events offered by the run-up to the Lincoln County War

offer far different impressions of the "ideal." Simple attempts at integration between the two archetypes prove impossible.[39] The actual fascist
state is marked by top-down control, cemented in place by a totalitarian
control that appears paramilitary in its execution. This is the actuality
of fascism, one that is opposed to both the ideal and the real historical
libertarian experience. Even theoretically, the fascist organic or corporate
model looks vastly different from the theoretical, libertarian model constructed by Robert Nozcik. Therefore, it is extremely difficult to see how
an enforceable, fascist corporate model could realistically be imposed on
the kind of quasi-feudal social structure concocted by Nozcik's extensive
work.[40] Integration of the two is impossible.

The only safe conclusion seems to be that there is no universal "ideal
state" for the Right, at least not one that attracts or can integrate both
extreme poles.[vi] But why is this so? What's the central hold up? It all
boils down to the right-wing image of human nature. This stumbling block
emerges with the touting of a human nature that rests on instinctual drives
that move people to extreme villainous behavior. This image leaves little
to offer a social order striving for equality, fraternity and liberty—in other
words, it affords little to a society basing itself on widespread democratic
values. This negative image of human nature severely limits either the
practical or theoretical possibilities for the Right. About the best that
the Right can do in arguing for the preservation of the status quo is to
advance political solutions that in part operate to counter the unfavorable
image of humanity.

The split in the theoretical ideals presented by the right (i.e., fascism
as contrasted with libertarianism) make impossible an amalgamation of
an exemplary social design. As pointed out above, the two ideals are simply too far apart. But this problem is not without a partially adequate, if
temporary solution. The existence of both ideals allow for the possibility
of one to provide cover for the other. As an example, let us begin by tack-
ling an obvious problem: The Right has always struggled with the idea

---

vi. In all fairness's, it should be pointed out that the same problem plagues
the Left. And while there is no two extreme positions, as there is in the Right, the
only safe conclusion is that ideological thinking, by its very nature, precludes
concrete expression.

of class, an image which the hierarchical optics of the pyramidal format supports. Economic and social class imply a structural foundation geared up for opposition and conflict rather than compliance and cooperation. The elimination of "class," so the thinking goes, will serve to ameliorate social conflict. In contemporary political science various theories of pluralism serve to move the focus away from class and onto the organism as a whole. Pluralist theory claims that political power is not concentrated, but spread throughout the social order and is based on numerous factors such as status, religious affiliation, education, etc.[41] According to the theory, there is no single, primary source of either social friction or political power. Obviously, pluralist theory is not without its critics, the same critics who disparage the organic model.[42] Regardless of whether pluralist theory is true, or an attempt at window dressing, the effort demonstrates the desire on the part of the Right to avoid conflict models in favor or accommodation models. This is the major problem with pluralism. It has often been pointed out that to achieve theoretical accommodation pluralism ignores both inequality as a source of friction and conflict and the groupings that activate the friction.[43] If the actual root cause (i.e., class) cannot be exorcised, then the window dressing is adapted to counter the energy for change. That the optics of the pluralist dressing is arguably some variation of the organic model seems indisputable.

To illustrate, and again point out the classic example of this type of cover image, take JFK's "Ask not . . ." speech. This single plea to sacrifice for the nation fully announces and promotes the primacy of the state. But again, we must ask, whose state are we talking about? It must be noted that the state summoned by JFK's speech is a state dominated by the top tier, or 1% as it is often dubbed. By the way, it is in no way snide to point out the obvious—that this is the same 1% from which JFK and family emerged. All this is hidden beneath the guise of the organic model served up with a dose of pluralism and patriotism to seal the deal.

At the end of the day, optics and political imagery aside, it is difficult to come to any other conclusion than what lies behind the right-wing ideal is a top down, authoritarian structure. This image is presented, of course, with the understanding that the contrasting image of the organic model be adopted to soften the sharper edges of the image. We have demonstrated the theory of libertarian society, when acted out in real-time, is shown to be a failure—an actual historical failure and not a hypothetical one. However, this does little to tarnish the theory as a cover story for the reality of a top-down status quo. The closer the social order moves toward absolute authoritarianism, the more libertarian—rather than fascist—talking points and canards are thrown at the rather grim optics. The ideal right-wing society, in real-time, is locked into a top-down, hieratical pyramid, with libertarianism adopted as more of an apology than a competing system. All of this starting with a decidedly dim view of human nature, a dim view that eventually shatters the fanciful and ideal social image of the Right, in favor of a harsher reality, that is, authoritarian rule with mitigating optics.

Notes

1. The idea of a "human nature" is itself a contentious one: Do human beings have an inbred nature at all? While recognizing the contentiousness, I will none the less use the term mostly for its familiarity.

2. Sigmund Freud, Found in *Nature of Man*, Ed. Eric Fromm, MacMillan Co. New York, 1968. p. 240/241

3. Thomas Hobbes, *Leviathan*, vol. ed by J.C.A. Gaskin, (Oxford University Press, Oxford) 1996; P. 35 (Ch. VI, §7)

4 Ashley Montagu, as quoted by Steven Pinker, *The Blank Slate*, Viking Press, New York, 2002, p. 24

5. Niccollo Machiavelli, *History of Florence*, Harper Torchbooks, Harper and Row, New York, 1966, p. 129

6. Leo Strauss, *"Thoughts on Machiavelli,"* University of Washington Press, Seattle, 1958, p 189, and to see the more materialist side of Machiavelli, see his "Discourses," I, 17 (142); 18. (146); III, 28 cf I, 24.

7. Leo Strauss, ibid, p. 249

8. Hayden, Brian, *Pathways to Power. Principles for Creating Socioeconomic Inequalities. Foundations of Social Inequality*, T.D. Price and G.M. Feinman (eds), pp. 15-86 New York, Plenum Press, 1995.

9. Bogucki, Peter, *The Origins Of Human Society*, (Blackwell Publishers, Malden, MA 1999) p. 262

10. John Locke, *The 2nd Treatise of Government*, (ch II, §13)

11. Thomas Hobbes, *Leviathan*, ed by J.C.A. Gaskin, (Oxford University Press, Oxford)1996, p, 66

12. Engles, Fredrick, Letter to Franz Mehrings (July 14, 1898) Found In *Marx—Engles Reader*, ed. Robert Tucker, New York, W.W. Norton, 1972, pp. 648-649

13. Moser, Muler & Trout, *The Theory of Knowledge*, (Oxford University Press, New York, 1998)

14. Obviously, Hegel's work can be cited here as right wing dialectics. However given the extreme difficulty of Hegel's phenomenology, and the fact that his work has largely faded away, except as the progenitor of the later Marxist dialectics, I will merely mention in passing that Hegel's influence has largely fallen out of favor. However, Hegel does remind us that philosophy (i.e., reason) can be employed to underwrite right-wing ideology. The fact that reason is not more often employed in this context rests with the difficulty in handling esoteric and cabalistic notions in an era of materialism and science.

15. Ingersoll, D, Matthews, R, & Davidson, A., *The Philosophic Roots of Modern Ideology*, Prentice, Hall, New Jersey, 2001, p.43.

16. For a detailed examination of Pareto and his studies on residues (i.e., "residues" being his word for ideology) and the circulation of elites see McLellan, David, *Ideology*, University of Minnesota Press, Minneapolis, MI 1986 p 40-44

17. One example of this absurdity and the root of the myopic cul 'd sac is found in a statement by Nelson Rockefeller, at the time one of the richest men in the world. In addressing a collection of wealthy donors, Rockefeller claimed, in all sincerity, "that the tax burden falls equally on the average Joe—people just like you and me." (Sophy Burnham, "Why The Rich Don't Care", *The Washington Monthly*, vol 10, #2, April, 1978, p. 11)

18. Alejandro Portes, *Economic Sociology, A Systematic Inquiry*, (Princeton University Press, Princeton, 2010) p, 79

19. For the orthodox Marxist perspective, see: Marx, Karl, *Capital, Vol 1*, New York, (Vintage Books, 1977) p. 344

20. See "Fascism and Race," Ingersol, *The Philosophical. Roots of Ideology*, ibid, pp. 227-28

21. From Herman Finer, *Mussolini's Italy* (New York, Grosset & Dunlap, 1965) p. 502

22. See Sternhell, Zeev, "Fascist Ideology," from *Fascism, a Reader's Guide*, ed by Walter Laqueur. University of California Press, Berkeley, 1976 p. 357

23. Libertarianism is frequently identified as "right-wing anarchism." This title (anarchism) is only negative until one realizes that "anarchy" does not correspond to chaos, but to an actual political theory, and one not at all violent.

24. Mussolini, Benito, "The Doctrine of Fascism," found in *Social and Political Philosophy*, Somerville and Santoini, editors, Doubleday and Company, Garden City, NY, 1963. P. 44

25. David Boaz, *Libertarianism: A Primer* (The Free Press, New York, 1997), p.2

26. Steven Maloney, //whatisbeingblogspot.com/2006/01/my-problem-with-libertarianism.html

27. Sternhell, Zeev, "Fascist Ideology", from *Fascism, a Reader's Guide*, ed by Walter Laqueur, University of California Press, Berkeley, CA, 1976; p. 345

28. Burke, Edmund, as quoted by Ingersoll, D, Matthews, R, & Davidson, A., *The Philosophic Roots of Modern Ideology*, Prentice, Hall, New Jersey, 2001, p.43.

29. Sternhell, Zeev, ibid, p. 354

30. One might argue, however, that this is the same approach as taken by Plato in the *Crito*. This is where Plato famously pushes back against escaping

his fated execution for treason by declaring the primacy of the state over the individual.

31. Burke, Edmund, *Reflections on the Revolution in France*, ed. O'Brien, C.C. Penguine, Baltimore, 1969, p.28

32. I refer here to Plato's and More's classic works, *The Republic* and *Utopia*, respectively

33. Robert, Nozick, *Anarchy, State and Utopia*, Basic Books; First Edition (November 17, 1974)

34. Hebert, Auberon, *The Right and Wrong of Compulsion by the State and Other Essays*, Liberty Classics (New York, 1978). Hebert was an early (19th century) promoter of libertarianism and the originator of a theory of social compliance as resting on something he called "voluntaryism." In the end, voluntaryism had no secondary material causation other than force; a contradiction that was ether unseen by Herbert, or ignored by him.

35. Fulton, Maurice, *History of the Lincoln County War* , University of Arizona Press; 1st Edition (March 1, 1980)

36. Davis, John W. *Wyoming Range War*. Norman: University of Oklahoma Press, 2010.

37. See, Mercer, Asa, *The Banditti of the Range*, Independently published (September 15, 2017)

38. For example, see, *High Noon in Lincoln: Violence on the Western Frontier*, by Robert Utley, University of New Mexico Press (February 1, 1990), and *Wyoming Range War: The Infamous Invasion of Johnson County*, by John W. Davis, University of Oklahoma Press; Reprint edition (August 1, 2012)

39. The attempts that are made tend toward a kind of evolutionism, which suggests that fascism is a precursor to libertarianism. I know this sounds awkward—radical individualism being the end product of a totalitarian state, but there are multiple attempts to put forward exactly this type of position. For example, see: https://radicalcapitalist.org/2018/04/10/fascism-is-a-step-towards-liberty/

40. See Robert, Nozick, *Anarchy, State and Utopia*, Basic Books; First Edition edition (November 17, 1974)

41. David McLennan, *Ideology*, University of Minnesota Press, Minneapolis, MI, 1986 p. 59

42. Greenberg, Edward, *Serving the Few: Corporate Capitalism and the Basis of Government Policy*, John Wiley and Sons, New York, 1974, see pp. 239,240

43. Robert Paul Wolff, "Beyond Tolerance," in Wolff, Moore, and Marcuse, *A Critique of Pure Toleration*, Beacon Press, Boston, 1965, pp. 43-45

TERROR AND TORTURE

The Philosophy and Ethics
of Asymmetric War

ANTOINETTE BERGSON

Abstract: Can torture ever be justified? This article by Antoinette Bergson attempts to answer that question without resorting to the much overused "ticking bomb" scenario. Instead, the article takes both a moral and ethical approach to uncover a new landscape in this contemporary world so much shaped by terrorism. This paper argues that the terrorist reshapes and fashions the ethical landscape in such a way that he invites and exonerates the practice of torture; this is to say that the terrorist voluntarily steps outside the boundaries of humanity; the doing so leaves behind the moral and ethical world developed along lines of humanistic principles designed to reduce torture as an interrogation technique. Be advised, this article stakes out a moral and ethical position, and not one relying on practicality, as is typically the case in discussions of torture.

Historically, torture has been put to many uses, most of them completely unjustified and for reasons as corrupt and scattered as they were vague and irrational. However, in today's world torture has claimed higher ground by dint of a narrower focus. Today, torture is primarily associated with the "war on terror."

Very little has been written adopting the approach taken by this study, *viz.*, to analyze the link between terror and torture to uncover any *necessary* connection. To do this we will explore a specific question: in some little understood way does terror reflexively and ethically condone torture? As this is a highly charged issue, I will be systematic in a way that might seem overly detailed and redundant. However, the detail is less about loquaciousness than it is about offering alternative perspectives.

In addition, this paper considers only contemporary associations. That is, torture will only be discussed as part of its relationship with terrorism. Torture to extract confessions, gain a recant of thought or action, or a forced implication of others, etc., are not part of the current discussion. The position explored here is intended to be very specific, and therefore whatever ethical questions arise regarding torture as related to terrorism, can only be understood within a certain context. In this case a context of *asymmetry*—asymmetric because of torture's association with an anti-terrorist campaign. So, first to understand terror it is crucial that we fully understand the concept of asymmetric war.

Further, there is a dynamic link between terror and torture that must be carefully analyzed before any ethical conclusions can be drawn regarding the use of torture—or in today's sanitized terms, "enhanced interrogation." Such an examination of this relationship between terror and torture will lead us to an uneasy conclusion concerning ethics, a result that is not at all apparent at first glance. Before we can look deeper, the controversial position taken by this paper demands accurate and practical definitions.

TERROR

Terror and the moral universe. All terror is not alike. First, it must be stated that the tactics terrorism employs are as varied as the personalities behind the attacks. In addition, it cannot be stated forcefully enough that terrorism is not a political doctrine, a political theory or an ideology.

It is a huge mistake to offer terrorism this kind of coherency. Terror is *not* a strategy for any systematic or comprehensive political change, for revolution, nation building, or a coup d'état. Terror, as such, has no end-game. Terror is a tool, a tactic. Terror is a *means,* not an end. Understand this and you can begin to understand the reason that so many different political persuasions can use terror in the pursuit of their policies. The fascist can use terror, and so can the left-wing anarchist. The imperialist can use terror, and so can the guerrilla insurgent. This raises a question: is it possible to discuss the ethical implications of terror without referring to either the strategic intent or the political ends for which terror can be employed? In other words, can we discuss the means separately from the ends? The answer is emphatically yes. If we are to uncover any ethical conditions endemic to the tool, the ends must be excluded.

Terror, as a tool, has no automatic and necessary relationship to a fixed end. This is not to say that terror has no impact, but rather that the aim and direction of that impact are extraneous to the tool. Terror can be analyzed as an action, a deed, separate from any desired ends. Consider, for a moment, a truck. Whether the truck is driving east or west, or whether the driver is a communist or a fascist, has no immediate meaning for the truck itself. This paper will take the point of view that the best way to understand the ethical relationship between terror and torture is to grasp the *ethical conditions* established by the tactic of terror, *per se*, that is, when terror is used as a means, used as a tool, independent of an end.

In one way or another—like it or not—actions always reflect the thinking and moral values at work behind the deed, again independent of the ends. It is very difficult to claim that the ends do not justify the means when there is no objective schism between the goal and the tactics. The means of terror generate such blind rage and confusion that the goal often vanishes into the tactic. The twin towers were attacked on 9/11, but how many of us can state the goals of the hijackers? At best, those goals were obscure; as in most terror, the means had become indistinguishable from the ends. The relationship between means and ends is an ever-evolving dialectical relationship. It is difficult to imagine that the *means,* do not eventually shift the way in which we conceive of ethical considerations, or simply put, questions of right and wrong. This ethical shift does not mean that one's moral standards are thrown up for grabs, or go out the window, or that those standards are merely a condition of the actor's sense of right and wrong. Rather, the old standards must be adjusted to meet the demands of the new conditions brought about by *tactical* considerations. Let me assure you that this is not a relativist position as the following example will illustrate. Consider the arrival of a new tool on the modern battlefield: the machine gun. This new, mechanized development caused the old standard of taking on an enemy combatant as an equal to become a ghost of the past. The machine gun greatly unbalanced the conflict, or to use the contemporary parlance, brought asymmetry into the conflict. The asymmetry demanded ethical redress. So, what is this asymmetrical pressure that insists on a reset of ethical standards?

a. Asymmetric warfare. This is a phrase that will be used and alluded to throughout this paper. So, what does it mean? How must we define asymmetric warfare? In a phrase, what makes warfare asymmetric is a lack of balance. The primary goal of the weaker opponent is to address his own weakness (lack of balance) through attempts to exploit and undermine one or more characteristic weaknesses of an opponent: it is weakness exploiting weakness. Asymmetric war is the attempt to exercise weakness to overcome strength. Find a characteristic weakness of the stronger opponent and exploit that characteristic weakness.

The key word above is "characteristic"—that is, a characteristic feature endemic to one or more of the elements defining the stronger opponent's structural model. For example, most governments, especially totalitarian ones, feature a characteristically strong police presence. A strong police presence typically provides both security and oppression, often justifying the later by providing the former. The two, security and oppression—characteristics of totalitarian regimes—suggest enough of a contradiction to present the opportunity for exploiting a weakness –in this case the paradox of security vs oppression. This can be done by presenting the police with problems they will fail to solve or cope with. Typically, the totalitarian regime will lash out with oppressive measures while accomplishing little in the way of security. This serves to cripple the image of the all-powerful state, while at the same time bringing brutal oppression to the native population. Random violence is a simple way to do this.

The very act of random violence will demonstrate that state police are unable to provide for general security. This failing will quickly drain the claim of police to be the guardians of public safety. Consequently, random violence will undermine fear of the police as an agency of oppression while at the same time weaken the perception of the government as a benign institution providing security. Consider how our view of government has changed as police become increasingly paramilitary, as our prison population explodes, as air-marshals put police everywhere, even in the next seat, etc. Yet, despite all the policing, safety eludes developed society: mass shootings go on unabated, random explosions occur in public places, planes are delayed because of unruly and violent passengers . . . positive views of government erode as government appears helpless to contain the chaos.

Unanticipated material developments in the art of killing clearly mutilated any sense of symmetry and thus affected the ethical context and conditions of the battlefield—and society. Between equal combatants, the ethical conditions can appear to be the same regarding the goal: killing the enemy. Often, there is a certain symmetry at the start. Asymmetry is achieved by exploiting a lack of balance in material conditions.

Developing conditions mentioned above: In WWI, the wide use of entangling wire, coupled with the introduction of the machine gun, unbalanced the conditions and destroyed the predictability of combat. This reconfigured ethical norms. Machine gun crews now feared for their lives in a new way. On capture, machine gun crews were viewed as little better than mass murderers, and they were very often bayonetted on the spot (bayonetting was considered to be a more painful and gruesome death). Note that the old ethical standards were not lost, but were adjusted to meet the challenge of asymmetry introduced into in warfare's material conditions. The introduction of a new tool of war did not cause the old standards to disappear, but rather, it unbalanced and mutated them in a way that brought forth a new set of ethical conditions. Revenge by bayonet became the remedy. Asymmetry demands its anthesis. New ethical considerations will arise to atone for the lack of balance and symmetry. It is not much of a stretch to say that asymmetry in and of itself provokes a need for rectification, especially in life and death situations. The ethical universe of the soldier had shifted under the weight of newly developed tools for his destruction. But while the conventional battlefield can be used to demonstrate asymmetry, it is hardly the place to illustrate terror or terrorism. Terror combines asymmetry with secrecy.

Like the machine gun, the tools of terror, in-and-of-themselves, possess no more ethical predisposition than a hammer or a fork-lift. Thinking

191

coolly and rationally—and objectively—terror is merely one of the tools used in conflict. However, terror, when taking the form of an asymmetrical tool of conflict, projects *asymmetrical ethical conditions* that are influential in the development of responses—often responses desperately reached for by governments to remedy the asymmetry. These would include martial law, suspension of *habeas corpus*, or torture, etc. Exactly how these asymmetrical ethical conditions arise to produce torture as a consequence is our focus.

Now consider terror more closely. Terror as a tool of conflict is designed to destabilize a populace and compel a government to respond in asymmetrical ways. The tool of terror is a psychological assault on the social and political security of a defined group. This assault is designed to compel the established order to behave in ways not completely of its own choosing. The ambitions of terror have been analyzed elsewhere at great length.[1] Terror, as examined here, is discussed as a *means*, a *tool* to achieve certain goals. This tool of terror is wholly dependent on secrecy and stealth, which gives terrorist violence a façade of randomness, at least to the victims. Secrecy and apparent randomness are the defining characteristics of terror. Secrecy and a seeming randomness create the appearance of arbitrary conditions—conditions that generate fear and widespread frustration. Note the similarity between terror and the introduction of the machine gun. It was the appearance of a random condition brought about by the machine gun that so frustrated and enraged infantry soldiers.[2] The WWI victim of the machine gun felt waylaid—unfairly and randomly ambushed by a soulless and unethical creature that lay in wait.

The appearance of randomness lies at the dark heart of terrorism and cannot lay claim to steady moral principles. But randomness, which terror has raised to an art form, can generate asymmetrical ethical conditions that greatly impact an entire moral universe. This means that a seemingly random act of terror directly provokes questions of right and wrong and thereby brings our capacity to judge good and bad into question. Morality, in this case, becomes a variable dependent on ethics rather than the other way around, as is the usual perspective.

b. Ethics: The above suggests that in order to make analytical sense of the tool of terror, a distinction needs to be drawn between morality and ethics. Quite simply, ethics represent a code of conduct that has its roots in a culture's moral principles. It is not too much of a stretch to say that ethics is cultural morality in action. Ethics involves the code we choose to put our moral principles into action. We might say that ethics is the study of the rightness, or appropriateness of a deed, while morality, as such, is the consideration of the "goodness" at work behind the deed.[3] For the sake of ethics, a moral principle must be clearly seen as a factor within the result of the deed. The ethic conceptually links the moral principle with the deed. Or in other words, ethics is the study of a choosing of actions, but in a *needful* relationship with the morality of a preestablished rule or principle. At the risk of whipping a dead horse, another way to grasp this relationship is to say that morality is the provider of ends, while ethics is the strategy of means. However, the relationship is dialectic, and they can only be *fully* understood separately as they appear in a dialogue with each other.

At this point an example will be helpful. The ends: It is *immoral* to lie. The means: Jill's *ethics* forbid her from lying. Jill did not lie. Jill's ethics act out the moral principle that lying is not good, with the result that Jill does not lie. Because ethics is the action, or means, the moral principle, although *a priori*, is revealed in the ends of the action (i.e., Jill did not lie). The ethics of the deed, as the fulfillment of a moral principle, is only fully comprehensible as it is revealed in relation to that principle. To merely state that Jill did not lie reveals the means, but nothing regarding her actions vis-à-vis intent or motivation—it is immoral to lie. The statement that "Jill did not lie" alone explains nothing about the morality behind the ethics. That explanation is revealed only by the relationship between the two.

I am making a big deal out of the relationship of ethics to morality for the following reason: Unless we are to argue for a metaphysically fixed set of moral principles that show little attachment for the real world, we must recognize that this dialogue between means and ends is a metamorphic process that takes place within a living context. Ethics is the translation of a culture's morality into concrete action within a living world. This living context is a fluid development guided by larger social and historical considerations. In other words, moral principles are a pointless headgame unless they are acted out ethically in a real-world scenario, which means that a real moral universe must bear a real time relationship to earthly reality. Ethics must therefore be seen be as contextual in the face of changing circumstances. Thus, ethical vision can sometimes expose a weakness, or sometimes provoke a revaluation of the moral principle the ethic is based upon. It is certainly possible for one to argue for a universal set of moral principles,[4] but it must be conceded that ethical conditions (i.e., the boundaries governing the actualization of the moral ends) must accommodate reality in the implementation of those principles. However, the changes necessary for implementation are often beyond the reach of human action. These shortcomings appear most obvious in medical cases where the high moral standards of the preservation of life and health are routinely beyond current human capabilities. Human calculation, as it addresses circumstance, often factors out the changes necessary to achieve some approximation of fixed moral standards. An event such as the fire bombing of the German city, Dresden, an ethical *cause célèbres* of WWII, epitomizes such a human calculation that sends existing moral standards into a tailspin. There is no way around this reality. Any change in the means, which is to say a change in the ethical conditions, must necessarily impact, and sometimes overwhelm, the ends—that is, the moral universe it purports to actualize.

c. Ends justifying the means. For clarity on this take an example from history: To ready a nation for war, for a life and death struggle that will determine the fate of an entire nation, any means necessary to acquire that end appears to overwhelm other moral principles. This was at least part of the reasoning underlying the approach taken by Joseph Stalin when confronted by Nazi Germany in the 1930s. The single mindedness and ruthlessness of Stalin's frequently cruel methods in this regard are well known. Such an approach is sometimes reported to be an example of the "ends justifying the means." This platitude that questions the ends as justification is not an altogether irrelevant point, but more aptly we can see it as an inaccurate perspective. It is more precise to assert that ends as justification, are, in many realities, *extraneous* to ethical action. From a moral point of view, as opposed to ethical, it is better to argue that the underlying weakness of this argument, as exampled by Stalin, raises the question of whether or not the survival of a particular nation state (or any nation state), as an end, has any "moral" standing whatsoever. This brings to light the dynamic of a hidden moral question and its relevance to existing conditions. As a universal moral principle, the survival of the nation state is circumstantially questionable; the moral universe in which the viability of the nation state is a "good" can be said to be more historical than universal. Such an example illustrates the uncertain and sometimes enigmatic nature of the dialectic between the moral universe and the unpredictability of possible ethical conditions.

Let me clarify the meaning of stable dialectic by offering an instance more universal in its strength of dialogue. When the "ends" for a soldier on a battlefield are the survival of himself and his comrades, then the "means," i.e., killing enemy soldiers, is understood as ethically justified. In the moral universe of war, it is ethically appropriate for a soldier in battle to seek survival, which often means killing the enemy. The moral claims of individual and group survival are not questioned in this circumstance; battlefield conditions make for a vigorous means-ends connection that justifies the means by any realistic line of reasoning. Ordinarily, of course, the taking of a human life, as a fixed principle, is morally reprehensible; but given the material realities on the battlefield that alter conditions radically enough to create new ethical conditions, the fixed moral universal is interrupted, arrested, and deferred. Any question of murder is extraneous to this moral universe of war. The interruption of moral principles here is not only supported by the conditions, but more to the point, the ethical conditions also reshape a consideration of the fixed moral ends. This example illustrates what I have been laboring to present: that preestablished moral notions of good and bad may be immensely satisfying, but in reality, are often ethically impossible to translate into action without stepping beyond that preestablished moral universe.

Thinking that ends (moral principles) are fixed and dominant in the dialogue with means (ethical action) is unsustainable. The reciprocity observed in the above battlefield illustrations demonstrates the kind of balanced dialogue that must exist between moral principles (ends) and ethical action (means) for any sustained sense of symmetry. I will add that if either is dominant, it would be the ethical conditions that command the reevaluation of the practical side of the moral coin. This is because the material world will always trump the metaphysical world.

d. Ethical Conditions—Terror and Torture: In a very general way, and regarding torture, changing ethical conditions are what bring revision to the playing field of morality. This is another way of saying that changing ethical conditions can insist on a reconsideration of the right and wrong of torture. Mutable ethical conditions, if I may repeat, are the result of morally driven actions as they are massaged by social context and historical circumstance. However, ethical conditions do not merely create a dialogue between action and circumstance; changing ethical conditions result in the development of new circumstances that provoke new moral considerations. Within that scope, ethical conditions are an ongoing and continually developing set of moral relationships between the ends of action and the kind of day-to-day reality with which we deal. In our contemporary world, these types of relationships obviously pertain to both terror and torture.

To the point: the relationship between terror and torture serves to define the *strategic,* ethical correctness—as opposed to moral correct-ness—of the actual deed. The strategic, ethical correctness of either terror *or* torture, with reference to the goal of the action, must always be understood and analyzed within the current social context. This is no chicken and egg question regarding terror and torture. Clearly, ethical conditions are circumstantially generated by the terrorist. This is to say that the circumstances established by the terrorist generate the condi-tioned ethical response. Morality cannot be ignored. However, while any pre-established and fixed system of moral intention has a role to play, of course, that fixed moral system ultimately must adjust to fast changing ethical circumstances (recall the introduction of the machine gun). In turn, the ethical conditions, as a part of that sequence of circumstance, cannot stand on fixed moral principles. Ethics must become an elastic mode of reaction that drives reaction as it responds to a dialogue with the goal—in this case, combating terror.

If I seem to be harping on this distinction between means and ends, it is because of the analytical advantage gained from separating a moral principle from the circumstantial difficulties in acting out that morality with principles of fixed ethical actions. This should be readily apparent. Such a situation would be found where there is a conflict of fixed prin-ciples. Take, for example, Kant's famous pronouncements on the moral duty to always tell the truth even if that duty collides with the murderer standing at the door and demanding to know if his intended victim resides at this address.[5] This is not such a fanciful scenario when you consider the Nazi Gestapo standing at the door of a boarding house demanding to know if there are any Jews inside. What is one to do in these cases? If you cannot slip out of an outright lie about the whereabouts of the intended victims, then there is a clear-cut conflict of moral ends—to lie or abet the murder of an innocent. It is all well and good to say telling a lie is a universal moral negative, until circumstances present this fixed principle with a conflicting moral principle—in this case, saving the life of another person. What irrevocable rule can dictate which of the moral principles should be chosen and acted upon? Kant himself attempts to weasel out of the moral dilemma by advocating subterfuge and misdirection (i.e., avoid answering the Gestapo's questions: instead of a direct answer, report to the Nazi inquirer that there might be Jews on the next block). The weaknesses in such a response are obvious, and it is just as obvious that there is no universal rule to resolve the antagonism.

Applying any hard and fast prescription to the special circumstances of torture is even more complicated. First, note that even extreme conditions do not imply any "ethics of torture" (or terror). Extreme conditions only lend criterion to a wounded social atmosphere that makes torture one type of possibility. [Think of the extreme conditions immediately aroused by the fall of the Twin Towers]. This is an aroused circumstance not easily dismissed as illegal or personally offensive. Such an aroused social atmosphere that allows for the possibility of torture represents a new criterion that develops into actual responses, responses that are more or less predicable and inevitable. That to make clear the relationship between the ethical conditions and the predictable responses an illustration will be helpful.

Let us again sketch a picture of a soldier (let's say this time from WWII) and look at what happens when he puts on a uniform to go out onto the battlefield. What are the ethical conditions that the soldier has set in motion? First, his action has allowed for the possibility of his death or physical injury. The high probability of death or injury is an unavoidable condition of the role the soldier has elected to play. In a manner of speaking, we might say that this is part of his job description. Then too, if the conditions he set in motion cause the death of an enemy soldier, this too can be thought of as a predictable response to the situation given the existing ethical conditions. If our World War II soldier is killed by an enemy soldier, his death must also be considered one of the predictable (i.e., symmetrical) responses given the ethical conditions our soldier has set in motion by his participation. "Thou shall not kill" is a moral precept that is awkwardly out of place on a battlefield. I think it is entirely fair to say that applying the terms right and wrong (and certainly good and bad), in the ethical sense of bringing harm to another, seems utterly misplaced in these circumstances.

None of this should puzzle the soldier. The professional soldier exists in an alternate moral universe, a universe that exists symbiotically through an ethical relationship with the material conditions of the battlefield. Any soldier at any time in history will have an intuitive grasp of these material conditions, as well as the impact of their ethical conditions on moral systems. The circumstances that he sets in motion have brought him to a point where the enemy that he has been sent to kill will try to kill him first. This is a predictable and inevitable response on the part of the "enemy." Further, to say that the enemy's response is a predictable and inevitable reaction sets it beyond the pale of moral judgments concerning good and evil. In a consideration of right and wrong it is clearly "right" that the enemy kill our soldier, while the question, "is it good that he kills our soldier?" seems irrelevant to the circumstances; it is right, but not necessarily good. Given the ethical conditions established by our soldier the word *correct*, or *right response*, seems more fitting in this case than "good." The bottom line here is that by his actions, the WWII soldier has willingly generated a set of *ethical* conditions, together with a predictable response, that are beyond the *moral* scope of good and evil.[6]

We can see that gathering "ethical conditions" places morality within a wider constellation of events and thus places greater circumstantial pressure on moral questions. The moral end of defeating the enemy and the ethical means of getting there are related, although they do not govern the immediate circumstances of the ethical conditions. The means of ethics by themselves must be in symbiotic (if not sympathetic) contact with the moral ends. However, as the illustration with the WWII soldier demonstrates, ethics cannot be governed to any great extent by abstract morality; this runs against the objective grain, for we instinctively grasp the extended implications. Again, an illustration will be helpful. The ethical conditions on a battlefield allow our soldier to kill with a gun, knife, or even a rock, but all things being equal, and for what should be obvious reasons, most of us would say that to kill with a gun is preferably humane to using a rock. Unfortunately, whether to kill with a gun or a rock is a circumstantial question of ethical means and stands far outside any larger moral consideration of killing, *per se*. Morality is present, but only in the very marginally capacity of minimizing pain and psychological duress

198

which softens the emotional difficulty of carrying out an act of violence. In this case, and many cases like it, ethical conditions typically render questions of morality merely academic. Material reality very often acts as a speed bump on the way to a *good* outcome.

Once the soldier has established and entered a dialogue with ethical conditions, conditions that exist beyond the usual boundaries of right and wrong, then why not the terrorist—does the terrorist not fall under the same material conditions as the soldier? Has not the terrorist generated a specific means that also establishes ethical conditions that have considerable bearing on subsequent moral questions? Unless conscripted, the soldier has freely chosen to step into a situation where the morality of everyday life becomes suspended in favor of a more fitting set of ethical conditions with often uncomfortable moral ends. Once the means are chosen, the ends follow as part of the package deal. The soldier has chosen and consented to the repercussions. Similarly, the terrorist has chosen and consented to all the possible consequence that might likely follow. It must be emphasized, however, that terrorism is different from a soldier's war and the conditions of that soldier's war. To understand the specific conditions established by terrorism, we must put terror as a tool under considerable scrutiny.

e. Terror as a tool. As I suggested at the very beginning of this paper, the tool of terror is deeply involved in the current generation of novel ethical conditions. These novel conditions are generated by a lack of balance and symmetry. To be sure, the terrorist is not a soldier in any conventional sense, but the terrorist dramatically alters circumstances in a similar way that engages one or more moral principles. We need to illustrate and analyze this "similar way" of engagement in order to better understand the way ethical conditions are affected by the tool of terror.

By way of illustration, it will be useful to draw a distinction between two events—the destruction of the Twin Towers, which is indisputably an act of terrorism, and the bombing of Hiroshima and Nagasaki, which are arguably war crimes, but not considered to be terrorism.[7] These two events are sometimes incorrectly compared.[8] Both attacks resulted in the wanton destruction of civilian life, but the key difference was this: the Japanese cities were bombed during an acknowledged state of war. Therefore, when Japanese civilian targets were hit there was no sense of ambush—horror and outrage, most certainly, and perhaps shock at the scope of the destruction—but there was nothing like utter surprise. What triggers accusations of terrorism and war crimes is the complete lack of balance that disturbs any sense of symmetry. One can argue, with some legitimacy, that the atomic destruction of a civilian population was so vast and indiscriminate that terror is an appropriate label. However, even though the bombing of Hiroshima and Nagasaki were shocking in the scope of the devastation, they did not seem a bolt-out-of-the-blue.[9] These elements of surprise and ambush represent the key difference between terror and the horror of war crimes. This single element of ambush, randomness or unpredictability, will surface again and again as a defining characteristic of terror.

The tool of terror does not primarily target enemy infrastructure—highways, pipelines, power grids, and so on—where the goal is to disrupt the political system's ability to deliver the material necessities underlying social cohesion. Targeting infrastructure lie within the purview of the guerrilla or insurgent. Instead, terrorism traffics in the horror of human blood. The source of that blood is not necessarily the strategic consideration. Within a specific context the terrorist appears to select targets at random, disrupting any sense of symmetry. The randomness itself is typically for symbolic and psychological purposes, which is a strategic consideration, not an ethical one. And it is this seeming randomness that shapes the ethical conditions set up by terror. The precise motives behind this-or-that random attack are beside the point here, partially because the motives are puzzling and unclearly expressed, we might say cloaked, by the perpetrator. However, the *ethical* point is that terror, through the initiation of apparent random violence, establishes ethical conditions unlike any other in human conflict. The soldier on the battlefield does not select targets at random. Even within dynamic and horrible battlefield circumstances there remains a predictable connection between the soldier and the target. For the terrorist, that balance or sense of symmetry is broken, with the outcome being an utter lack of predictability. This is a key point of the strategy and has a great impact on the resulting ethical conditions.

What are these resulting ethical conditions? If ethics consists of certain actions carried out pursuant to moral prerogatives, then there must exist—to adopt the words of C.D. Broad—a state of appropriateness or fitness in relation to the moral universals that guide them.[10] Whatever else can be said about morality, we understand that the fitness, or viability of the deed, as it relates to moral principles, must be universally understood by rational people. If we are to avoid complete incoherence, this implicit assumption must underly all our moral thinking. Were this not the case, then the fitness principle cannot be universally understood, and either there is some internal incoherence within the system, or we are dealing with an entirely alien moral universe. For example, throughout nearly the entire modern world, cannibalism and incest are today morally repugnant, isolated, and rejected as the most extreme of taboos; there is no ethical path in this modern world to guiltlessly carry out these forbidden activities. However, for some societies (nearly all in the past), both cannibalism and incest were morally acceptable and acted upon without hesitation. This is not to say that morality is relative to the individual, but only that the world that generated those moral systems has long disappeared. Cannibalism and incest were ethically viable (possessed moral fitness) only within a vastly different material universe. But let us be clear—the "fitness" of these acts did not spring full blown from the mind of the inhabitant of this different material universe; the sense of fitness grew large in the mind alongside some encouraging material context. Without context there can be no viability, no fitness. In the sense of coherence, cannibalism and incest cannot be said to lack balance or symmetry, but rather are symmetric, coherent, viable, even rational, but only when considered *contextually*.

So how do these considerations apply to the terrorist? The fact of randomness as a central strategy of terror distinguishes the terrorist's tool from the typical tools used by a guerrilla or a soldier. For the guerrilla or soldier, either infrastructure is targeted, or the human targets are more narrowly defined. These closely defined targets develop into rules of engagement, rules that restrain the soldier or rebel guerrilla. This provides a guide to an ethical context. Within this moral universe, targets beyond the scope of definition are called collateral damage—negative and unavoidable consequences of engagement. For the terrorist this is not the case. The terrorist stands these rules of engagement on their head. In the ordinary universe, what is considered random, collateral damage is a byproduct of an attack on a specific target. For the terrorist, "random collateral damage" is very often and deliberately the goal of the action, not a byproduct—*collateral* is the target, random is the tool. So, like the cannibal, this puts the terrorist in a different moral universe.

For in this moral universe, the ethics of randomness insists that blood may flow from a banker, a store clerk—or a child. The randomness is a perfect example of asymmetry at its best and is indicative of a symbiotic relationship with a moral universe distinct from modern warfare. Even in the ancient world, when the conquerors devastated a foe, killed off all the males, sent the females into slavery, and sowed salt into the earth, the target was always specific, and given the aim of the violence, appeared both coherent and rational, no matter how cruel the outcome. This indicates symmetry and balance.

The strategy of terror centers on apparently random acts of violence against civilian targets, that is, non-combatants. Whether the strategy is successful in moving the terrorist closer to a political goal is part of another discussion and I will ignore it here. What is relevant is that the terrorist's strategic design establishes a field of asymmetric ethical conditions, that is, a set of unbalanced, dialectical relationships, which are rooted, deliberately and with great calculation, in a lack of predictability, the heart of the asymmetry. Terror is a campaign waged by the stealth and chaos of asymmetry. This apparently erratic violence is a direct psychological assault on the sociopolitical psyche of a nation or group of people. Instability is the goal. Thus, the terrorist campaign is designed to undermine any confidence the citizenry might have in the ability of their government to protect them. The ethical conditions set in motion have far reaching implications and considerable impact on the psyche of most of the individuals within the targeted group.

For the polite and law-abiding citizen this apparent randomness of terror is highly unsettling. This appearance of randomness is what sets terror apart from the "normal" conditions of war; it should also be noted that terror does not (or should not) include specifically targeted acts of political violence, such as assassination. Terror serves the interest of a more general outcome. With what seems to be an unstoppable and random violence, terror seeks to destabilize faith in the governing authorities and undermine social cohesion. Out of the middle of nowhere, bombs explode, bullets fly, fires erupt, while government stands by all but helplessly. This promotes a widespread anxiety that removes the psychological foundation required for general security. It follows that to assert stability, the psychological conditions established by the terrorist demand a reaction leading to the reestablishment of predictability. The actual instability may be less than the *perceived* damage, but that is an analytical issue, not a psychological one. The bottom line is the urgent need on the part of the established political forces to reaffirm that sense of security undermined by the terrorist's attack on predictability.

TORTURE

Notice that I did not title this section "What is Torture?" This omission is for the simple reason that we all have a workable notion as to what torture is. We all know the rough outlines of physical torture without an elaborate description or haggling over the bloody details. Psychological and emotional torture is another matter. Here, lines are a bit fuzzy, making torture hard to define: for example, is shouting questions in someone's face emotional torture? Is there any way to clearly separate the objective from the subjective experience? The effort must be made—but elsewhere. In this discussion none of these definitional problems and issues are to be examined. The meaning of torture in this study is to be found in an analysis of the singular relationship torture has to the tool of terrorism—for there is a distinct and unique relationship that surrounds and influences the ethics behind any application of torture. Bear in mind that the application of torture in relationship to terrorism is situational and further, that the key word is *relationship*.

The usual questions asked of torture tend to ignore this relationship. Instead, torture is typically examined outside of its contextual meaning by using analytical devices drawn from a moral universe that do not necessarily apply to the *relationship* between torture and terror. This does not mean that terror goes unnoticed when discussing torture, but rather that the typical analytical strategy adopted in an examination of torture ignores the relationship as a contextual focal point. For example, "All torture is evil because it violates human rights," would be one way of framing the question, while at the same time side-stepping specific context. It should be obvious that in this type of framing, torture is pulled out of its specific context and condemned by the standards of a moral universe that only apply in the *absence* of a relationship with terror.

I realize that this emphasis on context remains somewhat unclear because torture is most often presented and defended as a response to terror. In general, it can be argued that torture is a moral issue coming at terror from outside the context of terrorism. This was the stated implication in the above section on terror. However, this is a different position than arguing an ethical connection between terror and torture. The first presentation—that of torture as a response to terror—is often a legal, constitutional, or human rights argument, or even a pragmatic argument—i.e., pragmatically, does torture work, does it combat the general anxiety over terrorism and reassert the government's ability to provide security for a population? This pragmatic position is often advanced in defense of torture. However, what is presented in this paper is not a pragmatic argument. This paper outlines the ethical relationship that draws terror and torture into a dialectical whole, based on a hermeneutic complex, if you will, and insofar as such an airtight complex regarding dialectics is possible.

Torture, as it is treated in this study, is analyzed, not pragmatically, but in the context of a *relationship*. Torture cannot be *morally* judged with any sense of completeness apart from the dialectical progenitor—in this case, terror. After all, moral speculation cannot take place in a complete vacuum. And further, let's be clear that torture, like terrorism, also generates ethical conditions, but these are conditions that are generated by its dialectical relationship with terrorism. This is not exactly saying that the one (torture) cannot be understood or judged without the other (terrorism)—though this is also a viable position—but that only the whole makes up the dialectic which facilitates a graspable moral understanding of the relationship.

Finally, this is a paper on ethics, yet strangely enough I am going to avoid the moral question of: Is torture right or is torture wrong? Like the WWII soldier in relationship with battlefield conditions, the issue of right and wrong is not simply contextually awkward but is misplaced.

TORTURE AND THE ETHICS OF RANDOM

Understand that the terrorist act of random violence is random only to the targets. The terrorist knows full well the objective nature and subjective value of the target. This is a separate question from one that considers the effectiveness or actual strategic significance of the target. The terrorist may be utterly misguided in the consideration of targets, but it doesn't follow that the targets were not plotted and carefully considered by the terrorist. The terrorist also realizes that the target is largely unsuspecting;

hence the violence unleashed is strongly enhanced by a lack of predictability, a feature at the center of terror. By design, the terrorist campaign depends on cloaking violence in a mantle of secrecy. Sub-rosa action is the heartbeat of terrorist violence. Ambush through stealth is the basic strategy for this kind of warfare. As I have been arguing throughout this paper, terror is a war of sudden and unpredictable violence meant to attack the psychological stability underlying the socio-political order, not by destruction, *per se*, but by secrecy and ambush.

The ethical conditions established by the terrorist create an atmosphere of fear augmented by secrecy. To regain a minimum level of stability necessary for social function, it is not the violence that the established governments must overcome, but the secrecy. Violence in war is commonplace and fully comprehensible to the citizen. Violence alone does not destabilize the social order or threaten political legitimacy, but fear of the unpredictable will unhinge the population. It is this element of the unpredictable, and the fear it generates, that established governments must seek to overcome. Governments exist and thrive by an image of total control. They will not long thrive in an environment of chaos. To overcome the level of fear achieved by the terrorist, the terrorist must be disarmed of secrecy. Disarming the terrorist of secrecy will realign predictability with the security mandatory for a stable functioning social order—in other words, symmetry and balance will be reestablished. The return to security through predictability would be the point of view—no doubt a correct one—of official governmental agencies. This is a *predictable* reply to the violence of ambush. It will be the inevitable reply to ambush.

Up until this point the focus of this analysis has rested largely on abstractions. This is the typical approach taken by researchers and theoreticians. Let us bear in mind that such abstract elements as civil security, terrorism, the national state, torture, etc., are all conscious impressions of real things and concrete events. However, abstractions are the *ideas* of things and events, not the actual thing and events themselves. We need to remind ourselves that the rules of ethics are not automatic and intrinsic to the conceptualizations swirling in our heads. The tendency to offer moral judgments on the abstractions of things and events, such as the state, or a revolutionary movement, is a neo-Hegelian metaphysical tool.[11] This incorporeal tool obscures the fact that it is people, in the individual and concrete sense, who lay out their personal moral prerogatives and render ethical judgments on both their own actions and the actions of others. It is with the individual action and actor that ethics must be analyzed. So, how does this play out with regards to the terrorist?

The job description of the terrorist includes eroding the power of the opposition by sewing insecurity. To reiterate, this insecurity is a product of fear deliberately created by apparent random acts of violence. For the terrorist, fear is the deliberate weapon of choice. This fear is instigated by a strategy of hidden warfare where the targets appear to be chosen at the whim of a madman, or the caprice of fate. This strategy lines up with feelings of success as defined by the terrorist. At the end of the day, success for the terrorist depends in large part on preventing the opposition from discovering a predictable pattern to the violence.

As I have already discussed, this lack of predictability is only from the perspective of the organized political state. For the terrorist this perspective may not be accurate at all. In fact, for the terrorist the target may not be arbitrary at all. The target may be selected with great care. However, this is a process known only to the terrorist. The shadowy nature of the standards by which the targets are selected is a calculated part of terrorist's strategy. This produces that lack of predictability that is a cornerstone of terrorist strategy, a strategy that is dependent on secrecy for success. When choosing this strategy, the terrorist knows full well the meaning and impact of secrecy and its vital role in the campaign of terror. Frequently, secrecy *is* the meaning of the target, with "erratic" being the goal.

All of this will come as no surprise to the terrorist who knows that the opposition will attack the heart of the campaign of terror by attacking the authority of secrecy. The terrorist has chosen secrecy as part of this war-by-ambush. The terrorist has chosen to create a condition where keeping secrets is a principle demand and meaning of the job. By choice, the terrorist may be called on to continue the terrorist strategy of secrecy during enhanced interrogation, i.e., torture. By choosing to be part of a secret war, the terrorist has consented to be put in that place where the combatants will use complimentary weapons of asymmetrical war. This is an attempt to regain symmetry and balance in the struggle against random violence. The terrorist has chosen the weapon of secrecy, and thereby consented to the possibility of the state piercing the veil of secrecy through its monopoly on violence—in this case, torture. As Thomas Hobbes so famously pointed out: "Nothing done to a man by his own consent can be injury."[12]

The soldier on the battlefield doesn't want to be shot and the terrorist doesn't want to be tortured, but both possibilities are inherent to the nature of their respective occupations. The soldier campaigning on the battlefield has a predictable target. That target, the enemy soldier, is fully aware that he is a target and takes anticipated steps and therefore responds appropriately to counter the enemy soldier. There is nothing hidden here, nothing secret; the intent is based on symmetrical understanding and is visible for all to see. Stealth can be employed, and most certainly is. But the soldier is certainly aware of the hovering bullseye, and routinely takes action accordingly. The ethical conditions of the open battlefield allow for openness by the participants. In general, the citizenry can remain on the side lines. Even where the citizenry is deliberately targeted (e.g., the WW II German air campaign over London) the citizenry knows they are the objective and for the most part know where and how the attacks will take place. Forewarned, they can respond rationally. Terrorism, on the other hand, built on secrecy and apparent randomness, disrupts symmetry, and allows for no such clarity and therefore, by design, the terrorist threatens any rational resolve on the part of the population. This is the condition that the established governmental forces must defeat.

The bottom line here is that the terrorist has chosen the path of secrecy and the appearance of randomness as tactics of the conflict. The terrorist has chosen to be responsible for this very secret nature of the terror campaign. Therefore, just as the soldier on the battlefield would not be surprised that his violence will be met by counter-violence, neither should the terrorist be surprised that secrecy will inevitably be met by measures of "counter-secrecy." To reestablish symmetry, predictability becomes a primary goal of any government's anti-terror campaign. This goal of reestablishing balance *is* predictable. Just as the soldier in combat can read the ethical conditions of the battlefield, and accepts them, likewise the terrorist must know the ethical conditions of his action when choosing the campaign of terror. If this sounds a bit like I am suggesting that the terrorist is responsible for the torture inflicted—this is correct. As we all choose our fate, so does the terrorist. The ethical conditions established by the terrorist do not just allow torture, they insist on it. Breaking secrecy is a key element to breaking the terrorist strategy, and the terrorist knows the asymmetrical ethical situation he is in as surely as the soldier on the battlefield knows the symmetry of his ethical situation.

The Issue of Human Rights. The question of human rights inevitably arises. These are typically *legal* questions, debated on numerous levels, i.e., the Universal UN Human Rights Declaration, US constitutional guarantees, etc. This is an attempt to move "soft" moral considerations into the realm of "hard" legal codification. Human rights are generally held to be rights or freedoms to which all people are entitled merely on the basis of being human. Human rights are also considered to be universal, applying to all humans equally, without consideration of their location or their station in life. However, there is absolutely no consensus as to the nature of what should or should not be regarded as a human right. To some extent this is due to the difficulty of agreeing on a legal definition of "human," at least one that is not grossly circular.[13] One need only point out the conflict between the United States and international treaties on the basic nature of human rights, which generally avoids "human" and devolves to wrangling over what constitutes a "right." The idea of "human" is assumed.[14]

For example, President Jimmy Carter, in his 1978 State of the Union address, announced that to earn a decent living was a basic human right. Much of the world agrees with Carter, yet there is much discrepancy on what constitutes a "basic right." This issue has never been resolved nor "basic right" defined and enshrined into law in the US.[15] There are, after all, political considerations.

Likewise, the abstract concept of human rights has been a subject of intense philosophical debate and criticism. From where do basic human rights come? Why are they a given? Are they by "nature?" Can "nature" be legitimately tested in court? As important: are human rights according to nature, or bestowed? If bestowed, by whom or what? These are just some of the examples of the philosophical puzzles that surround human rights. Interesting questions, to be sure, but they are also questions and issues that will sidetrack the basic thrust of this paper, which is the question of the ethical relationship between terror and torture.

This is not a dismissal of human rights. Human rights are profoundly important and are fundamental to a great many legal questions. However, the arrangement of any legality involving "human rights"—and legalities in general—are historically contextual and therefore shifting and contingent. As the details of every event and idea, whether legal or moral, contain elements of the contextual, so will the question of terror and torture.

However, certain characteristics of actions, and therefore characteristics of ethics, show great consistency. One of the characteristics would be the frame within which the event takes place. In this case: a dialectic. There are certain dialectical responses, I have been arguing, that are so utterly predictable that they cannot be considered in the absence of their counterpart. This arrangement sets up a certain inevitable dialogue that can be examined in a way that avoids the monologue of legal issues in favor of an ethical discussion.

~

Conclusion: Secrecy has been at the heart of the ethical position I have staked out. Here is a concluding way to get a line on the argument I have been making: there is something in the nature of secrets that offends. Secrets are a source of power. This is true both for governments and for those that would tear governments down. For both the terrorist and the terrorist hunter, secrets are a chosen ethical condition. However, for the terrorist the chosen ethical conditions are asymmetrical by design and based on the conditions of their struggle. This very frequently leads to asymmetry in the response to terrorism.

We think hardly at all about the spy who is executed for unearthing secrets and spiriting them off to an enemy. There exists a symmetry in the action and counter actions. What stands out here is the *relationship* to secrets. The spy is a conduit of secrets while the terrorist is the embodiment of secrets. With the spy, there is something underhanded and dishonorable about the work. We feel personally violated and threatened by the revelations of state secrets. Somehow, we think, the spy deserves what fate has in store. We even have a grim sort of satisfaction in seeing the deserts dished out to the spy. The terrorist, on the other hand, goes one step further than the spy. The spy is a secondhand threat. The terrorist is a primary threat. Secrets are the traffic of the spy, but they are a weapon for the terrorist. The terrorist directly menaces social cohesion and political legitimacy with a secret life; the terrorist is the living embodiment of the secret, a secret that kills. The spy is executed for transporting secrets. The terrorist must be pried loose from his secrets. There is an inevitability about this that marks the asymmetrical ethical conditions chosen and established by the terrorist.

Ethical consideration of torture cannot be rationally discussed in the absence of dialectics: actions and events that provoke torture as one of the responding remedies for asymmetry—the dialectical counterpart enacted by the ethical conditions generated by random acts of violence. This is not a simple chicken and egg question where all parties can wash their hands of the matter and walk away like crying victims of happenstance; the very existence of asymmetry agitates for redress. The tension produced by asymmetry insists on a rebalancing.

Taking part in a campaign of terror is a voluntary and intentional act. This voluntary act precedes any complementary reciprocity of "enhanced interrogation." The terrorist has voluntarily launched this dialogue with the "interrogator." Thus, it is a fair argument to claim that the *ethical* conditions for torture are present and are the responsibility of the terrorist, much more than the torturer. I do not claim that the "interrogator" is off the hook, for the interrogator must also make an ethical choice, though this choice seems far more circumscribed than that choice made by the terrorist.[16] It is also true that certain individuals possess a personality fit for the work of enhanced interrogation; in the need to get at the clandestine nature of a terror campaign these personalities are required, no matter how much we recoil at the imagery. From an established government's point of view, the secrets must be revealed for the redress of symmetry and for the sake of social stability. There is an undeniable inevitability linking the means as choice to the ethical conditions, to the ends.

Recall that the random acts of terrorist violence are only apparently random. For the terrorist, these acts are not at all random. They are by design. It is on the plain of secrecy that the battlefield of this war is fought. The ethics of this battlefield—the ethics of randomness—are made by the terrorist, not the interrogator. The terrorist generates asymmetry, the interrogator seeks redress through rebalance. It is the terrorist who is responsible for the way in which this war is fought. In the final analysis, and just as surely as the soldier chooses to be shot at and thereby chooses the possibility of death on the battlefield, the terrorist chooses the possibility of torture.

Notes

1. For example, see Michael Scott Doran, "Somebody Else's Civil War," found in *How Did This Happen?* Ed. by James Hoge and Gideon Rose of Foreign Affairs, Public Affairs Publishing, New York, 2002 especially pp. 31- 33.

2. Note that in WWI aerial combat the machine gun was used without this same sense of outrage. This is likely because the combat remained largely a one-on-one contest and the element of randomness was removed from the fight.

3. For an expanded coverage on this distinction you might look into such philosophers as David Ross, and his book *The Right and the Good*, (Oxford University press, New York, 2002)

4. The obvious example here is the moral philosophy of Immanuel Kant. See *Grounding for the Metaphysics of Morals*, various editions.

5. Immanuel Kant, *Grounding for the Metaphysics of Morals*, various editions, section 427.

6. At this point it is tempting to say that "ethics trumps morality," but such a statement, while philosophically important, opens a new line of discussion that is well beyond the scope of this paper.

7. As USAF General Curtis LeMay famously told his assistant Robert Mac-Namara, "If the Japanese had won the war we would've been prosecuted as war criminals."

8. For an elucidation, see: https://groups.able2know.org/philforum/topic/2764-1

9. It can be argued, successfully, I think, that there was hefty information and warning, none of which was acted on due to the sense of improbability that surrounded the pre-attack investigation. For greater detail, see: *How Did This Happen? Terrorism and the New War*, edited by James Hoge, Jr., and Gideon Rose, (Public Affairs, 1st edition, New York, 2001).

10. See C.D. Broad, *Five Types of Ethical Theory*, (Routledge & Kegan Paul, New York, 1971) pp.164—166.

11. As Hegel put it, "What is rational is real; and what is real is rational." [This famous quote from G. W. F. Hegel, *Elements of the Philosophy of Right* (1821)]. However, Hegel's extreme form of idealism tends to lose the species in a cloud of the universal, thus disrupting contextual analysis.

12. Thomas Hobbes, *The Leviathan*, various editions, Chapter 15, section 13. Before it is suggested that I am unfairly using Hobbes in this capacity, a reading of the entire section (#13, which falls under the Third Law of Nature, 'Justice') will show that Hobbes carefully suggests that all voluntary actions are

by individual will, and therefore consequences fall as a matter of the consent by will. It is also worth noting that this entire section (#13) seems slightly out of context, as though Hobbes was attempting to cover all his bases regarding volunteerism, ensuing consequences, and consent.

13. https://www.jstor.org/stable/1407800?seq=1#page_scan_tab_contents

14. This is becoming more controversial, as granting corporations legal "personhood" by the US Supreme Court has provoked an underlying question: is a person a human being? It takes but a little leap to discover what thorny legal problems this question can evoke.

15. It might be argued that US federal minimum wage laws provide for this basic human right. But clearly the minimum wage hardly qualifies for supporting a "decent living."

16. This is even truer when the interrogator selects the "terrorist" at random. Such fishing expeditions create vast problems, both ethical and practical.

THE *PARTICULAR* NATURE OF TRUTH AND CERTAINTY IN SOCIAL ISSUES

JOHN CONNOR

Abstract: This piece takes a deep dive into Wittgensteinian philosophy, and argues that the notions of truth and certainty in social issues are relative to time and place and the ideocracies of the thinker. The main topics are truth-value, fact and its corollary, certainty, as these subjects are often reflected in social issues. It is also argued here that "certainty" is drafted from truth and both have a value different from the thing we call "fact". It is also put forth that fact gains value from truth and not the other way around. (The position staked out is definitely Wittgensteinian, but not one tangled in the weeds). Where and when we find ourselves *determines the nature of truth* and its consequential impact on the "facts" surrounding social issues.

I t is on the basis of true witness that our actions are designed. There-fore, truth in action is a tricky business . . . but always an *assumed* business.

In debate and studies, especially of social issues, isn't there a ten-dency to bypass clear understanding of "truth" and speak around truth as though there is some immediate, intuitive and universal understanding of what truth is—its nature, its *supposed* infallibility? Writers, including professional philosophers, quite naturally also show a tendency to assume the truth of their subject. Doesn't every thought take for granted its own underlying supposition? Yes, it is almost impossible to discuss a subject without supposing its truth. Unfortunately, this tendency can stir up quite a few misunderstandings which lead people to talk right past one another. This is a crippling error when the subject is social justice.

Some statements seem so obviously true that there is an inclination to shuck them off as too ridiculous to ponder. For example, I can say: I pick up a stone from the ground. Then add: is it not a true fact that there is a stone in my hand? Such a blatantly obvious statement of objective fact might seem too silly to spend time with but notice the trigger that makes the statement a blatantly obvious truth: *Fact!*[1] We have an almost reflexive tendency to conflate the ideas of "truth" and "fact," blurring them as though one were synonymous with the other—fact makes truth obvious. This assumes that truth is a value that hinges on fact. People do this automatically all the time, because at first glance it would seem that what is "true" is also a statement of fact—a true, objective fact. Closer scrutiny shows that there is an important distinction to be made between truth and fact. Given precise stipulations, truth can have *value* while fact need not. "Fact" simply is. The value of truth, whether social, political or scientific, is granted to the holder with varying levels of certainty. Oddly enough, then, it is "certainty" that distinguishes truth from fact. The blur-ring of truth and fact has serious consequences for social justice. We have a strong inclination to confuse the two, and we typically, and understand-ably, tend to assume that fact has value rather than truth.

To get a proper handle on this distinction between truth and fact let me return to the stone and ask a question that is not so obvious: Is the stone an objective fact, or is the stone merely an image-thing in my mind? Carefully consider the stone. It seems clear enough that even without *contemplation* the stone possesses some kind of objectivity in my hand that is independent from my *regarding* of the stone in my hand. The stone was here before I picked it up and only transformed into a *thing in my mind* when I set it in my hand. My contemplation of the stone began after the fact of me regarding stone. It follows that how I *contemplate* the stone is very much a part of how I cognitively and subjectively organize the material objectivity of the stone. This subjective and cognitive organization is itself a result of a whole host of events and activities that were never overtly intended to intersect with the stone: education, culture, language, superstition, tradition, etc. All represent some of the many features that greatly impact both the regarding and the contemplation of the stone in my hand (not to mention social justice in my world). The actual *recognition* of the stone's objectivity enters into my contemplation of as an action only secondary to the subjective organization of the *regarding* of the stone. Remembering that it is possible to regard an object without contemplating its meaning, we may return to the problem: Is it true or is it a fact that I hold a stone in my hand? It appears that while both truth and fact seem correct, the truth of the matter originates from a place different from that of objective fact. Truth seems a matter of the *cognitive response* (triggering contemplation) to the stone in my hand based on all the personal and social activities and events cited above (education, culture, etc.). Truth is a subjective reaction to fact, which, as we will see, calls into question the nature of the subject doing the regarding rather than the nature of the objective fact.

I am fully aware that this fine hair splitting about a stone in my hand seems remote to issues of social justice. A bit of unnecessary philosophizing. Yet consider what the hair splitting implies: this thing called "truth" seems in some way dependent on how we have come to think about this thing called "fact." At the same time, the material objectivity, that is the "fact," (in this case the stone, while in the case of this study, social justice), possesses a certain independence from our cognitive process. This leads to a proposed general statement that truth is located in a cognitive process, distinct, yet not wholly separate from fact. More than that, truth is a screen that filters and manipulates objective fact. A serious implication here is that truth is a thing in our heads, while fact is something largely unknown, except through its connection with the "regarding" of the fact of the object. Therefore, it turns out that while truth is a value given to fact, it is a thing distinct from fact. They are intertwined, yet distinguishable.

Before proceeding, I should point out that it appears that I am care-lessly slipping into the old cliché of "Truth is relative." As clichés always hold a certain amount of validity this is correct, in a certain naïve way, which is to say a grossly unexamined way. So, what is at stake here is not the cliché, but one of the curiosities that lies behind the cliché: Why is truth relative? It might well be that the world positions us in such a way as to nearly force truth to be relative—or stated more accurately, *particular*. This suggestion leads to the observation that while truth might be relative, it is only so in a *particular* way.

The way in which questions concerning truth and fact are framed by professional philosophers can be located in any basic book on epis-temology (i.e., the study of knowledge) or truth.[2] It is the framing of the question that provokes a question about the relationship of truth to knowledge. For us non-professionals, moving about in our daily and practical routines, the consequences of a distinction between truth and fact are for the most part hardly considered or felt. Without in any way impugning the importance of professional, detailed discussions, it would seem that to facilitate this particular study I must take something of a shortcut. Here I will assume that in actions such as the picking up of a stone, we are allowed the shortcut of realizing that the stone will be recognized and regarded universally as a stone, that is, an objective fact—and never mind why. So, while there is fact-value in the stone in my hand, yet no particular truth-value in simply regarding the stone. Other issues are not so pedestrian, namely the importance of truth rela-tive to fact. This is not a tempest in a teapot.

There are particular social situations where truth commands our actions and fact does not. These situations can run from making decisions as a participant on a jury to lying to the boss about why we are going to be absent from work tomorrow, from cheating at solitaire to killing another human being. To be completely (and uncomfortably) on point, most of our actions *directly* concern truth just as they *indirectly* concern fact. Closely observing legal proceedings will demonstrate that good criminal lawyers never forget this distinction between truth and fact. Frequently courtroom drama swirls around the attempt to demolish truth by casting doubt on fact.[3] The other way around, the casting of doubt on truth to demolish fact, is also possible, and far more tempting; for example, casting doubt on the truth of an eye-witness in order to render moot the fact of what was

216

seen. However, regarding nearly all our human and social issues, and our human contemplations of these issues, are we not mostly concerned with truth rather than with fact? This is a temperamental statement, so to get at the disposition of truth I need to employ a slightly different, if not entirely original, approach to the issue of truth.

The phrase "this thing called truth" is used above casually, but deliberately, for "truth," although a product of cognition, has a thing-like quality to it in a sense similar to "facts." At least "truth" has this thing-like quality more than "certainty," which has the slippery feel of a distant abstraction. Just as truth emerges thing-like from fact, certainty weakens and in some cases completely undermines the thing-like quality and thereby can be enlisted to assault objective fact.

Ignoring for the moment such notions as certainty, this thing-like *feel* to truth offers us the *sensation* of possessing a handle to grasp whatever topic is under review. Unlike "certainty," a "truth" seems to offer something a little more "real," that is, truth appears to hold within itself something of value that we seem to be able to *possess*; that is, truth as a thing in proprietorship of "graspability" and "possessability." In other words, truth, and truth-value, must have some operational element linking both the cognitive setting of the mind with the material objectivity of the actual world.[4] A truth can always be linked to something independent of our individual cognition, either embodied in a reflection of *material reality*, as a glimpse into the many manifestations of a *relationship*, or revealed in a disclosure of *abstractions*. Yet at the same time it is we who do the reflecting, the disclosing, the manifesting, which are inner operations that can and frequently do function independently of the real, the actual and social world.

"Certainty," which I offered above as contrast, can be traced to "truth" as the portal to the actual and social world. The real value of truth is that truth represents the bridge between the real world and the realm of certainty. It might well be true that it is raining in Bora-Bora, or that there is life on Mars, or that Joan of Arc was a witch, but I can be certain about none of these things. The truth of these statements may, *if I choose*, lead me into the realm of certainty, but it is not a certainty that this will happen. Certainty, as distinguished from truth, is almost entirely part of a willful, cognitive world that is linked to the objective world only by the tenuous value we give to truth. This accounts for the greater difficulty with "certainty." Truth, by contrast, is a connective process, as described above, cognitively organizing the material objectivity into *"this thing called truth,"* therefore providing *"this thing"* with a truth-value, the "value" portion of which can imbue the realm of certainty with its powerful voice. However, it needs to be remembered that absence of certainty can also undermine truth-value, and thereby undermine objective fact.

Truth, in having this thing-like feel to it, also suggests something else—truth as property without ownership.[5] Perhaps a strange way to look at truth, but in this way it is possible to consider truth as something like a universal possession.[6] That is to say, truth as a cognitive property *available* to all of humanity. Not so strange after all. It is easy to consider that all humanity *can* possess truth, almost as though truth were something tactile as well as cognitive. This has an appropriate ring to it. Truth is a distillation and reorganization of the concrete world and as such draws that world directly into the process of reasoning. It is through that process of reasoning that the objective fact is infused with what it lacked before—the *value* of truth. This in no way defines exactly what truth is, but makes it plain that whatever truth is, it is a thing which, by its nature, is a cognitive property of some considerable value which is (or should be) universally available and shared by all.

We need, however, to exercise some caution when using the term "universal property," and especially note that "universal," paradoxically, implies certain particular situational elements which are sometimes at odds with its universal nature. A neutral subject, or objective fact, such as a "stone," might be universally (if superficially) understood as a stone, but it has no truth-value; considering or regarding the stone in my hand is what opens the door to truth. Fact issues from the stone, not truth. Of course this is different from saying that "the stone is in my hand," which raises a particular notion of truth as something distinct from the universal fact of the stone itself and opens the stone to the possibility of truth. That is, the value found in the regarding of the stone is *not* automatically transferred from the particular regarding or considering to the universal awareness of the stone as objective fact.

This situation can be demonstrated by the apparently innocuous and universal truth of the fact that "cats don't grow on trees." The only difference between a stone and the notion of cats-growing-on-trees is that you can handle the stone in your hand, while the latter reflection on cats and trees happens only in the mind. Therein lies a pivotal point concerning the transference of truth-value. At first glance the claim that "cats don't grow on trees" might seem an utterly obvious true and factual statement under any circumstance. It is, of course, universally true that cats simply do not grow on trees! Is there anything biased or controversial about this claim? It would seem not. The "cat" claim also seems to lack genuine meaning, as does any inaccurate statement or absurd assertion, which would suggest that an absence of meaning withdraws truth from the claim. While much of this seems overly silly, it does raise a salient point worth considering.

One influential philosopher (Wittgenstein) pointed out: we only know that it is true that cats do not grow on trees because we were taught this.[7] If we were never taught, or otherwise learned, what a "cat" was or what a "tree" was, we could not possibly know how "utterly obvious" it is that "cats don't grow on trees." Again, this seems a silly suggestion and a waste of time, for who does not learn about such things as cats and trees from childhood? Therefore, is not the example trite and the question consequently moot? Quite possibly not.

If one were to look up the word "cat" in a traditional Inuit dictionary, it could not be found, for the Intuits have no word for "cat' in their native vocabulary. Cats were not part of the traditional Intuit's life experience, at least not before the coming of "civilization" (admittedly, a charged and dicey term). Of the long list of things the Inuit value in their reality, cats simply do not appear, and therefore to teach an Inuit that cats don't grow on trees is at best pointless and in all probability an exercise in futility. As a consequence, without the word, (much less the value), and the experience that generated the word, it would be absurd to convince an Inuit of the obvious truth that cats don't grow on trees. The traditional Inuit's external or *objective* world simply does not allow for the obviousness of the claim's truth—that is, the Inuit's internal, or *subjective* world, will not allow for this particular contemplation of the objective facts. In the particular case of the Inuit and cats, fact and truth (object and subject) are not just at odds, but in fact truth is irrelevant to the regarding.

So, if there are exceptions to the "obvious truth" that "cats don't grow on trees" what are we to make of statements centered about such concepts as good and evil, human rights, racial inequality, democracy and social justice? It must be that "truths" concerning social issues, either simply, or in great complexity, have come into our heads as things that have been taught to us, and not necessarily by vaulted educational institutions. The teaching, or the learning, that facilitates the internal organization of complex reality into "truth," is of course, particular—that is, our learning has insinuated itself into our particular situation and assigned truth according to the complexities that that particular situation. While fact may be the same everywhere, truth is not the same everywhere. This raises basic social, cultural, and above all, historical connotations for our "particularity." Therefore, how we would learn to cognitively organize "truth" in one time and place will impact our social relations in a completely different way in another. What constitutes a social issue in one particularity will be completely absent or misunderstood in another. It follows that the degree to which we value what we are taught will also vary not only with time and place, but also with the individual's "particularity" within that time and place. Like the Inuit, I might live in the same time and place as a physicist, but not be particularly placed so as to understand the "truth" of, say, dark matter. Truth is highly particular, which renders its universality not only a failure to be reflexive in the way of "common sense," but possibly not even universally probable.[8] This sense of truth as being particular to time and place has obvious ramifications for social issues.

To offer a relevant example: Currently, social justice frequently seems to hinge on something that doesn't exist in either fact or truth: *Race*. While observing the human family as a whole it would seem that there are many varieties of people; that is, we often regard whole groupings of people that appear very different from each other as being different sub-species of *Homo sapiens*. By simply *regarding* the typical person from Sweden and then regarding a typical person from Kenya, we can quickly note definite and striking differences in appearance that seem to overwhelm the similarities. These differences appear to be facts in much the same way as it seems to be a fact when we regard the stone in my hand. Only concerted contemplation can reveal the truth of "race" as distinguishable from apparent fact. The truth is that despite the appearance of fact, race, as we normally consider it, is a social myth.[9]

But what is it we see when we regard the Swede and the Kenyan if not race? We see a social construct.[10] There are no biological markers that can reveal this thing we call race. There is no off-shoot, or sub-species, or kissing-cousins of *Homo sapiens*. The Swede and the Kenyan are

220

members of the same race, the only race, the human race. Of course, this is not obvious by simply regarding the two individuals. To get at the truth of what we are seeing, a complex system of study and contemplation must be put in the place of casual regarding. Thus truth gains increased currency from the value we place in study and reflection. Obviously, this difference between fact and truth has huge consequences for social justice. The justice we value in our courts turns on the value we gain from truth and not fact.

What does this suggest about truth found in social and political issues such as Natural Law, property rights, questions and issues relating to justice as fairness, of civil liberties, or for that matter, human rights in general? What if like the notion of cats and trees, the value of truth I place in rights, liberty, law or fairness is mostly particular to my time, place, and the scope of knowledge available to me? Then a basic "certainty" remains concerning truth. It would appear that truth seems to have a functional relationship not with fact, but with what we have been taught to value, or otherwise learned to value. This becomes the particular truth underlying our subjectivity. In this sense, it is the value we find in particular truths, rather than in facts, that is the integral part of that relationship between truth and the social issues that confront us. Like the Inuit, what we know and value about this world is based on a whole host of things that are not tied to material objectivity. Rather than truth, it is cultural and social value that defines and animates the ghost of value that lies within truth.

The truth of a matter clearly reflects "something" about society and societal issues, but that "something" is a complicated interplay of the things we value rather than objective facts. What we have learned (learning being a reflection of value, though not precisely the same thing), when we learn it, the depth and scope of the learning, the intention of that learning, and the material object of that learning, are all products of value and not directly related to facts. If what we are taught to value, or learn to value, has any bearing on truth, as it certainly appears to have, this "learning to value" casts a long shadow over any notion of truth as some pure and objective reflection of reality in a one-to-one correspondence. Such a one-to one correspondence may hold better for fact than for truth.

As it turns out, truth is often an ambivalent interplay between what we are taught to value—that actuality which is locked in the relationship with time and place—and the social issues that we witness, those

221

independent issues we euphuistically call "facts." Truth is not relative, *per se*. It is not *my* particular truth, but any truth that is not so much subjective to the cognitive process as it is relative to the subjectivity of a particular objectivity. This is to say that truth (as opposed to fact) is not relative to my subjectivity, but rather is relative to a materially objective time and place. The lack of consistency in truth is due less to objective factors than to unique social factors, which is to say, the particularity of our relative position within objectivity as a whole.

As strange as this may sound, all this relativity toward particular objectivity results in *truth-as-choice*. We choose the meaning of truth. From among the various presentations offered to us via our social subjectivity and based on the particular placement of our objectivity, we choose. Of course, truth eventually gains the status of relativity; that is, truth becomes relative to our total objectivity when it becomes a value. This is a fancy way of saying that we choose the truth of social issues, but only based on our social values.

Yet some confusion remains. Reflection leads to feeling, a feeling that truth, in any universal sense, begins to recede, replaced with what appears to be a relative truth. This feeling or sense of relativity is greatly governed by the interplay between our particular objectivity and particular subjectivity. These two particularities are constantly shifting, dissolving and reforming. It is as if truth were a thing built on sand. At first blush this appears to be a disaster. On second glance, it is a disaster with a silver lining. We can control the sense of particular relativity to a much greater extent than we can control the value from which it emerges. I have the choice to change my subjectivity through altering my relationship to my objectivity, thus changing my relationship to truth and therefore transforming the value of my truth.

The ability to change my subjectivity produces for me a special *personal responsibility* toward the shifting particularity of truth as it *regards* social issues. Along with the understanding of truth as choice comes a special realization that I am responsible for my relationship to social issues. I am responsible for my choices. This is my true particularity. Therefore, not only choice enters the realm of truth, but also responsibility for social issues.

In other words, circumscribed by what I know of social issues—the foundational structure of my particular situation—a kind of involuntary (often unconscious) bracketing goes on between my introduction to social value and the way I have learned to socially observe (both elements of our particular subjectivity). In that *involuntary* sense, a correspondence exists between what I have learned and how I assess the truth of social issues, between particularity and social truth.

All-in-all, riding on the shifting platform of changing context I bear a great deal of responsibility not only for my relationship with truth, but also for what I deem to be truth, and how the value of truth plays out in my understanding of social issues. This seems a strange and awkward position, that is to say that the truth of social issues depends on our adopted values, which within the particularity of time and place are largely our choice. Understanding this, the particularity of our situation, will have great impact on our reading of truth in social issues.

Notes

1. I use the term "objective" throughout this paper to indicate the world of objects existing outside of independent of our internal cognitive processes. The popular use of the word is deliberate.

2. For example, for a detailed summation of the subject, see Frederick Schmitt, *Truth, A Primer*, Westview Press (Boulder, 1995).

3. The famous OJ Simpson trial is a good example. The defense team was able to cast doubt on the facts surrounding the DNA evidence and thereby bring into question the truth of his guilt.

4. For the professional philosopher, note that I am conspicuously avoiding terms like idealist and realist, or metaphysical and physical.

5. The use of the word "property" is merely a convenient descriptive noun that allows us to handle aspect of "truth" with expediency. There is no intent to imply ownership.

6. For example, see Charles Fried, *Right And Wrong*, Harvard University Press, (Cambridge, 1978), especially the chapter: "On Lying."

7. Ludwig Wittgenstein, *On Certainty*, Harper Torchbook (New York, 1972) p. 36 (sec. 282).

8. G.E. Moore is most famous for his opposition to idealism as laid out in his work, *A Defense of Common Sense*, For an updated look at Moore's anti-idealist philosophy see the recent revaluation by Robert Tully, *Moore's Defense of Common Sense: A Reappraisal After Fifty Years*, Cambridge University Press, (Cambridge, 1976).

9. http://physanth.org/about/position-statements/biological-aspects -race/

10. https://www.psychologytoday.com/us/blog/busting-myths-about-human-nature/201204/race-is-real-not-in-the-way-many-people-think.

THE ORIGINS OF
CHRISTIANITY
AS POLITICAL IDEOLOGY

WILLIAM F. PRAY

Abstract: Christianity began as an obscure offshoot of Judaism, yet by the
10th century the religion had become deeply enmeshed in European politics
and culture. In fact, Christianity ultimately became the leading Medieval ideology. This paper maintains that the origins and rapid rise of Christianity are
due less to the appeal of the religion itself, than the result of Roman politics
and imperial Roman adventure; Roman politics, it is argued, gave Christianity
its unity and structural integrity. In turn, Christianity gave Rome religious
peace, and for a time, the ideological prerequisite for political peace. Later,
Christianity gave an unstable Medieval world the ideological foundation for
social stability, a stability that justified an inherently unequal political system.
Material evidence shows that Christianity emerged from a mixed plethora of
supernatural cults to become the leading religion because of specific political
conditions and not divine inspiration. These material and political conditions
are cited, enumerated and analyzed in-depth. There is also an addendum to
the article that offers an independent and deep diving analysis of ideology, in
and of itself.

INTRODUCTION:

C hristianity is not merely an "other-worldly" belief system. Christianity is very much a real-world, political actor. Christianity has been a potent driving force in the turning of human events—events that have brought about much human advancement and much human disaster. Both in the past and the present, Christianity cannot be considered a passive, historical interloper. The "religion" of Christianity developed as an active, then assertive, and finally aggressive historical force working in league with political persons to decide flesh and blood issues of moment.

In support of the above observations regarding Christianity this paper will argue for the following positions:

First, rather than the usual treatment of Christianity as a theology, this is a study which will identify and study Christianity as a political force complete with a formidable political ideology.

Second, it will be the position of this study that Christianity, as an idea-system, was, at its very inception, a manipulative political force. By manipulative it is meant that Christianity, along with being a spiritual factor in the lives of its congregates, was molded and fashioned by the political players of the time for ends which can only be described as social control. For the most part, this aspect of Christianity as co-opted for the purposes of social control is not readily apparent to the actors in the drama.[1] There is nothing particularly unusual in this, as existing within an historically developed idea-system, such as Christianity, typically renders the player unaware of the origin of the ideas. The ideas swirling in the player's head have a comfortable and a "natural" feel about them. So unless the ideas are closely examined, they can appear to the player as both obvious and natural and therefore existing on a plane beyond the immediate reach of steady analysis—or for that matter, *sans* analysis, beyond considerations of good and evil.

Any address of both of these historical points necessitates a short descriptive discussion of both politics and ideology. Following these short discussions, we will offer a phenomenological analysis of the concrete, historical roots of Christianity as political ideology. We will assume that the reader has at least some modest acquaintance with Roman history in late antiquity and the early European medieval period.

I. Defining Politics

Politics is a societal expression of will. At its most basic level politics are the rules and traditions that govern the willful expression of power. Typically, this power is exercised for the purpose of allocation of societal resources.

Expressed in blunter and more direct terms, politics is the determination of who gets what, how much of it they get, and how soon they will get it. We can say with certainty that politics is the willful expression of power that ultimately leads to the allocation of the goods and services available in any society, past or present. Expressed in more straightforward terms, you have food on your table and gas in your car by dint of the power arrangements existing within your particular social order—in other words, because of political arrangements.

However, let us be clear: because politics is a social expression of will does not mean that politics is about all the inhabitants of a social order surviving together, and certainly not surviving equally. As politics runs its course in any given society, it is the ultimate determiner of who survives the best and who barely survives at all. This has both physical and emotional repercussions. At its most basic, eating is an obvious consequence of political decisions. Self-esteem is also a derivative of political will, but a less obvious consequence. For example, look to the plight of racial minorities in any given society; condemned to second rate citizenry is to be condemned to second rate dignity. This ought to be lost on no one.

These questions of power relations between individuals are, in all societies, reflected in the structures of tradition and the law. Behind these structures, especially the structure of the law, is the threat of coercion, which in its rawest form is naked, brute force. Force and violence always stand behind the law, which does some damage to the notion of the law as the possessor of a superior ethics and morality.

It is important to note that politics in-and-of-itself is not coercion and violence. Far from it. In fact, politics is the concealment of coercion for the purpose of avoiding naked violence to settle disputes over the allocation of resources. This is so because the wanton and casual exercise of violence can lead to unpredictable, unstable and frequently unwanted results. It would seem obvious that open coercion, and certainly naked violence, can threaten the smooth distribution of social production. Raw uses of power in the form of open coercion and violence are therefore not desirable and wisely resorted to only as a last straw grasped by those in positions of political power.

The successful political act is that act which utilizes violence within its own concealment. The goal of politics is therefore the *force* of violence without the *use* of violence. For political efforts to be successful, a stable and predictable flow of distribution of social resources must take place without recourse to raw violence. This is usually a tricky and difficult goal to achieve, as the distribution of the social product is typically unequal and always has the potential to produce tension within the social fabric. To achieve the stable and continued unequal distribution of the social product, politics must call upon many resources. Chief among these resources mustered by any political apparatus are tradition and respect for the law. Both tradition and law have their roots in ideology. In the case of this specific study, we mean this ideological soil to be in large measure Christian political ideology.

II. Christian ideology[i]

We need to remind ourselves that we are engaged in a phenomenological analysis of Christianity as ideology and not as theology; that is, a pre-conscious world view as opposed to a detailed pursuit of a single study within the parent ideology. The two, ideology and theology have no doubt been often intertwined through historical contingency and given specific, concrete factors certainly reinforce each other, but for this study the *distinction* between a private belief system and an ideological redeployment of that belief-system is a pivotal one. Although the two may be rooted in the same historical circumstance, their separate development appears as a result of practical circumstance. Like a Venn diagram, the

---

i. Inasmuch as a treatment of ideology, *per se*, is both critical and yet only tangential to a more general discussion of Christian ideology, I have provided a lengthy analysis of ideology, in and of itself, in an addendum at the end of this paper. In addition, there is an article in this collection that treats with ideology as a separate study.

boundaries between ideology and theology frequently blur and coalesce. In spite of this, to fully understand the impact of "political ideology" we must struggle to analyze it as an independent and practical entity completely divorced from considerations of ecclesiology or Christian theology in general.

To illustrate this point of practicality we may look to the relevant example of a disruptive ecclesiastical issue which bubbled to the surface in the early 4th century. That would be the Arian controversy, although this is a controversy we will return to in greater detail below, we should note here that the Arian debate concerned the very nature of the founder of Christianity, Jesus Christ. Was Jesus divine or was he human? The controversy can only be described as a crisis of faith or a heresy that once threatened the structural integrity of the Christian belief system.[2] Although there is a flavor of existential explanation within the controversy, giving it a faint cast of ideology, the Arian controversy was only secondarily existential. More importantly for the descriptive analysis, this was a controversy which struggled with the fact that there was no discovered empirical or material basis to determine the answer to the divinity of Jesus. For reasons of doctrine, and ultimately for political motives, this controversy had to be resolved. This important squabble was finally decided at Nicaea in 325 C.E., at a synod called by the Roman emperor, Constantine the Great. This was a man whose tough, pragmatic sense led him to be one of the greatest of the Roman emperors. It is through Constantine that this theological dispute was turned into a political support network.

As pointed out above, the absence of an empirical and material base would seem to determine that the Arian controversy was a contest strictly internal to the Christian, spiritually driven belief system. Consequently, the issue would seem to be primarily a religious controversy, and only by extension a political (and ultimately, ideological) problem. Again, we should remind ourselves that ideology is marked by a material grounding with empirical dimension for description and discussion. What can be said of the theological decision regarding this Aryan controversy is that the resolution brought about by the synod called by Constantine (i.e., the Nicaean Creed[3]), offered substance to relevant political developments. While these theological developments were to eventually reify and impact imperial and medieval political structures, we need to underscore that the decision made at Nicaea in 325, which determined the divinity of Jesus, was theological and not ideological. However, the theology is for us only of secondary concern. It is the political and ideological outgrowth of the Nicaean Creed that concerns us here.

The time strictures are also relevant. We will be looking at Christian ideological development from a little before Constantine the Great's official establishment of the Christian religion to just before 900 C.E., with emphasis on the time frame from Constantine's conversion to Christianity through the mid-7th century.[4] During this period, events that led to the success of Christianity as a religion also transformed it into a serviceable political ideology.

In keeping with the descriptive analysis of ideology observed above, we would have to say that to qualify as any of the three types of ideology (existential, social, or political), Christianity must possess most, if not all, of the following earmarks. (1) It must have roots in empirically verifiable historical events or societal relationships; (2) to a substantial degree it needs to be an inherited idea-system; (3) as ideology, it must have the *potential* for intentional thought; (4) it must have at least the potential to be a closed idea-system whose internal logic can readily substitute for rational thought; (5) it must support a status quo that benefits certain socioeconomic groups as opposed to others; (6) as an ideology, Christianity would have the potential to restrict a clear view of material self-interest, especially that of a subjugated class.

Although we have listed empirical roots as the first qualifier, we will consider this element last as it requires the most careful description.

First, it seems difficult to avoid the conclusion that Christianity is part of an inherited continuum that issued from the Jewish sectarian history that predates Christ by at least two thousand years. This continuum flowed nearly seamlessly into a foundational relationship with that population living within the Judeo-Roman world of the first centuries. This same sort of continuum existed even for those not in any way directly caught up in Judeo-Christian orthodoxy. The later development of Islam will serve as an example.

In the beginning, Christianity was not a sharp break with the Judeo religious culture from which it emerged. Christianity drew its sustenance and authority from Judaism and only slowly surfaced, after many generations, as a distinct belief system, made real largely by the midwifery of Roman politics and Roman Emperors. Prior to the intervention of Roman politics, it is clear that the earliest developmental processes of Christianity are linked to Christianity's inherited Jewish theology. Christianity is therefore both inheritor and heritage.

Second, Christianity certainly qualifies as a purposeful and goal orientated system whose "thinking" can be consciously directed; it obviously has the potential for intentional, directed thought. Any of the ecclesiastical historical pronouncements, from that of the Synod at Nicaea in 325, through Luther's Ninety-five Theses, and on to the most recent of Papal Bulls, leave no doubt as to Christianity's capacity for intentional thought. In fact, it would be awkward at best to argue that any of the thinking behind church activities is without conscious purpose. This brings us to the next point.

Third, that Christian orthodoxy is a closed system, with belief substituting for rational thought. Christianity, like any spiritual system, is painfully slow to respond to outside empirical observation. For example, consider the Catholic Church forcing Galileo to recant his claims concerning the earth's position in the universe. It wasn't until near to the close of the 20th century that the Church formally recognized Galileo and his astonishing scientific accomplishments.

Fourth, one of the directives of an ideology is to legitimize the standing of one social group over another. The question of whether or not Christianity offers support for existing and unequal social orders is a hot button topic. To get our finger off the button, it is advisable to step back from contemporary social alignments. We can do this by fixing our view on historical arrangements which lie outside an immediate ideological distortion. For example, the unequal social relationships between both groups and individuals are easy to recognize if we consider a broad view of medieval, which is to say feudal, arrangements. That these inherently unequal relationships were supported by the Catholic Church is difficult to argue with. While this support was not uniform throughout the Church—that is, individual clerics might have rejected support of the Church's social positions (William of Ockham, comes to mind)—the official idea-system certainly qualifies historically as ideological support for the feudal social order, an order that clearly represented the interests of the few over the many.

This politicization of Christianity and its nominal support for certain conservative social and class arrangements is not accidental, nor is it a new twist on an older world view. Respect and obedience to the power of the state and its rulers is encouraged in all Christians, not just Catholics. Even the titular head of the movement, Jesus Christ, encouraged this: "Render therefore unto Caesar the things which are Caesar's, and unto God the things that are God's."[5] However, in all fairness it needs to be pointed out again that any ecclesiastical interpretation is not without its detractors.[6]

Following the progenitor of the movement came Paul, a man who never knew Jesus, yet was arguably one of the most intellectual, scholarly and influential of the apostolic church leaders. In many ways Paul created Christian doctrine and established the structural rules that grounded the Church. If we are to believe that he wrote much of the New Testament text, we must conclude that this great figure of the Church meant Christians to be satisfied with their station in life and obey and honor earthly authority. The State, at least during Paul's life, and according to scripture, was absolute and could command both loyalty and obedience.[7] All were to remain content with their lot in life, even to the point of excusing slavery for the good harmony of earthly society.[8] According to the founders of Christianity there is no obvious conflict between earthly and heavenly authority—both are to be obeyed. This is not to say that such conflict cannot arise, but only that it is not an inherent and integral part of the Christian idea-system. As the history of Christianity continues, just the opposite will unfold as the ideological status quo.

We can bear witness the supportive role of the official Church for conservative, even fascist elements in the Spanish Civil War (1936-1939), or the duplicity of the Church hierarchy in the rise and solidification of Nazi Germany, or the unwavering support of the Vatican for Augusto Pinochet's anti-communist Chilean dictatorship (1973-1990).[9] While individual members, or priestly sects such as the Jesuits, might press and act in support of social restructuring, the Christian idea-system, *per se*, does not support the overturning of existing social orders.

Given the effects of time and history on ideology, nearly all of the Christian sects came to support a hierarchal circumstance where the elect and the profane are clearly defined and identified with their social roles and their social positions. For accuracy it needs be noted that this is a somewhat later development of Christianity, but the seeds were present from the very beginning—for example, see Book Five of Augustine's *The City Of God*.

A careful theological reading of Augustine allowed certain sects of Christianity to avoid this life as a dead-end street through the notion of predestination. John Calvin offered such a reading of Augustine. According to Calvin, some are saved, and others are damned, and that—as certain Calvinist sects will argue—is preordained by God. The historical sects that believed in predestination are, generally speaking, direct off shoots of the anti-Catholic reformers (e.g., Calvinism and to a lesser degree, Lutheranism). More contemporary and popular sects, such as Presbyterianism, also offer forms of predestination, suggesting that those individuals that are predestined for salvation are marked by worldly success. In contemporary societies garbed by egalitarian ideology, none of this is elucidated in quite the same language as that used by John Calvin. However, the elements are still present in spirit nonetheless. This "spirit" can correctly be interpreted as ideological support for a hierarchal social order.

Fifth, one of the most powerful lures of the Christian religion is the other-worldly concept of heaven and hell and life eternal. Christianity would not have survived the first couple of decades after the death of the original leadership without these other-worldly structural elements, and without their politicization. It should go without saying that this emphasis on life after death found highly sympathetic ears within the Roman military. Up to the advent of Christianity any religious assertion of an eternal life, when offered at all, was available only to the rich and the powerful; the royalties and elites of most pre-Christian societies were often considered to be deities or quasi-deities. For a young legionnaire—often as young as sixteen—signing up for a twenty-year hitch, life after death for all, even the lowliest of the low, proved enticing in the extreme. It is fair to say that the expansion and spread of Christianity was greatly influenced by the Roman army and its legions moving throughout the empire. This is especially true in the later Empire when the army was to become mostly foreign recruits, peoples highly superstitious and susceptible to other-worldly claims.

This politicization is not a necessary element of Christian theology, but a byproduct that enters through the side door because of this other-worldly ingredient: A focus on successful living in this world can be bypassed in favor of eternal bliss in the next. One need not be overly concerned with being a slave or suffering social abuse in this world because of the freedom that awaits in the next, according to Paul.[10] Clearly, such a position can act to suppress immediate self interest in this material world in favor of gaining rapture in the next.

Sixth, in discussing ideology the lack of material roots poses a distinct problem. The key here is to carefully distinguish, as we have been doing, Christianity the theology from Christianity the ideology. Christian theology is a metaphysical belief system, and as such has no empirically propositional roots in the material world. However, as we will show, Christianity, *from the very beginning*, is also a real-world player among history's political institutions, and therefore has to be seen as having political roots in the material world. This cannot help but produce a real-world ideological system.

Developmentally, and in search of the material roots of Christianity, the Christian religion, like most religions, shows very uneven growth. The Christian religion began as a small cult, with the earliest commentary or writings on the cult beginning around 40 years after the death of the leader of the movement, Jesus[11]. Most people in the western world are familiar with the purported life of Jesus, at least enough so that a retelling of the most popular version is not necessary.[12] But the *material* beginning of the Christian movement is another story. The question is, how did the Christian movement get off the ground in the first place?

Discovering how Christianity was launched is not an easy a question to answer. Cults normally arise because they fit into an available niche in the social order. In the absence of close observation of the earliest spreading of Christianity, making sense of the development is difficult. However, historically two things appear to be clear.

First, the earliest beginning of Christianity took place in one of the most unstable and violent times in human history. This was especially true in Roman-occupied Judea, where the desire for salvation was not just a spiritual yearning, but one with brutal physical dimensions. This cannot be too strongly emphasized. For even though we might intellectually *understand* the bloodthirsty Roman occupation of Judea, being out of touch with the weltanschauung of the era makes it very difficult to fully *grasp* the bedrock ideology and the contributions this inherited element brought to *any* spiritual development. This brings up the second point.

Second, the birth of Christianity took place at a time when stories of miracles, demons, omens and apocalyptic visions were commonplace and fully believed. Today we scoff at the kind of magical stories and supernatural horrors that people of the time took utterly for granted. This inability on our part of put ourselves in the mental frame of mind of pagan antiquity prevents us from the clearly grasping on the power that "otherworldliness" had over the way people perceived their society and nature, and consequently how they organized their material outlook and the practical consequences of their lives. For us, living after five hundred years of rationalism and the dominance of science and empiricism, the fact that we are intellectually out of touch with this superstitious cultural outlook is not so remarkable.

It is important to look into the details to flush out the picture. In the beginning, Christianity was merely an offshoot of Judaism, fueled with some of the more magical aspects of paganism. Jewish messiahs and liberators of Judea were not infrequent. Stories such as walking on water, feeding the multitude with a few loafs of bread and a fish, or raising the dead, were commonplace in the day. No one, not the Romans, not the Jews, not even the practitioners of the new faith, considered Christianity as anything other than another pagan Jewish cult. The question arises, then: how did this tiny Jewish offshoot find its niche and develop into a worldwide phenomenon? What did Christianity bring to the historical reality of the time that allowed it to find roots and grow? To a large degree the answer lies in this inherited spirit of the times, at least during the time of Christianity's inception.

At its inception, Christianity was spread by word of mouth, reproduced again and again in face-to-face exchanges where the magic of this new Jewish cult was portrayed, personified and emphasized. Under the brutal Roman occupation that murdered over one millions Jews, nearly one fifth of the total population of Judea, the times appeared not just dangerous, but apocalyptic, and tales of an "end of days" were everywhere and seemed in no way far fetched. Again, it is difficult for us to imagine the wanton carnage that was brought by sword and spear to the people of Judea. The kind of bloodletting that the population witnessed, along with the terrible emotional and spiritual impact brought by the disaster, were traumatic indeed—a fertile bed for visions of apocalyptic solutions.

In the beginning Christianity appealed primarily to the illiterate, the poor, the enslaved, those people in greatest need of hope for an end to their this-world suffering, a hope offered by deliverance and rapture found in the next-world. Recall that for most of the world's pagan religions the chance for an eternal life was reserve for the deserving, that is, the well-to-do and high placed. At last here was a religion where the down-trodden and hopeless had hope; Christianity was a promise of salvation for the illiterate, the poor and enslaved—the vast majority of the world.

It is quite true that in the beginning, those at the bottom of the social pyramid were offered deliverance and a chance to worship in an atmosphere of charity and freedom. The new god was a god accepting of them because he was one of them. This "Lamb of God" was indeed seen as one of the poor and the meek, but also a man who brought with him salvation and an end to their suffering.

It is not entirely fair to characterize these poor as merely gullible. These poor of Judea were desperate and alienated from both Judaism and the dominant pagan religions. Judaism and the pagan religions were not for the poor and the under-classes. Judaism, for example, required (and still does) a hefty fee to become a member of a synagogue. Religions of the time were for the well-to-do, for the status seekers, those who were class conscious and for those from the ruling elite. The Christian cults began to develop first in Judean communities of the social flotsam, the base and outcast of the realm. Through this new Christian cult a sense of community began to develop where the poor could find refuge, assistance and the promise of an afterworld unconstrained by their poverty and lowly position. These things set the various Christian cults apart from Judaism and the many pagan religions where wealth and social standing presided over the blessings of the gods, and to a certain extent, protection from Roman might. In some ways Christianity was the revenge of the poor and the weak against the gods of the powerful and high born. Christianity grew out of the basest of material life, promising resurrection to the social living dead. For the Christians there was the promise of a glorious after-life. The Christians had, after all, a leader who had beaten the cruelty of Rome and had he himself risen from the dead. Most importantly, Jesus promised the same salvation to all who would believe.

In the hundred years after the death of Jesus the Romans, in the process of assaulting the Jews in Judea, inadvertently scattered the new cult of the Christian-Jews across the Middle East. The carnage the Romans brought to Judea affected not just the Jews, but the whole of Asia Minor, and eventually the empire itself. In the ten year period from 63 to 73 C.E., the Romans killed over a million habitants of Judea; and it has to be remembered that this was not mechanized killing. This was slaughter done with spear and sword. Given the lesser population of the time and the viciousness of the bloodletting, the fear and trauma must have been horrific. Many fled out of Judea, Jews and Christian-Jews alike. In the pursuit of two brutal wars against the inhabitants of Judea, Rome inadvertently spread the new religion among the Gentiles. There exists precious little record keeping concerning this mass scattering, but there is little doubt that the deportation of the Jewish people from Judea was widespread and extensive. In Jewish tradition, this dispersal is often referred to as the Diaspora.

Considering the weak beginning of the movement, it is not necessary to look into the question of whether or not Christian-Judaism represented any sort of overt revolutionary stand against the Roman occupation. Perhaps rebellion against Rome was a motivating factor, or perhaps it was just the Roman perception of Jews and Christian-Jews, or perhaps neither is correct. In all likelihood, the Roman military authorities probably thought very little or perhaps not at all about this new and obscure Christian-Jewish cult. For our purposes here, it is only important to recognize that throughout the ancient world religion and politics were not easily separated from each other; pagan rulers were routinely considered to be either gods or figures who spoke for the gods. From this bundling stems much of the modern wrangling over whether it was the Christian religion that was being persecuted, or a Roman attempt to stamp out the possible political derivations of the spiritual cult. We should also note that this lack of easy separation of politics and religion remained true in the western world until around the mid-18th century; this separation of politics and religion was one of the significant changes that helped speed the close of the Modern Era (1500 - c.1920).

It was during these Jewish Wars waged by the Romans that the Christian-Jews began to whither in Judea, leading the proselytizers of Christianity, such as Paul, to move into the Gentile world to spread the new religion.[13] Success in the Greek world was made all the easier by pagan traditions. In the Greek world, and the Roman, human beings becoming divine and gods taking on human form had a long tradition. Coupled with the belief in the possibility of a glorious here-after, something of only the dimmest mention in both pagan and Jewish traditions, the Gentile world proved fertile soil for the Christian seed.

Christianity began as a Jewish cult. By the turn of the 4th century this cult, during its early struggle with real world conditions, manifested some or all of the ingredients of a coherent, ideological framework. Even before wholesale intervention by the politics of Rome, Christianity had already developed (1) material roots in the Roman occupation, (2) inherited both Jewish and pagan spiritual traditions, and (3) possessed the potential for intentional thought. These first three were the general preconditions presented by history and cultural considerations that were largely beyond the immediate control of the players in the drama. Over time, the other three ingredients (analyzed in greater detail later) would emerge with the intervention of Roman politics. These three—(4) a closed system of thought that (5) benefited certain groups over others and (6) restricted those deposed social groups from a full understanding of the political agenda which controlled their material self-interest—would soon develop more willfully, a willfulness consciously directed by the elite players.

Between 100 and 300 C.E. this new cult had spread as far as Rome itself, but remained small, secretive, and hostile to the gods of the Romans. To be secretive was bad enough for the Roman authorities, but to be secretive *and* hostile to Rome's pagan gods, whose good will was necessary for the well being of the Roman state, was *politically* intolerable. Christianity was perceived as a threat to the rationale and viability of the Roman state.

III. Rome and Late Antiquity

One way to look at the history of late Rome, as well as late antiquity, is to see it as the unfolding and inauguration of Christian ideology. Of course, Christianity is not the sole historical legacy of Roman antiquity. The development of bureaucratic organization, structural engineering and the craft of war all stand as examples of important, if not always positive, contributions by Rome to modern human organization. These are, however, all legacies of a practical nature. The longest lasting immaterial, that is to say, ideological, residue left by the late Roman period is found in the evolution of the Christian idea-system.

The evolution of Christianity involved both theological and political aspects, with the theology, *qua* ideology, taking on an increasingly mediative role, and in the end, justifying political developments. Though the principle focus here is broadly ideological rather than narrowly theological, it is obvious that the two emerged together, and until toward the end of the Modern Era were always difficult to separate. From the Crusades to the Thirty Years War (1618-1648), there are numerous and overt historical examples of the impracticality of such a clear separation. To be sure, the kinds of ideologies at work in these events were overtly political, but they were also plaited through with Christian doctrine. Though Christian ideology acted as mediator and justification in these situations, the historian will typically prefer to focus on that ideology which best supports an unencumbered analysis of concrete political conditions. Even granting certain internal inconsistencies in religious thinking, which can hamper a full understanding of the overall political development of the West, the dominant religious idea-system must be considered and analyzed, along with the hosting, concrete conditions.

Before going specifically into Christian political ideology, it is a necessary preliminary step to investigate the nature of religion in Antiquity. Particularly relevant to this study is the state of religion in the society of the late period of the Roman Empire. But first, religion in Antiquity did not have the same relationship with political structures that was to develop in the Modern Era (1500 - c.1920). The legal, as well as conceptual, divorce of church and state is a relatively new phenomenon in Western history, as it only began to emerge in the mid-Modern period. In Antiquity, there existed no such separation between religion and the state. Religion and the state were one. Understanding this is critical if we wish to fully grasp the rise of Christianity as a *political* ideology in the late Roman period.

It was considered a symptom of political health in Antiquity when unity existed between the dominant religion and the state. The blending of church and state greatly facilitated the ease with which the ruling order could use ideology for mediation and justification of the hugely unequal social order. Just as the co-mingling of religion and politics offered a unified world view that those under its aegis took completely for granted, so too, did the use of religion for political justification, even though it was not a fully conscious process on the part of the ruling classes. In the ideological world all appeared as it was intended. That is, within the strictures of the idea-system, the player, whether ruler or ruled, saw nothing out of place or amiss. Such is the blinding power of ideology supplemented by official doctrine.

The Roman state religion contained the last three elements of political ideology we earlier promised to analyze in greater detail: (4) the state religion was closed and not open to general debate, (5) whether conscious or unconscious, the state religion certainly benefited the ruling classes in their manipulation of the subjugated classes, and (6) the state religion hid the agenda of the decision makers from the those outside the immediate circles of power. Understanding these three, key points will make clearer the threatened disruption to political control that could be brought about by unofficial, upstart religions—particularly those that professed to offer the exploited masses within the boundaries of the empire the support of a god and life eternal.

All three of these elements are found in the Roman pagan religions.

First: Debate was not tolerated. The Roman Emperors stood at the pinnacle, often taking on the mantle of a god, or calming to be a conduit to the gods. Roman emperors would claim to be the *Pontifex Maximus* of the gods, or the Vicar of Jupiter Capitolinus, both of these being common expressions for the religious function of the emperor. It should be noted, of course, that the similarity of these offices with later prelates of the Church is obvious. As the emperor spoke for the gods, to question his authority was to question the authority of the gods. In addition, as the priests of the pagan religions were in the service of the imperial government, the state political-religious system was effectively a closed system to outsiders and outside influence.

Second: none, except for those emperors who were completely insane, actually believed they were god; but the superstitious population never doubted that the gods spoke through the emperor. The Emperor's word was the word of the gods, and all who listened and believed in the pronouncements of the gods, believed in the Emperor and his divine abilities. That this belief in the emperor's divinity could be used to manipulate the population and legitimize imperial authority was obvious to all, except, apparently, the great masses of Roman subjects.

Third, how much of this ideology the ruling order actually believed in is secondary to understanding the power of the ideology to disguise the actual power relationships and the agenda of the elite from the general population. Control and sole proprietorship of the state religion, *qua* ideology, was one of the greatest of the imperial powers. Even if many of the emperors were not fully conscious that they possessed that power, that power was theirs, a power behind which to hide and control.

In general, the politics of Rome, which is to say the concrete power relationships, were always manipulative, dangerous and subject to unexpected demands from forces beyond the immediate control of the imperial machinery. We might add to this that Roman politics were almost always individualistic, opportunistic and cynical; this should come as no surprise. We will go into the particulars of this below when considering the historical context, but for the moment, it is enough to note that the atmosphere of power politics in Rome's late period was not conducive to any calm and reflective development of a coherent idea-system. Indeed, the study of ideology, *per se*, was well beyond the intellectual resources existent at the time. The rise and development of Christian political ideology as transformed into Roman political ideology was occurred in fits and starts, as mirrored, for that matter, the development of Christianity as an existential ideology.

The Christian idea-system roiled with the tumultuous politics of the time and only coalesced at the end of a long and often bloody birth process. This process took place within a definite reality, a well-defined, concrete historical process. For our purposes here, it is probably not useful to go into detail concerning theological debates within the Church at the time of the ascendancy of Christianity. The theological debates within the Church concern both those ideas that survived the historical process and those that did not. Some are more important than others, but none of them directly concern us here. For example, the question of who exactly Jesus Christ was is not as an important a question as who his followers *thought he was*. Dispensing with the theological issue makes possible the examination of those real-world struggles that launched Christianity as a serious ideological force. Recognize that although there were definite religious overtones to the many resolutions of these concrete struggles, our concern here is with the ideas that survived those political and historical entanglements of the time and not the otherworldly debates. Many fine works analyze the theological debates that took place in late antiquity in great and honest detail.[14] In this search for ideological development, our concern is with the shifting political dynamic, which is to say, the shifting power relationships, in late antiquity. For it is those shifting relations that nurtured the rise of Christianity in general and the Catholic Church in particular.

A. Historical context and the early development of Christian ideology

Right from the very beginning, the history of Christianity is the history of a declining Rome. The two histories are inseparable. In fact, if it were not for the historical and political disposition of the late Empire, Christianity, as a religion, and most certainly as an ideology, would have existed, then faded away as an obscure cultish offshoot of Judaism. As it was, the Empire and Christianity became so intertwined—the one a hardened political system and the other an otherworldly, developing spiritual system—that it is difficult to see the exact point where one ended and the other began. The fact that the end of Rome's western domination appears to slide so seamlessly into a Europe managed by a provincial feudalism was largely made possible by both the administrative structure of the church and Christian ideology. The ideology and the infrastructure of the new Church made the development of these harsh and oppressive feudal arrangements not just justifiably possible, but fully legitimized and integrated into the world view of the populace.

This raises a pertinent consideration that can clearly distinguish the world view of antiquity from that of later times. Empires, particularly Rome (though there were others, such as that carved out by Alexander) suffered from an absence of theme, or a consistent systematic worldview that we can only see as a lack of ideological coherence. Pagan religions hardly made up for this lack of a coherent world view. The works of Plato and Aristotle acted as critical reflections, but did not act to legitimize the raising of empires. This black hole of ideological coherence was to have far reaching practical considerations for many of the ancient empires. The absence of systematic political idea-systems undermined many of the ancient, imperial infrastructures. Internally consistent idea-systems are the philosophical glue binding political infrastructures to their concrete realities. Modern ideologies, as opposed to antiquity, offer contemporary political infrastructures a greater *sense* of coherence and stability; that is,

242

a complete and comprehensive ideology to buttress the claim of the social structure for legitimacy.

This missing coherence in political ideology meant that many of the ancient political empires possessed little or no sense of authority, other than outright violence. Many of these entities were simply military constructs held together by brute force. This lack of ideology became painfully obvious when the titular head was removed from the scene. Smooth transitions were impossible. Bloodbaths for control of the political infrastructure typically ensued, with all of the attending societal disruptions, but no lasting stability.

Both the cause and result of this lack of a legitimizing political ideology is that many of the empires of antiquity, such as Rome, were affairs of a personal nature, or a succession of personal affairs.[15] Some of these personal relations attempted to survive through some form of nepotism, held together by coercive power, with only a nod to tradition or pagan religious flimflam. While these traditional and dogmatic elements were always present in the Roman state sponsored religions, for the most part when the personal dictator of the Empire was removed, the Roman world was up for grabs.

This led to succession by coercion, force and war. Once the Roman Republic was overthrown, individual personality came to the fore once again as the central motif, always with the army as ubiquitous theme-maker. Recall that this is an army highly susceptible to the shifting caprice of spiritual idea-systems. Starting with Julius Caesar, power came at the tip of a sword, ungrounded in any consistent ideological justification. There was no natural law of succession, as there was no idea-system to support the political structure. Rome stumbled from ruler to ruler, a political vacuum in search of legitimacy. The difficulties, downsides, and drawbacks of this lack of ideological glue became all the more glaring as the Empire entered its long decline. The last great emperor, Constantine, made a great attempt to understand and reverse this decline and in so doing drew on all the available resources to bring legitimacy to his one-man rule. Constantine was the first to employ Christianity as a resource. In all likelihood, he understood neither the long-term implications of his political actions nor the power of Christianity as an ideological force. But he did understand its supporting and legitimizing role in his command of the army and therefore the empire.

Constantine ruled Rome from 306 (or 324, depending on one's definition of rule) to his death in 337. Constantine received a very decent education at the Emperor Diocletian's court and by his early 20's was campaigning to secure Rome's Danube bordor. By all accounts the matrial arm of his rule was honed and he was on his way to becoming a general of considerable talent. His political skills were yet to be developed.

Recall now that Constantine's mother and stepsister were both Christian. There is little doubt that this was an important fact in Constantine's life. The effect on Constatnine of his mother's choice to follow this new Christian religion will probably never be fully appreciated, but it must not be underestimated. Constantine's rule was marked from beginning to end by the emergence of Christianity.

In 303 Constantine witnessed Diocletian's ruthless persecutions of the Christians.[16] To fully digest the meaning of these Christian persecutions, it is necessary to have some understanding of the relationship between the Jewish people and the Roman state. Judea had always been a special problem for the occupying Romans. The Jews were always a stubborn and rebellious group. The Romans correctly understood this cantankerousness as emanating from Hebrew monotheism and otherworldly doctrines which were at the base of their religious ideology. In the hundred years following the birth of Christ, the Romans slaughtered nearly a million and a half Jews in order to bring the province under control.[17] The most heinious of these Jewish wars occurred shortly after the ministry and death of Christ (c. 66 C.E.). There was no mechanization for this slaughter—no explosives, no gas, only the sword and spear to accomplish this genocide. While the majority of these victims of Rome were Jews, many were from the new upstart religion that worshiped the Jew, Jesus Christ, as a God, a prophet, or godlike figure; at this point the nature of the Christ was yet to be defined. This would have to wait for the Synod at Nicaea in 325 CE.

There is in no real way to prove that Diocletian's anti-Christianity was not politically inspired. Diocletian was a reactionary of sorts and desired to rekindle the ancient glory of Rome, which meant revival of the old codes of conduct and of the pagan religion. To a certain extent, it would follow that stamping out upstart cults opposed to paganism was a definite part of the planned revival.[18] This revival was bundled with some very practical concerns for the practical Emperor Diocletian. Religion was one of the pillars of imperial rule, and by extention, support for the emperor who held office. Christians held themselves apart and aloof. Diocletian correctly saw the rise of Christianity as a force undermining the legitimacy of Roman occupation of large sections of the eastern proviences. Christians, though still a relatively small sect, were nonetheless a visible, resistant minority, having migrated from Judea to as far as Rome and Iberia. They resisted legitimizing imperial standards by refusing to participate in traditional pagan ceremonies, advising against military training, and collecting together in secret societies praying to a god that demanded an allegiance before that due the emperor. By the end of Diocletian's rule Constantine must have seen the stress on the empire as epitomized by the Christian presecutions.

The history of Rome upon the entrance of Constantine was a virulent and confusing time. The year of the four emperors oversaw territories under almost constant siege. The reality of the time was an unrelenting frontier penetration by tribal raiders, coupled with the continuous friction between the four emperors. Assaulted from without and torn from within, the political system was always threatening to unravel. Controlling the historical forces behind these threats was probably beyond any one individual. Constantine did the next best thing. If Constantine could not dominate these historical forces, his greatness was revealed in his ability to manipulate them. Constantine's conversion to Christianity is perhaps the most forceful, and most fateful, of these manipulations.

Constantine's conversion to Christianity gave full vent to the development of a potent and unifying idea-system. It was through Constantine's good offices that the ideology of the Catholic Church was raised to political authority. Of course, there is no way of knowing what precisely was in Constantine's mind at the point of his conversion, and there is no rational reason to assume that his conversion to Christianity was not sincere and genuine in every respect. However, even given that, it is still critical to bear in mind that Constantine was a ruler in a situation fraught with struggle and danger for him and the Empire he ruled.

B. History, Politics and Constantine's Motives

The story of the emperor Constantine's conversion to Christianity is one of history turned legend. Legend has it that the emperor Constantine saw a cross in the sky and an inscription that promised victory in an upcoming battle (Battle of the Milvian Bridge, 312). Armed with this divine foretelling, Constantine crushed the opposition and was on his way to becoming the sole emperor of Rome. Of course, this is the legend. The actual reality of the event was almost certainly different.

By the turn of the 4th century four emperors (the Tetrarchy) came to rule the Roman Empire, a volatile and cumbersome system which evolved in response to the slow disintegration of control over vast and difficult holdings. This slow disintegration was reflected in the fragmenting of the state religion. Probably in response to the anxiety brought about by the increasing social instability and political uncertainly, numerous religions and cults were springing up throughout the empire. Most were of local interest only. The "victory" of one of these cults, these ideologies, over the others would greatly facilitate political control. The question is, if Christianity made up only about 10 percent of the entire Roman population, why did Christian ideology emerge victorious as the Roman state religion?

To get a grip on this question, it is far better to understand the political and material realities presented by Christianity than the theological aspects. These material realities are the elements that certainly would not be overlooked by a great political statesman like Constantine. They can be listed as follows: (1) Christianity stood outside the imperial circle and was therefore an opposition force contributing to the Empire's fragmentation. This fragmentation was a situation that could not be allowed to continue. Since the great persecutions of Christian sects had proven unsuccessful, and even counterproductive, co-option was the next bold step open to Constantine. (2) Christianity had a social and intellectual infrastructure that was both coherent and spread throughout the empire. (3) Christianity's governing structure was looking increasingly like that of the Roman state. The far-flung bishops, from Rome to Alexandria, were similar to the Roman Paretorian Prefects, the Dioceses would reflect the Metropolitans, and the Christian rulers of the provinces were the Archbishops, and the cities had their bishops. Certainly, this would have been recognizable to Constantine as a ready made, supportive political infrastructure. (4) Military cohesion and loyalty were being affected as increasing numbers of soldiers were taking up the new religion. As discussed before, this growing conversion by the army was no doubt inspired by the Christian promise of an afterlife, something that would naturally appeal to soldiers living always in the shadow of death. (5) The new religion was affecting the great sea of poor in the empire, potentially creating a mass of disloyal population—or of loyal supporters. None of these elements of control would have been overlooked by a politician as ambitious and intellectually astute as Constantine. If nothing else, he was a strong and decisive leader who had proven in the past that he understood all his options.

At the time of his famous "Christian vision" (312 C.E.), Constantine was locked in a life or death struggle for control of the western empire with a second emperor the Tetrarchy, Maxentius. Constantine's army had marched and fought from Gaul, across the Alps, and down through northern Italy. When Constantine at last arrived at the gates of Rome, his army was exhausted, outnumbered five to one, and demoralized by a march far from home. Constantine, a more than adequate military commander, certainly recognized the need to offer his troops a morale boost.

Before going on, we need to reflect on the existing idea-systems of the time, particularly those among the tribes of the Rhine where Constantine recruited most of his troops. Unlike Roman soldiers, these pagan soldiers were not only uneducated and illiterate, but were also strong believers in ideologies of animism and the "magic of the sign". These pagan soldiers organized their lives around the magical intervention of the gods. Everywhere they looked there were symbols and signs foretelling the future. From a reading of the entrails of goats, to the sudden death of a bird falling out of the sky and landing at their feet, the interpretations by pagan priests were fully believed and acted upon. It is exceedingly difficult for us, with our strong lineage of science and empirical study, to comprehend the system of ideas that gripped these men, or to have empathy for their worldview. Theirs was a system where the sun, the moon and the wind in the trees were easily recognized as gods, or divinely driven signs to be carefully listened to and obeyed under pain of a death without the option of an afterlife. Theirs was a fearful world dominated by magic and spirits, a fanciful realm full of devils and demons in which they fully believed. Into this superstitious morass comes Constantine's miraculous vision.

As history turned legend goes, on the day before the battle with Maxentius Constantine looked up in the sky and saw a potent vision. The exact when-and-where was not accurately recorded and consequently those details are a little fuzzy. But it was generally held at the time that Constantine looked up at the noonday sun on the day before the battle and saw the first two letters of the Greek spelling of Christ. The Emperor also saw the words "Conquer by this."

Constantine's first reports were of these letters. He did not report that he had seen a vision of the gibbet upon which the Christ was hung, as was later claimed. Only after much time had passed was this revised version of Constantine seeing the cross in the sky presented. However, it was never clear whether Constantine authorized the change from the letters to the gibbet, or whether it was the work of church revisionists. But by either measure the result was the same. A new and potent symbol was introduced to the Roman world.

One thing seems certain about the actual reality of what Constantine saw (or fabricated). He might have had some sort of vision, as he described, or he might have seen a fairly common meteorological event for that time of year called a solar halo; perhaps the brilliance of the sun, underwritten by some deep psychological connection with his Christian mother and step sister, may have caused him to see things that were not there. Or more cynically, we might consider that he might have simply made the whole thing up for practical purposes based on his understanding of his pagan legionaries. It was not the first time Constantine had claimed visions, only before it was Apollo (C.E. 310) who foretold of his victory.[19] For the purposes of the coming battle with Maxentius it did not really matter what the Emperor saw. What was important for Constantine's troops was the perception of what happened and the belief in divine intervention. With their shields now painted over with the labarum Constantine claimed to have seen,[20] his troops, now reenergized by the certainty of divine guidance, the comfort of an after-life, and the blessings of a god, marched to victory.

Of course, it helped a great deal that Maxentius had strategically blundered in the arrangement of his troops. He deployed his men in such a way as to take advantage of their superior number. Inexplicably, however, Maxentius had placed his troops with their back to the river Tiber. He had done this in such a way that he had left his forces only a single narrow bridge to fall back on. Finally, Maxentius himself was killed early in the battle, sending his troops into panic.

Superstitiously, the defeat of Maxentius was expected by the legions of Constantine and by the people of Rome, for it was all foretold to Constantine by the new Roman god, Jesus Christ. At this point it mattered little what Constantine himself might have believed. The pieces on the political chessboard were all in play and he could not back out of this changing game if he had wanted to. History now had him reading from a Christian script. Constantine was now beholden to the new faith for his victory, the Christian faith. Of course, the emperor's conversion might have been authentic, but from the standpoint of the history surrounding Constantine's foray into Christianity, it is entirely possible that the conversion was not so much based on belief as it was on desperate, political circumstances.

Constantine was an immensely successful ruler during one of the most sinister and unstable of times—the approaching end of Roman hegemony. It would be difficult to imagine a successful ruler of Rome who was not utterly calculated in his handling of power. If he was to stay in power he had to carefully weigh every move, every thought in the most worldly and down to earth manner possible. Constantine survived battlefields and a ruthless political system to die in a bed—an almost unheard of accomplishment for Roman emperors in late antiquity. Again, while there is no reason to doubt the sincerity of Constantine's conversion to Christianity, the political implication and ramifications of this conversion would not have escaped so intelligent and capable a political strategist. There is little doubt that his conversion was also propitious for political survival.

Christianity's rise to dominate European thought for a thousand years was nearly exclusively the result of the political effects of Constantine's conversion. So, whether Constantine's conversion to Christianity was sincere or merely a ruse is beside the point of its political impact. When considering the rise of the Christian ideology as a unifying political force for the next thousand years, it is the blend of the ideology and its impact on the state that we must study and not the emperor's personal beliefs. However, the emperor's political activities help tell the story behind his personal regard for the new Christian ideology. For that, we must look again, and in some detail, at the Council of Nicaea in 325 C.E.

At the top of the 4th century a powerful schism was threatening to tear the young religion apart. This was the "Arian Controversy." This schism arose over the nature of Jesus Christ. Was Jesus a man, simply a prophet of God? Was Jesus like John the Baptist, or the later Mohammad, or was he divine, a god? Was he a god in his own right, a part of the godhead, or an earthbound, wise and compassionate Rabbi? Constantine, who ordered the gathering of bishops for the synod, needed a resolution to the looming schism. Constantine's actions regarding this threatened schism are telling of his interest in (and interpretation of) the new ideology's political implications. Today, the political impact of Christianity is obvious. In the fourth century it was not. The recognition of Christianity's political importance marked Constantine's true genius.

The Arian controversy appeared, at least on the surface, simple enough. The wrangling over the issue focused on the theological work of the Alexandrian priest Arius. Arius logically considered that if Jesus was the son of God, then God must have preceded the Son and therefore there was a time when the Son did not exist. This would mean that Jesus was not of a divine nature. One of the many implications here was that belief in Jesus could not ensure forgiveness of sin and eternal life. This conclusion threatened to hollow out two major defining points of Christianity. The first is the pivotal importance of eternal life to the Christian idea-system: an offering of salvation to all, even the poor, the sick and the powerless, and most importantly, the common foot soldier. Without the notion of life after death for all, Christianity threatened to slide back into the sea of forgotten pagan religions. The second issue is one that would dog Christianity down through the centuries: the absolute necessity of orthodox thinking substituting for freedom of thought.

For the emperor Constantine there was also a political dimension. Roman emperors had always enhanced their ruling positions by assuming the mantel of the vicar of the gods. For Constantine to be in control of this religious support of the Roman imperial infrastructure, it was important that Jesus be indisputably declared divine. Roman emperors also took on the position of *Pontifex Maximus*, that is, the highest pagan priest among high priests. When Constantine arrived at Nicaea, determined to keep himself squarely in the legitimizing glow of the new religion, he did so as the highest priest of the Roman world, the Pontifex Maximus.

Constantine convened the Council at Nicaea in 325, with himself presiding as the Pontifex Maximus and the Vicar of God. Constantine arrived in all his imperial splendor, taking the seat at the head of the council. He intended to make an impact on the assembled bishops, most of who were from the east where Arius had the greatest influence. Constantine needed to override that eastern influence. His political position would tolerate no split in the ideology, no controversy. The emperor needed an unambiguous assurance from the Council that divinity played a direct role in the affairs of the empire, a direct role that would play out through him, Constantine, and all successive emperors. There could be no split in the ideology that shored up the empire's political hegemony. This concern would lead to a second and perhaps more pressing need of Constantine's: the emperor also needed unequivocal assurance from the high priests of the Church that a universal idea-system supported his direct role in ensuring the blessings of that divinity. He needed authoritative benediction from the Council that his was a rule reflective of divinity and that he, the Emperor, was still the Vicar of God.[21] Obviously, this need directly affected his political position and therefore it is easy to understand that correct orthodoxy became a prime mission of the Christian emperor at Nicaea. Constantine bent every effort to ensure that the followers of Arius would come to support his desired view that Christ was divine, and he pressed for a unanimous vote on the issue. In the end, all but two bishops signed on to the Nicaean Creed and Catholic Christianity became the official religion of the Roman state.

What Constantine and the empire gained from the resolution of this controversy was a coherent ideology. Though there is no conclusive proof, Constantine himself was probably disposed to see Jesus as divine. He certainly pressed for this conclusion. However, it might also be argued that his interest in divinity was secondary to his political interest in the unity of thought provided by Christ as a part of the Godhead. This interpretation certainly suited his political agenda as well and brought a coherent orthodoxy to his new state religion.

~

However, not all about the new religion was new, and not all about Christianity's fit was pure politics. Christianity landed in the midst of a healthy and fertile ecclesiastical environment. Like a Venn diagram, the points of overlap between the pagan idea system and the Christian system were many and varied. Ten points can be made regarding this susceptible and impressionable environment that was ancient Rome.

1. There was no interfaith hostility aimed at killing off a young Christian movement. Pagan religions were pantheons themselves and could

easily assimilate new gods. Christianity, on the other hand, was hostile to the pagan religions, believing that pagan gods were demons and agents of the devil. This hostility gave Christianity a hard and often violent competitive edge *vis-à-vis* paganism's more accommodating attitude. One need only remember that the conversion of much of northern Europe was ruthlessly brought and bought at the tip of a spear wielded by such as Charlemagne. For that matter, both modern religions, Christianity and Islam, were born of sword and blood.

2. Christianity was missionary in intent. In the Roman world only Judaism was somewhat alike in this regard—and this was marginal. But unlike Judaism, Christianity made no demands of circumcision for converts, or dietary restrictions (both of these demands being obvious discouragements to potential converts). For the Romans, moving from one cult to another was easy and nearly seamless; the removal of the Jewish speed bumps along the way to Christian conversion only made the move a glide rather than a stumble and lurch.

3. There was the promise of a glorious afterlife, and not only for the rich who could buy their passage to the underworld. This gave Christianity great appeal to the masses of slaves and oppressed whose labor built the physical infrastructure of the empire. Even more importantly, the promise of an afterlife found great and special appeal to those makers-of-emperors, the military where sudden and violent death was an assumed job risk. One cannot too strongly stress the role of the army as the great advocator for the new religion. For the entire length of a legionnaire's enlistment, death was ever present and cast a long shadow. This was the first religion that offered the common foot soldier salvation in the form of an everlasting afterlife. Such a promise spread rapidly through the ranks of the army, cementing Christianity's political power with the rights offered by the purveyors of coercion.

4. Christianity appealed to the urban poor. Christianity filled that need for communication with the "other world" for the average Roman, the needy and even the destitute, which the pagan religions put out of reach. Pagan religions demanded sacrifices to curry favor with the gods. This was an expense that shut out the poor. Judaism demanded tithes from the members of the synagogue, also hindering participation by the lower classes. Christianity, however, made charity and support for the poor a universal duty. It was a religion not so much of sacrifice as of

enfolding, of welcome gathering rather than class dividing. In a sense, these ecclesiastical accoutrements made Christianity the only religion completely available to the great masses of the Empire and eventually the masses of Europe.

5. Christianity had universal appeal and was not bound by local myths, needs and customs. There was nothing exclusive about Christianity. It tended to absorb local customs rather than reject them. The Christian cult of Santeria stands as an extreme example of the flexibility of inclusive Christianity.[22] Another rather obvious example of Christianity's absorption of pagan rights is human sacrifice. Recall that Christ was called the Lamb of God, whose sacrifice was intended to appease a wrathful god and cleanse Christ's followers of all sin. But such human sacrifice was not completely pagan in origin. The Judeo-Christian bible is replete with reports of God's demands for human sacrifice.[23]

6. Christianity had built-in preconditions for an educated hierarchy. One conspicuous precondition would have been the demand for a literate elite in an illiterate world. This impetus for an educated hierarchy led to organizational structures unavailable to pagan religions. These educated leaders were missionaries and possessed the necessary organizational skill required to build a lasting structural order and take advantage of the near universality of ignorance and superstition.

It might be noted here that the church actively discouraged literacy, as this gave a huge advantage to Rome's prelates, *vis-à-vis* temporal rulers. In the end, and by the close of the 16th century, widespread literacy greatly facilitated the rise of Protestantism by disseminating the bible in common language. I refer here to Martin Luther and his translation of the bible into German. This effectively removed the priest as the intermediary and interpreter of god's word. It also effectively undermined the church's authority over the laity.

7. Unity and universalism were the great organizational en-framing of Christianity. Internal confusion, conflict and contradiction brought on by the multiple authors of the Scriptures, and their various interpretations, were largely confined to the literate elite of the church and did not interrupt the devotion of a following, illiterate mass. Of course, the rise of print and widespread reading by the masses ended the church's monopoly of the interpretation of god's word. God's word, or ideology, rapidly achieved a direct following with the masses of Europe.

8. Because of this fundamental universality of Christianity, it was almost inevitable that the political state (i.e., Rome) would seize and support this religion as an idea-system to underwrite the legitimacy of a far flung and autocratic empire. There is little doubt that the rising popularity of the new religion with the army was not lost on the ruling elite. These realizations by the elite soon lead to acceptance and promotion of the new religion, and eventually control.

9. The Roman emperor Constantine made Christianity the official religion of the empire. In so doing he made the bishops of the church men of power, offering them a political life as well as a religious one. The bishops soon eagerly accepted and replaced magistrates in civil matters, thus gaining local authority that was bound to leadership in Rome. This fusion of the new religion to the legal structure wed the fate of Christianity to that of the Roman political structure.

10. The physical, bureaucratic structure of the church began to take on the appearance of a shadow government. From the monasteries, to the top of the ecclesiastical structure, the church aped the Roman state, with bishops modeled on Roman Prefects, the Archbishops the provincial rulers, and the Pope as the emperor of this expanding spiritual community. The ideology became entwined with concrete political structures, providing the spiritual and political bridge between the waning imperial system and the new, emerging feudal system that would dominate Europe for a thousand years to come.

C. Transition to Christendom

The nearly seamless transition from Imperial Rome to feudal Europe was largely facilitated through Christian ideology and the shadowy, quasi-political material apparatus of the Catholic Church. Through this transition that we can begin to clearly see the reification of political institutions through the ideological function of legitimization. The rise of an Emperor or King was no longer a simple matter of his installation at the head of an army. Though naked power was still present, as it is in all political situations, it became obscured by the Christian ideology that acted to legitimize the ruling order. This is a pronounced change from imperial politics, where emperors came to power without the assistance of the state religion and merely assumed the mantel of pagan spiritual leadership. At around 500 C.E. the process seemed to complete itself. From this point forward political leaders came to their positions by the grace and good offices of religious institutions. Raw power was certainly still necessary to facilitate a transition in the ruling power, and was certainly still present in every day medieval, political struggles. However, from 500 C.E. onward the naked fist could be concealed beneath the velvet glove of Christian ideology.

Constantine the Great's death (337 C.E.) marked the last gasp of an assured Roman authority as a unified and coherent world power. The Theodosian dynasty (392–455) that followed witnessed the breakup of the Empire into an east half and west half. In Rome itself, following the 476 deposition of the young Emperor Romulus Augustulus by Odovacar, a barbarian chieftain of Hunnish background, the final chapter in the history book of the Roman Imperial period officially came to a close. Of course, the reality behind the shifting of social structures and their concomitant political arrangements is not so tidy as the closing of a book or a final exam in a history class. The living dynamic is a complex and time-consuming process to analyze. Our purposes here are to quit Rome in order to briefly introduce the power relations of feudal Europe as they were influenced and shaped by Christian ideology as well as the physical presence of the Catholic Church.

During the 5th century, the centers of European power began their shift north into the Germanic and Frankish territories. The city of Rome fell into ruins, being sacked multiple times by Germanic armies. The population of the city was reduced to about a tenth of the size it had been under the Imperial banner. This decaying situation remained the case until the new, northern centers of power re-invented Rome and infused it with both the new Christian ideology and the politicization of that theocratic ideology.

Through a series of *quid pro quos* between the Church and the first of the Carolingian monarchs, Pepin the Short (714—768), the Papal States, with Rome at the heart, were re-invented and established. Pepin's son, Charlemagne (742—814), converted thousands at the point of a sword, codified the states, and installed popes as rulers over these newly devised territories. There was nothing hidden here. Christianity was not just the political ideology in the new reality of the Papal States. Christianity represented a flowering of ideological thinking throughout Europe. It became the dominant worldview. It did not simply develop along with the shift in social and material relations emerging from the new centers of power. For a millennium, Catholic Christianity was the ideological engine which was to provide the primary support for the political arrangements of feudalism. Even if it is said that Christianity was not the "official state religion" as it had been in late Rome, it was an eager ombudsman, the apologizer and ideological justifier of the new European ruling order. Just as Christianity cannot be understood without understanding the politics of late Antiquity, the politics of feudalism cannot be understood without an understanding of Christian ideology.

Clovis I (466—511), the first of the great Frankish kings and founder of the Merovingian line of monarchs, was among the first to make fast and ready use of Christian ideology. He converted from paganism to Catholic Christianity (508), the religion of most of his subjects, and thus strengthened the hand of the Church. As with Constantine the Great, his conversion might or might not have been sincere, but that is beside the point of what conversion accomplished for him politically.

As Charlemagne was able to do several hundred years later further to the east,[24] Clovis was able to use the mantel of righteous Christianity to unite his people and undermine any support for his immediate enemies, the Visigoths.[25] Clovis recognized the contribution that Christianity had made and would be able to make in the future through the Council of Orleans in 511, which greatly strengthened the role of the Catholic Church in political affairs. Thus, the political process started by Constantine the Great made its way into medieval monarchies through Clovis, and finally culminated with Charlemagne, four hundred years later. By this point the ideology had matured to the point of offering final political justification through officially anointing the kings of Europe.[26]

Constantine's conversion and the legitimizing of the Christian ideology by the Roman Empire developed into a nearly unruffled transition to the new world order of the middle ages. This was a new order that led to a thousand years of undisputed Christian ideological dominance over the western world. This ideological hegemony only drew to a close after the challenge brought by the rise of the Enlightenment, rational thought and the advent of science.

This is not to say that there were no bumps in the road, for there was resistance and enmity, and some friction almost immediately arose between the Frankish kingdoms and German tribes. Other conflicts and contraventions could be considered more intellectual, as exemplified by the Arian controversy, Gnosticism and Manichaeism, or by the scholarly struggles within the ideology as represented by such intellectual figures as Luther and Erasmus. Politically, the Christian ideology was almost at once pressed into service for numerous purposes and adventures that would have certainly garnered mixed feelings from Christianity's founders. From Charlemagne famously converting the German tribes through a decade of bloodletting, to the Crusades, to the Inquisitions, it seems unlikely that Christianity's spiritual founders would have claimed bragging rights to the effects of Christianity's political ideology.

IV. Summary

By the 10th century Christianity, as an ideological player, was deeply enmeshed in the political landscape of medieval Europe. Christianity's ideological function was that of legitimizier and justifier for the socio-economic structure of feudal Europe. In accomplishing this ideological task Christianity did an unusually effective job. For a system as steeped in widespread exploitation as feudalism to have existed for over one thousand years was the genuine Christian miracle of the age. It certainly demonstrates the importance of a supportive ideology to the survival, even thriving, of an oppressive political system. This is not to say that Christianity acted solely as supporter for feudalism or that it did not have a separate agenda; but as ideology, Christianity acted as a provider of legitimization for a social system that almost exclusively served the interests of the few.

To sum up, Christianity began as an obscure offshoot of Judaism. Whether or not these Jewish-Christians were an actual political force in opposition to Roman occupation of Judea is not only questionable but is beside the point. What becomes less debatable is the development of the Christian religion following Rome's "Jewish Wars" (63-76 C.E.). Without the intervention of Roman politics, the fate of Christianity, as a religion, is uncertain. Since Christianity lacked the aggressive tendencies of a religion such as Islam, we can surmise that Christianity, in the Gentile world at least, might well have been fragmented by schism and in the end disappeared, melding with a glut of pagan religions. For the

Romans, the further away from the source of Christianity, in both time and distance, the less it would have resembled the original understanding by the original writers of the Gospels. Rome gave Christianity its unity and structural integrity. Christianity gave Rome religious peace, and for a time, the ideological prerequisite for political peace. Later, Christianity gave an unstable medieval world the ideological foundation for social stability that justified an inherently unequal political system.

Christian ideology did not fully succeed in making the transition from feudal and semi-feudal social structures to modern democratic social arrangements. Even without extensive analysis we can still briefly cite three likely reasons for the failure to make this modern transition: *First*, the egalitarian demands of democratic ideology conflict with the hierarchal nature of Christian ideology. *Second*, democratic ideology seems to be most at home in a dynamic environment which is at odds with the static picture of the universe presented by Christian ideology. *Third*, modern democratic ideology has a foundation of truth based on empirically grounded reasoning. This is in sharp conflict with truth by revelation as found in the Christian belief system.

As a result of this transitional failure, Christian ideology in the Modern Era (1500 to c. 1920) has been uprooted from its political soil and entered a period of long decline. At some point toward the end of the Modern Era, Christian ideology lost all connection with concrete social reality, and rootless, has drifted into a decadent phase. Having made its historical contribution Christian ideology can linger on indefinitely as a purely metaphysical entity; like many other decadent idea-systems, such as animism or astrology, the power of Christian ideology to mediate and justify now always in conflict with reality rather than in concert.

Addendum

IDEOLOGY

The notion of a "Christian political ideology" is an odd one. We are accustomed to thinking of religion as a belief process quite apart from most discussions of an ideological system, especially a political ideological system. This is a mistaken viewpoint, but (as will be demonstrated) a "viewpoint" with its own ideological mis-direction and purpose. Therefore, before we discuss Christian political ideology we need to arrive at a working acquaintance with ideology itself.

A. Determining ideology

It is most instructive to come to an understanding of ideology from a personal perspective. At its most personal and individual level, ideology is largely an inherited system of ideas that serves in three ways to establish cohesiveness in human life. This cohesiveness is best understood as a less than conscious shared world view; albeit, this established cohesiveness is not always successfully.

First, all ideologies serve to interpret and *explain* the human world around us. Ideologies can tell us the "who," and the "how," and, yes, even the "why" of our existence; this last—the "why" of us—being the prevue of religion. All these explanations involve the basic existentialist stuff that surrounds our lives: life, death, love, sex, and most importantly in the temporal world, our station and fit within our human community, both large and small. It would seem obvious that some of these ideologies would fall, loosely speaking, beneath a religious mantra, while others are more obviously philosophical or scientific. However, in general all these idea-systems, these ideologies, serve to create existential coherence and offer some small comfort for our emotional and psychological lives by offering explanation, no matter how absurd, for the mysterious and sometimes the outright unexplainable.

Second, at the social level, and sometimes historical level, ideologies not only explain, but go much further: they *mediate.* This is typically accomplished through the vehicle of explanation. Nearly all "social" ideologies explain how and why we fit into our *place*, not merely in the existential world, but also in the societal world. In so doing, these largely inherited ideologies serve the useful purpose of allaying not just our existential anxieties, but also our social anxieties. This is a very important function of ideology. Ideologies allow social systems to run smoothly through the vehicle of a dominant system of ideas that serves to mediate friction between social groupings. In a very real sense, ideological mediation serves the useful role of explaining away the kind of social and economic disharmony that so often leads to conflict. In a personal sense, ideology eases friction between the individual and social groupings. Ideology is the single most important factor in establishing and maintaining social cohesion. Without ideology there is only naked force.

Third, related to mediation, ideology mollifies. Societal friction is frequently aroused over the mal-distribution of social goods and resources. Ideology operates at its best when it mollifies friction by extending mediation via an idea-system that *justifies* through the *legitimizing* of particular power relationships. The form of the justification and the type of friction ideology smooths-over will vary from historical setting to historical setting, but both the source of the friction and the ideological makeover are typically reified in very definite political structures.

To summarize, these three types of ideologies, those that *explain*, those that *mediate*, and those that *justify*, correspond, roughly speaking, to the three most vital aspects governing human life: the *existential*, the *social* and the *political*.

While we will discuss all three types, it is with the last, the political, that we will be most concerned. It must be again noted that the types of ideology are not pure, except theoretically, and do not appear independently. Political ideology, our concern, does often "appear" to adopt or subsume parts of the other two types, almost always for political ends. Keep in mind that the tangential appearance of the other types of ideology is sometimes coincidental, but may also be part of deliberate manipulation. It is vitally important that we draw a distinction, when possible, between conscious rigging of the local political theater and the unconscious infection of the other, related ideological systems.

It is also important to keep ideology phenomenologically distinct from other studies into the human experience, such as culture and social psychology. This is not to say that there are not numerous points of inter-section and overlap, for there certainly are. But, in general, ideology man-ifests or reifies itself in a manner different from run-of-the-mill cultural or social-psychological experience. For example, racism, *as ideology*, finds reification as Nazi doctrine (though this is not all that Nazism is). On the other hand, cultural or social-psychological dimensions of racism do not rise to the level of reification or necessarily even conceptual expression but live on in the barely conscious tribalism of "them" and "us." Indeed, even by the very act of rejecting the "ideology" of racism we affirm its "cultural" existence.

To distinguish ideology, *per se*, that is, an idea system that defines a thinking-cluster different from other forms of "understanding" such as cultural understanding, we must make the following six descriptive observations.

First, ideologies interpret. Ideologies must reflect tangible happen-ings, or things, in the real material world. Ideologies must have common roots in actual events all humans can recognize as offered interpreta-tion. These things or occurrences might be distant, or historical, but they must be verifiable. This insistence on tangibility does not mean that the interpretations offered will be the same, or that all ideologies will be an accurate reflection of the real world, but this empirical qualifica-tion will distinguish ideology from less coherent systems—for example, belief-systems such as astrology or voodoo. Although there are very defi-nite similarities, there are good reasons to hold belief systems apart from ideology. Belief systems are idea systems, (i.e., ideologies in the strictest sense of the word); however, the grounding in empirical consistency is the single most important qualifier distinguishing ideology from systems of belief. Otherworldly beliefs appear to be ideology, but without a mate-rial foundation. To illustrate this, briefly contrast and compare a religion like voodoo with the rational ideology of science. Both claim to interpret and explain the world around us, yet these claims are based on wildly different assumptions about what underlies and supports the reality we see and feel.

This empirical qualifier is important if for no reason other than that it allows us to verify the accuracy of the ideological interpretation. All ide-ologies are correct interpretations *within their own systems* but are often utterly incorrect interpretations when measured against each other. By this empirical qualifier, I mean to say that some ideologies are simply more accurate at interpreting reality than others; e.g., other-worldly belief attempting to act as an "ideology" is less accurate at interrupting reality than ideology as a material system of ideas.

Second, ideology is to a great extent an inherited system, one that is absorbed without total consciousness of the social osmotic process. At birth we are arbitrarily flung into a particular setting and situation complete with a historically produced matrix of societal relationships. In short, we emerge in a rationalizing idea-cluster not of our own making. This idea-cluster has encompassing organizational functions that serve as home base for interpreting the world around us.

In many ways this home base forms the foundation for what we might call our *common sense*. It can be noted that *common sense* (i.e., the inherited system) is neither universal nor timeless. For example, it is no longer *common sense* that the sun revolves around the earth. However, the setting and historical situation in which we find ourselves is interpreted by idea-clusters and idea-systems (i.e., ideology) that are not only impossible to avoid, but not entirely desirable to avoid. Even when utterly wrong, these idea-clusters are part of our experiential world, offering us systems of thought that make sense of time and place and being.

We might also quickly draw a distinction between ideological interpretation and opinion. "Opinion," correctly used (and it is usually not correctly used), rests on conscious and intentional learning. We can see this in action when a chemist passes judgment on molecular bonding, or a farmer assesses the appropriateness of crop rotation, or a musician suggests harmonizing cords.

Third, ideology is not cultural inheritance. Although ideology, like culture, is not necessarily fully conscious of itself, it *can* become a consciously intentional thinking system. Culture is not at the outset any kind of intentional thinking system, though it can and often does become the servant of ideology as in the case of warping a folksy kind of communitarianism (i.e., the basic structure of tribalism) into something like racism. In addition, ideology is not, as culture is, a largely insensate system of shared *values* and unconscious *interpretation* of shared symbols, languages, and actions. Culture allows a smooth and seamless functioning with our social environment, and it does this without a hint of awareness; is the fish aware of the sea in which it swims? Ideology, on the other hand, serves to explain and mediate the concrete world through *legitimizing its content*. Cultural idea-clusters neither explain nor justify nor legitimize—culture merely *presents*. Culture also possesses vague concurrences of thought, but it is outside the conscious and deliberate development of ideas produced by thought. Culture possesses values without rationality, reaction without concrete cause, and triggers response without analyzed justification. Culture is a blindly automatic *process* of indoctrination and not a conceptual system characterized by conscious thought. As a totality, culture is simply the *irrational "we are"* that is beyond alteration through conscious manipulation.

Fourth, it is important to distinguish ideology from belief systems and superstition. While ideology is typically a closed system of ideas that *can* substitute for rational thought, it is not a system that is fundamentally or necessarily irrational. Ideology is not a system that has become detached from material reality and is rootlessly adrift. As a consequence, working through a conscious manipulation of the ideas within the idea-system, changes to the internal dynamic of the ideological structure, can be brought about. On the other hand, in an irrational system characterized by belief or superstition, intelligible internal change through rational manipulation of the idea structure is compromised by the prerogatives of non-tangibility. In other words, separation from the real world makes any superstitious notion possible, no matter how ridiculous or laughable. Tangling with ideology can be vexing, but ideology hails from an historically, concrete material base and is therefore not, *ipso facto*, absurd.

Fifth, ideology is a closed system of ideas that fosters a world view which tends to historically legitimize a given social order whose concrete existence most often benefits certain groups to the detriment of other groups. In addition, and primarily for reasons of self-interest, (but not always *because* of self-interest), ideological systems stubbornly resist outside scrutiny or analysis. An obvious example of the impact of self-interest would be the racialist or nationalist ideologies at work to legitimize slavery in the western world.

Sixth, ideology *can* function to greatly restrict an accurate vision of one's own self-interest. Although this is not an exclusive action, it is a very contentious process that lies at the heart of ideologies negative impact. However, to be more precise, ideology, when acting as an inhibitor to the understanding of self-interest, is more accurately a phenomenon best understood as *false consciousness*. This false consciousness, this deflection of understanding regarding the true position of the self, *vis-à-vis* society, is more a derivation of ideology than a fact of ideological perception, *per se*. To make this clear by gross example, it is nearly universally true that the common soldier of any era understands his mission in far different terms than the chieftain for whom he fights and dies. For example, take the 2001 invasion of Iraq—was it about Iraqi freedom, or about oil? For the foot slogger in the 11th century crusading armies—was the sacking of Jerusalem (1099) about God, or loot? To be clear, typically this false vision, or consciousness, of realty is not so finely cut and dry; there are nuance that, for the sake of facility, I am ignoring. And to be sure, I have selected examples that offer stark support for my position. Yet even so, ideology has nearly always restricted an accurate vision of the soldier who willing sacrifices his life for a cause (i.e., an ideology) bearing no direct benefit to himself—and of huge benefit to those directing his actions, and sacrifice. Typically, false consciousness is derived from a wrong impression of one's position within the social matrix. This idea of false consciousness is easily demonstrated by pointing to the lost lives of countless soldiers down through the ages—individuals who had little idea of the real reasons they were involved in a bloody conflict. As another example, we may look at losses on both sides of the American Civil War, with those willingly sacrificed lives of the Confederate soldiers being most egregious in this regard; these soldiers sacrificed everything in support of a social and economic system they had absolutely no stake in. One need not disrespect the sacrifice of Southern soldiers to understand this. The contention here is the argument that the self-sacrifice on the part of the soldier is the result of an alignment of self-interest *with* the ideology. A fast analysis of which social group(s) the ideology in question supports, and which group(s) it oppresses, should quickly put this contention to rest.

Although ideology does not always conform exactly to all of the points described above, we can still see that a correct understanding of ideology leads us way beyond the typical explanation of ideology as merely a theme or tool of a political party or a political system. Specific themes of political or other social parties can more properly be called theory, doctrine or dogma. This is for two reasons: *First*, ideology cannot be called dogma, doctrine, or theory, as all these make a *conscious* and literal claim on truth. Ideology represents a largely *unconscious* world-view and truth is not a direct, conscious concern.[27] Within the ideological world-view things such as truth have been rationalized through the idea-system with the result that they are either taken for granted or have become completely beside the point. *Second*, dogma and doctrine (not so much with theory) represent a defensive posturing consciously derived from belief or ideology as a hedge against potentially destructive alien systems of thought. Ideology operates more as unconscious social glue. While there can be points of intersection, ideology will typically precede doctrine in the same way that belief will precede dogma.

For our purposes in this paper it is enough to say that ideologies are, at the individual level, a largely unconscious processes that quiets the discomfort and anxiety we may feel within a given social environment. This is their existential function. When necessary to assuage anxiety, we can even jump from one ideological platform to another. This is because it is not only possible, but likely, that we carry several related ideological systems within our frame of mind simultaneously and without apparent conflict, even when analysis shows that these systems are at odds with one another. An obvious case of this would be where the Christian virtue of "loving thy neighbor" falls into sharp conflict with the cutthroat practices of "marketplace capitalism." We simply glide from one ideological platform to another, as necessitated by revolving and recurring situations. Thus, the trading of ideological platforms smoothly manages internalized societal tensions.

Ideologies serve not simply to mediate, but also to buffer us from apparent chaos in the world around us. In a very real sense ideologies bind us to a social order as well as help us successfully navigate through a social environment prone to friction, friction being one of the hallmarks of all social environments. This is a clue to the source of power for most ideologies: to alleviate socio-economic anxiety. In this sense, ideologies are actively pursued, not simply clung to.

On the other hand, those ideologies that accurately interpret reality may do the opposite of providing relief. Instead, they may fling us into terrible states of anxiety. These ideologies are less comfortable, even if more pointed and insightful; various modes of scientific idea-systems would qualify here. As an example of these stressful ideologies try the idea-sys-tems that produce knowledge of climate change, or generate the discovery of the unending adaptability of life threatening viruses. These and other results of a rational and materialist ideology cannot help but create a general concern and serious misgivings—and sometimes outright panic. This generation of anxiety is not the goal of the rational ideologies, such as science, but it is frequently the result. The cure for this acute anxiety is *more* science, not less, which is typically *not* the remedy offered by antagonistic belief systems.

Other ideologies, manipulating their ability to distort reality through various means of misinterpretation, make possible the avoidance of anx-iety. Nearly all forms of superstition or mysticism fall into this category. Nationalism, racial superiority, or attempting to appease the Gods through human sacrifice, etc.—all these distorting, superstitious ideologies allow those immersed in the idea-system the luxury of avoiding painful contact with the real world. This avoidance is largely accomplished through some internal dynamic of the ideology. That internal dynamic is one that causes the amelioration of existing tensions and anxiety to be the *goal* of the ideology and not the *result*. In this sense superstitious ideologies oper-ate in the reverse of scientific ideologies, where results are the natural outgrowth of the idea-system and not the goal the system. The energy for the dynamic (rather superstition or scientific) ultimately springs from the survival reflex, a struggle to find release from existential threats. This highlights the point that all ideologies are an attempt to understand the world in a non-threatening way.

I'd like to make clear that superstitious ideologies are not some form or another of *false consciousness*. False consciousness (a study in itself) is often energized by superstition, but in many ways false consciousness is hostile to individual survival. It offers few ways to mollify or offer res-olution to conflict. Extreme examples, such soldiers offering their lives for causes not their own, have been offered above On the other hand, distorting ideologies, in the sense of their power to mediate conflict and reduce pain, can, as exampled above, be said to have a "legitimate" social function.[28]

From where do all these idea-systems come? There is no uniform answer to this question, no exact formula, but it is safe to say that our making sense of the world comes from within an ideological matrix that itself springs from a synthesis of our inherited idea-system coupled with our daily contact with the world. In other words, the experience of our everyday, practical encounters with concrete reality are both impacted and impact the worldview we learned at our grandmother's knee, be she a witch doctor or an astrophysicist. At its core, ideology is a living process that emerges from our need to manipulate our environment through control of our living situation (underwritten by the goal of survival). Ideology is an evolving system, a system shaped by collaboration between the inherited idea system we learned as children as it collides with our everyday struggles with the material world.

Notes

1. It should go without saying that Christianity is not alone in being utilized by the powers-that-be for political purposes. Incorporeal ideas, by their very nature, have all lent their energy to unsavory, if unintended, political ends. In the modern age Islam and various pandering by supremacists may serve as examples of these "unintended" ends.

2. In brief, the Arian controversy concerned itself with the nature of Jesus Christ. Was Christ a mortal, a prophet of God, or was he divine, that is, of the substance of God. The Council of Nicaea in 325 decided in favor of Christ's divinity.

3. The Creed determined that Jesus was one with God, thus ending a schism that threatened to tear the church apart. The church is described in the Creed as "one holy catholic and apostolic church". It is intended that it should be one universal (catholic) church that represents God's will on earth. The Creed was meant to unite all Christians by providing a statement of belief that was acceptable to all.

4. For a more broadly developed overview of the period such work as the classic by Norman Cantor is highly recommended. Norman F. Cantor, *Medieval History, The Life and Death of a Civilization*, Macmillan Co. (Toronto, 1969).

5. The theocratic interpretation of this passage is spiritual; however, Christ, as the Jewish Messiah, most likely intended the statement to be a political claim that the world belonged to Caesar, except Judea, which belonged to the "Chosen People" of God.

6. It is worth repeating that a material and historical interpretation that supports Christ as a political rather than religions figure takes the position that the statement cited indicates that Caesar can have the whole world *except* Judea, which belongs to God (i.e., the Jews, as the chosen people). This was a rebellious claim, for which a traitor's death, as the crucifixion suffered by the Christ, was warranted.

7. For example, see Romans 13: 1-7.

8. See Corinthians 1 Cor. 7:17-24.

9. It need to be remembered that much of the Chilean catholic clergy strongly resisted Pinochet's human rights violations and suffered the same fate as many on the Chilean Left.

10. 1 Corinthians 7:22

11. Who Jesus was, historically, and whether or not he actually considered himself a leader of a movement, are, quite frankly, impossible to determine with the available scholarship, and no stand will be taken on these questions here.

12. It should be noted for the record that the writers of the gospels were people who, most likely, had never known or even laid eyes on the Jesus they wrote about. They were retelling stores they had heard. This probably accounts for the many discrepancies between the gospels.

13. It is important to note that Paul hardly accomplished his mission single-handedly. He had considerable support and traveled with a group of disciples that assisted him in his writings and sermonizing on the new religion. See: https://catholiccourier.com/articles/st-pauls-friends-aided-him-in-his-travels

14. For a sensitive and carefully considered treatment of this struggle within the early church see Elaine Pagels' *Beyond Belief, The Secret Gospel of Thomas*, Random House, (New York, 2005).

15. The "empires" of several of the Greek city-states (e.g., Athens) might stand as an exception.

16. Constantine played no role in these persecutions and later attempted to disassociate himself from them.

17. For details see James Carroll, *Constantine's Sword, the Church and the Jews*, Houghton Mifflin Company, (Boston, 2001), especially pages 85-90.

18. At around 300 C.E. sociological historians have estimated the population of Christians throughout the empire to be approximately 10% of the total. See: Hopkins, Keith, "Christian Number and Its Implications." *Journal of Early Christian Studies* 6:2 (1998) 185-226.

19. On July 25, 310, it was told that Apollo appeared to Constantine and proclaimed him sole ruler of the Roman Empire.

20. This sign was most likely crossed spears with a vertical P. A symbol that would match the first two letters of the Greek Christ: Chi (X) and Rio (P).

21. In contemporary terms, Constantine's need for spiritual reassurance to shore up his rule might be compared to a US President needing public assurance that he or she was not a member of the communist party, didn't collude with a hostile foreign power, or was born in the United States.

22. This is the unlikely amalgamation of Christianity and Voodoo. Santería, also known as Regla de Ochá or La Regla de Lucumí, is a syncretic religion of Caribbean origin which developed in the Spanish Empire among West African descendants. Santería is influenced by and syncretized with Roman Catholicism. Its liturgical language, a dialect of Yoruba, is also known as Lucumí.

23. Genesis 22:2; Exodus 22:29-30; Judges 11:30-39; etc.

24. See Sidney Painter, *A History of the Middle Ages, 284-1500*, Alfred Knopf, (New York, 1953) pp. 76/78

25. See Isaac Asimov, *The Dark Ages*, Houghton Press (Boston, 1968) pp. 57/58.

26. It is not at all clear who initiated the process of Christian popes anointing kings, but in all likelihood it was Charlemagne, who paradoxically established this nemeses of all European monarchies down to the advent of democratic institutions.

27. I deliberately avoid the use of the term *unconscious* to avoid confusing ideology with a psychological process.

28. For clarification see my paper *On The Nature Of False Consciousness*.

THE LEGITIMATE ROLE OF VIOLENCE IN POLITICS

RICHARD WU

Abstract: This is a discussion of the "legitimate" role and expression of violence in the political process. First, the article begins by carefully distinguishing between politics and government—government being the facilitator of the political relations at work behind the decision-making. The article argues that decision making concerning the sharing of the social harvest is inherently violent, which is consistent with any coercion found in the process of distribution; government merely offers the cloak of legitimacy. It is within this stage of decision-making that violence first emerges. The article presses the central point that force and legitimacy do not share a common origin. The combination of legitimacy and coercion do not emerge from a desire to obey the "Hobbesian Fundamental Law," that is, to seek peace, but rather from the desire to escape the unstable, incoherence found in the war of all against all; rather than peace, it is constancy and predictability that are the goals. In so saying, it follows that the origin of legitimacy, and legitimate coercion, is not often born of some voluntary political consent on the part of a population. Instead, legitimacy is most often derived from the overwhelming need to escape the unpredictable and unstable states of irrationality dredged up by force and violence.

Politics or Government

By distinguishing between the two, politics or government I mean to introduce the claim that politics and government are not the same creature and ought not be conflated. Government is more like the horse that is harnessed to the cart of politics. As the two ought not be confused with each other neither should the cart be placed before the horse, i.e., politics drives government, not the other way around. Much of this position seems to depend on a working definition of both "politics" and "government".

Given the above recommendation, it seems appropriate to open this paper with the simple expression: "politics" is the process that determines (1) who gets what, (2) how much of it they get, and (3) when do they get it. While this statement is a borrowed paraphrase from Aristotle, it remains an eternally accurate description of politics as the arbiter for the distribution of available goods and services. As we will see, this is very often a violent process.

However, "politics" does not descriptively address the means of distribution; that is, the machinery inherent in the decision-making process. For that matter, this definition does not even suggest that there is a formal structure (i.e., government) at work in the process at all. Therefore, it needs to be pointed out that the word and concept of "government" is absent from this description of politics for an excellent reason. What we casually refer to as "government" is merely the concrete expression of a particular mode of political relations. Consequently, "government" can and should be studied apart from politics. Such a study of government separate from politics might prove tedious and will not inflame the passions, yet it is this critical separation that allows for understanding both politics and the violence a governing structure places at its disposal.

Even given the absence of a fully organized and relevant governing structure a political determination will be made by some arm of the community. From the head of a family, to direct democratic counsel, to a corporate CEO, (positions showing up as *natural* to the situation), political decisions are determined and followed up by instruction given to others to act on those decisions. In most cases, especially where the transfer from decision to action appears seamless, the governing authorization appears *inherent* to the *natural* situation, (e.g., children doing their choirs as directed by the Dad, infantrymen carrying out the orders of their platoon sergeant). A point to be made here is that what may seem *natural* to a given political situation (e.g., Dad or Mom as boss) may be fully aligned with the *inherent* themes of boss-hood (e.g., the monopoly of force). The former (an ideology natural to the situation) being more-or-less esoterically positioned while the latter (the many inherent themes) is a concrete arrangement, materially fixed by current circumstance, and therefore determined by earthly circumstance.

The above considerations lend understanding as to why historians often see governments becoming inconsistent with the current conditions controlling distribution of the social product. A current governing apparatus might represent conditions existent over decades or even centuries prior to changing political relations, causing government action to vacillate between decadent reactionary policies and a morbidity rendering any action impossible. Any established "government," and the "politics" of the community it purports to enact, may have drifted apart, grown out of touch, and may be entirely separate or even antagonistic entities. At the extreme ends of this antagonism between government and politics there can develop a revolutionary situation exemplified by the French Revolution, or at the other end, a reactionary situation as seen in the rise of fascism in the mid-20th Century.

For the above reasons, in this study I will look upon government and politics as distinct analytical entities.

~

The determination of who gets what, how much, and when—i.e., politics—might only indirectly involve a governing super-structure. This governing superstructure, as such, may have meandered into an irrelevancy that is more of a distraction than a point of reference for socio-economic understanding, much less a deep analysis. This is particularly true in the current days of multi-nationalism, both corporate and political. The determination of social distribution may often be made by a political culture whose manipulations are out of sight behind some entrenched, traditional ideology—an ideology that makes the division of goods and services appear casually routine and cloaked from even conventional understanding. The community's *weltanschauung* can make many transfers of goods and services seem effortless, commonplace, and so routinized that they seem to be sown into the very fabric of life. In this sense the political culture appears *natural* to the situation, while the government may only *appear* as inherent to the natural; that is, government as a contrived structure that draws its sustenance from the *natural* situation but not its validity.

All deciding processes, rather natural or inherent, ultimately depend on the single, universal element of enactment. No matter what the decision-making process, the only consistent theme of politics is the fact of *facilitation*—that is, the concrete element that determines the ability of the deciders to carry out the political decisions. For those most affected by politics, how decisions are arrived at is less universally meaningful than the enactment of those decisions as their consequences. For much of a population the impact of political facilitation runs from harsh to violent. As enactment is the role of government, violence is often it companion.

All of this makes the formal study of governmental decision-making less informative than would be a study of some less visible, underlying thread of consistency in the facilitation and delivery of those decisions. Government, properly understood, may only represent an agency designed to obscure the *political process* underlying the actual delivery of social goods and services. This obscuring role of government is an especially critical and informative analysis for understanding how and why the distribution of the social product is grossly unequal.

Looking from a different angle, government, *per se*, serves as an agency and means of violence that is only hinted at by the political relations of any given culture. It can be stated with considerable consistency that any determining power authorizing distribution presupposes that this agency possesses an underlying monopoly of force necessary to press decisions into reality, i.e., the actualization of decisions. Political determination rests on the supposition that the deciding agency possesses the governing power to actualize their decisions. Ultimately, this type of actualization rests on the enactment, or the threat of enactment, of violence to gain compliance. The distribution of the social product is not so much an independent process in and of itself as it is as extension of the organized and controlled application of force, *qua* political violence. This is a disagreeable but important way to look at the underlying support for political power, and the true meaning of government: the implementer of political violence. This leaves open an important side-bar: The question of an "inherent legitimacy" of government as the custodian, articulator and instrument of political violence.

The Claim: *Legitimacy.* At the heart of political decision-making one sees a relationship of social forces that will always attempt to gain peaceful compliance. This peaceful compliance is facilitated through a widespread recognition of "legitimate" authority. If the political process is to avoid naked violence, then some belief in the righteousness of the deciding authority must be in place. There are clearly moral issues here. These are critical, but best meant for a different discussion. Moral and ethical issues will be sidestepped in favor of this study which concerns the material and ideological issues surrounding the relationship between violence, legitimacy and politics. An analysis of the political process that emerges from decision-making will find that legitimacy and violence function as the muscle and sinew of the facilitation. These are the purely practical consideration.

Allow me to state first what should be obvious: The authorization of a political decision necessarily implies the use of coercion, that is, connotes the latent awareness that the authorizing agency possesses a monopoly of violence. To some degree or another, the political process will always employ coercion, the awareness of a potential for violence. It should also be fully understood that while coercion is little more than the promise of violence, that promise lurks behind every decision. The very nature of political decisions—enfranchising some, disenfranchising others—makes the consideration of potential violence unavoidable. In every legislative act, some win and some lose, necessitating the implication of coercion and the force to gain compliance.

The first step in the coercive process is to disguise the potential for violence beneath the mantle of legitimacy. This hiddenness is an ideological precondition for the avoidance of violence. Although I call this a first step, a proper analysis insists on the inspection of a deeper issue: the question of antecedents: do force and coercion (i.e., government) flow from legitimacy, or does the legitimacy flow from force? The question is one that is more than just idle curiosity, for the answer uncovers the fundamental infrastructure of all governmental expressions of politics. It might also be asked, with somewhat more complexity, whether the answer to this question might be found in some dialectical relationship existent between force and legitimacy that springs from what appears to be their shared origins. While the two questions are intertwined, it is best to treat them separately for reasons that will become apparent.

In this paper I will not take a soft approach. The implications are too important for understanding the political process. I will argue that force and legitimacy do not share a common origin. The combination of legitimacy and coercion do not emerge from a desire to obey the Hobbesian Fundamental Law, that is, to seek peace, but rather from the desire to escape the unstable and unpredictable coercion found in the war of all against all. In so saying, it follows that the origin of legitimacy, and legitimate coercion, is not often born of some voluntary political consent on the part of a population. Instead, legitimacy is most often derived from the overwhelming need to escape an unpredictable state of force and violence. This is not standing Hobbes on his head so much as it is rearranging his argument to make clear that government is only the lesser of political evils. "Legitimate" violence springs not necessarily from a desire for peace, but from the need to swap an unpredictable form of coercion for a more predictable form of coercion. This is a subtle but important shift.

Almost as a matter or routine, we have been taught that there is a deep and nearly sacred relationship between voluntarism and the consent of the governed. We, in the Western culture, have some long-standing familiarity with John Locke's assertion that government is not legitimate unless it is carried on with the consent of the governed. This interpretation of the relationship between the people and the state has grown into something of a mixed platitude-conundrum for the concept of "legitimate." How can I possibly conceive of my relationship with the governing structure of an "equalitarian democracy" in the absence of "consent," that is to say, my voluntary consent?

If not voluntary, then how specifically is political consent derived from coercion, i.e., violence? The answer here is found in the latent fear we all feel when presented with a choice between compliance and disobedience to the dictates of the political landscape in which we find ourselves. From mild anxiety and trepidation to anger and outright terror, these human sensations speak to us of the suspicion that our consent is not voluntary.

Indeed, we spend much of our lives avoiding even the appearance of non-compliance with the dictates of the governing structure.

First, recognize (as discussed above) that government is an expression of politics (i.e., who gets what, how much, and when) and not the other way around. So to substitute politics for government in Locke's observation and restate that "*Politics* is not legitimate unless it is carried on with the consent of the governed" gives the expression an odd ring, a queer meaning difficult to decipher. This is because "politics," properly understood, weighs in as a more universal, absolute system of arbitration than "government." Politics is a concept not necessarily identified by the contrived formalities of government. Politics is a concept more identified by feelings of coercive pressure brought about by circumstance rather than laws. This is another way of recognizing that we feel less in control of political power than governmental power.

Then consider the outright reality that consent itself is clearly coerced. According to the Hobbesian argument, governments are the result of individuals escaping the violent "laws" of the state of nature. This means that I consent to the coercive power of the Leviathan. Unable to escape coercion from any direction I merely opt for predictable coercion over unpredictable coercion.

While the above is a tenable argument, the more immediate and less theoretical position is to go along with Rousseau: when I am born into a nation-state a contract is *assumed*. It is assumed that I "consent" to its laws and the expectations of the governing community. By virtue of living within the boundaries of a particular state I consent to be bound by all civil and criminal laws, be taxed, conscripted into the military, or whatever other adherences are deemed proper by the existing political apparatus. Am I therefore coerced by this assumed contract? The answer to this question seems as so obvious as to completely trivialize any suggestion of non-compliance. If there are any doubts, consider the response of any political entity's refusal to comply with its laws or directives. The response as dictated by the "contract" would range from mild social pressure to devastating police violence.[1]

Realize also that "consent" in this Rousseauian argument is merely a disguise for contractual entrapment, an ideological slight-of-hand that allows us to proceed comfortably with our everyday lives. Yet the feelings and concerns of which we take note when contemplating disobedience make us fully aware that the threat of outright violence always lurks beneath the placid surface of consent. It is not simply an irony that violence is a most potent source and medium for voluntary, political consent. Violence is a "tell" that booby-traps even the most benign of political ideologies. However, to gain legitimacy the violence at the heart of consent must be camouflaged by a velvet glove and hidden from view.

Of course, one can always argue that I am free to leave for another nation—to be bound by those laws. But unless I can separate myself completely from all political entities—a practical impossibility—it appears that I must make a choice between accepting one type of coercion in favor of accepting another. This makes a sham of the freedom to shake political coercion completely.[2]

To be sure, such a position on force and violence will cast the ideology of a fair and balanced decision-making process in a difficult light. However, it will also lead to the resolution of some apparently intractable issues concerning legitimacy: we might consider such issues as when regime-change can be made "legitimate," or when democratically elected governments are "legitimately" replaced by a military junta, or when dictatorship is legitimate and appropriate. These considerations concerning legitimacy and force may be uncomfortable, but decisive. I might also suggest that such an analysis of the relationship between legitimacy and force will raise awareness regarding more common place situation-resolution: think over such tricky situations as how "managed news" and "political correctness" can gain legitimacy, or lose it. The answer here is uncovered once we recognize that "politically correct" information is guided by the characteristics of legitimacy and not the other way around. This guidance slants information in the direction of what can be called, with a sense of genuine soundness, "managed news." This is merely another way of saying that "managed news" supports the coercion that supplies it with legitimacy; the dialectic that supports political correctness. Of course, all this is hidden behind the same veil of ideology that obscures political violence.

One last point concerning the question of obscurity: From the point at which the issue of political violence arises, a dialectic between coercion and legitimacy comes into play. This dialectic distorts the origin of legitimacy as a stand-alone issue. The syntheses of the dialectic between coercion and legitimacy allows the question of origin to disappear into a rapidly developing ideological *re*-configuration (i.e., the new configuration as the dialectical synthesis). The dialectic between coercion and legitimacy is therefore obscured, and with it the actual nature of the *origins of legitimacy*. In other words, the dialectic between coercion and legitimacy is submerged and disappears beneath the emerging synthesis, the idea of *legitimate force*. In effect this *assumes*, at the conscious level, *de facto* legitimacy and mitigates nagging but important questions surrounding origins.

The Subject: *What is violence?* Given the above assertions concerning politics, violence and legitimacy, it is appropriate to delve into the question of the nature of violence itself. What exactly constitutes violence? Disagreement on this question ("What is violence?") cleaves apart not only political parties, but very often separates social reality from the political process. Vital for the question of an "ideology of legitimacy" is the relationship between political reality and political process. Let me say emphatically that both political reality and process involve violence.

At first glance, "what is violence?" appears a silly question. After all, in a fashion similar to how we understand pornography, we all know violence when we see it—don't we? I witness physical violence enacted in books and on screen constantly. Where human beings are involved, we consider violence to be the shooting, beating, trampling, stabbing, crushing, burning, etc., of people by one or more other persons, or by what we typically refer to as natural occurrences. (To streamline the discussion I will, for a moment, place the very real category of "emotional violence" on hold.)

An obvious example: a robber walks into a convenience store and plunders the cash drawer, then shoots and kills the store clerk. Is there any doubt that violence has occurred? A second: a young girl is run over and killed in a city crosswalk. This is also a violent act. And finally: consider a doctor in a life-and-death situation. A doctor accomplishes an emergency tracheotomy on a suffocating woman. There is pain and physical trauma in the doctor's actions, is there not? All of these actions, from the robber's to the doctor's, bear some of the earmarks of a violent act. Yet at the same time I am compelled to recognize a difference in the acts. All three acts are violent acts, *per se*, yet it is obvious that when the actions are compared the situations reveal not just a quantitative difference, but a qualitative difference. Although the acts are violent, they are each colored by "intent." While I recognize that there are other differences between violent acts, the *culpability* of the perpetrator of the violence—and hence the real meaning of the act—hinges on intent.

It is difficult to imagine that a trigger is pulled by accident. Of course, it might be claimed that the robber's gun discharged accidentally, but that claim can be dismissed as the death dealing action was part of a larger system of decision-making that few people would fail to recognize. The robber intended to take money, and even if the killing of the clerk was a secondary (perhaps unintended) consequence of the primary action, the principle intent overwhelms the secondary and "unintended" violent action; Anglo-Saxon law reflects this understanding in the prosecution of capital crimes.

The driver of the auto that runs down the child might not have been a transgressor of a larger moral issue, e.g., fleeing a crime. For example, suppose the child leaped unexpectedly into the path of the auto and the unintended death was seemingly beyond the control of the driver. In this case it is difficult find the automobile driver "guilty" in the same manner that I would find the robber. The driver is guiltless due to lack of intent. I might even call this an "accident."[3] We might also consider that the driver was being distracted by an electronic gadget (e.g., radio, cell phone, GPS, etc.). In this case the violence was an unintentional byproduct of an unrelated act. These are not the same types of "accidents," but neither are they intended to cause violence. Unfortunately, the result is still a violent death of the child. Violence has still occurred regardless of intent.

The doctor's actions, while inflicting pain and physical damage, are certainly intended to promote a higher cause, i.e., the furtherance of a human life. The doctor, in committing the violence, is carrying out his sworn obligation—a duty, if you will. The doctor's actions are intended for a good purpose, regardless of appearances. I am forced to recognize, however, that the doctor's effort on behalf of the woman does *appear* to be a violent act, with intent being the overriding, ameliorating element.

Either consciously or unconsciously, I factor the notion of intent into all these actions. Because of intent I tend to graduate the culpability of the actors in the violence. I am guided in deciding guilt or innocence by my understanding of the intent of the purveyor of the violent act. However, a key factor in this study is that violence in all these cases has occurred regardless of intent and culpability. There may be no guilty party associated with many brands of violence, but violence has occurred, nonetheless.

For a moment, allow me to get even closer to the point by putting "intent" completely aside in order to focus on violent acts, *per se*. All three of the above described actions, regardless of intent or outcome, have certain things in common. Physical violence toward humans inflicts some degree of pain and some manner of objective damage. I would argue that unless we drift off into some ultra-metaphysical realm, where action takes on spiritual trappings, violence must have at least these two elements in common, that is a degree of pain and a degree of damage. However, this raises some interesting issues. For example, what if I were to blunder outside in the midst of a tornado and get swept away to my death. Has violence occurred? Or suppose that on a hiking trip in the high desert of New Mexico I become lost. I spend days wandering about in search of water and eventually die of dehydration. What if, in playing a round of golf, I am struck by lightening? Again, the question arises: has violence occurred? We are not accustomed to thinking of violence in quite these terms, yet it seems that even in the absence of human action (save the possibility of that provoked by my own careless or stupidity) a violent act can play out in even where direct human instigation is not present. Other factors than those caused by direct and conscious human decisions can cause violence to human beings.

Under the heading of "what is violence," there remains only one other item to discuss: the emotional damage and emotional pain that the above events inflict. The entire area of emotional violence is murky. Subjectivity plays such a crucial role in establishing emotional pain and suffering that it is better for this paper to avoid it. I am not suggesting that such things do not exist, not at all, or cannot be devastating to the people involved, but only that the exact nature of internal, emotional pain is difficult to establish and assess. For the sake of a manageable thesis I am offering emotional violence recognition without direct treatment.

It might seem repetitive, but I need to make it clear that any event that results in physical damage and pain is symptomatic of violence, regardless of intend or mitigating factors such as miscalculation, natural disasters, or outright stupidity. This brings me to the point: the consideration of politics and violence. It seems obvious that in whatever manner the social product is divided amongst the members of a social order, some are going to be damaged by the division, as the distribution is never equal.

The Problem: *Politics and Institutional Violence.* There at least three issues to be dealt with in any treatment of the relationship between violence and politics.

First is the issue that politics, as the process for determining the distribution of social products, can be counted on to make certain rulings that will discriminate between social groups or factions. The discrimination advances the needs of one group and puts aside, ignores, or suppresses the needs of other groups. There are moral considerations here, but the fairness of the discrimination is beside the immediate point of this project. What I am after here is not what is "good" or "bad" in the distribution, but the integration and magnitude of the force used in the process of distributive discrimination. Political decisions will ultimately result in favor for some, and pain, discomfort, or injury for others. This study is about a political process that is intrinsically violent in its distributive discrimination. This kind of violence is inherent in political decision-making and is formally institutionalized in governments.

It seems clear that the sheer effectiveness of discriminatory rulings depends on the amount of pressure the structural manifestations (i.e., government) of the political process can bring on bear on the group(s) involved. At the top of this chain of coercion is the notion of "legitimacy," which is found to a greater or lesser degree in all governments. At the bottom of this chain of coercion lies the governmental authority to bring naked violence into full swing. Naturally, these are uncomfortable considerations. We prefer to rely on the governmental rituals that disguise the coercion and violence (e.g., in the form of legislation, courts, etc.), rituals that mute or hide the uglier fact of naked violence. But ultimately, there seems no way around this recognition. When the light of analysis is cast we can see that the violence institutionalized in governmental coercion is inherent in the process of social distribution.

A second issue now arises that insists on an examination of the intent of political goals, *per se*, as misdirected behind the governmental process. This issue will present the reality that not only is the governmental processes violent, but so also are the political goals. This is not the usual perspective—in fact the governmental process is often mistaken for the political goal. This confusion is often the foundation for the mistaken assumption that the governmental process prevents political violence. This mistaken notion achieves easy support because the governmental process spirits the precise intent of political goals behind a system of negotiation that seems to preclude political violence. This is to say that the violence is hidden behind a governmental process that misdirects our understanding of political intent. For instance, take the governmental process to balance the budget in order to lower tax rates on corporations. Frequently this process serves to hide the violence: for example, the chronic underfunding of health and welfare costs for the poor. Politically this is violence against one segment of the social order for the benefit of another segment. Another example: anti-labor legislation restricting union organizing. Ostensibly, this is couched in terms of attracting capital investment and thereby increasing employment possibilities. Politically, however, this is a wealth distribution to one group (corporate investors) by sacrificing another (labor). These common paradigms are harshly presented here, and never in the governmental arena would the presentation be made so blunt, but the point is made. The political intent is typically screened behind the governmental process.

All political decisions involve dispersion. Recall that just as in the examples of violence cited above, the actual governmental process is beside the point, the pain and suffering in distribution are real, and institutionalized. For example, a whole host of apparently unrelated political decisions are involved in creating homelessness—from government decisions that restrict housing development by raising interest rates, ostensibly in order to control inflation—to government decisions to cancel contracts for building public housing to head off deficit spending to shifting resources away from assistance to the needy in order to bolster police agencies fighting crime. The irony here ought not to be overlooked: with each decision for what appears be a good and just purpose, the ultimate achievement found in the growing institutionalization of homelessness in an increase in crime by the dispossessed. Of course, the institutional goals are be made to appear devoid of any inherent violence in their character, and the deciders utterly guiltless of bad intent. So of course, one point of the decision-making process is to claim that these decisions forestall violence and thus comes to sanitize any violence found buried within the goals themselves. In political parlance appearance is everything. So if decisions are made that ultimately lead to limited access to education, health facilities, nutrition, housing for certain groups, and some degree of social violence results, the connection between the decision-making and the ensuing social violence is difficult to see. The negative results come to light only after some considerable lag time and a detailed study that the average citizen will remain ignorant of.

A third issue comes about when I consider that there is a strong dynamic in the political process for the centralization of decision-making. This characteristic found in the centralizing process limits access and thus institutionalized centralization leads to alienation and disenfranchisement as secondary by-products of the dynamic. Institutionalized alienation and disenfranchisement bring their own considerable weight to the issue of violence. Centralization allows for limited input by divergent groups, facilitates ease in capturing the deciding apparatus, and overwhelms and absorbs the weaker by the stronger (i.e., better organized, and more violent) elements at work in the process. All this centralization facilitates the natural political process of violence in discriminatory distribution. This topic of centralization, and its role in political violence, necessitates a closer look.

Centralization. Political power demands an exclusive monopoly on violence that is both facilitated and is aggravated by increased centralization. It follows that monopoly grows with an exclusiveness made available by that centralization. This centralizing tendency seems to be inherent in the nature of the political process, but it is not necessarily natural to it. Inherent in political struggle is the favor of circumstance. Historical circumstances inherently show favor to one faction over another, making possible the growth of one faction at the expense of another. Of course, skill and manipulation of the circumstance on the part of the political players is key to the monopolistic growth.

For example, what I mean is this: the formation and strong centralization of the Soviet Union was to a great extent favored by historical circumstance. WWI and the threat of counter revolution (which was over by 1921) presented the leadership of the Bolshevik revolution with historical circumstances that made monopolistic centralization not only possible, but practical. For a time the violence of the counter-revolution and the fear of encirclement kept the widely diverse republics under the central authority of the Kremlin. Inherent in this process was that fear of the unpredictable elements of both internal and external violence. This centralization was to remain for nearly a century, a forced union of the republics. This was not a natural inclination toward centralization, but one generated by the circumstance of survival. At the first sign of the loosening grip of centralization, which occurred toward the end of the Khrushchev era, the centralized structure quickly fell apart. The diversity of the Soviet Republics led to what would seem a natural decentralization based along historical and cultural lines.

On the other hand, the unification of Germany in the late 19th century sprang from the increasing power of Prussia and was not directly forced upon the German states, although it must be noted that the overall historical situation was skillfully manipulated by Prussia, and in particular, Bismarck. Following the circumstances presented by the defeat of Napoleon and the centralizing forces of German industrialization, the later war against the Danes (1864), followed closely by the war against the Austrians (1866) and finally the war against the French (1870-71), demonstrated that only the Prussians possessed the power to lead a united Germany against foreign foes. In a sense, through manipulation of circumstance, Prussia presented the German states with a *fiat accompli*. Where the internal liberal and democratic efforts at German unification failed in 1848, industrialization and trade, and above all, the external contests of arms, succeeded in a kind of natural centralization by 1871. Here, as opposed to Soviet centralization, the common factors of culture and language greatly facilitated the political realization of German unification. The centralization of the German state was both intrinsic to the historical circumstances and natural to the situation.

Why and how do these tendencies work out so that centralization occurs? Loosely speaking, the key motivation seems to be a desire for stability—to avoid the unpredictability of forces beyond control of the individual, or organizations—that seems to rest beneath the shelter of a centralized authority. Once more, this conjures images of Hobbes, but again I must insist that this is not an overt desire for peace. We as individuals, or members of larger political groupings as suggested above, desire predictability rather more than peace, and will accept a coercive state to avoid some unpredictable and unstable situation along with the anxiety and fear it brings. The state, as a representative of certain factions that may not operate in the highest interests of the general population, and may be downright violent in bringing about these interests, but at least the coercive state promises principles that are predictable—or in a somewhat softer vernacular, dependable.

Let me offer an easy example of how the need for predictability inclines us toward centralization. I've already mentioned large scale situations above, but on a somewhat smaller scale we might look to a country such as the United States there are fifty states, each of which may have different traffic laws, some of them quite obscure. Obviously, this is can be very confusing to people traveling coast to coast. To escape the unpredictability there arises a natural desire for uniform traffic codes so that the unwary motorist can avoid feelings of being openly extorted by an alien entity. Feelings of being preyed upon produced anxiety and are strongly related to feelings of alienation. The various police agencies maybe entirely correct in the traffic enforcement, yet the size and remoteness of any central and uniform authority almost guarantees a sense of victimization.

There are many examples of the desire for uniformity found in a central authority. Yes, centralizing enhances predictability, but there are also dangers. One obvious danger is that the more remote the centralized power, the greater is the tendency to obfuscate the true nature of factional interests. Without a doubt, centralization, while desirable for uniformity and predictability, it also leads to a remoteness and alienation which can only enhance the institutionalizing of political violence. The irony here is a source of frustration and cannot be overlooked.

A Suggestion: *Fragmentation.* It is absurd to take the position that people will stop distributing social products. Politics, as measured, deliberate distribution, is one way in which human beings have chosen to socialize their lives. The argument I have presented makes it clear that politics is both intrinsically and inherently violent, and further that violence becomes increasingly abstract and institutionalized with political centralization. If we can all agree that violence is not an attractive feature of human relations, then the question becomes how is politics, *qua* violence, to be mitigated? How is it possible to control institutional violence and minimize it, which is another way of saying, control and minimize the harsher aspects of politics?

Inasmuch as politics, as distributor of social product, cannot be done away with, how can the process be amended so as to limit its more violent aspects? I am going to suggest an old remedy. I will call it fragmentation. It has been called other things at other times. To make my suggestion plausible, and easy to analyze, I will sketch it as a derivation of the argument presented by James Madison in his now famous Federalist Paper #10.

Federalist #10. Broadly speaking, Madison takes the position in Federalist #10 that (1) among human organizations, politics is a given, and (2) that a goal of political organization should be to limit the ability of factions. Feuding factions will attempt to co-opt the governing apparatus and thus advance that particular faction's agenda. Often, these factional agendas adversely affect the well-being of everyone else. Madison argues that there are two ways to control factions. First, eliminate the cause of factions, and second, control the effects of factions. Madison dismisses the first (that is, causing everyone's self-interest to be identical) as impractical. Madison is left with controlling the effects. There are two things about Madison's overall position to note.

First, Madison is fearful of any one faction achieving a majority. In general, he ignores minority factions as rendered moot where popular sovereignty is the rule. For example, a faction desiring the preservation of the monarch butterfly is likely to be lost in the roaring cacophony of competing factions.

Second, Madison takes two positions regarding the establishment of factions. The first is an argument for elites to define and refine the popular conception of self-interest. By this it is meant that in Madison's perception people are generally ignorant of what is in their best interests and elites are necessary to protect and advance the self-interest of the general population. The second is Madison's supposition that the more factions there are in existence the less chance there is of a few combining into a majority to capture the helm of government. It is this last that I want to focus on, with some passing discussion on the minority factions Madison dismisses.

Clearly, one result of an increase in the number of minority factions is that a great number of competing groups will tend to slow down the political process. This has been noted often enough.[4] It has also been remarked that slowing down the process can frustrate the popular will and possibly the common good.[5] This "slowing down of the process" is a correct assumption, and possibly a thought in the back of Madison's mind. Increased number of factions would certainly make amassing a majority of factions very difficult, and without a functioning majority the oppression of the minority would not be possible. It should be remembered that the minority Madison was out to protect was found in that very elite he saw as protecting the self-interest of the general population.

Regarding minority factions, we *might* consider these factions to be small democracies, where, as Madison points out, the majority of this minority can take over the faction and run its agenda through the faction. This is plausible enough. However, what seems to go unstated here is the fact that rule by majority is also the essence of democracy. This is a sort of take-it-or-leave it situation. It is well known by scholars that Madison was afraid of direct democracy, as were most of the elite thinkers in the 18th century, or any century. Madison, among others, was attempting to shape and blunt the force of direct democracy.

The question arises: is Madison correct? Is this democratic situation oppressive? Clearly from the point of view of many minorities it is. But unlike the nation state, the individual dissatisfied with the small faction's agenda is presumable free to move between small factions until they locate a faction with an agenda better suited to their talents and desires. In this case, the smaller the factions the easier it should be to move between them. It should also be pointed out that the smaller the faction, the greater the probability of the individual grafting his or her relationship and self-interest to the faction's internal structure and external manifestations.

We tend to think of factions as overtly political and something of an abstraction. They need be neither. As an example, factions can represent demographic entities. This situation exists now, but on a very large scale, large enough so that the individual can well feel helpless to figure his or her role vis-à-vis the entity, or how the entity impacts personal situations and other entities. This is particularly true where these entities are the nation, the region, the city, etc.

The sense of helplessness can be ameliorated where the scale is reduced. I am suggesting a scale much, much smaller, a scale more in keeping with a practical grasp of the individual. This could be a demographic entity as small as a city block. Factions can also be occupational, as regional sections of school teachers, or fire fighters, or butchers, bakers and candle stick makers. If human beings control the entity it can be democratized, and democratized on any scale, but the smaller the scale the better equipped the individual is to regard and understand personal relationships and responsibilities. This indicates that meaningful democracy is often a matter of scale.

Factions as economic entities. The mention above of occupations as entities points out that political factions need not be limited to types of lobby groups such as PETA, Neighborhood Watch, or The Hoover Institute. Political factions could also be *economic entities*. If politics is the process of who gets what, how much, and when, then at least one obvious place to properly establish democratic factions is where the social product begins its journey. Madison understood perfectly well that the most common and durable source of factions is the unequal distribution of property. As already discussed, the politics of unequal distribution operates through concrete government entities in distorted and disguised ways—ways that conform to the ideological expectations of the society. This always leads to misunderstanding, bickering, strife, and ultimately some degree of institutional violence. Openly politicizing these economic factions, for the sake of transparency and to allow them less distorted operation, would seem a good place to start.

It is certainly possible to democratize small to medium sized productive enterprises. This would create the types of democracies that Madison knew would present the possibility of capture by the majority—that is, become democratic entitlements. However, this arrangement would work toward mitigating Madison's fear about the common individual not having a clear grasp of their self-interest. Working within the enterprise, who but the producers would be better acquainted with the inner working, demands and expectation of keeping the enterprise productive? Would not self-interest press toward moving the enterprise forward for the betterment of the majority within the faction?

The possibilities seem endless. Economic, democratic entities can be formed with consumer groups; for example, a faction or union of local auto-insured tied to a faction of local mortgage holders. In these cases the auto-insured would control the business of insuring themselves, while the mortgage holders would control the business of their own mortgage companies. The only conditions would be based on size of the entity and whether it was local, something facilitating every participants' understanding. No entity should be so big as to be beyond the range of the individual to understand his or her relationship to the other members of the faction and to the whole. This moves democratic control forward and presents a barrier to top down coercion—a coercion in the interests of the few at the very top of the chain.

Would such fragmentation end politics as institutional violence? Or would it completely end politics as coercion? No, to both questions, but fragmentation would make centralization much more difficult, which in turn would reduce the level of violence augmented by the alienation inherent in centralization. And "yes," democratic majority in the smaller group would become oppressive to the minority within the group. But need it be pointed out again that majoritarianism is a central principle of democratic rule? Then too, the oppressed minority would be free to move to other groups, or for that matter, form a separate group of its own.

Economic factionalism has the added benefit of promoting cooperation. As opposed to centralization where cooperation could be coerced, small entities would find outwardly directed coercion difficult if not impossible. The overall consideration here is that while small, democratically run factions would potentially be coercive against their own members, small entities would also make more difficult any translation of factional politics into institutional or naked violence against the social order. The coordination of the decision-making leading to overt violence would be less abstract and in democratically run entities require greater overall voluntary participation.

Practical concerns: In this paper practical implementation of alternative political designs is not the focus. This paper was designed as a study of politics as violence. The suggestion presented above of fragmenting the social order into widespread democratic factions is merely intended to present a counterpoint to the current structural situation. So one might well ask, how would anything massive, like dam building, highway construction, or flood control, ever be accomplished? The answer is that large scale enterprises would be accomplished through factional common interest and cooperation rather than coercion. This study is a description of an intolerable situation, that being politics as violence.

The suggestion of fragmentation is only meant to demonstrate that there is always an exit to social situations that seem intolerable. We only need the imagination.

As a matter of praxis, I must recognize that the full implementation of fragmentation would be a difficult matter. Democratizing enterprises such as insurance companies present obstacles every bit as formidable as democratizing nations; it's merely a matter of scale. As it stands, then, being formidable alone should not stop us. It should encourage us to recognize that we are presented with yet another possibility in the struggling toward democratic ends. The idea of fragmentation I have presented here, I hope, is greeted in the spirit of possibility and trust in human imagination to find a way out of politics as violence.

Notes

1. Implied consent is also present in Plato's Crito, wherein Socrates accepts his own execution in part because he has implicitly agreed to live under Athenian law; he accepts the coercion in exchange for the benefits of living under the authority of the Athenian state.

2. One can always argue that I can exit the situation by ending my existence. While this is correct, I leave it up to the reader to draw their own conclusions.

3. Whether there is such a thing as an 'accident' I will put aside for the moment. The important thing to note here is that regardless of any other consideration, violence has occurred.

4. For example, see Garry Wills, *Explaining America*, Penguin Books, (New York, 1982)

5. For an elucidation of this one might look into the dispute between C. Wright Mills and Robert Dahl in the early 1960s. While disagreeing strongly on the details, both agree that manipulation of faction has lead to the frustration of the popular will.

WHAT IS IDEOLOGY
A PHENOMONOLOGICAL
STUDY

WILLIAM F. PRAY

Abstract: This article offers a detailed, descriptive analysis of ideology. What precisely is ideology, and from where does it derive? How does ideology operate, and what are the individual and social effects of ideology and ideological thinking? The limits of such a study are discussed, along with a clear distinction drawn between political doctrine and ideological thinking—as the two are often confused; the article stresses that the terms political doctrine and ideology are often used interchangeably, which is a serious and distorting mistake. Doctrine concerns itself directly with the politics surrounding resource distribution. Ideology is a far vaster system that encompasses and arranges all our daily experiences into how we understand the world in general. As the analysis is phenomenological, there is a heavy analytical reliance on examples and illustrations, and above all, the *experience* of the phenomenon known as ideology.

T his paper offers a phenomenological study of ideology. By this it is meant a descriptive analysis of ideology through a careful study of the characteristics found within the *experience* of ideology. Through this descriptive analysis the effects of the phenomena of ideology on human activity will become more understandable. Throughout this paper numerous examples will be offered in support of the descriptive understanding, and a consistent attempt will be made to achieve this understanding without any preconceived notions as to the outcome of the study.

1. PERSPECTIVES AND LIMITATIONS

From nearly any perspective, the concept of ideology proves to be one of the most widely used, yet intractable, of all modern concepts. For starters, the concept of ideology is charged with certain meanings that it does not inherently possess. While these false meanings will be discussed below, there is one inaccuracy that is particularly irksome. It is an inaccuracy that seriously limits a clear understanding of ideology. That inaccuracy is the misguided notion that ideology is solely present in political action. Ideology is much more than politics and any view that suggests that ideology and politics are synonymous is incorrect and must be discarded immediately.

What we see in active political arrangements is a *conscious doctrine*, which is to say, a very *conscious* codification of notions that carefully spell out the desires and arguments of different sides in the struggle for a commanding position in the social order. This thing called doctrine approaches dogma, an unshakable belief in the bullet-points that support a call for position in the social order. Ideology is absorbed largely by experience and ranges far beyond politics in its unconscious and automatic processing of day-to-day living.

While political doctrine may act as an ombudsman for ideology, ideology, *per se*, is much broader than politics and allows for a much more general theater of activity and interpretation that a mere evaluation of ideology as power relations. For example, we can say that ideology mediates much of our social lives and much of our ethical thinking. This is a large statement, but if this perspective can be satisfactorily established, then it follows that fully understanding the subject of ideology is a vital one for grasping how we understand, or misunderstand, societal relations along with the dynamics of political power and social change.

As we look into the perspective model of ideology, we will have to limit the subject to that of the ideal sketch. And it is ideal. There will be nothing in reality that conforms precisely to this sketch of ideology. This is partially inevitable; the vagueness of the concept of ideology is largely brought on by the nature of ideology itself. Unlike conscious political doctrine, ideology defies precise codification in the same way that an individual's dreams defy universal interpretation, modeling and codification.

When discussing different models of ideology, the same limitations as found in dream interpretation will apply. Each model will be an epitome. Getting into detailed discussions of different, concrete ideologies, rather than a general theoretical model, approaches a level of social and political debate that is best to avoid in this context. Such a political debate is a mischaracterization of this overall project which is, ironically, to deny ideology its subconscious source of power. It must be kept in mind that ideology is in many ways a misinterpretation of reality, or perhaps more accurately, as in dreams, a misrepresentation. Ideology does not report events in a way that are not true, but rather allows for the processing of events and actions is a way that distorts or hides the meaning behind the actions. In another context, this distortion is sometimes referred to as "false consciousness."

For the sake of grasping the real impact of ideology on human activity, we need to always consider a few perspectives and limitations that can add shape and substance to this quite complicated and not fully conscious subject.

First, we need to consider ideology a "system of ideas." This system of ideas emerges from the concrete situation in which we find ourselves, with "we" meaning us as a grouping, or a sub-grouping of active social systems. As we are not born with ideas in our heads, so all idea systems must begin life as an organized reflection of our experience. This organized reflection can afford us a genuine and authentic representation of our social constellation. However, note that the word "accurate" is not used to describe the representation, nor is the word "knowledge" used in conjunction with representation. That is because both "accurate" and "knowledge" border on a claim to "truth," and as we will see, truth plays little overt role in ideology. Being genuine or authentic carries a different meaning: to be these things means to be an actualization of the original, but not necessarily a true image. For example, myths may be integrated into our situation, and so into our ideology, yet these myths are nowhere to be found in a true image of reality. Ideology is an arrangement of ideas that come very close to a reflection of the way things *appear* to be. As an obvious example: the sun *appears* to rise in the east and set in the west, *appearing* to travel across and around the earth, making earth the center of the solar system—this representation well serves certain theological ideologies, and by extension the political institutions that ideology supports. This is another way of saying that such an ideological reflection is not true or factual, but rather an interpretation of the way we experience things and events. It is quite true that as human beings we often come to interpret things through myths and tradition rather than scientific hypotheses and testing. This last is a way of intimating that while science is not an ideology, science possesses its own ideology.

Second, we need to realize that our reflection of experience is more than a manifestation of our inheritance of ideas—the *zeitgeist*[1] goulash into which we are flung at birth. The reflection and interpretation is itself part of the *becoming* of the historical process which is to emerge as our "ideological heritage." In other words, just as we are part of our own experience, we are also a part of our own *reflected experience*; we are always a Becoming of future historical experience.

This interaction between experience and the *process of experience* sets up a difficult situation. On the one hand, judging ideology to be an ethereal process, rather than rooted in the real social circumstance makes it more difficult to analyze correctly; in the end such a view draws us back and away from the real power of ideology. On the other hand, forgetting that there is an intangible element to ideology that we might call "a reflection of the times" also represents a loss; ignoring this loses an overall grasp on our flowing historicity.

Thus, there are two overriding perspectives on ideology. The first is concrete, but if viewed one dimensionally it causes us to lose sight of the forest for the trees. The second is ideal and oppositional, which if viewed as the sole perspective, makes us loses sight of the trees for the forest.

We need to be also aware of another perspective and limitation that suggests ideology cannot be coherently studied at all. This position argues that ideology is in the grip of an inherent contradiction: after all, if everything is ideological how can we study the subject outside of its own light? What results is a naturally occurring paradox. If all views are ideological in some sense, then how is it possible to get a truly unbiased and objective view of the subject? Cannot one be forever accused of the circularity of examining ideology ideologically? Can one think objectively about something so intrinsically and subjectively "inherent"? While we must recognize and acknowledge this important claim, at the end of the day it seems that all we can do is be aware of the *probability* that ideology itself is a fundamental motivating factor in our study and (to borrow from psychoanalysis) one must be fully conscious of this quasi-neurotic probability and thereby steel against its unwanted influence. For if we are unguarded against ideology as a motivator, ideological influence will surely creep in. Hence a phenomenological investigation seems the best route to take to gain the best understanding.

2. WHAT IS IDEOLOGY?

Ideology is how we interpret and understand our world and our place in that world. But what is it—what is ideology?

It is important to disentangle this question from a second, tangential issue: where does ideology come from, from what circumstances does it emerge? In this study the *'from where'* will be cleaved off from the *'what is.'* This separation can be done clinically, but we need to keep in mind that the two issues (what it is and from where does it emerge) are in fact intimately connected, and this is one of the fundamental difficulties in coming to grips with the subject.[2]

It is useful on a practical level to consider ideology as fundamentally a living idea-system. This is a system that emerges from the interplay between two forces: first, an inherited matrix which frames the system into which the living experience must fit, and second, that self-same living experience itself. A lack of fit often leads to the alteration and eventual evolution of the inherited framework. This is a way of saying that the idea-system is like a living thing which is subject to a slow evolution in the manner in which it interprets experience. To see a slowly evolving idea-system in this way is somewhat over simplified, but it is a good starting point.

Next, the specific nature of the idea-system is uncovered by looking into the purpose of the system. In general, the purpose of all inherited idea-systems is to interpret and explain the world around us. At its most basic level, the idea-system is energized by a pursuit of survival, both actual and societal. Yet there are other, very human levels. For example, much of this ideological interpretation can be found in responses to existential anxieties, anxieties provoked by such questions as: *Why are we here?* Such fundamental existential questions and interpretations tend to be a concern of philosophical and theological systems. For the purpose of this paper, the most immediate meaning of these ideological systems is to interpret the *social world* in which we find ourselves. As already stated, this is partly for survival, but ideology also makes one feel at home, comfortable with the social setting. Ideology can tell us who and where we are in this social world, and more importantly *why* we occupy some particular niche in that social world. Most of this ideological interpretation is automatic and goes on at a subconscious level.

Looking closer, ideologies go further than merely interpretation. Ideologies have the important function not only of explanation, but also of *mediation*. Ideologies allow social systems to function smoothly by mediating friction that can arise between various social groupings. In this function of mediation ideology not only explains the social world but acts as a support for that social world. Typically, the supporting mediation often takes the form of *justification* for the social system, or social ordering. In this sense ideology, through its justifying function, tends to *legitimize* a particular social order (hence the source of confusion between political doctrine and ideology). Looking back on many historical situations much of the justification and legitimizing offered by ideology appears absurd. For example, until very recently, it was a given that the rulers of peoples did so as the living will of God on earth; while there remains a residual of such thinking, it has been mainly discarded in favor of other justifications. However, this does not lessen our interest. On the contrary, the function of justification and legitimization for the social order by these idea-systems is what most concerns us and arouses our interest in ideology. How these ideologies work to mediate and justify and legitimize will form the basis for the phenomenological approach to this study.

As suggested above, we are far too accustomed to think of ideology as synonymous with political doctrine and ideologues as mere characters in a political drama. This is a serious misunderstanding and a source of confusion. There is a definite difference. In addressing this difference, we need to acknowledge that ideology frequently secretes political overtones and encourages political involvement together with political action. Political doctrine, on the other hand, has it roots in ideology, and is often an expression of ideology (a kind of manipulated exegesis, if you will) but political doctrine, *per se*, is different from ideology. For one thing, ideology, as opposed to doctrine, does not necessarily make any claim on truth. Doctrine, as it might be expressed in a political party's platform, (or in a Papal Bull), typically does make strong claims on truth. Another difference is that political doctrine is overtly goal orientated, while ideology is less concerned with goals than it is with justification—although sometimes justification is a political goal. Therefore, while there are points of overlap and points of common interest, do not confuse political doctrine alone with political ideology. Ideology is much more than doctrinaire formalism. While a party's platform, as expressed through its doctrine, may have some connection to ideology, the source of energy and focus of the doctrine, (and therefore the claim on truth and goals), is the self-interest of the faction driving the party. It is the claim on truth and goals, therefore, which distinguishes political doctrine from ideology—even political ideology. Both doctrine and dogma will be considered at greater length later.

Looking more closely at ideology as mediation in the form of *justification*, we need to recognize that justification is a fundamental organizing principle exercised by nearly all ideologies. This is particularly apparent in justifying a social order where the distribution of goods and services appears grossly and painfully unequal. We can easily see that certain ideologies appear to justify the inequality. This principle of justification is vital in the ideological process. It is this feature that sidetracks the pandemonium and violence that may otherwise result. Much of ideological mediation is facilitated through justification and not vice versa, as doctrine may make it appear.

For example: the interplay between ideas and experience, as they were reified in the medieval church, serves well as an example of this kind of mediation. That is, the prevailing religious ideology serves to mediate, through justification, the established inequities found in the medieval European feudal system. In this system, the individual was at ease with his or her place in society, which was identical with their function in the social order. The individual became the *idea* of the social function. Each of the "functions" carried out the assigned task for the survival and betterment of the whole. It is impossible to understand the operation of this thousand year old system without understanding the medieval mind, which is to say understanding the feudal ideology. The individual was a sacrifice to his or her function, and this sacrifice was for stability and the common good. The repression, exploitation and social violence perpetrated by the medieval social hierarchy were justified by an idea-system that purported to be the word and hand of God. Eventually this was to become Church doctrine, and from our contemporary vantage point, must seem extreme and all but preposterous. Yet this ideology of other-worldly interpretation, coupled with of the material experience under which the vast majority of people suffered, is the only way to understand the widespread feeling of legitimacy toward the feudal system; this is the seed of monarchist doctrine.

To one degree or another, all exploitive political systems have depended on a doctrine, which in the grand sweep of history has very often meant religious doctrine. But European feudal ideology is not only religious doctrine, but an encompassing superstitious worldview (belief in demons, witchcraft, etc.) of which religious ideology was almost an inevitable by-product and cohabitant. At the same time this religious doctrine functions as a reinforcement of that ideology *and* the superstitious worldview. It is fair to say that while many political systems utilize religion to bolster their sense of legitimacy and justification, no past social system depended on religious ideology for social stability so much as did the European feudal system. In many ways, religious ideology and doctrine gave a sense of constancy to a grossly unstable world.

Of course, it goes without saying that while some ideologies function to prevent violence, many other ideologies act as a midwife for violence. The first kind—where ideology is present to mediate against violence—is typically found in societies where there is some reverence for law as a means of constraining and modifying both individual and intra-group violence. In analyzing the nature of the prohibition to violence, the ideological roots can be uncovered.

In general, where the ideology and the law co-mingle, justice gains some spiritual or metaphysical stature. This causes the law and justice to be separate and rise "above" the individuals or societal groups that promulgate these laws in the first place. Law gains some trapping of the sacred. In this sense the law becomes a kind of alien entity to be revered without regard to the concrete relations that might reside (or did reside) behind the new metaphysical presence. As a consequence of this kind of elevation, any hidden intent of the law inherent in its ideological roots is supplanted by the sacred meaning. It is not at all easy to see or understand this separation in our modern "frame of mind." This is because such a metaphysic is a transposition of an ideological component that *is our living frame of mind*, just as the Christian frame of mind was the living medieval frame of mind. The reason it is easy to grasp the medieval fixation with the metaphysic of the Divine, or Revelation as Truth, and not *see* our reverence for the modern current of the legal metaphysic, is our emersion in the fog of contemporary ideology. Getting away from abstractions might help us break through this "fog of ideology." An illustration will demonstrate this.

Let us look at taking a human life. Such an action seems to be a straightforward subject, clearly devoid of any ideological meaning or metaphysical components. So, let us examine the notion of homicide as being illegal—that is *murder*.

Murder is illegal in nearly all societies, but, we need to note, not under all circumstances. With the possible exception of self-defense (and this is also conditioned by the current idea-systems) the idea of "murder," *per se*, relies on factors of social self-interest, a pillar of ideology. That is to say, the idea of homicide, defined as murder, is closely related to questions of who is in command and in whose interest the killing is done. These questions appear most obvious when the killing of another human being is done in the interest of the state, which leads to the second ideological component that acts to promote violence.

When the executioner, the policeman, or the soldier, carry out homicide at the behest of the state they are not held to any reckoning as the act is never defined as murder (at least not in any legal sense). When homicide is done in the interests of the state, we usher in the concrete component that lies behind the metaphysical or ideological factor: in this case, the historically defined social relations that form the state.

To delve deeper into the nature of this metaphysical distortion surrounding the idea of murder, we must ask: "Whose State?" That is, The State, like murder, also has an ideological component that hides the concrete realities of its social relations. So, we must ask: In whose name is murder permitted? And further, what concrete societal entities lie behind the metaphysical mask of the state? When phrasing the question in these terms it is possible to bring into focus a certain mythical quality aroused by this entity, the state; we can see that what appears so obviously a non-metaphysical action, such as murder, has inherent ideological roots that can transpose the concrete into the metaphysical. This revelation forces us to focus on the nature of the state for answers relevant to the spiritual essence revealed within the ideological structure of the law.

While analyzing the nature of rhe state is beyond the scope of this study, we can understand the relevance of the state in legitimizing numerous strands of violence. To promote legitimate murder from the outset, the needs of the state are pressed into service. To take but one obvious example, most imperialist doctrine would fall into this legitimizing pattern by coaxing some ideological balm from the rampant bloodshed. Here political doctrine and ideology co-mingle, with ideology providing the legitimacy and justification for the doctrine. Yet even with the co-mingling it is important to note that we can isolate and examine the ideological support given to a doctrine of imperialism. To illustrate: in some cases imperialist doctrine is supported by one of the many faces of racism, or economic determinism, or some form of nationalistic manifest destiny—and all of these idea-systems can co-mingle to drive the political doctrine of imperialism.

It is most important to recognize that in both these above senses (i.e., to forestall social violence, or to justify violence) ideology offers support for certain elements in the social order through administered mediation of opposing social interests, a mediation that inevitably takes some form of justification. Through the lens of justification we can begin to see a certain subjective characteristic of ideology that causes certain social groups benefit more than others. Ultimately, of course, nearly all ideologies carry strong, elusive subjective forces within them. That is, in practice, ideology tends to favor the agenda of certain societal groups as opposed to other societal groups. Oddly, this does not seem to detract from the influence of the idea-system but adds to it.

This aspect of the influence of ideology can be seen where the ruling order is claiming some descent from the gods. In pre-Dynastic Egypt, for example, the Pharaohs were considered gods. No further justification was required to exploit the lives of those existing beneath. Later, in Dynastic Egypt, the use of religion enhanced both the role of the priests and the Pharaohs in that through mystical ceremony the kings became one with their 'ka' and were *transformed* into Gods.[3] In such an intensely super-stitious community this idea-system which supported the notion of trans-formation offered ultimate legitimacy to the ruling Pharaohs *and* firmly established the priestly class in an indispensable supporting role for the ruling order. The evolving idea-system added another supporting layer for itself *and* enhanced the agenda of another exploitive social group. The exploitation of certain groups is justified by the ideology of other-worldly transformation, and at the same time, the justification reinforces the other worldly ideology.

3. IDEOLOGY, OR DOCTRINE AND DOGMA

It is not helpful to consider ideology wholly as a form of doctrine or dogma. There are many times when ideological systems can lead to doc-trine, which in turn can lead to dogma, but they are distinct modes of thinking. Working through a descriptive analysis will help in clarifying our understanding of the three.

About dogma we may say the following:

First, by definition, dogma goes beyond an appeal to the real and appeals solely to authority, as exemplified by religious dogma where appeal is made to some scripture rather than reason and evidence grounded in the concrete world. So while dogma is typically separate from material reality, idea-systems, and any doctrinaire outgrowth of those systems, remains rooted in concrete experience and therefore appeals to expe-rience rather than authority. It follows that ideology and its doctrinaire expression remain socially and politically relevant. Dogma, on the other hand, due to its separation from concrete reality, becomes increasingly irrelevant in addressing actual issues and concrete situations.

Second, dogma represents a decided viewpoint on *truth*. Truth is an inherent demand of dogma. Dogma claims this right to truth by authority, usually by divine authority, or authority that has achieved some form of divinity. These views on authority and truth seem an obvious result and byproduct of dogma's detachment from concrete situations.

Third: Truth is not an inherent demand of ideology, as ideology represents a largely unconscious worldview where such things as truth are not necessarily a part of the discussion and are very often beside the point. Unlike dogma, ideology arises out of concrete, historical situations, and the players are most often utterly unaware of ideology's deciding influence on how they address their problems and issues. If considered carefully at all, everyday ideology is seen as some form of "common sense," which tends to be an inhospitable environment for truth, *per se.* Ideology, typically, makes no such claim on truth. Where it appears as a claim to do so, (e.g., beginning a discussion with: "According to Marx and Lenin . . .") it is doctrine or dogma which is called upon and not ideology.

Ideology, doctrine and dogma are not static systems of thought and ideas. They are a constant, free flowing dynamic, evolving (or sometimes devolving) according to the synthesizing of changing historical conditions. To illustrate: in the western world, modern ideologies, as they have evolved in contemporary times, have come first to co-mingle and then to eventually supplant theological doctrine and dogma with political modes of analysis and thought. This is because of the manner in which the crystallization of power relations have come about in the modern social order. The expression of power relations in the Middle Ages was satisfactorily expressed by a fixed, theological mode of thought, where each individual was in their fixed and proper place as an harmonious expression of God's design. This mode of thought, which we might call a type of existential dogma, obviously proved unsatisfactory in modern times, where due to the rapidly shifting relations of production and trade no one individual's place and no socioeconomic entity could be fixed or predictable. Permanence in social relations (as in feudal arrangements) was a thing of the past; the new order of the day was rapid changes in commodity production and distribution, together with concomitant social transformation. Modern and contemporary expressions of power relations, as they rose out of a rapidly changing scientific and engineered means of survival, found an unsatisfactory expression in Divine Ordination. Newer ideological expressions of reality were needed to organize the gathering of the far less stable world of capital formation, industrialization, and marketplace distribution. That ideology became overtly political, a mode of thought as concrete as the relations from which it sprang.

To offer another example, we might view nationalist ideology in such a light. The nationalistic system of thinking, like all ideologies, draws its form and energy from historically evolved, material relations. The closing of the Middle Ages was precipitated by changing forms of wealth that demanded new systems of transportation, commerce and trade, along with specie exchange, which allowed for capital formation and industrialization. These developments meant that the centers of power began to drift away from the local level to the regional level, and the nation state began to emerge. These shifting material relations rendered an ideology dependent on a static universe increasingly irrelevant and decadent. These relations demanded new, dynamic and vigorous ideological frontiers. Along with this move away from the static provincial to the dynamic and novel national, idea-systems appeared to replace the parochial ideologies and their theological supporting apparatus; among these new idea-systems was Nationalism (not to mention liberalism, constitutionalism, equalitarianism, capitalism, etc.). This is not the place for a detailed discussion on the emergence of the nation state, but it is appropriate to use its emergence as an example of changes modes of ideological thought.

4. POSITIVES AND NEGATIVES OF IDEOLOGY

Ideologies offer either positive, systematic and soothing explanations, or they present negative, critical evaluations for the more tumultuous and apparently contradictory events in the world. Ideologies are either constructive and supportive of material relations, or destructive and iconoclastic toward those relations. For the most part, positive and socially supportive ideologies tend to be of the inherited variety, while negative and critical ideologies usually arise during the process of concrete, material changes.

On the positive side, many ideologies of the inherited type, unlike party doctrines, lend themselves to an established stability of outlook.

Positive ideologies offer a comforting ideological point of view: all is as it should be, even during inexplicable chaos. Positive ideology establishes a fixed meaning of intention to offer a sense of personal security through a permanent and fitted frame of reference. Positive ideologies offer mediation, a go-between that acts as a cushion between us and our place in the historically produced social environment—an environment which is frequently nasty and hostile. How and why certain ideologies do this is quite another matter. For the moment it is enough to say that ideologies generally involve, not a fully conscious process, but rather a comforting mode of interpreting the world that allows us to feel at ease in a specific historically conditioned social environment.

On the negative side, ideologies of the acquired variety will inevitably arise when existing conditions intensify social friction that feed into factional antagonism. Because these emerging ideologies typically will stand on the outside of, and in opposition to, an interpretation of existing material relations, they can offer sharp insights into weakness and contradictions within those social arrangements and the ideologies which support them. These insights may eventually discredit and overturn previous idea-systems and the socio-political institutions they purport to support. We might offer as an example the rise of a rational, scientific idea-system that emerged alongside a democratic nationalism. Both rationalism and nationalism stand in direct opposition to the theology that encouraged and supported feudal arrangements. Not only did rational ideology undermine the theology that supported feudalism, but it also supported the steady emergence of capital formation for industry, social equality, and nationalism.

At the same time, these newly acquired oppositional ideologies can offer other models of social relations—that is, ameliorating models that offer solutions to existing antagonisms. That these negative ideologies might fail is beside the point of the idea-system. It is entirely possible that either the antithetical ideology is premature in its development, or utterly behind the flow of history. In this regard, we might see the political theories of William of Ockham (1288-1348), or the scientific theories of Copernicus (1473-1543), as ahead of their time,[4] and the vast majority of racist ideology, and now nationalist ideology, as behind the times.

Also consider the fact that nearly all ideologies of the inherited type are, to one degree or another, resistant to outside influence, and therefore withstand dramatic and sudden alteration to their various interpretations of social milieu. Indeed, many inherited ideologies are utterly impervious to outside influence, and even any kind of meaningful outside exchange. This becomes an increasingly given position as the ideologies approach decadence, where the roots of the ideology, and its doctrinaire expression, begin to come loose from the material soil from which they sprang and drift into dogma. Along with the possible decline of the idea-system, these ideologies are closed systems of thought that are, to a great degree, self-serving. These ideologies are their dogmatic expressions that often show signs of fierce resistance to any type of breach to the boundaries of their system. One illustration that comes to mind in this regard are religious ideologies (as expressed through religious dogma). History is replete with examples of religious ideologies, the dogmatic expression of which responds violently to rumors of change (recall, dogma's expressed claim on truth). Witness the numerous Inquisitions from the 12th through the 16th centuries. These were specific, violent, authoritative reactions to the threat of rational thought then arising in Europe, a rational thinking that stands in direct opposition to religious dogma. The violence cited here is in proportion to the underlying decadence of the ideology that propped up the dogma. However, while the truth of the dogma was at issue, the greatest contributing factor was the changing material conditions that no longer watered the ideological roots; these changing material conditions caused a withering of vital thinking and gave impetus to the emergence of a decadent dogma. A purely authoritarian claim on truth is always more vulnerable than the dynamic claims of an expanding, growing and robust rational ideology.

Understand, however, that religion is not alone in this violent resistance. Political, racial, social, and economic ideologies, and their doctrinaire expression, all have shown signs of defiance and violent reaction to change. Because history is a dynamic and moving system, there has never been a time in history without idea-systems struggling to remain rooted in a shifting, material landscape. At least one implication of this struggle is the enormous drag ideology places on events moving toward anything we might even remotely call progress. Here decadent, nationalist ideologies, and their dogmatic expression (e.g., monarchist or fascist doctrine), serve as apt example.

5. THE ALLURE OF IDEOLOGY

How it is that ideology casts such a long shadow? It does so because, in general, many (but not all) of these idea-systems allow us to avoid the anxiety that thinking creates.[5] This may sound tongue-in-cheek, but the statement is earnest. Ideology, especially the inherited variety, serves as a substitution for anything resembling closely reasoned analysis. Some of these ideologies are familiar as political schemes, for example Marxism, (when taken as dogma)—but many other explanations can range from decadent social ideologies (e.g., racism) to economic (e.g., capitalism, when taken as dogma) to theology (e.g., Islam).

It is important to note that not all ideologies are dead wrong or provide a false image of reality. Many ideologies, typically the *acquired* variety, as opposed to the *inherited* type, provide critical insights and powerful tools to organize our social reality into a cohesive whole that can defeat blind frustration (for example, a rational, scientific idea-system might serve as such an acquired ideology). Obviously, these are largely pragmatic benchmarks rather than ethical ones, as would be the case when considering ultimate rational idea-systems which might be lumped under the general heading of "scientism." Many other of these "isms," these powerful acquired idea-systems, can increase anxiety rather than forestall it. One such non-scientific, critical idea-system that would tend to arouse anxiety rather than appease it would be, loosely speaking, existentialism[6]. If I may quote Rollo May:

"Anxiety is not an affect among other affects, such as pleasure or sadness. It is rather an ontological characteristic of man, rooted in his very existence as such. It is not a peripheral threat which I can take or leave, for example, or a reaction which may be classified beside other reactions; it is always a threat to the foundation, the center of my existence. Anxiety is the experience of the threat of imminent nonbeing."[7]

Although ideologies show resistance to change, not all ideologies are equally "idea-tight." Some ideologies are quite porous, even to the point of seeking outside influence and the consequent alteration that can follow. Here, many of the democratic ideologies come to mind. Some of the more extreme types of democratic ideology (e.g., as in some forms of anarchist theory) allow, by intent, for so much input that the ideology's sense of cohesiveness is threatened. This can be detrimental to the ideological system as a whole. In this specific case, the practical application of anarchist democratic precepts is swept aside by its own ideological demands, the crippling irony being that which generates the appeal of the anarchist movement is also its Achilles heel. Non- authoritarian, direct democracy can lead to a lack of focus, cohesion, coherence and direction, threatening the group's necessary and adequate response to objective pressure. As an example, we might look at the Spanish Civil War (1936-1939) where the anarchists, avoiding central command, found it increasingly difficult to find a consensus in fighting the forces of Fascism, clearly one of the major causes of the Republican defeat. This paradox has always been the cruel, theoretical irony at the heart of anarchist theory.

However, overall we must say that the great majority of ideological systems are, by their set of internal demands, "closed." For example, it is difficult to imagine an idea-system such as Nazism, where Aryan superiority functions as an internal demand of the system, being open to "new information" on genetics and DNA. This causes most of these systems to posses their own internal systems of logic, some of them quite quirky. We might illustrate this with a bizarre practice found in idea systems adopted to uncover witches and worshipers of Satan. An accused witch or succubus would be tied and bundled with weights and tossed into a body of water. If this luckless "devil" floated to the surface, they were pronounced guilty and burned or hanged. If they drowned, they were pronounced innocent. That this logical incongruity survived for centuries can only attest to the blinding power of ideology. Then also, the fact that this absurd practice survived into the 18th century United States should cause us to pause and reflect.

This tendency toward a closed system of logic leaves vulnerable the outcome of even the best of analysis by the most open of these ideologies. We might explore this implied contradiction by returning for a moment to a specific democratic ideology: liberal democratic ideology. While it can be noted that in general democratic ideologies are more open than many other ideologies (e.g., fascism), a closer look can, in specific cases, reveal a tendency in ideologies toward closure through various mechanisms of transformation. For example, at the core of classic liberal ideology is the belief in the individual's right to pursue his or her goals unmolested by the political state. When coercive necessities arise, such as a government claiming the necessity to arbitrate conflicting goals, the subsequent repression is nonetheless analyzed in terms of the ideology, i.e., governmental repression is not seen as a repressive apparatus, *per se*, but as means to conflict arbitration. The internal logic of the ideology transforms government repression into a progressive factor *facilitating* the individual's right to pursue desired goals. Surreptitiously, and by the cunning of its internal logic, the ideology transforms a negative into a positive. Even extreme forms of liberalism, such as Libertarianism, cannot entirely escape the implied contradiction brought on by "necessity." Of course, the liberal ideologue will hotly argue the necessity of government intervention to forestall civil conflict. While this position may have some validity, it is beside the point we are making concerning ideological logic. Successful ideologies will often make use of their own internal logical systems to absorb powerful oppositional constructs and flip them into useful elements of their own.

Any effective and successful ideology is highly capable of dipping into the analytical wing of its idea-system to transform the *negative* aspect that comes into social experience into a *positive* thing, or at least something compatible with its patterns, and in this way protect the integrity of the ideological model as a whole. Thus, as in the above example, the flexible ideology cleverly masks resistance to change beneath the cloak of accommodation to change. In this, liberal democratic ideologies are not alone. Accommodation and transformation of negatives into positives is a favorite tool of Christian ideological logic. We might look at the absorption and transformation of even hostile characteristics, as is seen in the strange case of Vodouisant, where the pagan practice of voodoo is absorbed and transformed by the primary Christian ideology, although the two systems appear grossly antithetical and ill-suited for marriage; not surprisingly, Vodouisant is roundly condemned by orthodox Christianity.

To restate and summarize: inherited or acquired, many ideologies are powerful organizing tools. Liberal democratic ideologies are but one example, showing greater flexibility and adaptability than, for example, the monarchist ideologies they replaced. Even so, as illustrated above, any ideology, from the most liberal of democratic ideologies to the most conservative of religious ideologies, will show degrees of resistance to outside evaluation—bearing in mind that the resistance is often hidden, appearing instead in the guise of adoption, which in actuality is cooption.

Ideologies, no matter how flexible, reflect patterns of thought from which they are unlikely to deviate wholesale. This differs from say, *opinion*, as personal or public opinions do not represent models of an interpretive system of ideas possessing a logical set of analytical tools by which to explain or justify social phenomena. Opinions, as opposed to ideologies, are merely hazy notions, like flickering shadows on the wall of the cave, distorted representations of the surrounding reality. Though opinions may be an extension or development of an ideology, opinions in and of themselves neither analyze nor provide the tools for justification.

6. Ideology's Bad Name

At least one conclusion that can be drawn from much of the above description is that ideology is little more than a hindrance to human progress. Ideology represents a great stumbling block, a tangled system of muddled thinking that undermines clarity of reason and prevents convincing analysis. In many ways this is a correct perspective, and in other ways not so much so. This way of thought leads to repeated failures in basic problem solving and disastrous attempts at social engineering and controlling historical forces. But if ideology deserves much of its bad name, we should be able to coherently point out the central reasons.

First ideology is a system of ideas that not only serves as a substitute for rational, unrestrained and creative thought, but a system which is stubbornly resistant to outside analysis and change. At least one disturbing corollary of this position is that ideology can and does promote violent action in the world while only pretending to understand that world.

Second, this closed system of ideas has shown consistent historical tendency to support and prop up certain given social orders together with the generally uneven social relations that result. And, of course, the role and meaning of the ideology in support of these uneven social relations is justification. That is, the exploitive nature of many social relations is explained away by supportive ideologies. Organic models of society such as feudalism and classical fascism come to mine. However, even revolutionary ideologies that would topple existing social orders would set up another order that favor certain social elements and suppress others. Of course, whether this new setup is a positive step toward justice, fairness, and human advancement, depends a great deal on who considers the question. This consideration by the viewer is, in turn, influenced by the position occupied in the "new social order," together with the analytical expression provided by the ideological tools of this new social order.

Third, ideology can obscure an accurate vision of our self-interest. Ideology can leak a dense fog that absolutely hampers our connection with events and situations confronting us. Ideology can deflect our focus into dead end channels and thereby severely limit our choices and leave us at great risk. Scapegoating is the obvious example of this kind dead end channeling. For example, the Jews, Blacks and Hispanics, these groups are the causes of all our problems. Through scapegoating we may turn off thinking and need look no farther.

These three attributes of ideology frequently overlap and reinforce each other. But alone or in tandem, the main thrust of ideology is to substitute a prefab idea system for rational thought and analysis.

It has probably not escaped notice that we have yet to discuss "false consciousness," as a topic of ideology, where "the real motive forces impelling (the actor) remain unknown to him . . . Hence, he imagines false or seeming motive forces."[8] This is because while false consciousness is certainly related to ideology, false consciousness is not the same as ideology, *per se*. To consider false consciousness and ideology as one and the same is a common error, but the subject needs to be taken up in a separate treatment.

7. SUMMARY

To sum up, we can state the following descriptive characteristics about ideology: (1) Doctrine and ideology are different entities. We must not fall into the trap of believing that ideology only represents a perspective in political doctrine. (2) Ideology is not knowledge, in some traditional sense of a catalogue of facts and figures, but a mode of thought, or a system of ideas. (3) This system of ideas is typically inherited. However, acquired, critical ideologies are possible and even probable. (4) The primary intent of both positive and negative ideologies is to offer interpretation of the world around us. (5) A secondary intent of a ideology is to mediate conflict. (6) An adjunct of mediation is to justify aspects of the world around us. (7) As opposed to political doctrine, ideology makes no claim on truth. (8) Ideology is largely an unconscious worldview that arises out of our concrete, historical situation. (9) Ideologies can offer either positive and soothing explanations, or negative, critical analysis (the latter being largely an acquired system, rather than inherited). (10) Nearly all inherited ideologies show a marked resistance to outside influence. Acquired ideologies can follow the same pattern, but to a lesser extent. (11) Ideologies, particularly the inherited types, are an attractive alternative to thinking. The prefab notions found in any idea systems allow us to avoid asking the difficult questions that thinking can arouse. (12) Not all ideologies are wrong or offer an incorrect interpretation of reality. (13) Ideologies differ from opinion insofar as opinions, even when correct, typically lack the intellectual tools necessary for explanation and justification.

Notes

1. Spirit of the times

2. In another paper the origins of ideology will be treated in depth.

3. For an in depth look into these practices, see http://www.touregypt/ GODS1.HTM

4. For what should be obvious reasons surrounding controversial sugges-tions, I deliberately avoid using contemporary ideologies and movements.

5. Keep in mind that thinking is not a skill we are born with. While we possess, at birth, the necessary hardware, the skill of thinking must be taught and learned.

6. Even a casual introduction to the way existentialism fathoms our exis-tence as merely an accidental case of happenstance, that we lack any foundation for our state of being, is a study in itself and beyond the scope of this paper.

7. *The Discovery Of Being*, by Rollo May, W.W. Norton and Co. New York, 1983, p. 109

8. Fredrick Engels, *Selected Correspondence*, Progress Publishers, Moscow, 1965 p. 455

WHAT STANDS BEHIND
THE LIBERTARIAN

JACK ARAMBULA

Abstract: This article offers an analysis of the primary ideological "givens" standing behind the political doctrine of libertarianism. First, Arambula offers an explanation describing the difference between right-wing libertarianism and left-wing libertarianism, leading to the focus of the paper being on the more common right-wing, libertarian doctrine. The three leading right-wing assumptions are closely examined: (1) The libertarian view of human nature. (2) The libertarian idea of natural rights. (3) The libertarian claim of a natural right to property, sometimes called "entitlement theory." This is an in-depth analysis, concluding with the somewhat negative impact that these assumptions have on the theory of right-wing libertarianism.

When I take up a social issue and passionately debate its pros and cons, ninety-five percent of the time I am debating a super structural ideological point. For example, is capital punishment justified? Is socialism bad? Should we scrap affirmative action? These are all important issues, but they are all superstructure issues sitting atop far more fundamental and largely unspoken givens. Standing behind all social and political positions there are one or more unannounced but assumed givens. These assumed givens behind arguments are similar to axioms in geometry. If these axioms are correct then the logical derivatives that follow, such as a position on flat-tax or abortion, stand a much greater chance of being correct. On the other hand, if the axioms are incorrect then whatever is built upon them is not worth the ink to write them. So it is that a good way to approach social and political positions is to first examine these primary givens that stand behind the ideological superstructure.

I do not mean to imply that an advocate of a social position, or an ideologue for a political point of view, would always be deliberately dishonest. Of course, sometimes it is true that the ideologue is little more than a snake-oil salesman. However, more typically, the ideologue may completely believe in the position he or she is advocating. They may do this without questioning or examining their underlying assumptions. The advocate may not even realize that the assumptions are there, standing behind the position and out of sight. This last is very often the case.

Before I move directly into an examination of the assumptions that stand behind the libertarian let me offer one note of caution. There are several different versions of libertarianism, starting with so-called Left and Right Libertarianism. Left-Wing Libertarianism, sometimes called mutualism, is definitely a minority position within the Left and only deserves the title "libertarian" with the greatest circumspection. Consequently, I will not treat it here. I will deal only with Right-Libertarianism as it is the predominate theory at play, and from this point forward I will drop the "Right" in libertarianism with the understanding that it is implied. It should also be noted also that libertarianism is sometimes called Right-Wing anarchy. Calling libertarianism anarchy is completely wrong. I feel confident that by the end of this work calling libertarianism any type of anarchy will have been demonstrated to be a misnomer.

What are these assumed "givens" that underlie the libertarian position? There are several givens. I will only consider the most basic three:

(1) The libertarian view of human nature. (2) The libertarian idea of natural rights. (3) The libertarian claim of a natural right to property, sometimes called "entitlement theory." Along with this discussion I will attempt to fully illustrate the implications of these assumptions and the difficulty that comes with handling their internal consistencies. Unfortunately, restriction of space must be considered.

(1) Human Nature. As any political scientist will tell you, the issue of human nature—that quasi-involuntary baseline for our behavior—is one of the pivotal issues on which *every* political theory hinges. How we act, what we think, and why, and the way we perceive the world is, at bottom, based on certain assumptions about "human nature." It is also one issue that is much overlooked, and thus unspoken. We can go no further in a discussion of libertarianism without giving the subject its due.

With respect to human behavior, there is no libertarian writer that I know of who has not, or does not, use this term, "human nature." Indeed, it would be difficult to tease out the contingent libertarian concepts (e.g., natural law, natural rights, etc.) if they did not rest on some sort of belief in the baseline nature of humanity. The concept of human nature is a tricky one and libertarians approach the subject gingerly. However, rather than dropping the term entirely, the tendency amongst libertarians is to say very little about human nature, and with good reason.[1] Controversial comments about the nature of our species do not auger well for the delicate tripod which supports the libertarian ideology (i.e., the *natural right* to life, liberty and property) and which seeks to minimize the role of the political state. To illustrate: if libertarians were to claim that human nature is intrinsically wicked, they find themselves vulnerable to the ultra-conservative argument that a coercive state is required to check the human propensity to violence and pillage. On the other hand, if they claim that our species by nature is good, they find themselves falling in line with communist and anarchist theories that lead to doing away with the state entirely—something libertarians do not want to do, and indeed, cannot do.[i] Consequently, libertarians must position themselves somewhere in between these alternative views on human nature. As I will demonstrate, this accounts for some of the problems with consistency

---

i. This obviously runs counter to common assumptions about libertarianism, and I will treat with it a bit later in this paper.

found in the libertarian's sensitive positions surrounding the existence of the political state.

As a general rule, libertarians carefully avoid the difficult view of our species as possessing any inherent nature. In general, they say that the basic essence of a human being on this plane of existence is simply a creature animated by an egoistic and rational "will-to-survive."[2] And except for this built in will-to-survive a human being arrives on this earth—a blank slate, a *tabula rasa*, as John Locke put it at the end of the 17th century. Further, whether this very human "will-to-survive" produces good acts or bad acts depends on rationality as man comes into contact with alternative choices presented by the world outside of him. This all sounds rather neutral and boring, but I am attempting to cast the widest possible net to gather the greatest agreement on libertarian sentiments regarding the nature of our species.

The bottom line is that when pushed, the libertarians will say only that by nature man is an *egoistic and rational* creature with a *self-interested "will-to-survive."* This is a minimal declaration on the nature of man, and one difficult to debate. That we as humans are primarily concerned with our own selves (are egoistic), are thoughtful (are rational), and desire to survive (are self-interested) appears obvious. In addition, the minimalism of this position possesses the attractive feature of being both resilient and flexible. However, this brand of minimalism also possesses a difficult side. The issue of flexibility, (consider a point of view supporting only a few markers underlying human behavior) can quickly transform into a sponginess when it comes to supporting the hard specifics of the libertarian ideological superstructure. This disadvantage of the minimalist position is the crux of our discussion and we will go over it shortly. For now, let me just add that classic and contemporary liberals also suffer from this handicap, though not to the same extent. By this I mean that classic and contemporary liberals, unlike libertarians, do not attempt to connect human nature (i.e., egoistic, rational self-interest) with some "natural right to property." This difficult connection will come up repeatedly for libertarians. At this point let me note that while a minimal declaration on human nature will solve one or two problems, it will engender other, less tractable issues.

Issues with a minimal declaration on human nature. There are several issues concerning the minimal position on human nature. To begin with, a minimalist position necessarily has only minimal applications. Describing a human being as merely a creature of egoistic, rational self-interest engenders instability because such a declaration lacks the authority to support a firm ideological structure. Egoistic, rational self-interest *might* be a correct assessment of human nature, but the political direction such an assessment takes is far from as obvious as libertarians might like it to be.

First, as the issue will come up repeatedly in this paper, it must be stated that to say that human beings are self-seeking and self-interested in no way distinguishes them from the lesser animals. All animals are concerned with their individual well being. It is the nature of *all animals*—and these include human beings—to be self-absorbed in this way. Obviously, animals, like people, may be concerned with other things, such as protective parenting, grooming, and so on, but all animals are self-serving in regard to their own survival; it's instinctual and baked into the cake. The only libertarian claim concerning the nature of humanity that truly sets us apart from the lesser animals is our faculty of reason. It is with the faculty of reason that the libertarian problem with human nature makes itself felt.

The problem question now becomes: does "reason" influence "egoist self-interest" in the way libertarians claim it must? As libertarians frequently cast an eye toward Aristotle in search of support for their position on rational man (and to a lesser extent, self-interest)[3] allow me to use Aristotle to demonstrate the libertarian problem with "rational man."

It is quite true that Aristotle claimed that what separates men from the lesser animals is the ability to reason. However, the faculty of reason led the Greek philosopher in a far different direction than the one libertarians have in mind. Aristotle's view of natural-man as rational-man meant political-man—that is, a man integrated and functioning as a part of the greater community. Aside from the view of humanity as social and political, there is no apparent conflict between the Aristotelian view of natural man and the libertarian view. However, Aristotle does continue on, claiming that the best of political-man, the best of rational-man, of natural-man, means placing virtue ahead of all else. The force of Aristotelian virtue reveals a problem for the libertarian. Aristotle clearly takes this ideal of virtue as found in the rational-man, *qua* political-man, in the direction of the common good and not the individual good. For

Aristotle, virtue and the rational individual find expression only in the common good.[4]

To be more specific: the rational human species, according to Aristotle, has an innate propensity to develop complex communities. In Aristotle's philosophy there is teleology to this development. The goal of these communities is, according to Aristotle, is a cultivation of virtue for the sake of justice. By virtue and justice Aristotle meant the betterment of the common good of the whole, which Aristotle saw as having primacy over the individual's good.[5] In these communities, the purpose of reason is for the excellence of common, community life, not individual rights or needs. The needs of the community supersede the needs of the individual.[6] The individual derives personal good from the excellence of the common good. If nothing else, we can see that rational man does not *necessarily* operate in the service of the self-serving, egoistic man as the libertarians would have it.

Of course, the libertarian is not struck dumb by this. The libertarian will respond that there is no conflict here. The common good is actually *enhanced* by rational, egoistic self-interest. The libertarian will insist that although it will *appear* that egoistic, self-interested individuals may be pulling in opposite directions (i.e., the direction of their individual self-interest), such appearances are deceptive. Rather than producing pandemonium, this individual, rational self-interest will actually bring about a stable and healthy "common good."

How does the libertarian argue that this apparent conflict between egoistic individualism and the common good is an illusion? The libertarian can present one of two positions: (1) a metaphysical argument, or (2) a pragmatic argument.

The metaphysical argument. Without entering a debate as to whether Aristotle's reasoning is superior to that of the libertarian, or visa-versa, we can easily recognize that a troublesome issue with the libertarian claim to "common good" is that one of the arguments rests on a metaphysical foundation.[7]

For Aristotle, the "common good" sits atop reason alone. In the libertarian metaphysical argument, the "common good" is reason as it is *revealed* through a secondary, underlying esoteric medium. But what is this esoteric medium, and exactly how rational is this claim that reason can be revealed through any such secondary medium?

In modern times this metaphysical medium often takes one of the many forms found in Adam Smith's "invisible hand' (i.e., The Market as the chief constituent of the Hand)[8]. It would be inaccurate of me to suggest that simply because the libertarian explanation for the "common good" is metaphysical and often mystic (e.g., the invisible hand) that the argument is wrong. It is more precise to say that giving phenomena a metaphysical foundation tends to make empirical verification difficult at best, and at worst, inconsistent. This problem with verifiability is a corruption inherent in the nature of metaphysics: it lacks the concrete expression necessary for factual study. To avoid the corrupting charge of metaphysics, the libertarian will tend to introduce "the market" in a way that makes it appear as empirical fact.[9] But the market, even spoken of as a thing representing the exchange of multiple goods and services, remains an unwieldy abstraction. Like all abstractions, The market remains troubled and indeterminate in this "appearance" in the garb of empirical fact. As an example of this troubled abstraction, one thorny and corrupting indeterminate is that market projection and prediction have always eluded the best minds in the field; another is that the market cannot be tested under controlled conditions. These and other anti-rationalist positions (e.g., "trickle-down theory," "supply side economics," "a self-correcting market," etc.) found at the heart of libertarianism generate a black hole swallowing the verifiability necessary for scientific study. This alone is a symptomatic indicator of the lack of any concrete foundation for the market as a real and material empirical phenomenon. Is the market actually driven by Smith's invisible hand? It can't be proven by any other argument than that driven by the metaphysical.

As any philosopher will tell you, metaphysical solutions are notoriously slippery, and this reliance on a metaphysical entity has been a persistent thorn in the side of libertarians. But given their view of egoistic self-interest as the heartbeat of human nature, is it difficult to see how they can pluck it out. At root here is the distinct possibility that the libertarian view of human nature might itself be a metaphysical concept, thus affecting a torturous double bind.

In the interest of "compare and contrast," examine a much less torturous view of egoistic self-interest as it relates to the common good. Take, for example, one such as the right-wing, statist view of the fascist position. The fascist does not dispute that human nature is driven by egoism and self-interest. In fact they embrace this point of view. However, along with this embrace comes the claim that a strong state is necessary to control a self-interested human nature, an egoistic nature that if left unchecked will produce chaos. Rational self-interest, according to the fascist, must be rationally controlled and channeled by a neutral and disinterested elite. The energy produced by the destructive forces within self-interested human nature must be harnessed to service the betterment of a *collective of individuals*. If necessary, this harnessing must be done by coercive means. It is the fascist's claim that it is for everyone's good that a corporatist state arise to take charge of the chaos produced by egoistic self-interest; a clear-sighted, autocratic state must forcefully steer individual self-interest in the direction of the common good. This coercive state is for the betterment of the self-interested individual. To be sure, such a notion of a strong state violates the unshackled freedom of the individual, an unrestrained freedom which is at the pinnacle of the libertarian ideal. We see, though, that an argument for rational self-interest can lead in directions not intended by the libertarian.

This brings the libertarian's view of human nature to a fork in the road: Is it to be the nature of humanity as acted out individually or is it the nature of humanity as acted out collectively. That is, is it the primacy of the individual or the primacy of the aggregate (i.e., the state). Given the libertarian view of an egoistic self-interested man, the apparent answer is the primacy of the individual. Here the weakness of their minimal declaration of human nature makes their argument for the primacy of the individual over the collective a shaky one, a claim held together more by metaphysical faith than Aristotelian reason.

The pragmatic argument. Approaching the issue of the collective from a pragmatic angle the libertarian does not, and cannot, reject the well being of the community. This is a very real and practical issue for the libertarian. The libertarian depends on a healthy collectivized humanity to satisfy the needs of a privatized self-interest. This is another way of saying that the primacy of rational self-interest demands a collective laid bare for egoistic exploitation. Restrictions of any kind that protect against the exploitation of the collective are intolerable to the libertarian. On the other hand, wholesale exploitation will quickly eat up the material foundation so necessary for the survival of egoistic self-interest. At this point it is easy to see just how attractive a magical solution such as the

322

"invisible-hand" appears. Yet, at the end of the day, practical libertarians will recognize any metaphysical solution such as the invisible hand of the marketplace as problematic.

Libertarian theory is purportedly based on the individual, but the assumptions standing behind the theory emphatically require ready access to a well structured and well behaved collective. The question confronting the pragmatic libertarian is in what proportion are the needs of the individual and those of an orderly social collective to be balanced? Also of importance: how is the order of this collective to be enforced? The structure and maintenance of the social order is a tireless political issue, but given the libertarian's perspective on human nature it is an issue that produces a particularly acute ideological thorn. Even in the face of a human nature defined in terms of extreme individualism, no practical libertarian can reject the state, not entirely, or the coercive legal framework it can provide. The practical libertarian clearly understands that despite any strong belief in that ethereal, metaphysical entity, "The Market," the collective must participate in preventing its own disintegration, or outright collapse, and this participation must be given freely. If this participation is not given voluntary (always a tricky proposition) then it must be policed in some fashion. Here the coercive political state enters through the back door out of necessity. Despite all the rhetoric to the contrary, the libertarian seems to need a coercive state to enforce an orderly and predictable collective, a collective necessary for the support of the egoistic and self-interested individual.

According to Adam Smith, the forces of the market are not enough to keep society from falling apart. The pragmatic Adam Smith points out that it is government's proper role to see that the collective remains in good order.[10] Just the same as any other political theory, the exact nature of the coercive political state is defined in relative terms—in this case, relative to libertarian philosophy. Given the minimal declaration on the nature of the human species the libertarian finds himself operating from a political platform precisely the same as other statist philosophies with the only difference being found in the style and purpose of the state.

To draw all this together: the gravest weakness of the minimal libertarian declaration on human nature as justified by egoistic, rational self-interest is that it causes the libertarian to be unable to define the libertarian state with any real sense of internal consistency. What I mean by that statement is the following: The *egoistic* part of the libertarian view of human nature wants to reject the coercive, political state, but the *rational self-interested* part of the libertarian view demands it. Within the libertarian matrix the *egoist* often stands at odds with the *rationalist*, an inconsistency not found in Aristotle's vision of the political state.

Natural Rights. In political and legal circles the term "natural right" (*qua* natural law) is used and exchanged endlessly. There seems to be no need to explain these natural rights, much less consider them in any analytical light. The common and automatic use of the phrase "natural rights" seems to put it beyond any normal sense of conjecture or controversy. The right to "Life, Liberty, and the Pursuit of Happiness," is a phrase deeply embedded in the consciousness of many. We hardly give it a thought. Humans are thought to have natural rights before they have political rights. We are born with them, are we not? Indeed, modern political rights rest on the ideological concept of rights according to nature. The only question seems to be: precisely what are these natural rights?

In an effort to find an answer, we might say that it seems reasonable, since we speak of *natural* rights, that they must be rights according to some law of nature. If not a *law* of nature, then at the very least these rights should emanate in some way from the natural world. Much of our political and legal thinking is based on these rights that we are told somehow spring full blown from the nature of things. It is simply how things are. Indeed, the very notion of these rights is both an assumed and heralded foundation of many a modern political institution, including those of the United States and much of Europe. Natural rights are presented as immutable and eternal. Only what if things are not quite as they appear?

(2) Issues with the claim to Natural Rights. The fact is that the idea of "natural rights" has a very skimpy history. Until the 17th century and works of John Locke, rights according to nature played no role in political thought. In the western world,[11] and prior to the 17th century, only the Greek and Roman stoics carried on any philosophical treatment of the subject, and that was a modest treatment at best.[12] The fact that natural rights arose in political thought at such a late time would suggest that some analysis is warranted.

Any kind of human rights, natural or legal, must have roots. Hopefully these roots of natural rights are sunk in the natural world rather than the supernatural world. Since we are not looking into the natural rights of ducks or wart hogs, these natural rights must be rights according to the nature of humans. However, given the libertarian assumption regarding human nature, this creates a problem. For if we are to take the libertarian point of view at face value, *viz.*, that the nature of our species can be reduced to a simply egoistic, rational self-interest, or a "will to survive," then excepting for human intellect man's basic nature is hardly different from the duck or wart hog. It would follow that putting "reason" aside, the claim should be valid that the lesser animals too should enjoy the same natural rights as humans. This leaves us "reason" as the turning point for natural rights. Only, as we will see, it is not clear in which direction the spear-point of reasoning is aimed.

Simply because homo sapiens can reflect on a "right" does not automatically support a logical process that leads to the possession of that carefully considered "right." As opposed to the lesser animals, the fact that I am a rational man means little more than that I can intellectually summon forth "natural rights" as a hypothesis. The mere "summoning" alone is no formal proof that natural rights can reach the level of theory, let alone fact. I can think that I have a "right to life" according to nature, but what animal in nature has a "right to life," or a "right to exist?" Just because I can conceive of a natural "right to life," it does not automatically follow that animals have such a right—or for that matter that animals, including homo sapiens, have any "rights" according to nature. It is fair to say, along with John Dewey, that "Natural rights and natural liberties exist only in the kingdom of mythological social zoology."[13]

Formal logic has definite rules. In this case, logic demands that there be two or more true premises leading to the conclusion that humans possess natural rights. There is nothing in nature, or "human nature," that supports the required premises. Reflection alone allows me to consider human nature not conjure one up. If I am being honestly rational, I must recognize that there is more desire than logic behind the claim of natural rights. At the very least, the claim that natural rights are truly natural must remain highly controversial and existing more in the realm of wishful thinking than nature. Consequently, we are left with only the vague feeling that "natural rights" seem to be innate, forgetting of course that prior to the 17th century we would not have had this vague feeling of possessing "natural rights." Speculation on human rights as natural rights is more a matter of time and place than an proposition good for all eternity.

Consider now what one leading libertarian, Lew Rockwell, had to say on the fundamental natural rights of man:

"Libertarians believe that liberty is a natural right embedded in a natural law of what is proper for mankind, in accordance with man's nature. Where this set of natural laws comes from, whether it is purely natural or originated by a creator, is an important ontological question but is irrelevant to social or political philosophy."[14]

Although Rockwell undoubtedly recognizes a very real problem in claiming natural rights as innate, most libertarians would not be so blunt in dismissing a forthright analysis of their origin. John Locke, for example, was very much aware of this disconnect between man's "natural rights" and rights in nature. Like the above writer, Locke glossed over the disconnect by claiming that natural rights were of supernatural origin. That is, God created man with "natural" rights both in and according to nature.[15] It was just this kind of supernatural, metaphysical support for natural rights that caused the leading empiricist of the day, David Hume, to refer to natural rights as "nonsense on stilts."[16]

The only pragmatic solution to this dilemma is to disentangle the nature of man from natural rights, which leave the idea of rights as natural with no empirical footing. To avoid this problem most libertarians would simply not open the door to a strictly analytical inspection of natural rights. "Rights" in nature simply cannot be rationally or empirically claimed. Natural rights can only be claimed through a supernatural medium such as God-given, which greatly reduces their intellectual appeal.

If human rights are not present according to nature, then human rights are only granted by the grace of the legal framework provided by the political state. If human rights do not arise from nature, then to speak of rights as derived from nature is a matter of political ideology, not a matter of empirical fact. Once again, this introduces the unwanted political state into the libertarian equation. The political state can easily accommodate natural rights, but not in a way that will cohere well with libertarian theory. The need for the coercive political state as the guarantor of "natural rights" is a bit awkward for the libertarian to accept, but he can live with it. To claim that the state is also the *originator* of "natural rights" is to expose much of libertarian theory as more of a collection of self-serving platitudes than a coherent ideology. We can see that in considering natural rights the libertarian can ignore the need for the political state only by ignoring these subtle contradictions.

(3) **The right to property.** While this "right" may seem to many the weak leg of the tripod, (i.e., the *natural right* to life, liberty and property) this "right to property" is actually the leg that shows the greatest stability. This is so because it can be argued that this claim to property does not necessarily rely on a right according to nature or some supernatural entity. The claim to property makes more sense as a right when it is accorded by the logic of our particular human situation rather than a right according to some definition of nature. So note here that I stress "situation" and not "nature." This is an important distinction for the libertarian position. And note also that I put the accent on the libertarian "position" and not the libertarian "doctrine" or "ideology." There are serious problems with this position, so a further treatment of this situation is necessary. I'll work out the pros before I cite the cons.

The claim to property as a "natural right" goes roughly as follows: since I possess my body, I possess what is produced by my body, as my labor has made what I have produced an extension of my person. Or concurrently, since I have a right to my own body, I have a right to what my body produces. The origin of this claim to property as a natural right stem first from the ownership of the self (i.e., a derivative of the natural right to life). Then citing John Locke, property is that which has been mixed with the labor of the builder or shaper of property. Human labor has infused human value into the product or property; as a result of human labor, a human value now exists in the property produced. I use the phrase human value as "property" here in its loosest sense. Intellectual property qualifies, as does the acquiring of "unclaimed" property, which would then be worked for the production of products.

However, in spite of the above, or perhaps because of it, the libertarian right to property does not necessarily depend on any claims to natural rights, or on rights granted by a supernatural entity. Speaking concretely, the right to property is often called the *labor theory of value*[17] thereby bypassing any appeal to a metaphysical premise. Whatever I produce with my labor acquires the value of my labor, a value which by virtue of my labor I own. As property is the physical extension of the value produced by human labor, the product and the *value of the product* (i.e., property) belongs to the producer of the product, as his labor has made it an extension of his person. I am repeating this in several different ways for two reasons. First, this concept of property as labor-value gets a little tricky when attempting to dispose of this labor-value, as it must be converted into alternate types of value. And second, this concept of ownership of property rests at the center of the libertarian idea of freedom. Freedom is rooted in the right to property. It is the freedom to dispose with property (i.e., labor-value) as the owner of the property desires, without precondition or interference.

This rather straightforward materialist position resolves two weaknesses found in other libertarian claims. (1) God is left out of the argument, and (2) so is nature, at least as such. The claim certainly seems to make sense given the human situation. If I make an arrowhead, or compose a sonata, whatever labor-value the product possesses is by the dint of the value of labor inherent in the creation. It follows then that I should freely be able to do whatever I wish with my creation and the labor-value it possesses. I can freely give this value away, trade it for services, and at my death, freely pass this value along to anyone I wish. As I said, this seems to make prefect sense—at least as far as it goes.

There are two secondary problems with this position when it comes to the manipulation and exercise of labor-value as property. First, how would one secure his future—that is, protect himself against the caprice of time? One obvious answer is by accumulating this human labor value. One must build a storehouse of labor-value against an uncertain future. While this answers the first question, it exposes a second issue: How is the accumulated labor-value to be stored up? This, the second problem is how to convert material possessions, or their labor-value, into other commodities when outright barter is unavailable? This is a problem that arose early on in human history.

John Locke was keenly aware of the accumulation of unequal wealth in the England of his day. Given the extremes of his day, it was difficult to miss. He was also aware that this wealth could not possibly have been created entirely by those individuals who possessed this accumulated wealth. It was no easy trick for Locke to see what was going on around him. Locke recognized that accumulated wealth was not so much the result of human labor and labor-value, *per se*, as it was of the business of trade and sale. Locke's answer to both of the above questions, as well as the conversion of labor-value into trade and sale, was the invention of money and contract: that is, the reliable storing-up of past labor-value and the predictable transfer of future labor-value. In effect, what Locke was describing was the conversion of hard labor-value into liquid, *abstract-value*.[18] This conversion of value was intended to produce predictability. The conversion also led to a little understood and unanalyzed consequence: the turning of abstract-value into *political* and *social* power. Thus, with the conversion of the concrete into the abstract, the new variable of political power was introduced into the social equation.[19] It goes without saying that this conversion was historical as well as contemporary to John Locke. Wherever and whenever the abstract-value of money presented itself, the conditions for coercive power were formed. Locke merely described, analyzed and laid the ideological groundwork for the emergence of new forms of concentrated wealth, together with their impact on evolving societal and political relationships.

If one accepts this labor-value as the foundation for the claim of property rights, then this right possesses greater empirical verifiability and a logic more coherent than the previously discussed claims. Further, the conversion of labor-value into abstract-value makes the accumulation of both wealth and political power nearly inexhaustible. This last, the concentration of wealth (*qua* abstract-value) with its potential for political power, once again raises a problem of ideological consistency for the libertarian. Abstract-power implies the coercive, political state—not its opposite. How are we to deal with this apparent inconsistency: if property is freedom, what are we to make of its abstract-value as the progenitor of laws, the contract, their implementation and enforcement—in short, the coercive state?

Issues with the right to property: The issue with property rights that loom above all other issues is the problem of the political state. This is not a metaphysical or supernatural issue; the state is not a metaphysical entity. The emergence of the political state presents the libertarian with a very real dilemma: How to justify the political state without making it appear obvious that the concentrated power of the state is the servant of concentrated wealth? The attempt to solve this thorny problem has filled volumes of libertarian literature.[20]

In libertarian theory, the individual's right to property and the freedom to exchange that property must be politically protected from the collective interest, even though that collective might be the original source of labor-value. It is fundamental to libertarian theory that the individual's rights supersede any collective rights. Not all libertarian thinkers agree on the details, but in general an individual's property or the exchange of property cannot be managed, regulated or taken away even in the interest of the larger community. There must be no violation of the individual's freedom, especially in regard to what he owns or has produced, even when it is at odds with the collective interest. All actions surrounding property must be voluntary and unrestrained. The interests of the collective must be secondary to the rights of the individual to preserve the free exercise of exchange and accumulation by the individual. It is this suppression of the community in the interest of unrestrained accumulation that eventually leads to a few awkward ideological results.[21]

The suppression of the needs of the community seems to represent state power rather than man acting as an independent, rational animal. For example, it is difficult to explain by what trick of reason one can argue that an individual's possession of a vital social resource, such as water, could be reasonably denied to the collective, while at the same time insisting that the collective enforce its own destruction by self-inflicted coercive means if necessary.[22] The potential for outright contradiction underscores the awkwardness of claiming democratic authority in favor of economic power as reified through the political state.

Initially, this coercive power was seen by John Locke as merely an enhancement of personal security and survival, but the new *abstract* power of concentrated wealth necessarily went further. To fully guarantee the security offered by the coercive power embodied within concentrated wealth, it must be tethered to a platform that will both reify and *legitimize* the conversion to coercive power. That platform is the political state, with its monopoly on coercive power. As Locke presented it, the political state was a voluntary binding together of people for the purpose of "peaceably living amongst one another, in secure enjoyment of their properties, and a greater security."[23] It is through the political state that what begins as an enhancement of personal security becomes the power to maintain concentrated wealth through the monopoly of coercive power. So the essence of the conversion to the abstract is really one of changing concrete property into the property of power as reified and legitimized through the political state. The difficulty with this comes when attempting to reconcile the coercive state with freedom for all. In an attempt to maintain the primacy of libertarianism, there are at least two possible outcomes to this "difficulty" with reconciliation. Keeping in mind that in a democratic model, where the great mass of the community may be hostile to huge concentrations of wealth, the libertarian would be compelled to dismiss an openly urber-democratic and equalitarian model. Ironically, the committed libertarians would have to turn to a statist option. In order to blunt equalitarian impulses, the libertarian would turn in favor to (1) an oligarch model, or at the very least, (2) a fascist model.

Let it be said at the outset that the conversion of labor-value into concentrated wealth makes the political state not merely desirable but inevitable; it would seem obvious that the need for reliable and predictable security for all that concentration of wealth makes the existence of the state inevitable. The existence of the political state does appear to solve certain immediate concrete problems connected with the libertarian idea of freedom, but not without internal inconsistencies regarding that same sense of freedom. The transformation of abstract-value (i.e., money, or a form thereof) and future value (i.e., the contract) into coercive power (i.e., the state) creates what was first thought of as a guarantor of the free exercise of wealth and power for *all*. That last word, "all" is the problem. By the inclusion of "all," what in effect had happened is that the state had become not simply a guarantor, but a broker. Because of the necessity to guarantee security and the rights of property for "all" the state has become a legal arbitrator of wealth and power. The state, as arbitrator, has suddenly developed the potential to be an independent identity reflecting the values of the power it brokers. As those values primarily reflect self-interest, the state shows every inclination to become another self-interested entity with the ready availability to stand directly in the way of other rational, self-interested freedoms. Unfortunately, this independent state model shows some of its greatest reflection in fascist ideology, an ideology which appears, at least superficially, to be at total odds with libertarian philosophy.

So what is it to be, the state as arbitrator of wealth or the agent acting on behalf of concentrated wealth? Either the fascist model emerges as the best example of an independent state acting as a broker between the interests of wealth and the balance of society, or the independent state is seen as an *agent* of the "right to property." The meaning of this last is that the state emerges as the subordinate *facilitator* of the interests of those few who would accumulate the greatest amount of wealth.[24] This last type of political state is best represented by the oligarchic model. Of course, some might wish to argue that oligarchy is at the root of fascism. While there is some truth to this claim, it should be pointed out that an uncorrupted fascism frequently concerns itself with the community as a whole, that is, with the government acting in the role of adjudicator of conflict between the various competing sections of society. The fascist fully believes that the government's role in conflict resolution will keep the wealthy from devouring themselves and thereby undermining the society as a whole. Of course, the oligarchic model the state could easily stand in opposition to the interests of the community, however, unlike the fascist model, oligarchy would primarily facilitate the interests of the wealthy.

This suppression of the community in the interests of property rights is an issue of power that depends not so much on "nature" as on the "nature of the political state." Here lies the rub: what the "right to property" might gain for the libertarian in logical and empirical coherence, it loses to ideological irony: i.e., for the state to be able to guarantee the "right to property," and also be able to enforce this right. In either the fascist or oligarch model, the rule of the state must come first, thereby making the "power of the state" the primary consideration, not the "right to property." It should be clear that both the fascist or oligarch models of the state adjust more comfortably to these issues than the democratic model.

Final remarks: At the beginning of this paper I asserted that identifying libertarianism with any form of anarchy is wrong. By this point it should be clear that to one degree or other the three underlying and fundamental assumptions of libertarians all lead to the existence of some form of a coercive political state.

To summarize the statist positions drawn from the assumptions that stand behind the libertarian:

First, the libertarian claim of human nature as egoistic, rational self interest is not stable enough to support the philosophy's contingent claims.

As I demonstrated above, the introduction of "reason" trumps instinct and opens the door to other radically different claims on social organization that can be supported by the same view of human nature, (e.g., the Aristotelian view of the social order and the political state). Without passing judgment on which of the two views, Aristotelian or libertarian, is more logically coherent, it can be said that the type of social order (i.e., political state) envisioned by the libertarian must depend on factors other than those which emerge from their image of human nature as rational, egoistic self-interest. That is, if natural egoistic self-interest is trumped by human reason, the libertarian vision of the social order (i.e., political state) does not reflexively follow. Therefore, if human reason rather than instinct is the key to the nature of the social order, the libertarian view must allow for its development on factors other than rational, egoistic self-interest.

Second, a "natural right" in any form is at best a metaphysical claim. At worst a natural right is a completely arbitrary claim. In either event, natural rights clearly do not exist in nature. As these rights do not exist in nature, then they must be seen as legal rights established by a political entity and only graced with the ideological dressing of *natural*. It follows that whatever rights libertarians claim are more a matter of historical circumstance than universal principles. Consequently, as these rights are neither universal nor instinctual, disagreements will arise—quite possibly bold disagreements that will necessitate the intervention of a political state with strong coercive authority. It goes without saying that the reliance on a legal and coercive framework stands in contradiction to the libertarian claim to be anti-statist.

Third. The right to property is clearly the most contentious of the libertarian claims. Since rights in any form do not automatically spring from the nature of the human species, nor are they found anywhere in nature, they are mere legal claims. These legal claims depend on the nature of the political state, not on any agreed upon or immutable universals found in nature.

Given the libertarian insistence on the legal "right to property" libertarian philosophy depends on a coercive state to both grant this "right" and enforce it against those who would take issue with the "right to property"—namely, the laboring and propertyless classes.

In conclusion. In spite of their superficial claims of individual freedom and their anti-statist rhetoric, all the underlying tenets of libertarian philosophy support the existence of a coercive, political state. Libertarianism only differs from other political philosophies in the kind of state that they desire. This "libertarian state" would support, by coercive means if necessary, the maintenance of property in all its forms: property and capital, both liquid and real, in whatever accumulated and disproportionate amounts these forms might reach.

The libertarian state is not necessarily an oligarchy or fascist state. However, inasmuch as the rights of property supercede the collective rights of the majority, the libertarian philosophy is decidedly anti-democratic. It is not fair to call libertarianism a form of totalitarianism, as the libertarian state would not involve itself in the total management of individual lives. In fact, it would try to avoid this, if only from the standpoint of economy and efficiency. However, there is little doubt, despite the libertarian claims to the contrary, that libertarianism represents a form of state tyranny. No matter the possible legal afterthoughts, the presumptive "givens" standing behind the libertarian all lead to suppressing the needs of the many in favor of the wealth of the few. As stated above, the only apparent difference between libertarian tyranny and other forms of state tyranny are the goals and methods employed.

Notes

1. A notable exception to this avoidance of discussion on human nature is Ayn Rand. While it is not my intention to discuss individual philosophers, I will say that Rand's philosophy of Objectivism is not precisely the same animal as Right-Libertarianism. Rand's philosophy is a sometimes uneasy combination of Aristotle and Locke. Many Right-Libertarians show a tendency to take the Lockeian-Rand and ignore the Aristotelian-Rand.

2. See Ayn Rand, "Galt Speaks," in *Atlas Shrugged*, and Rand, *The Virtue of Selfishness*. I use Ayn Rand here as she is a widely respected spokesperson for libertarianism, and not because she represents a unilateral perspective on the philosophy. In fact, her philosophy would more properly be called "objectivism," and while objectivism shares many points in common with libertarianism, there are also numerous points at variance.

3. To claim that Aristotle supports self-interest in the general way that most libertarians claim, most philosophers would agree, is a tortured claim. To live the virtuous life that can achieve the *eudaimonic* character is clearly in the individual's self-interest. But it is equally clear that Aristotle never intended virtue to mean that life should be lived for selfish and egoistic ends.

4. There are many other points of difference between Aristotle and libertarian thought, as for example, the exchanges of goods for profit, of usury, and the accumulation of wealth, are all, according to Aristotle, unnatural acts, and not worthy of rational man. See Aristotle, *Politics*.

5. See Aristotle (1276b20)

6. See Aristotle (1280b39, and 1281a4-8)

7. Metaphysics is the study of principles that are claimed to either transcend or underlie reality. The essence of "mind," is one example, what would be the nature of God is another example. To the metaphysician both "mind" and God claim to have a relationship with physical reality, but rise above physical reality in a way that would appear to give them a separate life or a reality of their own. This is a correct definition, but also a simplification. If one is interested, there are numerous philosophical dictionaries available for a more detailed definition.

8. Adam Smith: "Every individual intends only his own gain, and he is in this, as in so many other cases, led by an invisible hand to promote an end which was no part of his intention."

9. The "market" is a largely metaphysical entity with empirical roots. In mainstream economic theory a market represents any exchange of goods or services for money, or other services or property. The principle of the market emerges spontaneously from human interplay and is not restricted to a specific place or time.

10. Adam Smith, *Wealth of Nations*, Book 5, 1, para 178

11. Beyond the 17th century western world, only Islamic law has several specific references to natural law.

12. By both the Greek and Roman stoics. This was largely in reference to slavery, *viz.*, that no man was by nature a slave.

13. See John Dewey, *The History of Liberalism.*

14. http://www.lewrockwell.com/rothbard/rothbard12.html

15. For an extended treatment of this, see Michael Zuckert, *Natural Rights and the New Republicans*, (Princeton University Press, New Jersey, 1998) especially pp. 256-258

16. Hume certainly thought that many rights, including property rights, together with an unequal distribution of wealth, were just and proper, but saw no need to infer them from "natural laws," which he felt was pure invention.

17. See John Locke, *Second Treatises of Government.* See also, Adam Smith, *On the Wealth of Nations*, Book 1, Ch. V

18. By abstract-value I mean more than coin and currency. Abstract-value extends to securities, bonds, and contractual arrangements between people and economic entities. For a treatment of money as abstract value see John Smith in *What is Money*, (Routledge, London, 2000) especially, pages 20-22.

19. By political power I do not necessarily mean the political state, although this is implied. By the use of the phrase political power I intend the more basic definition of political power: *viz.*, abstract-power means the power to determine who gets what, how much of it they get, and when they get it.

20. To see the amount of effort that has gone into reconciling concentrated wealth and political power one might look into either of the two contemporary classics on the subject: *The Libertarian Reader* by David Boaz, or Robert Nozick's *Anarchy, State, and Utopia.*

21. To be balanced, it should be noted that esteemed libertarian economist Fredrick Hayek found room to place limits on *laissez-faire* capitalism through a regulatory role for government. In his book, *Constitution of Liberty*, Hayek argues for a government intervention through such things as work-hour regulation, manipulation of the monetary system, regulating the institutional flow of information and communication. See, F.Hayek *Constitution of Liberty*, (University of Chicago Press, 1960)

22. For an excellent attempt at resolving this type of conflict you might see Robert Nozick, *Anarchy, State and Utopia*, especially chapter 5.

23. John Locke, *Two Treatises of Government*, Chapter VIII, sec. 95

24. For the sake of space I am ignoring other state models, such as the political state based on communist principles.

Epilogue

A POINT OF HONOR

The Role of Honor in Contemporary Civic and Civil Discourse

WILLIAM RANDOLPH

Typically, epilogues are intended to bring closure to the words just read. After having worked through a dozen articles that delve into the philosophical underpinnings of political positions, honor may well be the ribbon to tie up whatever cynicism that might have been unleashed.

Abstract: Honor is a word, a concept, an idea, irritatingly and utterly out of favor in our contemporary times. Even so, this article will take this arcane subject seriously. There are two perspectives on our topic. First, there is a brand of honor that is an externally awarded gift. This is a type of honor that is bestowed from without by accolade and treasure. The second type is a self-possessed sense of honor, one that is felt inwardly, sometimes deeply, and depends less on outward signs of recognition than it does on a sense of self-appreciation. In this essay we are primarily concerned with the second type. We speak of honorable so-and-so, keeping one's word of honor, doing the honorable thing—but what does that mean? What does this most ancient of sentiments have to offer in our contemporary age? Is it appropriate and fitting? Is the concept of honor gender neutral, or gender specific? What is the evolution of honor and how does it impact our current thinking? We would like to think of politics as being an honorable calling, but is it? Can it be? This paper by Randolph, even while recognizing the difficulty, argues in the affirmative: honor does have a place in contemporary political discourse and action.

337

66 "P oint of Honor!" Definition: an expression indicating a matter seriously affecting one's personal integrity and self-worth. What exactly does that mean, and what role does that meaning play in politics and philosophy? I'll take the position that for politics, the short answer is, *everything*. For philosophy, it seems obvious that *any* answer concerning honor will instigate an intriguing and contentious debate. As a topic, honor plunges deep into the recesses of right behavior and wrong action, a debate on good vs. bad, a general stirring up of questions and issues concerning morals, ethics, integrity, courage, and most awkwardly of all, gender chauvinism.

The word "honor" is bandied about often enough, carelessly, it seems—typically in a mocking and a flippant manner. Honor is a word, a concept, an idea, irritatingly and utterly out of favor in our contemporary times. Even so, this article will take the subject seriously. Given that seriousness, we will launch the topic in a direction not only controversial, but one that will downright rub many people the wrong way. However, before we get going with these rubs and complications it is important to more narrowly define the subject of honor, then point out, in greater detail, the relationship of this subject to politics, philosophy and general civil discourse.

There are two perspectives on our topic. First, there is a brand of honor that is an externally awarded gift. This is a type of honor that is bestowed from without. This brand is sometimes referred to as "vertical" honor—that is, the elevation of someone, by accolade, award and treasure, above the common herd; examples would range from a Boy Scout merit badge to an Oscar. The second type is a self-possessed sense of honor, one that is felt inwardly, sometimes deeply, and depends less on outward signs of recognition than it does on a sense of self-appreciation. In this essay we are primarily concerned with the second type. The origins of this inward sense of honor are unclear, but hopefully this paper will go some considerable distance to reveal and clarify those beginnings. This second type of honor (the self-possessed) follows close on the heels of a positive sense of the self that is routinely and deliberately maintained and privately carried; a positive sense of self that can be recognized by outsiders or by a peer group. This second type is sometimes referred to as "horizontal" honor.[i] This is a

---

i. Horizontal, as use here, is not to be confused with class ranking or class structure itself. Horizontal, as used here, indicates the directional flow of awards and rewards.

type of honor that is peer supported, self-recognized and respected by those surrounding the individual with no need for laurels or accolades.

In searching for a quick way to distinguish between the two types, we might look to the way in which the two forms of honor can be taken away, and the impact on shame. The first, the vertical, is typically removed by some form of external character assassination—gossip, for example, or factual public claims of misdeeds, or even accusations of malfeasance that directly undermine the external reward atop which honor rests; rather than shame, this external impact results in ridicule. The second type, the horizontal, can be endangered by an inner sense of shame brought on by behavior that compromises the meaning of honor. This inner sense of shame that compromises horizontal honor, will figure in later discussions. The other kind of honor—that is vertical honor—which is bestowed from without, will not be extensively considered in this paper, except as a possible byproduct of the second. Understand then that references to honor in this paper will nearly always relate only to this the private, internal sense of horizontal honor.

Regarding honor's relationship with politics: I think that we would all agree that politics is often a brutal, aggressive and nasty business, thus setting up a delicate and strained relationship with our subject of honor. Politics, in any and all its forms and arenas, are almost exclusively concerned with the distribution of societies' wherewithal, be those resources in the form of material goods or claims to rights and duties. Politics has usually been a devil-take-the-hindmost world concerned only with surviving; this is an intensely brutal world where successful politics is all about the self-interest of living well. Diving into such a mosh pit of knavery would seem an awkward placed to speak righteously of virtue, morality, or any other form of human decency—all of which are claimed to be elements of honor. Yet, do we not speak of political figures as "The honorable so-and-so . . ." or refer to a judge as "Your Honor . . .?" Given the routinely corrupt nature of political and legal business, gracing the referents by the title of "Your Honor" seems a bumbling burlesque that snickers aside at the irony. But lodged within the folds of the irony we find the "tell." Regardless of how you might define "honor" it is apparent from any characterization of it that corruption and honor can't happily co-exist. Consequently, it would be difficult for us all not to agree with the sentiment that only the honorable should be in positions of political power. This claim is a platitude, if not an outright fiction, for we can hardly imagine a truly honorable individual stooping to that seedy world inhabited by most politicians. Honor and corruption appear antithetical. Given that reality, we find ourselves hoping that the former conquers the latter, making honor a proper venue and antidote for political corruption. Idealistic? Perhaps, but then, as we shall see, theoretical notions of honor are rooted both in the ideal and the material.

So, if honor is all to the good, why does this stopgap to corruption rub people the wrong way? What is it about honor that relegates it to a compartmental doghouse reserved for those antiquated clichés that survive only in the twilight world of the arcane and enigmatic, such as modesty or prudence? What's the problem? If honor is something of a barometer for ethical behavior, why consign it to the cultural dust bin? The answer, I will argue, is both completely understandable and understandably wrong.

A Gender Problem?

Many years ago, after presenting my master's dissertation, one of my committee's readers, a professor of philosophy (I'll call her Dr. Barnes), took exception to my use of the term honor—an exception that bordered on umbrage. I understand the source of her displeasure, at least in part. The idea and concept of honor is woven through with notions and the "feel" of what we might call "maleness." Dr. Barnes is not alone in hitting this exclusive gender speed bump which to many seems like it grants the "honor" of honor exclusively to men. In today's world such male "exclusivity" cannot help but generate irritation, suspicion, and even anger for many women. In this era of women's struggle for the same basic rights as men, which depends on a justifiable rejection of male dominance, such apparent exclusivity to a virtue that grants prestige is understandably irritating. We can understand how women intent on equality might be allergic to it. So, what exactly is the source of Dr. Barnes' irritation? Exactly where does this annoying sense of "maleness" come from?[ii]

The answer, in a single word, is *physicality*. One feels a sense of the intractable, even an orneriness, lodged in a stiff backbone that runs

---

ii. To satisfy the curious, my graduate committee, in its entirety, accepted my thesis without reservation.

340

implicitly through honor. There is a ponderousness about honor that signifies magnitude and muscularity—indeed, even an *inherent* muscularity. And there's more. This muscle and sinew of physicality acts as harbinger for a violence that underscores that stiff backbone of honor. No doubt Dr. Barnes, and indeed anyone who has grasped the reality of male violence against women, has the not unreasonable impression that "honor" has historically been tied to a predominantly male reliance on muscularity and physical aggression to settle conflict. However, violence against women is only a degradation of what honor can and should be, namely, that one be ready to back up what is properly honorable with force. So, as I will use it here, "physicality" means the toughness, the muscle, the dexterity, and the skill to credibly back up one's claim to honor with the threat or the application of force. "Physicality" foreshadows a lurking potential for force and violence that is lacking in synonyms and substitutes for the word and idea of honor. Physicality can and even should be intimidating, at least when there is a proper point of honor at stake to defend. Substitutes such as integrity, dignity, fidelity, conscience, etc., simply will not do. The more casual, common and routine definitions of honor—words that routinely pop up—words such as "valor" and "chivalry," are but a velvet glove stitched with a kind of posture and vigor that do little to cloak an iron fist.[1] There is little doubt physicality is a significant feature buried deep within honor that irritates many people, though the exact causal trigger will vary from individual to individual.

Back in the day—and given my standing in the department as a candidate for a Master's—I didn't debate the source of Dr. Barnes' individual reaction. Dr. Barnes was a thoughtful and disciplined intellectual and I am certain that there was a rational and thoughtful argument underlying her reaction, and she did choose to share some of that with me.[iii] But underlying the rational I caught a glimpse of something else, the gender problem.

There is an understandable gender reaction to honor. While acknowledging the gender specific reaction, I will not take it as my task to argue against it. In fact, I think such an argument would be an utterly fruitless waste of time, something like arguing that women shouldn't think or react as women. That last statement alone opens a nasty, chauvinistic can of

---

iii. Primarily, and briefly, she felt that honor was in some way anti-existential; it hampered, or even denied freedom of choice.

worms that would sidetrack the point of this paper. It is enough to leave open the possibility that gender reaction is not happenstance but contingent, an exigency I will attempt to accommodate. I will also pursue the question of why the physicality, why the muscularity, and why the concepts of honor implicitly (and sometimes explicitly) entail a willingness and an ability to use physical force to defend what honor requires one to defend?

Before proceeding with that pursuit, we need to clarify something. Besides physicality, it ought to be evident that not every man possesses the kind of bellicosity typically associated with that adjunct to honor, *valor*, which is to say a bold determination in the face of great danger, very often physical danger, though not exclusively so. It should also be noted that such mildly chivalric behavior as displayed in such efforts as opening doors for women and refraining from cursing around them, are fast becoming relics of the past. On the other hand, there are women with the physicality and pugnacity required to demonstrate the brute force underlying valor—MMA fighters are no less lethal because they have a vagina.[2] The difference seems to be how the male and female MMA fighters deal with their own survival instincts.[3] On balance, it would seem that men lacking physicality is a more common reality than powerful female warriors, the latter category being more of an outlier than the former. Yet, even with those exceptional women who are possessed of a high degree of physicality, they recognize the "maleness" inherent in fighting and are chagrined that a male's sense of honor is a vital feature that keeps them from engaging with each other—male vs. female.[4]

If properly presented, I believe an examination of the origins of honor might take some of the "wrong way," mentioned above, out of the rub. This can be done, while at the same time recognizing that the kind of male dominance inherent in gender chauvinism and misogyny is never automatically triggered by a sense of honor, or even inherent to the design of honor. I will insist that it is only in the "civilized" version (i.e., corruption) of honor, that honor has any role to play in misogyny.

The Origin of Honor

It seems obvious that understanding the origin of a thing is critical to being able to follow its later developmental path. This is a material understanding and not a semantic one. Therefore, I'll avoid using "origin" as though we are on some sort of scavanger hunt for the meaning and history of the word, or as a cultural casting, or as something learned at mother's knee. Instead, I'm going to suggest we view origin from a platform of Darwinian evolution. However, first, let me make perfectly clear that I am keenly aware of the possible knee-jerk reaction to this approach. Suggesting evolution in the same breath as anything perceived as exclusively male and physical is likely to set teeth on edge. I understand this. Consequently, I want to repeat and stress that I am not arguing that honor is genetically linked in some one-to-one correspondence, or any other kind of measurable relationship with gender violence, gender chauvinism, misogyny, or bigotry, in the generally understood sense. Given the nature of claims of superiority adopting the words "dominance" and "chauvinism," it might be helpful in this sense to replace these charged words with the word and idea of "function." In this sense we would have male and female functions, or roles, at the most basic levels, and not power and repression, even though modern optics may make it appear so. Keep faith with your passion for parity and an end to a world of male dominance and bear with the reasoning and direction taken in this paper.

It is safe to say, then, that honor, *per se*, is not a survival trait, not directly, nor is honor, as such, "baked into the cake." However, I will argue later in this paper that there are valuable and rewarding gender traits that are linked to early evolutionary design. I'll take an immediate pass right now, as it is vital that we first define, in a general way, what honor is, and define it as closely as possible—surprisingly, something that is rarely done. A most useful way to approach this is to look at how honor was considered in three different eras: Ancient (beginning of recorded history to 500 CE), Middle Age (500 to 1500), and Modern (1500 to 1945), then see if there are many, or even any, points in common—points that might be used to identify honor or its salient features.

Ancient Greece. First, we move backward in time to the Greek city states, to a time when horizontal honor was tied to "the deed."[5] In ancient Greece glorious and heroic actions were looked upon as being very similar to honor, though not precisely the same. Glorious action was how honor was earned. Glory was an external commodity, one granted by men and gods, while honor was a personal commodity, though a commodity both earned and enhanced by glory. The individual, the hero, that doer of deeds, was very much a person living within the community, yet apart.

In Homer's *Iliad*, for example, we see an ongoing struggle between external, vertical honor and personal, horizontal honor based on battle-field valor. It is clear that Agamemnon, king of the Greeks, is waging a war against Troy to reclaim his brother's stolen, personal honor—purloined along with his wife, Helen, Queen of Sparta. Despite the damage to the Greek "community," the war to erase Menelaus's dishonor lasts ten long years. It needs to be added that in ancient times the two, personal honor and community honor—the worldly and the personal, the vertical and horizontal—were often joined at the hip, often making it unclear where one left off and the other began. Let me be clear, this is no chicken-and-egg debate over what comes in what order. In the ancient world, the individual's honor comes first, always prior to vertical honor. Honor was not awarded by the community; it was earned by the individual through "the deed" without regard to the vertical bestowed by the community.

Let us refresh ourselves on the storyline: Achilles, the central figure of the Iliad, suffers a personal blow when his worldly superior, King Agamemnon, strips Achilles of his prize, Briseis.[iv] By taking Brieis, the king demonstrates that his vertical power as ruler of the host is greater than the individual, heroic status of Achilles. This sets up an important question for the Greeks: Is worldly, vertical power more meaningful and decisive than personal, horizontal honor. This raises the question of the individual vs. the community, that is, puts the individual in rivalry with powerful social relations. Is the external world, that is, its political power structure, with its fickle volatility, greater than the "glory" we have the power and will to achieve for ourselves? In the end, as Homer tells it, King Agamemnon is reduced, the vertical bows to the horizontal. The bloodied warrior Achilles, the hero, is mightier than a mere king. That king, having forfeited his own honor, must eventually grovel before the greater prestige of the status and greatness of the doer of glorious deeds. The earned horizontal triumphs over the granted vertical. Yet, we have the sense that even though King Agamemnon has lost his perch, the honor of the Greeks, the community, the context, as it were, remains unscathed. Not only the honor of Achilles, but also the honor of the host, rises above

---

iv. There are several versions as to how Briseis came into the possession of Achilles, (legend and the poem conflict slightly) though in the end this matters little to the unfolding plot of Homer's poem.

Agamemnon's fall. The horizontal, that is the hero, rises above the vertical in status and authority.

But all this becomes ambiguous later when the raging Achilles slays Hector, Prince of Troy—in an act of revenge for Hector's killing of Patroclus—we find ourselves losing sympathy for Achilles. In his defilement of Hector's body, an act in which one can find neither glory nor valor, we see an act of extreme wrongfulness. There is right and wrong played out here as ethics collide with honor. We must understand the whole picture: the two combatants, Hector and Achilles, fight for different reasons: Hector for the glory of Troy (the community), and Achilles for the self—for selfish, personal revenge. The thirst for revenge undermines and weakens the glory (which is to say, the honor) achieved and possessed by Achilles. This sudden loss is mainly due to the enflamed hubris that engulfs Achilles—and his honor. We see here the corrupting influence of madness and fury. In the end, Achilles partially redeems himself and his honor by abandoning rage and returning Hector's body to his father, King Priam, together with promises of a truce for the duration of the funeral. In the end Achilles does the right thing and honor is given a second wind. In this tale we see honor as resting on physicality, valor, and on the shoulders of the hero, that individual doer of deeds.

In the ancient western world, glory and valor were dramatically and undeniably intertwined in support of honor. Blood and disorder underwrote the personal story of the hero and his glorious deeds. This association of honor with blood and mayhem quickly invalidates proxies for honor such as "dignity" or "integrity" or "virtue." It is the "deed," underwritten by violence (or at least the potential for violence), that moves honor into a wholly different category than any polite sense of parlor room decency. However, this categorizing does not account for the origins of the melding of violence with the deed in such a way as to enframe honor; this blending will be discussed in detail later. For now, digging more deeply into the *Iliad*, we can see other, more positive attributes heralded by honor. Warfare and chaos are clearly there, but there are also multiple moral and ethical issues raised by the poem, important matters that are concerned in many ways with the identification and role of honor. Throughout the poem there are questions regarding justice, truth, reliability, duty, etc., but hanging over all these questions is the ambiguous imperative to "do the right thing." Ambiguous yes, but fully center stage as we see Agamemnon humble himself before Achilles, and Achilles humble himself before King Priam. This definition of honor as dominated by "right action" will gain increasing importance and influence in the Middle Ages.

Question: is this understanding of "doing the right thing" a simple and unreliable cliché or platitude? We will dive into the mysterious issue of "right action" a bit later. At this point it is most important to take note of the two key elements of honor in the western, ancient world: glory (*qua* violence), and the "deed." Before the rise of feudalism, it was by these two components—glory and the deed—that the western world understood honor and the culture it supported. This understanding will undergo a series of changes, not the least of which is the eventual triumph of the vertical over the horizontal.

Middle Ages (500—1500). This period demands close inspection. For it is during the Middle Ages that changes take place reflecting an exchange of individual effort in favor of class and status. The vertical granting of honor replaces the horizontal earning of honor. This coincides with a significant change in social structure. A cosmopolitan, Mediterranean Roman system is replaced by the smaller, isolated, self-sufficient manorial system. This is a system where a petrified hierarchical structure based on birthright locks out social mobility. Such a rigid system is seen as commanded by God. Charlemagne instructed his subjects at the turn of the 9th century, "Let everyone serve God faithfully in that order in which he is placed."[6] There were those who prayed, those who fought, and those who labored, all three stations ordained by the laws of the universe.[7] In such a frozen world, roles and function are handed down by God and the laws of the universe. Honor is still there, only it now becomes a thing granted by birth, a thing to be possessed, not earned. For the first time too, a code and rules of conduct are devised with the intent of controlling individual efforts at glory and achievement—and some would add, controlling mayhem.

Two new ingredients arise during this period to address these changes in social development. In addition to these, there is a distinct adjunct to the changes that center on the culture of honor. The two new components are "Christianity" and "chivalry." More than anything else, these two notions serve to separate the medieval concept of honor from the ancient. The tangential adjunct to the social change is that honor now becomes a feature that the nobility is born with, a feature of class position within the feudal hierarchy. This kind of bestowed honor can be lost largely through inaction, to be replaced by shame. During the Middle Ages—and beyond—honor comes, *ipso facto*, as a thing branded into social rank and position. Aside from being born into the right class, the aristocracy now does nothing to achieve honor. It is an unearned feature that comes along with position, status and property. However, loss of honor, and shame, remain possible, with subsequent impact on social position.

Perhaps more than anything else, this birthright of honor reflects the influence of feudalism's calcified class structure. For the first time authority and class and honor become features of inherited property rights. From this point forward, only rarely would social advancement be achieved through martial prowess. The Middle Ages was a time where upward social mobility—when possible at all—followed a path of contrived marriages, ecclesiastical advancement, clever bureaucratic maneuvering, etc., not through honor achieved on the battlefield. The glorious deed is on its way out and social position is ushered in.

Something else was also thrown into the mix. At this time there appears a recognizable, though rudimentary "code of honor." In the beginning, the code—or pre-code, if you will—was unwritten, though it grew out of the elements of Christianity and chivalry and served as an accessory of class and social position. This code of honor, particularly as an addendum to chivalry, was (and is) generally accepted as legitimate. However, likely due to the fact that the pre-code was unwritten, both the origin and details expressed are questionable. Even so, belief in the pre-code appears to have been widespread, so keep the feudal class structure in mind as we start by examining the development of a hardened code born of the two new elements surrounding honor: Christianity and chivalry.

The pre-chivalric code—sometimes referred to as the *noble habitus*—was a code, given current research, that was never written down.[8] Yet *noble habitus* was generally known in the early medieval world (ca. 600—700) and could be considered a precursor to later, more carefully defined restraints on knightly conduct. The chief feature of the *noble habitus* seems to have been what we might call loyalty.[9] During the medieval period, however, "loyalty" was a clever device intended to direct the knight's warlike tendencies in the "right" direction.[10] This hypothesis is due to the reasonable assumption that loyalty during this period also meant prowess on the battlefield in the interests of certain feudal chieftains. Loyalty always played out in the interests of the liege lord.[11] As we'll see next, *noble habitus*, in the main, was always in the interests of a top down social order serving the ranking nobility and clergy.

Another element of the *noble habitus* gives further evidence in support for an ideology intent on controlling the warrior class.[12] That element was *forbearance*, which acted as another means of corralling the knight's—and men-at-arms in general—passion from running amok: forbearance must be practiced in the face of not only your betters, but also your inferiors, and even your enemies.[13] This is referred to as the "Davidic Ethic," by many researchers.[14] There were a few other elements, such as largess, protecting the weak, bravery and fighting skill, suggested by scholars, but by and large the code *noble habitus* was a pre-code, or at least that part of it that was most widely known and practiced. There was, however, no mention of either the Church or Christianity in this pre-chivalric code. The inclusion of religious authority came later as the Church spread its political influence and ideology over western and northern Europe.

Following the *noble habitus*, there arose a more or less intentional code, a citing of rules identified as Charlemagne's Code of Chivalry. The code listed seventeen rules for the conduct of knights and men-at-arms.[15] If Charlemagne was behind it, and that's not entirely clear, the code must have been issued around the year 800.[16]

To fear God and maintain His Church
To serve the liege lord in valour and faith
To protect the weak and defenseless
To give succor to widows and orphans
To refrain from the wanton giving of offence
To live by honour and for glory
To despise pecuniary reward
To fight for the welfare of all
To obey those placed in authority
To guard the honour of fellow knights
To eschew unfairness, meanness and deceit
To keep faith (i.e., keep one's word)
At all times to speak the truth
To persevere to the end in any enterprise begun
To respect the honour of women

Never to refuse a challenge from an equal
Never to turn the back upon a foe[17]

There is deliberate intent here. The code is intended to control the behavior of men-at-arms in times that were unruly and chaotic. In addition, and for the first time, the Church is mentioned in official rules of conduct: to defend and maintain the Church and Church prelates now becomes the number one duty of the knight and men-at-arms.[18] Obedience to the liege lord becomes the second. Both the rivalry and frequent conflation of religion and temporal politics are a critical development overshadowing much of western history, at least until the close of the 17th century.

First, and perhaps more than anything else, what these early codes demanded of men-at-arms reflects the growing power and influence of the Roman Church—and the importance of both religion and the Church to emerging European rulers. Secondly, loyalty, more than ever, is directly tied to obedience to the liege lord—do the lord's bidding and keep faith with him; do not be lured away by pecuniary reward, and at all times, protect the honor of women (i.e., protect the blood line of the nobility). We see in this code the emergence of the intentional primacy of the vertical, the community (i.e., the ruling order) over the personal. For the first time, honor is a vertical feature beholden to the community (i.e., the power structure) and not earned by the individual (i.e., the hero). This represents a significant change from the horizontal honor of antiquity. The codification of honor is not by accident. It is by intent that the individual is reduced to adhering to the code or losing honor through disobedience with subsequent impact on position. There is little doubt that the overall importance of the code was for the benefit of the ruling classes. However, quite a few of the seventeen rules of conduct can be imagined under the heading of "right action," that is of "doing the right thing," seemingly independent of social status. Whether this "right action" is by intent or happenstance is beside the point. The point is that with "right action" there is a thread of continuity with the ancient code of an earned, horizontal honor. This unintentionally goes beyond the desires of the ruling order and sometimes pits the code in direct conflict with the powers that be. As stated sometime later by Michel de Montaigne: "There are two sets of laws, those of honor and those of justice, in many matters quite opposed."[19] This, of course, implies that justice is only what the powerful say it is.

349

One way to look at Charlemagne's Code is that as an indirect result of following these medieval dictates, the powerful are drawn to a way of standardizing and preserving one's honor—bearing in mind that the origin of honor is found in birthright and no longer as a doer of glorious deeds. It is a reminder that one can lose their honor by violating the code, now more widely understood. From this point forward the individual's quest for glory and honor falls under the sway of the political structure's desire for predictability and stability and control.

It was during this medieval period that Christianity achieved its greatest influence in the western world. The pagan religions that preceded Christianity never possessed the cohesiveness, uniformity and unilateral authority (both political and spiritual) as that possessed by the newly emerged Catholic Church of Rome. How this unilateral authority was achieved by the Roman Church is beyond the scope of this paper, but that the creed and dogma of Catholic Christianity became Western Europe's *weltanschauung* is beyond dispute. The dominance and ideology of Catholic Christianity filtered into every aspect of life. This included the life of the armored knight, which, given the superstitious nature of thinking at the time, is not surprising. It was also obviously useful to the Church that the knights often swore oaths of honor and allegiance to the church prelates. Officially, the Church and the Pope had no corporeal power in the form of standing armies or any policing agencies. Volunteer forces and mercenaries were periodically employed in defense of the Papal States, but standing armies were a rarity in Papal history until around the 12th century. The temporal powerlessness of the Church is especially true at the point of transition from the pagan pontifex maximus to its Catholic form of Supreme Pontiff. The Church gained considerable martial influence and authority by the 12th century, but prior to that period found the voluntary allegiance, or at the very least, the forbearance of men-at-arms not merely useful, but necessary.

Cemented into this corner of the Christian outlook was the knight and the notion of knightly honor. The difference between the ancient notion of honor and that of the Middle Ages is that honor is no longer won as a result of battlefield glory, as it can now be lost through action contrary to the code of chivalry. It is tempting to think of personal honor as being a creature of chivalry, though it is not. Recall that medieval chivalry arose alongside medieval Christianity. This would make knightly honor not so much born of personal inclination and effort as it was a creature of Catholic thinking, a thinking that was revealed through the code of chivalry; an organized code of conduct surrendering individual's discretion to the rule of an external code. This was a code whose origins reflect Christian principles rather than pagan. The knights and men-at-arms must adhere to this new the code of chivalry or face the loss of personal honor and possible excommunication. Due largely to the absence of widespread literacy among the men-at-arms, the gap between the ideal of the chivalrous outlook and actual practice of the principles of chivalry remains unclear. But what is noteworthy is that Christian principles were woven throughout the notion of knightly honor and knightly notions of chivalry. Honor secured by the deed now takes a back seat to honor secured by birthright and adherence to ecclesiastical edict. Vertical honor trumps the horizontal honor of antiquity.

The rise of chivalry was also a symptom of the times. The word, chivalry, derives from the old French understanding of *chevalier*. This translates most readily into "a horseman," but more thoroughly into the phrase: "A man of aristocratic standing, and probably of noble ancestry, who is capable, if called upon, of equipping himself with a war horse and the arms of heavy cavalryman and who has been through certain rituals that make him what he is."[20] In the real medieval world there were two forms of knighthood. There was the aristocrat, of course, that is, the nobleman, but let it be pointed about that the second type—the ordinary knight—was an individual who was a long way from a "man of aristocratic standing." The difference between the typical mounted knight and a common man-at-arms (foot solder) was largely the possession of a horse, good weapons and rudimentary, heavy armor. The cultured and charming knight of Hollywood fame did not exist to any great extent beyond a few members of the nobility. The real medieval knight was an illiterate hooligan on horseback who was constantly on the prowl for his next meal, next liege lord and next war.[21] The commonplace medieval knight was a footloose mercenary with little to recommend him, other than prowess on the battlefield. Among other things, the code of chivalry was intended to put guard rails around this thug and guide his martial activities into useful directions—that is, useful to the nobility.[22]

At the close of the late Middle Ages, a list of "knightly virtues," which brings us closer to the actual meaning of honor, is found in a curiously composed list of chivalric qualities. This list comes by way of the third Duke of Burgundy, Philip the Good (1396—1467). These are the words the duke chose to use in describing the twelve virtues, as he saw them, exhibited in the Knight's Code of Chivalry:[23]

Faith
Charity
Justice
Sagacity
Prudence
Temperance
Resolution
Truth
Liberality
Diligence
Hope
Valour (sic)

Although in many ways similar to Charlemagne's Code of chivalry, what we see in the list is an absence of intent. Philip's list of virtues offers no direction or guidance. The lack of intent opens the door to a deeper inspection and understanding of chivalry and personal honor. There are other, much longer ways of setting down these guideposts designed to curb an excitable temperament.[24] But this simple list makes the point that by 1500 a code of conduct had arisen to offer self-evident guardrails for the more violent prone in feudal society. These were important guardrails, if the knights wished for continued employment and an honorable life. How widespread the adoption of this list was is not important to the direction of our research. Likewise, there is little way to know how many knights and men-at-arms actually followed this code of conduct, or thought to reaffirm their personal honor through its adoption. What is not beside the point is recognizing the glue that binds the whole list together. This entire list of virtues can be reduced to a single meaning: do the good through right thinking and right action. The sentiment of "right action" remains the same, whether one speaks of ancient or medieval notions of honor. Rather than glorious actions, the deed has reemerged as right action, right thinking, and right attitude.

What is lost by 1500 is the mystical, though compelling link between glory and honor. You'll notice that the duke's list shows only one item in the code that openly calls for a glorious reward ripped from violent experience. That single element cited by the duke would be *valor*. Of course, it could be argued, given the lack of direct intent, that the connection between valor and warfare is not exclusive. Valor, as a virtue, can certainly be shown to have other meanings aside from violence, such as resisting a ruthless, totalitarian regime (e.g., Sophie Scholl)[v], struggling against slavery (e.g., Harriet Tubman), refusing to accept oppression (e.g., Rosa Parks), acting with bravery on the battlefield (e.g., Florence Nightingale, Clara Barton, Anna Etheridge).[vi] What we will see is that by the modern era (ca., 1500—1945) what remains of the connection between glory and war, and therefore, glory and honor, is again weakened by material factors. In the end, the role of violence is reduced to rump exercises such as the duel. What is strengthened is the link between social position and honor, class and honor, where honor is neither earned nor properly acknowledged.

The Modern Era (1500—1945)

"The essential thing is not why we are fighting, but *how* we fight."[25]

It's violence and physicality all over again. Or so it seems. The above quote from Ernst Junger[vii] concerning WWI typifies the rear-guard sentiments expressed by many who railed against the shifting fortunes of the individual challenged in combat. There are rules to fighting, fumes Junger, rules of honor for the individual that go beyond temporary political motivations and causation. It is individual's honor that is eternal, not the current political "cause." But unfortunately for Junger and the men of his

---

v. Sophia Magdalena Scholl was a German student and anti-Nazi political activist, active within the White Rose non-violent resistance group in Nazi Germany. She was convicted of high treason, and executed, after having been found distributing anti-war leaflets at the University of Munich with her brother, Hans.

vi. It is not an accident that I chose women as illustrators of valor. The concept of women and honor will be discussed at greater length ahead.

vii. Ernst Jünger was a highly-decorated German soldier, author, and entomologist who became publicly known for his World War I memoir *Storm of Steel*.

generation, things were changing rapidly on the battlefield. Junger speaks of an honor alive in the ancient world, won by valor and glory, but not in the modern world where it is awarded by ribbon and accolade and class. [26]

One of the outcomes of these changes on the field was a flagging sense of duty and honor that was keenly felt by professional solders on both sides of the Great War. Ernst Junger, a German officer during WWI, was searching in vain for glory and honor amongst the blood-soaked ground and tangled wire. The sense of loss felt by Junger had more to do with how warfare had changed than how soldiers had changed, a shift that had begun in Western Europe a thousand years before his venting of frustration. If anything, Junger was trying to forestall the rapidly shifting attitudes toward honor, a change growing in the face of the utterly impersonal violence mushrooming around him. For Junger and the other soldiers of WWI, modern combat was a true game changer. The mass grinding of human flesh loosened and finally stripped any notion of individual valor from amongst the rolling waves of mass carnage.

Not only has the nature of war changed, but also how the violence is portrayed, which is mightily important. In the modern age, representation of war has gone from verbal and literary expressions to being immortalized by both still and motion pictures; in our contemporary era that is nearly all we get. It is one thing to read or listen to tales of bravery, martial skill and high adventure—it is quite another to see the gory landscape littered with corpses, blood-soaked earth and body parts having been ripped loose and flung about by high explosives. It is difficult see modern scenes of devastation through the lens of glory. It is also difficult to award valor to an artillery man who fires shells at an enemy he cannot see, or a drone pilot who kills from a control room thousands of miles away from the battlefield. These observations alone deftly affect our perception and meaning of "the deed."

Much that was key in the ancient western world has been upended in the modern. Gone are the days when men faced men on the battlefield, men wielding individual weapons requiring great prowess and skill. Nowadays men confront machines of enormous and impersonal power; no skill required[viii], no bravery, no resoluteness—no honor. Faced with this new,

---

viii. One might argue on behalf of fighter pilots as individuals of great skill, but the days of individual aerial combat were largely ended by the conclusion of WWII.

mechanized reality the mantra of "do the right thing" seems to have lost all meaning, swallowed up by the vortex of automated butchery. Amongst the new routines of industrial madness, the individual is lost, and so is "the deed." Modern warfare changed everything, took everything, depersonalized individual effort, leaving glory and the deed tossed asunder in its wake.

At about the time of the French Revolution (1789), and to a lesser extent, the American War of Independence, entire populations were mobilized for what Carl von Clausewitz dubbed total war.[27] This involved appeals to the masses and instigated harsh conscription laws. Serfs and slaves make poor soldiers. Those classes had little invested in outcomes of wars of antiquity and scuffles between the nobility in medieval times. But with modernity came both the means to arm the masses and the ability to make them feel that they had a stake in the outcome. The Battle of Agincourt (1415), for example, the battle that finally doomed the knight and the age of chivalry, was won by less than 7000 English at a cost of 600 men, as opposed to 8000 French killed or captured. Although professionals, the superiority of 15th century English technology, the simple long bow, was wielded by lowly English yeomen. Technology and the under-classes brought down the Medieval notions of a glory reserved for the mounted knight and nobility. Compare this with the first day of the battle of Somme (1916), when the English had 400,000 men under arms and lost 57,000 men in a single day. These were not professional solders striving for glory, but the masses either conscripted or brought willingly to the fray and armed with weapons requiring far less skill than of old. Literacy, democracy and nationalism gave the "citizen" a stake in the outcome, and the technology of mass production brought the means. This had a decided impact on the idea of honor.

Three thousand years ago glory, replete with its stepchild, honor, was found at the heart of the bloody deed. Today, we still have the word—honor—and we have sensations of status and power marshaled behind its use, but the nature of what it is, how it is to be achieved and preserved, have substantively changed. As pointed out above, an individual sitting at an air-conditioned workstation, pressing a button that obliterates hundreds of human beings on the other side of the world, strikes no one as a glorious deed, nor does it make the operator a hero. Today a new definition of "the deed" must emerge if honor is to find any kind of place in the contemporary world—indeed, if it even should find a place.

I mentioned several women above: Scholl, Tubman, *et al.* I did this to make the point that harking back to Philip the Good and the list of twelve virtues making up his code of chivalry, women need not be excluded, *ipso facto*—and certainly not in our contemporary world where physicality and direct violence play a much reduced role. There are few of these twelve virtues of Phillip's that the women named above did not demonstrate through their individual heroics. We might also note that their activities did not involve bloody violence. True, Sophie Scholl was guillotined by the Nazis, but this was not violence she committed or chose. Given what we know of Sophie, it is not at all difficult to identify her actions both as heroic and honorable—and the same for the other women as well, each of whom, in their own way, paid tribute to many of the virtues extolled by the chivalrous system. Consequently, we need to ask if a violent and bloody experience is an absolute requirement to turn the "virtuous" deed into one of honor. It looks very much as though in this contemporary era we need an alternate definition or a different set of guidelines supporting and interpreting "the deed"—that is, if honor is to be saved in any form that might assist right action. Also, we need to ask if given the changes brought about by modern warfare, can honor survive independent of "glory?" Then too, as the defining characteristics of the deed and honor change, we are faced with an important adjunct: can women routinely possess honor in the same way as a man?

Above I used the wording "alternate definition" to suggest that the way in which the deed is understood need not be brand-spanking new. Rather, the definition might be tweaked and adjusted to meet the demands of contemporary circumstance. This means that suggesting wholesale changes are unnecessary. Most of the virtues outlined by Philip the Good back in the 14th century are still adequate as a guide to "right action." The position of the observer needs adjusting to afford some slight re-coding. For example, "faith," Philip's first virtue, need not be a religious faith, but a faith in humanity maintained in the face of adversity (e.g., Dorothy Parker, Mother Teresa, Ida Tarbell), or even the simple act of keeping one's word. Valor on the battlefield can be redesigned and designated as courage in the face of evil (e.g., Sophie Scholl, Edith Cavell, Malala Yousafzai). It will not escape anyone's notice that all the examples I have offered are women. This brings up the obvious point that the contemporary world has broadened the scope of honorable behavior to allow for the inclusion of heretofore improbably actors. Our world has become a place of such rapid change that much of what we were comfortable with is no longer available. To access honor again, we must redefine and re-exhibit our topic.

Let us first identify the primary and self-evident element that have survived all three eras. As mentioned several times, a central tenant that skewers the centuries, and all actions of "the deed," is that in face of adversity and evil, one must do the right thing. Somehow, we sense that the actions and persons cited all have one thing in common: right action. This brings us to the nature of "right action" as a central pillar upholding our notions of honor and offering a narrow focus on individual actions in that regard.

Honor as right action

Going back to the 9th century code of Charlemagne, as the code dictates right action for the honorable knight, we can see that fully two thirds of the elements are, for most of us, self-evidently grasped as "right action." Actions such as protecting widows and children, keeping one's word, or rejecting unfairness, meanness and deceit, would be seen by most people as right action. Going beyond the self-evident, how does the code more narrowly define right action? Diving deeper, the answer as to what makes "right action" is found in the nature of the outcome of the action. It is difficult to see the outcome of most of these actions indicated by Philipp's list as leading anywhere but to a beneficial result. As opposed to Phillip's "right action" words, the code elements lifted from Charlemagne's list, (such as obedience to authority, or living for glory), are not so automatic or straight forward in their path to a good outcome. Therefore, lacking a good outcome these principles may not be animated by right action. To be clear: instinctive, reflexive, automatic, self-evident, are not entirely satisfying adjectives, in and of themselves, by which to highlight "right action." What is "right action" agitates for raising the question of what a good outcome is, or more to the point, what is "the good."

Without drifting off into a lengthy philosophical debate, it is fair to say, along with most philosophers, that what is good is what is valuable, or a thing held instinctively to be of value by most human beings. That is, a thing of self-evident value. Note, we are not saying that all that is valuable is good. Good and valuable are not interchangeable. The Hope Diamond is valuable, but it seems silly and meaningless to say it is self-evident that the diamond is good. To get to the point we might say, therefore, along with Aristotle, that "if there is an end for all that we do, this will be the good achievable by action."[28] So far then, we have honor as right actions leading to a good outcome, a result most humans would recognize as a thing of value. While this does not satisfy the meaning of "the good" it does suggest, however, even to consequentialists such as E.G. Moore, that right action means to bring as much good into the world as possible.[29] This does seem to satisfy the meaning of self-evident. So, what then is "the good" to which honor as right action strives?

We should also point out the trap of relativism. For example, along with Moore above, we might reject "the good" as it is identified in the way most utilitarians would have it—that is, meaning pleasure or happiness.[30] The sadist finds pleasure in torture, and the Nazi found happiness in the conquering of France, but can we honestly define these events as good in a way most humans would recognize? Is goodness in these events self-evident? Obviously not. As utilitarian standards of goodness can never be evenly applied, or represent value shared by humanity at large, Moore's rejection of hedonistic utilitarianism is beneficial for the purposes of analyzing honor.

Yet there are things that remain self-evident, and utilitarian. For example, eating, when one requires nutrition, would seem an action leading to a self-evident good—a right action to sustain a thing of value, one's own life. Satisfying nutritional needs is then a right action leading to a good outcome: sustaining life. This is almost childish in its self-evident and utilitarian simplicity. So, there is such a thing as self-evident goodness. Let us look again at the list attributed to the Duke of Burgundy to see what is self-evident, then roll onto evolution and the evolution of right action and the good.

Is there anything in the list attributed to Phillip that would lead to a bad or questionable outcome? I have adopted Philip's word list rather than Charlemagne's Code for a reason that is not immediately obvious. A single word has the benefit of allowing the mind to grapple freely with the idea of "good," and "good outcome" according to reflective, self-evident standards; a sort of free-wheeling hermeneutic approach if you will. Charlemagne's Code, on the other hand, is replete with adjectives that flush out intent, sending interpretation of the elements of the code in deliberate directions. It is this directed intent which hampers our ability to come to grips with the idea of an ethically laden word itself. What I mean by all this is that the word "truth," for example, conveys a meaning that the statement, at all times speak the truth, does not. Truth, of course, has value. We sense this as self-evident. Truth, as an idea, is good. However, to: "At all times speak the truth," is not self-evidently good. This is not apparent at first, and many philosophers and writers have plunged into this debate. Let me flavor this debate with one of the more famous: Immanuel Kant and his famous declarations concerning the telling of truth. Is telling the truth always good?[31]

Kant maintains that duty and rational morality demands telling the truth at all times: "To be truthful (honest) in all declarations, therefore, is a sacred and absolutely commanding decree of reason, limited by no expediency."[32] That seems definitive. Further, Kant declares that a lie "always harms another; if not some other particular man, still it harms mankind generally . . . ,"[33] In support of these declarations Kant proposes the case of the murderer at the door, demanding to know if his victim is in the house. Kant's illustration is somewhat fanciful—this from an individual we would hardly find to be more rational. So, what does this man of reason suggestion to us about real situations? Should the victim be revealed to the murderer? To offer a real life example, what was Hermine Gies to say to the Gestapo agents standing at the door demanding to know if she knew of any Jews hiding in the neighborhood?[ix] Kant's short answer is, "Yes," Gies should tell the truth—it is her duty to mankind—and so presumably she is to become an accomplice to the removal of the Frank family from her home. But is this a right action that leads to a good outcome for mankind? I will allow the reader to pour over Kant's own words from his brief remarks, but it seems terribly obvious that unless you are an anti-Semitic murderer, the answer cannot possibly be yes. Can anything be more self-evident? The point of all this is not a critique of Kant, but rather a faith in the humanity of the reader, and that he or she will squirm mightily trying to muddle through Kant's tortured reasoning on this point. The main point of this is that Philip's words have an instinctive veracity about them that Charlemagne's Code does not.

---

ix. Hermine Gies, a Dutch citizen who hid Anne Frank and her family from the Nazis.

An immediate consequence of the above is that the simple equation of violence = glory = honor, is thrown into question. Honor as defined in antiquity finds itself at odds with modern and contemporary realities, certainly as anything self-evidently springing from violence. The Middle Ages was the turning point. This was a world where horizontal honor was replaced by vertical—where male dominated violence as progenitor of honor was supplanted by honor granted by class and social rank. The notion of honor at the beginning in the medieval world, and the ways of losing it, come increasingly under the sway and aegis of "right action," not violent action, which often leads in questionable directions on behalf of questionable individuals. If horizontal honor is to be preserved in any form for the individual, a different understanding between right action and good outcome must be discovered or fashioned.

So, are there any words in Phillip's list that might foster a bad outcome? I would submit that "faith," "liberality," and "valour" need qualifiers: perhaps faith as in faith in the human spirit, liberality, as in liberality toward the poor and downtrodden, valour as in bravery in the face of wrongdoing. The rest of the list easily yields self-evident interpretation compatible with "good outcomes." I won't belabor this, as the point I am trying to make is that honor, as cultivated by Phillip's list, spreads it ideal mantle over more than the nobility and male gender. Modernity has unfurled the cloak of honor to encompass all of humanity. This has resurrected honor as horizontal, leaving vertical honor to accolades and rewards granted for narrowly defined achievements. Regarding horizontal honor's rebirth, I return to Hermine Gies.

Honor, Gender and Evolution

Can there be any doubt that every day that Gies sheltered the Frank family was a threat to her life—that the Dutch woman demonstrated a profound bravery (*qua*, valour) in the face of grave menace and adversity? It seems clear that Gies acted daily out of a sincere faith in her good deeds in an ugly world, in a humanity pinned on an iron cross, and her actions contributed to the burial of that cross. In fact, this woman routinely acted in a way that exemplified the goodness found in every single one of the words in Phillip's list; where to act out those words in Nazi occupied

Holland was a dangerous enterprise? Hermine Gies' life was one of deep and impeccable honor. It is entirely possible to say the same of Sophie Scholl, Harriet Tubman, and hundreds, even thousands of other women whose names and deeds have not been recorded. I believe that Dr. Barnes, my thesis proctor who appeared years ago to take offense at my use of the word honor, was reacting to honor as defined by antiquity and Medieval Europe. As we have shown, those monopolistic male-only notions of horizontal honor ended abruptly with modernity. In this sense, I believe that Dr. Barnes represents a transitional mentality, a mentality that has not yet freed itself from traditional themes of quasi-romantic honor rooted in the powerful male, the hero, that doer of good deeds. Although modern history has upended these idealized concepts and offered a new understanding of honor that would serve to include women as well as men, we still have one issue we can't dodge entirely: the issue of *physicality*.

Way back at the very beginning of this paper, I identified physicality as one of the obvious undertones running through honor, a feature that, for multiple reasons, hampers women in a complete realization of personal, horizontal honor. Size and strength do not directly factor into the elements of Phillip's list. Yet the physical is there, lurking in the background, and not simply as a hangover from antiquity. Words such as justice, resolution, and valor, clearly suggests a toughness and backbone that appeals to a physical dimension. And of course, we cannot ignore the physicality implicit in most of the features of Charlemagne's Code, not to mention a generally semiconscious, sub-systemic understanding of honor. This is more than simply a footnote from antiquity and medieval times. Physicality as an element of honor is obviously there, if nowhere else, it exists as a part of the cultish charisma surrounding "the hero."

Even though there are fewer and fewer social roles that demand a strong physical presence, there are those roles that do remain, and they are very often associated with "the hero." I refer here to police, fire fighters, soldiers, etc. We cannot ignore this or pass this off as a simple fascination with mystical figures of the larger-than-life, but unrealistic, hero. This does not exclude women from traditional "hero" roles, but the women involved in these traditional roles where physicality plays a significant role are an extreme minority. For example, since the ban on females in combat roles was lifted in 1993 only 92 women have completed the

US Marine Corp's combat training.[x] As of mid-2018, only eleven women remain fully qualified for combat duty in the United States Marine Corp.[34] Of these women, it is reported by the Marine Corp that of "the women serving in combat billets, most of them are in less physically demanding roles such as light air defense and artillery, commonly referred to as a non-load bearing job field, according to data obtained by Marine Corps Times."[35] Only 11% of the US police and prison agencies are populated by female officers, with the majority of these women being prison matrons in female facilities.[36] As in the armed forces, women in police agencies likely face enormous obstacles. Commenting on females in policing, one researcher observed that, "women who do breach the boundary to penetrate this masculine world can only ever be partially successful and will often have to subsume 'male characteristics' to achieve even a limited social acceptability."[37] While this discrimination is very real, it is also apparent that one of the reasons for the treatment is that female recruits for these types of jobs are the exception. Women who take on traditional male "hero" roles are statistical outliers. The point here is that the type of muscularity and body size required by many traditional physical jobs sharply restrict the type of women who enter the field. I believe that this physical dimension is a fact in gender relations that—at least at the current time—must be lived with.

Additionally, there are recent studies that point to a direct relationship between male sexual attractiveness and hero status. In several studies, women have shown a marked preference for alpha-hero status.[38] The opposite, that is, of males finding female heroes more sexually attractive, seems not to be the case.[39] This evokes a deep, abiding feeling of unevenness that we all sense. The inequity leads to a desire to reject the strong, male "hero." Unfortunately, it is also a concrete disparity that cannot be easily brushed aside.

Then too, due to a lopsided ratio regarding size and strength, there exists a nearly primeval assumption about males protecting or assisting females under dangerous and threatening circumstances. There is also a theme representing a bias against harming women, and this is not exclusively male thinking. In some well documented studies, women show a marked preference to protect females over males; this preference in

---

x. This writing is fall of 2020

protective behavior appears to be a society wide norm, and not simply a gender bias.[40]

We are entering the field of gender function and sexual dimorphism, but not exclusively of a physical nature. The issue that concerns us is a protective dimorphism at work in gender behavior. How is it possible, for example, to explain the huge disproportion of male to female lives saved on the Titanic, (1/14, male to female)? Or viewed from a different perspective: 80% of the male passengers died, as opposed to 25% of female passengers who perished.[41] For that matter, economic class seems to have been completely ignored in relation to gender: third class women were 41% more likely to survive than first class men.[42] All of this is factual, even though men outnumbered the women on board the Titanic by a whopping two-to-one margin.[43] Or how do we explain the 2012 Aurora theater shooting where five men died actively and intentionally protecting women?[44] In the former, the actions of male passengers were hardly instantaneous. With nearly three hours before final sinking there was considerable time to think through the behavior and selection process. In the case of the Aurora shooting, the action of the men in the theater gives every appearance of being reflexive, automatic, even instinctual.[45] Are these two different examples best understood as social engineering, or a thousand generations of natural selection where males protecting females insured that their genetic material would survive and be passed on—material that included protective adaptations? There are also studies that show that females demonstrate reproductive preference for mates based on such factors as height, muscularity, size, even aggressiveness.[46] There is nothing 100% conclusive in these illustrations or the extrapolated conclusions. Science is not in the business of certainty, but of the probable, and this goes for studies in evolution.[47] So, regarding women's increased stature in the world of honor, how best are the elements of physicality and gender protection to be analyzed and dealt with? I suggest that we can best relate to this with a more detailed understanding of evolutionary development.

The basic premise of evolution is well known: character traits are sewn into a species' DNA by the successful transmission of genetic material from one generation to the next. Useful traits enhance the possessor's chances of survival, failing traits do not, and therefore these failing traits do not get passed on to subsequent generations; nor, for that matter, are the successful traits distributed universally. For us humans, the transmission of traits varied from place to place, and was hugely influenced by environmental and cultural manipulation. However, long before the arrival of civilization, millennium upon millennium of generational selection has instilled dispositions and traits that do represent general patterns of inclination that underlie and support many of our human adaptations and characteristics.

Okay, so what is baked into the cake? The short answer is everything and nothing. Everything that makes us human is there—yet nothing there is identical to anyone else. Nearly all of us have ten toes, but none of our toes look exactly like anyone else's toes. The same holds true for many survival traits. We all possess survival traits (e.g., fight or flight). They evolved with our primal ancestors but did so to differing degrees (e.g., the varying degrees of melanin in our skin). This last, "differing degrees," is important. While we all possess survival traits, the strength and types of the evolution of these traits is hugely impacted by the place and manner of their evolution (e.g., the sickle cell trait as a reaction and defense against blood borne pathogens such as malaria which evolved in tropical areas plagued by mosquitos). General remarks can be made concerning evolved traits, specifics cannot. Not all tropical populations possess the sickle cell trait, but this does not detract from a general understanding of sickle cell as an evolved adaptation to tropical, blood borne diseases. While it is currently impossible to know exactly what environmental factors guided the evolution of a specific survival trait, the existence of these traits—even a shadowy existence, such as sickle cell—is rarely disputed as the result of evolutionary adaptation.

In the *Descent of Man*, Charles Darwin pointed out that sexual selection hinged on "the advantage which certain individuals have over others of the same sex and species, solely in respect of reproduction."[48] In other words, amongst our prehistoric ancestors, mating for reproduction shows a bias for selecting characteristics that enhance a species' advantage in the natural world. In the primeval period it is unlikely that this selection was rationally thought out, but rather driven by an unconscious instinctual impulse for reproductive protection beneath the aegis of a powerful protector. Consequently, it is not a stretch to suggest that those advantages include self-survival and survival for the transmitter and incubator of genetic material. Further, Darwin noted that "the sexual struggle is of two kinds; in the one it is between the individuals of the same sex, generally the male sex, in order to drive away or kill their rivals, the females remaining passive; whilst in the other, the struggle is likewise between the individuals of the same sex, in order to excite or charm those of the opposite sex, generally the females, which no longer remain passive, but select the more agreeable partners."[49] Again, Darwin points out that primal females tend to pick out a mate that will enhance their chances of survival and successful reproduction. This is the essence of physicality.

At the end of the day, all the above-mentioned aspects of selection by our early ancestors represent right action and good outcome for the greatest number—that is, if you count survival as a good outcome. Given that time in pre-history, we must accept the level of violent behavior that goes along with these right actions by the successful progenitors of our species. A strong physical presence and physical violence did have a place in the selection process. Physicality and individual violence still do have a place in right action, but it is a place that is continually shrinking in size. So, bear in mind that modernity and civilization have a huge impact on altering behavior adhering to any crude primordial interpretation, even for the intentional meanings in Charlemagne's Code. Modernity impacted both genders, but primarily women, as technology has consistently diminished the role of physical size and strength. Phillip's list offers raw visceral understanding, while Charlemagne's Code shows the massaging of civilization. Civilization is the great agent of moment, though current research makes it highly probable that evolution lays a thumb on the scale of honor, although the size and weight of that thumb remain ambiguous.[50]

In Summation

I have avoided the word "conclusion" in favor of summation. What material evidence we have on the subject of honor allows us to deal with probability rather than the certainty implied by the word conclusion. As with many things human, passion and emotion often interfere with objectivity and reason. With that in mind, it seems that history has caught up with the concept of honor everyplace but our hearts. Even while struggling with this interference, it is still fair for us to conclude that over the past 5000 years honor has dramatically changed its defining characteristics.

It seems clear that the honor of glory found in Homer's day no longer fits or is appropriate in our day. Except for the shrinking number of social positions that require physicality, that is, size and strength (which technology will one day overcome), horizontal honor has become far more recognizable in a wide swath of humanity. Horizontal honor is available to us all, and not restricted to class or status. The nobility with its monopoly on the gifts of rank and privilege are no longer the sole repository of honor as understood in the modern and contemporary ages. Modernity may have brought horizontal honor to the masses of people, but it has also brought with it the sense of shame that is the loss of honor. If right action, is inherent to the mass of humanity, then so is shame, a loss of honor through wrong action.

The wave of technology arriving with modernity has removed the glorious hero of antiquity. Advances in technology and resultant thinking have removed the frozen ranks of the Medieval World where honor was an unearned, automatic feature of the feudal class structure. Modernity, with its technological leap into mechanized warfare, was the first nail, literacy and democracy the final nails. It would seem that with the residue of physicality isolated to a few pockets of occupation, horizontal honor is available to us all, big and small, male and female, young and old.

Technology in the hands of motivated masses has destroyed the blind notion that blood and guts equals glory equals honor. Literacy and democracy, creatures of material advancement, have been the agents of that destruction. They have also brought philosophical idea of "right action" forward for consideration by the average person. Democratic thinking requires an independent thinking that goes beyond blind obedience to the law. Honor guides us toward "right action" that often alienates current convention. Reminding us again of Michel de Montaigne's famous remark back in the late 16th century: "There are two sets of laws, those of honor and those of justice, in many matters quite opposed."[51] If right action brings us into conflict with convention, then so much the worse for convention. It follows that shame is the reward for a reflexive obedience to a dishonorable convention. Today, every more so than in the past, doing the right thing is required of us all. Bluntly, honor is demanded of us all.

366

No doubt history—that is, technology and the changed thinking arriving with it—will catch up with the rump factors of male exclusivity—material reality and physicality—but at the current time these will be features we have to live with. But know this: What we do not have to live with, and indeed, need not live with, is shaming the human spirit inside us all by suppressing the honor we all can express and achieve: the ability to right action leading to a good outcome for the greatest number.

"The honorable are habituated by virtue as a way of life. Honor proceeds out of honesty. There can be no honor in deceitful and shameful acts. The honor found here is inherent to us all." Robert Ashley, c. 1596[52]

More than ever before, living an honorable life is demanded of us all.

Notes

1. For example, see, https://en.wikipedia.org/wiki/Honour

2. https://www.bing.com/videos/search?q=female+mma+fighters+fighting+men&view=detail&mid=F10FB4545DD251214691F1 0FB4545DD251214691&FORM=VIRE

3 To see male vs. female fighters: https://www.mmafighting.com/2014/4/6/5587032/for-female-mma-fighters-training-with-men-an-inevitablity-that

4. http://www.scifighting.com/2013/12/24/21670/3-reasons-men-vs-women-mma-fights-wont-work/

5. It is important to note that although this paper is focused on the culture of honor in the west, the east also had similar standards for the warrior class, for example, see: Inazo Nitobe, *Bushido, The Warrior's Code*, Ohara Publications, Burbank California, 1979 (Original manuscript published 1889), and Daidojo Yuzan, *Budoshoshinshu, the Warrior's Primer,* trans by William Wilson, Ohara Publications, Burbank CA, 1984

6. As quoted by David Herlihy, "Three Patterns of Social Mobility in Medieval History," *Journal of Interdisciplinary History,* Vol 3, #1, (Spring 1973), p. 623

7. Ibid. p. 623

8. See Mills, Charles (2004). *The History of Chivalry or Knighthood and Its Times,* Volume I of 2, first published 1825.

9. For a more detailed paper outlining the basic elements of *noble habitus*, see: https://mcbainmanor.com/2019/03/25/noble-habitus-loyalty

10. For further clarity on this, see: Crouch, David (2005). *The Birth of Nobility: Constructing Aristocracy in England and France 900–1300.* Harlow, UK: Pearson.

11. See: Mills, Charles (2004). *The History of Chivalry or knighthood and its Times*, op.cit.

12. For a complete list of the suspected elements of the *noble habitus*, see https://en.wikipedia.org/wiki/Chivalry

13. As a matter of interest, it was a lack of forbearance that separates Achilles, and his vile treatment of Hector's body, from any knightly code of honor.

14. Crouch, David, op. cit., P. 78

15. https://errantsvigil.wordpress.com/2010/03/30/charlemagnes-code-of-chivalry/

16. https://www.baronage.co.uk/chivalry/chivalla.html

17. As enumerated in http://www.medieval-life-and-times.info/medieval-knights/code-of-chivalry.htm

18. For details, see: https://www.baronage.co.uk/chivalry/chival1a.html

19. As quoted by Frank Stewart in his book, *Honor*, by Frank Henderson Stewart, University of Chicago Press, Chicago, 1994, p. 79

20. Keen, Maurice, *Chivalry*. New Haven, CT: Yale University Press. (2005). P. 1

21. See: *Vengeance in Medieval Europe: A Reader (Readings in Medieval Civilizations and Cultures)*, ed by Small and Kelly, University of Toronto Press, Higher Education Division; 1 edition (June 1, 2009)

22. https://www.history.com/news/chivalry-knights-middle-ages

23. There are several versions of this list. This one came off the web site: http://www.medieval-life-and-times.info/medieval-knights/code-of-chivalry.htm. And rather Philip the Good, third Duke of Burgundy, was the actual author of the list is open to question, but this list did come about during the lifetime of this Duke of Burgundy.

24. For example, see the literary scholar, Léon Gautier, for a vastly more extensive list (*op. cit.*).

25. As quoted in *Honor Among Men and Nations, Transformations of an Idea*, by Geoffrey Best, University of Toronto Press, Toronto, 1982 (p. 91)

26. See Ernst Junger's *Storm of Steel*, first publish.ed in 1920, for an excellent account of how both the nature of war and the idealization of it shifted dramatically in WWI

27. The writer of the classic, *On War* (1832)

28. Aristotle: *The Nicomachean Ethics*, translated by David Ross, Oxford University Press, Oxford, UK, 1998, p.11

29. See, William Shaw, *Moore on Right and Wrong*, (Dordrecht, Kluwer Academic Publishers) 1995 p.94

30. Ibid, p. 180

31. I refer here to Kant's famous "On a Supposed Right to Lie from Altruistic Motives," From Immanuel Kant, *Critique of Practical Reason and Other Writings in Moral Philosophy*, ed. and trans. Lewis White Beck (Chicago: University of Chicago Press, 1949), PP. 346-50

32. Ibid, p. 347

33. Ibid, p. 347

34. https://www.marinecorpstimes.com/news/2018/03/05/where-are-the-female-marines/

35. Ibid.

36. Heidensohn, Frances, *Women in Control?: The Role of Women in Law Enforcement*. Oxford: Clarendon (1992).

37. Ibid. p.132

38. https://www.sciencedirect.com/science/article/pii/S1090513815000239

39. Ibid.

40. https://www.thejournal.ie/more-likely-to-protect-women-2812888-Jun2016/

41. https://titanicfacts.net/titanic-victims/

42. https://www.anesi.com/titanic.htm

43. https://www.historyonthenet.com/how-many-people-were-on-the-titanic

44. https://abcnews.go.com/US/women-survived-theater-shooting-grieve-hero -boyfriends/story?id=16840623

45. Eighty-two casualties were reported. Seventy were hit by bullets. Ten victims died at the scene and two more were pronounced dead in local hospitals. Four men—Jonathan Blunk, John Larimer, Matt McQuinn, and Alexander Teves—died protecting their girlfriends. Gordon Cowden died saving the lives of his two teenage daughters. For details, see, wikipedia.org/ wiki/2012_Aurora,_Colorado_shooting#Casualties

46. Feinberg, D. R.; Jones, B. C.; Law Smith, M. J.; Moore, F. R.; DeBruine, L. M.; Cornwell, R. E.; Hillier, S. G.; Perrett, D. I. (1 February 2006). "Menstrual cycle, trait estrogen level, and masculinity preferences in the human voice". *Hormones and Behavior*. 49 (2): 215–222.

47. To understand the probabilities inherent in evolution, see, https://www.new-scientist.com/article/dn13694-evolution-myths-evolution-is-just-so-unlikely/

48. Darwin, Charles, *The Descent of Man and Selection in Relation to Sex*. (London, first published 1871) p. 256.

49. Ibid, p. 398

50. Extensively discussed in, https://sciencemeetsreligion.org/evolution/ probability.php

51. Op.cit.

52. *Of Honor*, Robert Ashley, ed by Virgil Heltzel, The Huntington Library, San Marino, CA 1947. P. 107

Other works by William Pray

Fiction:

Green Fields, Apollo Publications, Sacramento, CA

A Dozen Miles of Unpaved Road, Firebird Rising, Venice, CA

Terminal Cure, Firebird Rising, Venice, CA

Non-fiction:

What Can I Do, Rhino Publications, Venice CA

William F. Pray, was one of the original founders of the journal *Politics and Philosophy*. He served first as Assistant Editor and then Chief Editor of the journal for over ten years. William Pray has advanced degrees in both Political Science and Philosophy. His primary residence is in Nevada, where he continues to write both non-fiction and fiction.

Contact Information:

William Pray lives in Reno, Nevada. He can be reached at
www.WilliamPray.com or at **www.Thefirebirdrising.com**

Made in the USA
Middletown, DE
30 October 2022

13751343R00227